GERALD COREY is Professor Emeritus of Human Services and Counseling at California State University at Fullerton. He received his doctorate in counseling from the University of Southern California. He is a Diplomate in Counseling Psychology, American Board of Professional Psychology; a licensed psychologist; a National Certified Counselor; a Fellow of the American Psychological Association (Counseling Psychology); a Fellow of the American Counseling Association; and a Fellow of the Association for Specialists in Group Work. Along with his wife, Marianne Schneider Corey, Jerry received the Lifetime Achievement Award from the American Mental Health Counselors Association in 2011 and the Eminent Career Award from ASGW in 2001. He also received the Outstanding Professor of the Year Award from California State University at Fullerton in 1991. He regularly teaches both undergraduate and graduate courses in group counseling and ethics in counseling. He is the author or co-author of 16 textbooks in counseling currently in print, along with numerous journal articles. His book, *Theory and Practice of Counseling and Psychotherapy*, has been translated into Arabic, Indonesian, Portuguese, Turkish, Korean, and Chinese. *Theory and Practice of Group Counseling* has been translated into Korean, Chinese, Spanish, and Russian.

Jerry and Marianne Schneider Corey often present workshops in group counseling. In the past 30 years the Coreys have conducted group counseling training workshops for mental health professionals at many universities in the United States as well as in Canada, Mexico, China, Hong Kong, Korea, Germany, Belgium, Scotland, England, and Ireland. In his leisure time, Jerry likes to travel, hike and bicycle in the mountains, and drive his 1931 Model A Ford. The Coreys have been married for 48 years; they have two adult daughters and three grandchildren.

He holds memberships in the American Counseling Association; the American Psychological Association; the Association for Specialists in Group Work; the American Group Psychotherapy Association; the American Mental Health Counselors Association; the Association for Spiritual, Ethical, and Religious Values in Counseling; the Association for Counselor Education and Supervision; and the Western Association for Counselor Education and Supervision.

Recent publications by Jerry Corey, all with Brooks/Cole, Cengage Learning, include:

- *Theory and Practice of Counseling and Psychotherapy*, Ninth Edition (and *Student Manual*) (2013)
- *The Art of Integrative Counseling*, Third Edition (2013)
- *Theory and Practice of Group Counseling* (and *Student Manual*, Eighth Edition, 2012)
- *Becoming a Helper*, Sixth Edition (2011, with Marianne Schneider Corey)
- *Issues in Ethics in the Helping Professions*, Eighth Edition (2011, with Marianne Schneider Corey and Patrick Callanan)
- *Groups: Process and Practice*, Eighth Edition (2010, with Marianne Schneider Corey and Cindy Corey)
- *I Never Knew I Had a Choice*, Ninth Edition (2010, with Marianne Schneider Corey)
- *Group Techniques*, Third Edition (2004, with Marianne Schneider Corey, Patrick Callanan, and J. Michael Russell)

Jerry is co-author (with Barbara Herlihy) of *ACA Ethical Standards Casebook*, Sixth Edition (2006); and *Boundary Issues in Counseling: Multiple Roles and Responsibilities*, Second Edition (2006); he is co-author (with Robert Haynes, Patrice Moulton, and Michelle Muratori) of *Clinical Supervision in the Helping Professions: A Practical Guide*, Second Edition (2010); he is the author of *Creating Your Professional Path: Lessons From My Journey* (2010). All four of these books are published by the American Counseling Association.

He has also made several educational DVD programs on various aspects of counseling practice: (1) *DVD for Theory and Practice in Counseling and Psychotherapy: The Case of Stan and Lecturettes* (2013); (2) *DVD for Theory and Practice of Group Counseling* (2012); (3) *Groups in Action: Evolution and Challenges—DVD and Workbook* (2006, with Marianne Schneider Corey and Robert Haynes); (4) *DVD for Integrative Counseling: The Case of Ruth and Lecturettes* (2013, with Robert Haynes); and (5) *Ethics in Action: CD-ROM* (2003, with Marianne Schneider Corey and Robert Haynes). All of these programs are available through Brooks/Cole, Cengage Learning.

ABOUT THE CONTRIBUTORS

ALVIN N. ALVAREZ, PhD, is Associate Professor and Coordinator of the College Counseling Program at San Francisco State University. His professional interests and scholarship focus is on Asian Americans, racial identity, and the psychological impact of racism. Dr. Alvarez is the current president of the Asian American Psychological Association (AAPA) and recently received the Early Career Award from AAPA.

JAMES ROBERT BITTER, EdD, is Professor of Counseling in the Department of Human Development and Learning at East Tennessee State University and is the author of *Theory and Practice of Family Therapy and Counseling*. He is a consultant in the areas of individual and group therapy and in the application of Adlerian principles to the counseling of children and families. Dr. Bitter has written many journal articles on family mapping and family constellations, created memories versus early recollections, and family reconstruction.

WILLIAM BLAU, PhD, has a private practice and teaches as an adjunct instructor at Copper Mountain College in Joshua Tree, California. Although his theoretical orientation is psychoanalytic, he often uses techniques from other approaches. His specialty areas include clinical biofeedback and the psychotherapy of psychotic people. Dr. Blau and his wife, Cathey Graham Blau, LCSW, BCD, work together in providing biofeedback training and couples therapy.

DAVID J. CAIN, PhD, ABPP, CGP, is the editor of *Humanistic Psychotherapies: Handbook of Research and Practice* and of *Classics in the Person-Centered Approach*. In addition, he is the author of *Person-Centered Psychotherapies* (APA, 2010). Dr. Cain teaches at the California School of Professional Psychology, San Diego (Alliant International University) and in the psychology department at Chapman University. Dr. Cain's primary professional commitment is the advancement of humanistic psychology and psychotherapy. He maintains a private practice in Carlsbad and San Marcos, California.

GRACE A. CHEN, PhD, is a licensed psychologist at Counseling and Psychological Services at California State University, East Bay in Hayward, California. Her professional interests include Asian Americans, identity development, multicultural counseling, and college student development. She earned her PhD in Counseling Psychology at the University of Texas at Austin. Currently Dr. Chen serves on the directorate body of the Commission for Counseling and Psychological Services, a division of ACPA–College Student Educators International.

ROBERT C. CHOPE, PhD, is Professor of Counseling at San Francisco State University, and the founder of the career specialization. He is the author of four books and a Fellow as well as the 2004 Outstanding Career Practitioner award winner of the National Career Development Association. Dr. Chope holds the Robert Swan Lifetime Achievement Award and Outstanding Career Practitioner Award from the California Career Development Association.

ANDRÉS J. CONSOLI, PhD, is Professor of Counseling at San Francisco State University and former coordinator of the marriage and family specialization. He has written articles on client–therapist matching, psychotherapy integration, stress and anxiety, and Latino/a mental health. Dr. Consoli's research interests are in multicultural supervision, access and utilization of mental health services by Latinos/as, and the social representation of psychotherapy.

SHERRY CORMIER, PhD, is Professor Emerita in the Department of Counseling, Rehabilitation Counseling, and Counseling Psychology at West Virginia University. She is a licensed psychologist with a part-time private practice in Morgantown, WV. Dr. Cormier has co-authored several books, including *Interviewing and Change Strategies for Helpers; The Professional Counselor;* and *Counseling Strategies and Interventions.* Her areas of training and consultation include clinical supervision, cognitive behavioral therapy, stress management, and wellness.

FRANK M. DATTILIO, PhD, ABPP, is on the faculty of psychiatry at both Harvard Medical School and the University of Pennsylvania School of Medicine, has been a visiting lecturer at many universities internationally, and is a clinical psychologist in private practice. Dr. Dattilio is the foremost authority on cognitive behavior therapy with couples and families and has authored or co-authored 17 books and more than 250 professional publications worldwide. His works have been translated into 27 languages and are used in 80 countries.

ALBERT ELLIS, PhD, ABPP, is considered to be the father of rational emotive behavior therapy and the grandfather of cognitive behavioral therapy. Dr. Ellis remained professionally active until his death at age 93 in 2007. He published more than 75 books and more than 800 articles, mostly on the theory and application of REBT. He gave workshops throughout the world and saw individuals in his counseling practice.

KATHY M. EVANS, PhD, is Associate Professor at the University of Southern Carolina and the Coordinator of the Counselor Education Program. Dr. Evans received her PhD in Counseling Psychology from The Pennsylvania State University in 1989. She is a licensed professional counselor and a licensed psychologist. She teaches in both the entry and doctoral level counseling degree programs, with an emphasis on the acquisition of social justice skills and multicultural competence in counseling and supervision. Dr. Evans's research interests and presentations focus on multicultural, career, and feminist issues.

JON FREW, PhD, ABPP, is Professor of Psychology at Pacific University's School of Professional Psychology and is in private practice in Vancouver, Washington. He has published extensively in the field of Gestalt therapy and is on the editorial board of the *Gestalt Review*. Dr. Frew co-authored *Contemporary Psychotherapies for a Diverse World*. He is co-director of the Gestalt Therapy Training Center Northwest and has conducted training workshops in the United States, Canada, and Australia.

WILLIAM GLASSER, MD, is Founder and President of The William Glasser Institute in Chatsworth, California, and is the founder of reality therapy. Dr. Glasser's practical approach continues to be popular among a variety of practitioners and teachers. He has written a number of books on reality therapy and choice theory.

ELIZABETH A. KINCADE, PhD, has practiced and taught in both counseling and psychology fields for more than 20 years. She is the Chair of the Counseling Center at Indiana University of Pennsylvania. Her research interests are in feminist therapy, social justice, ethics, and group dynamics. Dr. Kincade is a licensed psychologist and received her doctorate in Counseling Psychology from The Pennsylvania State University in 1989.

KELLIE N. KIRKSEY, PhD, is Professor of Counselor Education at Malone University, as well as a clinician in private practice. She is a licensed clinical counselor, supervisor, and a rehabilitation counselor who blends traditional modalities with spirituality and creative expression for healing and wellness. Dr. Kirksey infuses wellness and the multicultural competencies into all of her courses.

ARNOLD A. LAZARUS, PhD, ABPP, is Distinguished Professor Emeritus in the Graduate School of Applied and Professional Psychology at Rutgers University and president of the Lazarus Institute in Skillman, New Jersey. He is a Diplomate in Clinical Psychology of the American Board of Professional Psychology. Dr. Lazarus developed the multimodal approach, a broad-based, systematic, and comprehensive approach to behavior therapy, for which he has received numerous awards. He is considered a pioneer in the field of clinical behavior therapy.

MARY MOLINE, PhD, Dr.PH, is Professor of Counseling and Family Sciences at Loma Linda University. Dr. Moline serves as the Program Director and the Director of Clinical Training for the Master's in Marriage and Family Therapy Program. She is a licensed marriage and family therapist in California. She received her PhD in marriage and family therapy from Brigham Young University and her doctorate in public health from Loma Linda University. Dr. Moline is a clinical member and an approved supervisor of the American Association for Marriage and Family Therapy.

GERALD MONK, PhD, is Professor of Counseling at San Diego State University and teaches a range of conflict resolution and counseling courses. He has played a significant role in the development and international expansion of the narrative metaphor in therapy and mediation over the last 15 years. Dr. Monk has published numerous articles in the areas of narrative therapy, social constructionism, and mediation, and has co-authored three books. He has conducted workshops on narrative therapy and mediation in Canada, the United Kingdom, Iceland, Ireland, Cyprus, Mexico, Austria, New Zealand, Australia, and the United States.

MELISSA L. MORGAN, PhD, is Assistant Professor in the Counseling, Clinical and School Psychology program at the University of California, Santa Barbara. She teaches counseling theories, psychology of gender, and racial diversity courses. Her scholarly agenda focuses on resilience and thriving in the Latino/a and migrant population, social justice, prevention, and subjective well-being.

JOHN J. MURPHY, PhD, is Professor of Psychology & Counseling at the University of Central Arkansas, a licensed psychologist, and an internationally known author and trainer of client-directed brief therapy approaches with families, children, and adolescents. Dr. Murphy has authored numerous articles and two books, one of which is *Solution-Focused Counseling in Schools* (ACA, 2008). Dr. Murphy is a popular workshop presenter who has trained thousands of practitioners throughout the United States and overseas.

WILLIAM G. NICOLL, PhD, is Professor and Chair of the Department of Counselor Education at Florida Atlantic University in Boca Raton, Florida. Dr. Nicoll provides training in Adlerian-based interventions across the United States as well as in Europe, Asia, Latin America, and Africa. His writings focus on the applications of Adlerian brief counseling with individuals and families and with the school-related problems of children and adolescents.

JOHN C. NORCROSS, PhD, ABPP, is Professor of Psychology and Distinguished University Fellow at the University of Scranton and a clinical psychologist in part-time practice. A long-time advocate of psychotherapy integration, his 22 books include *Psychotherapy Relationships That Work; The Psychotherapist's Own Therapy; Leaving It at the Office;* and the *Handbook of Psychotherapy Integration.* Dr. Norcross has conducted training and workshops in 27 countries. He served as president of the American Psychological Association's Division of Psychotherapy and the Society of Clinical Psychology.

J. MICHAEL RUSSELL, PhD, PsyD, is Professor Emeritus in both the departments of Philosophy and of Human Services at California State University, Fullerton. He is a Research Psychoanalytic and Training and Supervising Analyst for the Newport Psychoanalytic Institute. His academic and research interests include existential psychoanalysis, philosophical assumptions of psychotherapy, existential group, and philosophical counseling. Dr. Russell has received numerous awards for excellence in teaching from California State University, Fullerton.

SUSAN R. SEEM, PhD, is Professor in the Department of Counselor Education at The College at Brockport, State University of New York. She is a licensed mental health counselor, a national certified counselor, and an approved clinical supervisor. She has taught courses on practicum, internship, group counseling, supervision, and diversity perspectives. Dr. Seem is particularly concerned with issues of privilege, power and difference, and the experience of marginalized groups.

JOHN WINSLADE, PhD, is Professor of Counseling at California State University San Bernardino and is Associate Dean of the College of Education. He is committed to the development of narrative practice and to social constructionism in counseling and in mediation. Dr. Winslade has co-authored six books in these fields, one of which, co-authored with Lorraine Hedtke, describes the practice of remembering conversations as outlined in this text. He has taught numerous workshops on narrative practice in North America, Europe, Australasia, and the Middle East.

ROBERT E. WUBBOLDING, EdD, is Professor Emeritus of Counseling at Xavier University. He is the director of the Center for Reality Therapy in Cincinnati and also the director of training for the William Glasser Institute in Los Angeles. He has taught reality therapy cross-culturally throughout Asia, Europe, and the Middle East, and frequently gives workshops in the United States. Dr. Wubbolding has written numerous journal articles, book chapters, and has published numerous books on reality therapy, including *Reality Therapy for the 21st Century*, and most recently, *Reality Therapy* (APA, 2010).

To the 26 talented contributors (consultants) in this book who worked with Ruth, illustrating the many alternative approaches to client care.

CONTENTS

PREFACE

Case Approach to Counseling and Psychotherapy reflects my increasing emphasis on the use of demonstrations and the case approach method to bridge the gap between the theory and practice of counseling. Students in the courses I teach have found that a demonstration in class often clears up their misconceptions about how a therapy actually works. This book is an attempt to stimulate some of the unique learning that can occur through seeing a therapeutic approach in action. It also gives students a chance to work with a case from the vantage point of 12 counseling approaches: psychoanalytic, Adlerian, existential, person-centered, Gestalt, behavior, cognitive behavior, reality, feminist, postmodern, family systems, and multicultural approaches. In addition, the book provides students with the opportunity to consider a single case from two integrative perspectives.

Readers will see how each of the various therapeutic approaches is applied to a single client, Ruth Walton, who is followed throughout the book. A feature of the text is an assessment of Ruth's case by one or more consultants in each of the 12 theoretical perspectives. In this edition six consultants address counseling Ruth from multicultural perspectives. Highly competent practitioners assess and treat Ruth from their particular theoretical orientation or their integration of several approaches; they also provide sample dialogues to illustrate their style of working with Ruth.

The various theory chapters use a common format, allowing for comparisons among approaches. This format includes a general overview of the theory, the guest commentary or commentaries, followed by my way of working with Ruth from that particular perspective. I discuss the theory's basic assumptions, an initial assessment of Ruth, the goals of therapy, and the therapeutic procedures to be used. I have revised and streamlined these sections illustrating my counseling style with Ruth for the eighth edition of this book. The therapeutic process is concretely illustrated by client–therapist dialogues, which are augmented by process commentaries explaining the rationale for the interventions. Questions for Reflection at the end of each chapter help readers apply the material to their personal lives and offer guidelines for continuing to work with Ruth within each of the theoretical orientations.

Chapter 13 provides a unique perspective on working with Ruth as if she were a member of various cultural groups. Contributors show how their approach with Ruth would incorporate cultural themes if Ruth were Latina, Asian American, or African American.

Chapter 14 presents two different perspectives on integrative counseling and brings all of the approaches discussed in the book together. One contributor demonstrates the value of an integrative counseling approach with Ruth. Then I demonstrate how I would counsel Ruth in an integrative fashion by drawing on various therapeutic approaches. Students are assisted in thinking about designing their integrative approach to counseling practice.

Supplementary Resources

Ideally, *Case Approach to Counseling and Psychotherapy* will be used as part of an integrated learning series I have developed for courses in counseling theory and practice. In a separate book, *The Art of Integrative Counseling,* I describe how to develop your own integrative approach to counseling and provide guidelines for acquiring a personal style of counseling practice. Ruth's case is used to illustrate this integrative perspective. *Case Approach to Counseling and Psychotherapy* can supplement the core textbook to enhance students' learning of theory by letting them see counseling in action. In the textbook, *Theory and Practice of Counseling and Psychotherapy,* Ninth Edition, students are given an overview of the key concepts and techniques of the models of contemporary therapy. The accompanying *Student Manual for Theory and Practice of Counseling and Psychotherapy* contains many experiential activities and exercises designed to help students apply the theories to themselves and to connect theory with practice.

A self-study program, *DVD for Integrative Counseling: The Case of Ruth and Lecturettes,* illustrates my own integrative perspective in working with Ruth through video recorded counseling demonstrations. Look for the icon throughout this book that signals the coordination of the counseling sessions in the video program with the topics in this book. The video program brings together several of the therapies and provides concrete illustrations of my ways of working with Ruth. The videos are also available on the *Premium Website for Integrative Counseling* for students and faculty who prefer to access the videos online. A printed access code can be bundled with the textbook, or an instant access code can be purchased online at www.cengagebrain.com.

A new lecture program now complements *Theory and Practice of Counseling and Psychotherapy* (9th ed.). The *DVD for Theory and Practice of Counseling and Psychotherapy: The Case of Stan and Lecturettes* ties in well with the theory chapters in *Case Approach to Counseling and Psychotherapy.*

What's New in the Eighth Edition of Case Approach?

Every chapter of the eighth edition of *Case Approach to Counseling and Psychotherapy* has carefully been reviewed to refine existing ideas and provide new material. Twenty-six guest contributors (consultants) demonstrate their approaches to assessing and treating Ruth, and all but two of these selections have been updated and revised to reflect current practices. Four new contributors are included in this edition—Sherry Cormier (behavior therapy), John Murphy (solution-focused brief therapy), John Winslade (narrative therapy), and Melissa L. Morgan (multicultural counseling)—three writing major new pieces on their approach to counseling Ruth, and one joining existing authors in revising a multicultural perspective on Ruth. I have revised my sections in each chapter and added Some Final Thoughts at the end of each theory chapter. Changes in this new edition included the following:

Chapter 1, Introduction and Overview
- Revised discussion of basic assumptions of several of the therapies
- New material on solution-focused therapy and narrative therapy
- Revision of Drs. Palmer's and Nystul's discussions of diagnosis

Chapter 2, Case Approach to Psychoanalytic Therapy
- Revision of symptom substitution, assessing for suicidal ideation, free association, and Ruth's diagnosis
- New discussion of brief psychodynamic therapy
- Revision of goals of therapy

Chapter 3, Case Approach to Adlerian Therapy
- Revision of social interest
- Expansion of multiple therapy
- Revision of assessment of Ruth

Chapter 4, Case Approach to Existential Therapy
- New material on how Ruth creates her moods
- Revision of how techniques are a creative process

Chapter 5, Case Approach to Person-Centered Therapy
- Added emphasis on diversity of therapeutic styles
- Expanded discussion on role of diagnosis
- New discussion of experiential focusing
- More on individualizing each client's therapy
- New discussion on primacy of the client as agent of change

Chapter 6, Case Approach to Gestalt Therapy
- Revision of key issues in Ruth's life
- Revision of some therapist–client dialogue

Chapter 7, Case Approach to Behavior Therapy
- More emphasis on empirically supported techniques
- Revised discussion of DSM diagnosis for Ruth
- A new major piece by Dr. Cormier on working with Ruth
- New discussion on the basic features and process of behavior therapy
- Making a functional diagnoses based on the behavioral analysis process

Chapter 8, Case Approach to Cognitive Behavior Therapy
- New section on overview of cognitive behavioral approaches
- Retained Dr. Albert Ellis's piece, a classic contribution to cognitive behavior therapy
- Minor revision of family therapy using CBT framework with Ruth

Chapter 9, Case Approach to Reality Therapy
- Revised general overview of reality therapy with emphasis on the therapeutic alliance
- Clarification of the role of symptoms
- Discussion of the linkage between assessment and treatment
- New section on using metaphors in therapy

Chapter 10, Case Approach to Feminist Therapy
- Revised overview of feminist therapy
- Revision showing three feminist therapists working as a team with Ruth
- Revised section on traditional diagnosis from a feminist perspective

Chapter 11, Case Approach to Postmodern Approaches
- A new major piece by Dr. Murphy on working with Ruth from a solution-focused brief therapy perspective
- A new major piece by Dr. Winslade on working with Ruth using narrative therapy and a remembering conversation

Chapter 12, Case Approach to Family Therapy
- Dr. Bitter joins with Dr. Moline to expand applying family therapy to Ruth's case
- New dialogue by Drs. Moline and Bitter in demonstrating family therapy with Ruth

Chapter 13, Counseling Ruth from Multicultural Perspectives
- New and expanded introduction to multiculturalism
- New co-author for "Ruth as Latina" segment
- New section on therapist multicultural competency
- More emphasis on understanding and respecting Ruth's unique experiences as a Chinese American woman
- Increased coverage of the role of religion in working with Ruth as an African American woman
- New section on Jerry Corey's multicultural perspective on Ruth

Chapter 14, Integrative Approaches and Developing Your Own Therapeutic Style
- Difference between integration and eclecticism
- New major piece by Dr. Norcross on integrative psychotherapy and his style of working with Ruth
- Expanded and broadened view of the meaning of evidence-based practice
- Revised comprehensive discussion of my style of integrative counseling

Acknowledgments

I appreciate both the support and the challenge given by those teachers of counseling courses and clinicians who read the revised manuscript for this eighth edition and provided specific helpful comments for improving the effectiveness of the case presentations. These people are:

- Jonathan Alex, Lehman College/SUNY
- Barbara Beaver, University of Wisconsin–Whitewater
- Patrick Callanan, California State University, Fullerton

- Pornthip Chalungsooth, University of Scranton
- Peter Emerson, Southeastern Louisiana University
- Melodie Frick, West Texas A&M University
- Robert Haynes, Borderline Productions
- Amanda Healey, Sam Houston State University

Special thanks are extended to Marianne Schneider Corey, my wife and colleague, for her contributions to this revision. Based on her clinical experiences as a marriage and family therapist, she reviewed the case of Ruth and the guest contributors' pieces as well.

Special appreciation goes to Kay Mikel, the manuscript editor, whose sensitivity and editorial skills contributed in important ways to the readability and interest of this text.

I am particularly indebted to those individuals who reviewed a chapter in their area of expertise and who also contributed by writing about their way of working with Ruth from their particular therapeutic perspective. These 26 guest contributors (consultants) demonstrated their approach to assessing and treating Ruth, and you can learn more about each of them in the About the Contributors section. To these contributors I dedicate this book.

— GERALD COREY

CHAPTER ONE

Introduction and Overview

Structure of the Book

In *Case Approach to Counseling and Psychotherapy* you will encounter 12 different therapies and see how various therapists use these approaches in their work, selectively borrowing concepts and techniques to form their own unique style of counseling. I encourage you to follow this model and to integrate techniques that are appropriate to your client population in a style that is an expression of who you are as a person. Effective counseling combines your personality with the technical skills that you employ. To apply techniques appropriately, it is essential to consider your personal style and theoretical orientation in relation to each client's unique life situation.

Before this large task of developing a personalized approach can be accomplished, however, you will need to know the basics of each of the theories and acquire some experience with these therapies. My aim is to provide a balance between describing the way therapists with a particular orientation might proceed with a client and challenging you to try your hand at showing how you would proceed with the same client.

In this chapter I describe methods for conceptualizing a case and provide background material on the central figure in this book, Ruth Walton, who is also the "client" in the accompanying video program published as the *DVD for Integrative Counseling: The Case of Ruth and Lecturettes* and online as the *Premium Website for Integrative Counseling: The Case of Ruth and Lecturettes.* Refer to Ruth's intake form and autobiography frequently as you work with her in each theory chapter and in Chapter 14, which describes integrative approaches in counseling Ruth. "Ruth" is a composite I created by combining many of the common themes I have observed in my work with clients. I believe the life themes ascribed to Ruth are representative of clients you may meet in your practice.

Chapters 2 through 13 begin with commentaries by one or more "outside consultants" on Ruth's case. Twenty-six guest contributors (consultants) demonstrate their approach in assessing and treating Ruth. Each consultant was given Ruth's background information and also read my perspective on her for the theory under discussion. The consultants were asked to include these points in their section:

- The core concepts and goals of the consultant's therapeutic approach
- The themes in Ruth's life that might serve as a focus for therapy
- An assessment of Ruth's dynamics, with emphasis on her current life situation
- The techniques and procedures that would probably be used in counseling Ruth
- Illustrations of the therapy in action through dialogue between Ruth and the therapist

After the guest contributors' discussions of their perspective on Ruth in each chapter, I look at the basic assumptions of the approaches, make an initial assessment of Ruth, and examine the theory's therapeutic goals and procedures. The therapeutic process is made concrete with sample dialogue I have with Ruth, along with my process commentaries, which provide an explanation of the direction therapy is taking. In addition, I provide my own version of the theory as I draw from key concepts and selected techniques in my way of counseling Ruth.

You will notice that there are two invited consultants for Chapter 7 (behavior therapy), Chapter 8 (cognitive behavior therapy), and Chapter 9 (reality therapy). In a few instances, two or more guest contributors worked as co-authors in describing their collaborative approach in counseling Ruth. In Chapter 10 (feminist therapy) three consultants work as a unified team with Ruth. In Chapter 11 (postmodern approaches) three invited consultants write about working with Ruth from the perspectives of solution-focused brief therapy and narrative therapy. In Chapter 12 (family therapy) two family therapy practitioners join forces to demonstrate how they apply principles and procedures in working with Ruth and her family. Chapter 13 (multicultural perspectives) focuses on how to apply an integrative perspective when working with clients from various ethnic and cultural backgrounds. Six contributors show how they would counsel Ruth if she were a Latina, an Asian American, or an African American. In each case, the counselors demonstrate how they would adapt their own approach to multicultural themes and to Ruth's perceptions relating to her culture. In Chapter 14 (integrative perspectives) a contributor describes his integrative approach, which is followed by my own integrative perspective for working with Ruth.

With the contributors' and my work with Ruth, you are exposed to 27 different therapeutic styles in helping Ruth challenge her self-imposed or external limitations and shape her new identity. In a sense, all counseling is aimed at helping clients transcend their limitations and tap their inner resources for change. In our various ways, we each assist Ruth in reaching to the sky to tap the limitless possibilities in making choices to become the person that she never dreamed she could be.

You are encouraged to become an active learner by evaluating the manner in which the consultants and I work with Ruth from the various theoretical perspectives. You are asked to show how you would work with Ruth using the particular approach being considered in the chapter. To guide you in thinking of ways to work with Ruth, each chapter ends with "Questions for Reflection." In addition to thinking about these questions by yourself, I suggest that you arrange to work with fellow students in small discussion groups to explore various approaches.

You can further enhance your learning by participating in a variety of role-playing exercises in which you "become" Ruth or her counselor, and also by participating in discussions in small groups based on various ways of working with her. Rather than merely reading about her case, use the various perspectives to stimulate reflection on ways in which you have felt like Ruth. In experiential practice sessions, you can draw on your own concerns in becoming the counselor. Think of as many ways as possible to use this case to stimulate introspection and lively class discussion.

In Chapter 14 you are encouraged to consider the advantages of eventually developing your own integrative approach and counseling style. Such an integrative perspective of counseling entails selecting concepts and methods from various sources and theories. An integrative approach does not necessarily refer to developing a new theory; rather, it emphasizes a systematic integration of underlying principles and techniques of the various therapy systems. I encourage you to strive to build a unified system that fits you and is appropriate for the particular setting in which you practice. It is essential that you be willing to challenge your basic assumptions, test your hypotheses as you practice, and revise your theory as you confirm or disconfirm your clinical hunches.

Video Programs as Supplements to Case Approach to Counseling and Psychotherapy

I demonstrate my integrative approach to counseling in *DVD for Integrative Counseling: The Case of Ruth and Lecturettes,* which shows segments of individual counseling sessions in which Ruth explores key themes in her life.[1] Throughout this book I will refer you to specific sessions in the video program that demonstrate the application of these diverse theoretical perspectives from the initial to the ending phase of therapy with Ruth. The videos and this book are ideal companions. Throughout this book I will refer to the DVD when citing the video demonstrations, but these videos also are published on the Premium Website for Integrative Counseling, which can be accessed with a printed access card or online at www.cengagebrain.com. The material on the DVD and on the premium website are identical, so you will not need both to use all the material.

The Art of Integrative Counseling also uses the case of Ruth as the central example in illustrating an integrative approach to counseling practice.[2] This book expands on material presented in Chapter 14 here, which is devoted to bringing the approaches together and illustrating how you can develop your own therapeutic style.

In addition, a DVD and online program titled *DVD for Theory and Practice in Counseling and Psychotherapy: The Case of Stan and Lecturettes* may enhance your understanding of each of the chapters in this book. In this series I counsel a client named "Stan" from 11 different theoretical orientations to demonstrate selected techniques introduced in this book as they are applied to a different client.

Overview of the Therapeutic Perspectives

In the chapters that follow, the case of Ruth will be analyzed and discussed from various therapeutic perspectives. We will consider the basic assumptions of the perspective, its view of how to assess clients, its goals for therapy, and its therapeutic procedures. This section presents the essence of the various approaches. As a way of laying the foundation for developing an integrative approach, we will look for common denominators and differences among the 12 approaches.[3] For further study, I highly recommend the following books on psychotherapy integration: *Handbook of Psychotherapy Integration* (Norcross & Goldfried, 2005), *Psychotherapy Integration* (Stricker, 2010), and *A Casebook of Psychotherapy Integration* (Stricker & Gold, 2006).[4]

Basic Assumptions

When therapists make initial contact with clients, their theoretical perspective determines what they look for and what they see. This largely determines the focus and course of therapy and influences their choice of therapeutic strategies and procedures. As you develop your counseling stance, pay attention to your own basic assumptions. Developing a counseling perspective is more involved than merely accepting the tenets of a particular theory or combination of theories. Your theoretical approach is an expression of your unique life experiences.

How do theoretical assumptions influence practice? Your view about the assessment of clients, the goals you think are important in therapy, the strategies and techniques you employ to reach these goals, the way you share responsibility in the client–therapist relationship, and your view of your function and role as a counselor are largely determined by your theoretical orientation. Attempting to practice counseling without at least a general theoretical perspective is somewhat like flying a plane without a map and without instruments. But a counseling theory is not a rigid structure that prescribes the specific steps of what to do in therapeutic work. Instead, a theoretical orientation is a set of general guidelines you can use to make sense of what you are doing.

One way to approach the basic assumptions underlying the major theoretical orientations is to consider six categories under which most contemporary systems fall. These are (1) the *psychodynamic approaches*, which stress insight in therapy (psychoanalytic and Adlerian therapy); (2) the *experiential* and *relationship-oriented approaches*, which stress emotions and subjective experiencing (existential, person-centered, and Gestalt therapy); (3) the *cognitive* and *behavioral approaches*, which stress the roles of thinking and doing and tend to be action-oriented (behavior therapy, rational emotive behavior therapy, cognitive therapy, and reality therapy); (4) *feminist therapy*, which stresses egalitarian relationships and social and political activism to combat oppression; (5) *postmodern approaches*, which include solution-focused brief therapy and narrative therapy; and (6) *family therapy*, which stresses understanding the individual within the entire system of which he or she is a part.

Although I have separated the theories into six general groups, this structure is somewhat arbitrary. Overlapping concepts and themes make it difficult to neatly compartmentalize these theoretical orientations. What follows is a thumbnail sketch of the basic assumptions underlying each of these 12 approaches.

❧Psychoanalytic Therapy   The psychoanalytic approach views people as being significantly influenced by unconscious motivation, conflicts between impulses and prohibitions, defense mechanisms, and early childhood experiences. Because the dynamics of behavior are buried in the unconscious, treatment often consists of a lengthy process of analyzing inner conflicts that are rooted in the past. Longer-term analytic therapy is largely a process of restructuring the personality, which has broader treatment goals than most approaches. Brief psychodynamic therapy approaches address more modest goals in a limited time frame.

❧Adlerian Therapy   According to the Adlerian approach, people are primarily social beings, influenced and motivated by societal forces. Human nature is viewed as creative, active, and decisional. The approach focuses on the unity of the person and on understanding the individual's subjective perspective. Adler holds that inherent feelings of inferiority, or feeling less than one should or need be, initiates a natural striving toward achieving a higher, or greater, level of mastery and competence in life. Like all living organisms, humans strive throughout life to grow, evolve, and become more fully developed and capable. The subjective decisions each person makes regarding the specific direction of this striving form the basis of the individual's lifestyle (or personality style). The style of life consists of our views about others, the world, and ourselves; these views lead to distinctive behaviors that we adopt in pursuit of our life goals. We can influence our own future by actively and courageously taking risks and making decisions in the face of unknown consequences. Clients are not viewed as being "sick" or suffering from a psychopathological disorder and needing to be "cured." Rather, they are seen as being discouraged and functioning on the basis of self-defeating and self-limiting assumptions, which generate problem-maintaining, ego-protective behaviors. Clients need encouragement to correct mistaken perceptions of self and others and to learn to initiate new behavioral interaction patterns. Counseling is not simply a matter of an expert therapist making prescriptions for change. It is a collaborative effort, with client and therapist actively working on mutually accepted goals and the facilitation of change at both the cognitive and behavioral levels.

❧Existential Therapy   The existential perspective holds that we define ourselves by our choices. Although outside factors restrict the range of our choices, we are ultimately the authors of our lives. We are thrust into a meaningless world, yet we are challenged to accept our aloneness and create a meaningful existence. Because we have the capacity for awareness, we are basically free. Along with our freedom, however, comes responsibility for the choices we make. Existential practitioners contend that clients often lead a "restricted existence," seeing few if any alternatives for dealing with life situations and tending to feel trapped or helpless. The therapist's job is to confront these clients with the restricted life they have chosen and to help them become aware of their own part in creating this condition. As an outgrowth of the therapeutic venture, clients are able to recognize outmoded patterns of living, and they begin to accept responsibility for changing their future.

🍃 Person-Centered Therapy   The person-centered approach rests on the assumption that we have the capacity to understand our problems and that we have the resources within us to resolve them. Therapists focus on the constructive side of human nature and on what is right with people. Clients can move forward toward growth and wholeness by looking within rather than focusing on outside influences and by conducting their own problem-solving dialogues. They are able to change without a high degree of structure and direction from the therapist. Therapists provide understanding, genuineness, support, acceptance, caring, and positive regard.

🍃 Gestalt Therapy   The Gestalt approach is an existential and phenomenological approach based on the assumption that individuals and their behavior must be understood in the context of their ongoing relationship with the present environment. The therapist's task is to support clients as they explore their perceptions of reality. The fundamental method to assist in this exploration is awareness of the internal (intrapersonal) world and contact with the external environment. Clients carry on their own therapy as much as possible by doing experiments designed to heighten awareness and to engage in contact. Change occurs naturally as awareness of "what is" increases. Interruptions in the process by which clients develop awareness and move toward contact with the environment are monitored. Heightened awareness can lead to a more thorough integration of parts of the client's reality that were fragmented or unknown.

🍃 Behavior Therapy   Behavior therapy assumes that people are basically shaped by learning and sociocultural conditioning. This approach focuses on the client's ability to learn how to eliminate maladaptive behavior and acquire constructive behavior. Behavior therapy is a systematic approach that begins with a comprehensive assessment of the individual to determine the present level of functioning as a prelude to setting therapeutic goals. After the client establishes clear and specific behavioral goals, the therapist typically suggests strategies that are most appropriate for meeting these stated goals. It is assumed that clients will make progress to the extent that they are willing to practice new behaviors in real-life situations. Continual evaluation is used to determine how well the procedures and techniques are working.

🍃 Cognitive Behavioral Approaches   From the perspective of rational emotive behavior therapy (REBT), our problems are caused by our perceptions of life situations and our thoughts, not by the situations themselves, not by others, and not by past events. It is our responsibility to recognize and change self-defeating thinking that leads to emotional and behavioral disorders. REBT also holds that people tend to incorporate these dysfunctional beliefs from external sources and then continue to indoctrinate themselves with this faulty thinking. To overcome irrational thinking, therapists use active and directive therapy procedures, including teaching, suggestion, and giving homework. REBT emphasizes education, with the therapist functioning as a teacher and the client as a learner. Although REBT is didactic and directive, its goal is to get people to think, feel, and act for themselves. Therapists consistently encourage and challenge clients to do what is necessary to make long-lasting and substantive change.

Other cognitive behavioral therapies share some of the assumptions of REBT. For example, cognitive therapy assumes that people are prone to learning erroneous, self-defeating thoughts but that they are capable of unlearning them. People perpetuate their difficulties through their self-talk. By pinpointing these cognitive errors and correcting them, clients can create a more fulfilling life. Cognitive restructuring plays a central role in the cognitive therapies. People are assumed to be able to make changes by listening to their self-talk, by learning a new internal dialogue, and by learning coping skills needed for behavioral changes. Cognitive therapists are structured, active, and directive, yet they strive to enlist clients as collaborators in the therapeutic endeavor. Cognitive therapy is present-centered, psychoeducational, and time-limited.

Reality Therapy   Reality therapy operates from the premise that all relationship problems are in the present and must be solved in the present. Problematic symptoms are the result of clients trying to deal with a present unsatisfying relationship. Once a significant relationship is improved, the troubling symptom will disappear. Reality therapists challenge clients to consider whether their current behavior is getting them what they want. Clients are encouraged to explore their perceptions, share their wants, and make a commitment to counseling. Because clients can directly control their acting and thinking functions more than they can control what they are feeling, their actions become the focus of therapy. Clients explore the direction in which their behavior is taking them and evaluate what they are doing. They then create a plan of action to make the changes they want.

Feminist Therapy   A basic assumption of feminist therapy is that power inequalities and gender-role expectations influence individuals from a very early age. Gender socialization has negative effects for both women and men, as all individuals are capable of possessing a range of characteristics and behaviors that go beyond rigid and restrictive cultural stereotypes. Therapy is conducted in a gender-sensitive manner. This includes having a positive attitude toward women and being willing to challenge patriarchal systems, empowering both women and men by helping them transcend gender socialization, and assisting women in finding their voices and discovering meaning in their lives. The therapist's role is to sensitize clients to the impact of gender, class, race, ethnicity, and other aspects in their lives. Feminist therapists are aware of the potentially destructive power dynamics in the client–therapist relationship and build mutuality into the therapeutic process. Therapy is viewed as a cooperative and collaborative relationship.

❧ Postmodern Approaches   The postmodern approaches (solution-focused brief therapy and narrative therapy) challenge many of the assumptions of traditional therapies. Like feminism, postmodernism is marked by acceptance of plurality and the notion that individuals create their own reality. Some of the main assumptions are that people are competent and healthy, have the capacity to find their own solutions to difficulties they face, and are the experts on their own lives. The postmodern approaches have in common the basic assumption that we generate stories to make sense of ourselves and our world. People are empowered by learning how to separate themselves from their problems. Clients learn that the person is not the problem—the problem is the problem. Therapists help clients to free themselves from problem-saturated stories and open space to co-create alternative stories. In essence, clients reauthor their stories about themselves and their relationships. Therapy is a collaborative venture aimed at helping clients construct meaningful goals that will lead to a better future.

Solution-focused brief therapy moves from problem-talk to solution-talk and focuses on keeping therapy simple and brief. By talking about the exceptions to a problem, clients are able to conquer what seem to be major problems. Clients learn to pay attention to what is working, and then do more of this. Change is constant and inevitable, and small changes pave the way for larger changes. Little attention is paid to pathology or to giving clients a diagnostic label.

In *narrative therapy* the discussion centers on how a problem has been disrupting, dominating, or discouraging the person. The client is asked to find evidence to support a new view of being competent enough to escape the dominance of a problem and is encouraged to consider what kind of future could be expected from the competent person who is emerging.

Both solution-focused and narrative therapists adopt a "not-knowing" position, replacing the therapist-as-expert with the client-as-expert. Therapists do not assume that they know more about the lives of clients than clients themselves do. Clients are the primary interpreters of their own experiences. Therapists attempt to create collaborative relationships based on the assumption that collaboration opens up a range of possibilities for present and future change.

❧ Family Systems Therapy   Family systems therapy is grounded on the assumption that the individual cannot be fully understood apart from the family system. A basic principle is that a change in one part of the system will result in a change in other parts of the system. If the family unit changes in significant ways, these changes will have an impact on the individual. Likewise, if the individual makes changes, the entire family unit will be affected. Thus, therapy involves assessing and treating an individual's concerns within the context of the interaction among family members. From a systemic perspective, being a healthy person involves both a sense of belonging to the family system and a sense of separateness and individuality. Some of the assumptions of family therapy include the notion that a client's behavior (1) may serve a function or a purpose for the family, (2) may be the result of the system's inability to function effectively, and (3) may result from dysfunctional patterns that are passed on from generation to generation. The family therapist intervenes with individual clients in ways that will enable them to deal more effectively with significant people in their lives, whether or not these other people are physically present in the therapy session.

🦋 **Multicultural Perspectives**   The contemporary theories of therapeutic practice are grounded on assumptions that are part of Western culture. Many of these assumptions may not be appropriate when working with clients from non-Western cultures. The basic assumptions of many of the theoretical orientations described in this book reflect values such as choice, the uniqueness of the individual, self-assertion, personal development, and strengthening the ego. Therapeutic outcomes that these models stress include improving assertive coping skills by changing the environment, changing one's coping behavior, and learning to manage stress. In contrast, non-Western orientations focus on interdependence, play down individuality, think of the collective good, and emphasize losing oneself in the totality of the cosmos.

Western therapeutic approaches are oriented toward individual change. Non-Western approaches focus more on the social framework than on development of the individual. The techniques associated with some of the contemporary counseling models may need to be modified when they are applied to other ethnic and cultural groups.

Seeking professional help is not customary for many client populations, and individuals typically first may turn to informal systems (family, friends, and community). In an increasingly pluralistic society, there is an ethical imperative to avoid forcing all clients to fit a mold that may not be appropriate for their cultural background. As counselors, we need to be aware of how our assumptions and underlying theoretical orientation influence practice with diverse clients.

Using Techniques From All Approaches

Whatever techniques you employ, it is essential to keep the needs of your client in mind. Some clients relate best to cognitive techniques, others to techniques designed to change behavior, and others to techniques aimed at eliciting emotional material. The same client, depending on the stage of his or her therapy, can profit from participating in many of these different techniques.

As a therapist, you would do well to think of ways to take techniques from all of the approaches so that you are able to work with a client on *all levels* of development. For example, when working with Ruth (whom you will become very familiar with in this book), your initial interventions may be directed toward getting her to identify and express *feelings* that she has kept bottled up for much of her life. If you listen to her and provide a place where she can experience what she is feeling, she is likely to be able to give more expression to emotions that she has distorted and denied.

As her therapy progresses, you may well direct interventions toward getting her to think about critical choices she made that still have an influence in her life. At this time in her therapy you are likely to shift the focus from an exploration of feelings to exploring her attitudes, her *thinking processes*, her values, and her basic beliefs. Still later your focus may be more on helping her develop *action programs* in which she can experiment with new ways of *behaving,* both during the sessions and outside of them.

In addition to working with Ruth as an individual, there may be significant therapeutic value in bringing in members of her family of origin, her current family, and significant others. It could be useful to work with Ruth as someone who has been oppressed by gender-role stereotyping. Seeing Ruth as part of a system will provide another dimension that can deepen therapy. An important part of Ruth's therapy could involve encouraging social action on her part, geared to changing certain aspects of the *environment* that are contributing to her problems. It is not a matter of working with one aspect of Ruth's experiencing while forgetting about the other facets of her being; rather, it is a case of selecting a focus for a particular phase of her therapy. The challenge you will face as you encounter Ruth is how to utilize an *integrative approach* as you draw on a variety of techniques to help Ruth work through her struggles.

In working within a *multicultural framework,* it is especially important for you to use techniques flexibly. Clients should not be forced into a strict mold. Rather, techniques are most effective when they are tailored to what the individual client needs, which means you will have to modify your strategies. Some clients will resist getting involved in techniques aimed at bringing up and expressing intense emotions. Confrontational techniques may close down some clients. In such cases it may be best to focus more on cognitive or behavioral techniques or to modify emotive techniques that are appropriate for the client. Other clients may need to be confronted if they are to move. Confrontation at its best is an act of caring. It is designed to motivate clients to examine what they are thinking, feeling, and doing. Relying strictly on supportive techniques with certain clients will not provide the impetus they need to take the steps necessary to change. Techniques work best when they are designed to help clients explore thoughts, feelings, and actions that are within their cultural environment. Again, the value of bringing the client into the counseling process as an informed partner and a collaborator with you as a therapist cannot be overemphasized.

Perspectives on Assessment

Some approaches stress the importance of conducting a comprehensive assessment of the client as the initial step in the therapeutic process. The rationale is that specific counseling goals cannot be formulated and appropriate strategies cannot be designed until a thorough picture of the client's past and present functioning is formed. In this section I describe various views of the role of assessment in therapy. I also present some ways of conceptualizing an individual case, emphasizing what information to gather during the initial stages of therapy.

❧ Psychoanalytic Therapy　Psychoanalysts assume that normal personality development is based on dealing effectively with successive psychosexual and psychosocial stages of development. Faulty personality development is the result of inadequately resolving a specific developmental conflict. Therapists are interested in the client's early history as a way to understand how past situations contribute to a dysfunction. This approach emphasizes the importance of comprehensive assessment techniques as a basis for understanding personality dynamics and the origin of emotional disorders. However, some analysts shy away from gathering information, preferring to let it unfold during the process of analytic therapy.

Adlerian Therapy   Some Adlerians prefer to engage in a more structured assessment process utilizing a detailed lifestyle questionnaire to gather information regarding the client's family of origin, parental relationships, sibling relationships, and family values so as to begin to see the client's perceptions of life and the context in which his or her unique style of life developed, which includes one's view of self, others, and the world. Others prefer to use a more informal process, incorporating aspects of the formal lifestyle assessment (for example, family-of-origin information, birth order) as well as any of a variety of other assessment techniques that help to reveal the underlying cognitive framework of the client's personality. Early childhood recollections, family genograms, favorite childhood stories, family-of-origin stories, art therapy activities, and other such projective techniques can all be utilized in the assessment process by Adlerian therapists.

Existential Therapy   Existentially oriented counselors maintain that the way to understand the client is by grasping the essence of the person's subjective world. The primary purpose of existential clinical assessment is to understand the assumptions clients use in structuring their existence. This approach is different from the traditional diagnostic framework, for it focuses not on understanding the individual from an external perspective but, instead, on grasping the essence of the client's inner world. Existential therapists prefer understanding and exploration of the client's subjective reality, as opposed to formulation of a diagnosis.

Person-Centered Therapy   In much the same spirit as existential counselors, person-centered therapists maintain that traditional assessment and diagnosis are detrimental because they are external ways of understanding the client. They believe (1) the best vantage point for understanding another person is through his or her subjective world; (2) the practitioner can become preoccupied with the client's history and neglect present attitudes and behavior; and (3) therapists can develop a judgmental attitude, shifting too much in the direction of telling clients what they ought to do. Focusing on gathering information about a client can lead to an intellectualized conception about the person. The client is assumed to be the one who knows the dynamics of his or her behavior. For change to occur, the person must experience a perceptual change, not simply receive data. Thus, therapists listen actively, attempt to be present, and allow clients to identify the themes they choose to explore.

≈ **Gestalt Therapy** Gestalt therapists are interested in the "backgrounds" out of which the "figures" that guide their work emerge. Assessment is an on-going process embedded in the dialogue between client and therapist. Many Gestalt therapists gather certain types of information about their clients to supplement the assessment and diagnostic work done in the present moment. Gestalt therapists attend to interruptions in the client's contacting functions, and the result is a "functional diagnosis" of how individuals experience satisfaction or blocks in their relationship with the environment. A functional diagnosis allows the Gestalt therapist to assist clients to understand how they experience interruptions in the natural process of fulfilling their needs.

≈ **Behavior Therapy** The behavioral approach begins with a comprehensive assessment of the client's present functioning, with questions directed to past learning that is related to current behavior patterns. It includes an objective appraisal of specific behaviors and the stimuli that are maintaining them. Some of the reasons for conducting a thorough assessment at the outset of therapy are these: (1) to identify behavioral deficiencies as well as assets, (2) to provide an objective means of appraising both a client's specific symptoms and the factors that have led up to the client's malfunctioning, (3) to facilitate selection of the most suitable therapeutic techniques, (4) to specify a new learning and shaping schedule, (5) to predict the course and the outcome of a particular clinical disorder, and (6) to provide a framework for research into the effectiveness of the procedures employed.

≈ **Cognitive Behavioral Approaches** The assessment used in cognitive behavioral therapy is based on getting a sense of the client's patterns of thinking. Attention is paid to various beliefs the client has developed in relation to certain events. Therapists are not merely concerned with gathering data about past events but are also alert to evidence of faulty thinking and cognitive distortions the client has incorporated. Once self-defeating thought patterns and beliefs have been identified, the therapeutic process consists of actively challenging these beliefs and substituting constructive ones.

≈ **Reality Therapy** Assessment of clients is typically not a formal process; psychological testing and diagnosis are not generally a part of this approach. Through the use of skillful questioning, reality therapists help clients make an assessment of their present behavior. They have little interest in learning the causes of clients' current problems or in gathering information about clients' past experiences. Instead, the focus is on getting clients to take a critical look at what they are doing now and then determine the degree to which their present behavior is effective. This informal assessment directs clients to pay attention to their pattern of wants, needs, perceptions, successes, and personal assets to evaluate whether their lives are moving in the direction they want.

≈ **Feminist Therapy** This approach is less than enthusiastic when it comes to traditional diagnosis. Feminist therapists criticize the current classification system for being biased because it was developed by White, male psychiatrists.

Also, the classification system tends to focus on the individual's symptoms and not on the social factors that cause dysfunctional behavior. The assessment process emphasizes the cultural context of clients' problems, especially the degree to which clients possess power or are oppressed. Some assessment and treatment approaches include gender-role analysis, power analysis, assertion training, and demystification of therapy.

Postmodern Approaches   Like feminist therapy, the postmodern therapies do not emphasize assessment, diagnosis, or categorization of individuals. Postmodern therapists do not want to assume the role of judging clients or thinking and talking about them in terms of pathological categories. These therapists do not get caught up in totalizing descriptions of an individual's identity, especially if these descriptions are anchored in terms of a problem. Instead, the emphasis is placed on an individual's competencies and establishing relationships with clients whereby they become senior partners in the counseling venture. Rather than looking at what is wrong with people, this approach focuses on the client's strengths and resources.

Family Systems Therapy   In most systemic approaches both therapist and client are involved in the assessment process. Some systemic practitioners assist clients in tracing the highlights of their family history and in identifying issues in their family of origin. The premise underlying the significance of understanding and assessing one's family of origin is that the patterns of interpersonal behavior and communication learned therein will be repeated in other interactions outside the family. Individuals may be asked to identify what they learned from interacting with their parents, from observing their parents' interactions with each other, and from observing how each parent interacted with each sibling. Clients may also identify the rules governing interactions in their family. These family precepts include unspoken rules, messages given by parents to children, myths, and secrets. Family rules may be functional or dysfunctional.

Multicultural Perspectives   Cultural sensitivity is essential when conducting a comprehensive and accurate assessment. It is important to consider ethnic, cultural, and diversity factors in patterns of behavior; otherwise a client may be subjected to an erroneous assessment and diagnosis. An accurate assessment and diagnosis involves consideration of the realities of discrimination, oppression, and racism in society and in the mental health disciplines. It is critical to consider the ways in which clients' socioeconomic and cultural experiences can influence behavior, including the presentation of symptoms.

Assessment should include questions regarding the religious and spiritual background of the client as well to determine how these factors in a client's history may be important to a client. Assessment begins during the intake session, but it is an ongoing process. Because a client's spiritual or religious beliefs and practices may have been factors in the development of the problem, these beliefs are potential resources for helping clients find solutions to their concerns. If clients indicate concerns about any of their beliefs or practices, this can be a useful focal point for further exploration in therapy sessions.

THE PLACE OF ASSESSMENT AND DIAGNOSIS IN COUNSELING AND CASE MANAGEMENT Assessment consists of evaluating the relevant factors in a client's life to identify themes for further exploration in therapy. Diagnosis, which is sometimes part of the assessment process, consists of identifying a specific category of psychological problem based on a pattern of symptoms. There are several types of diagnosis. *Medical diagnosis* is the process of examining physical symptoms, inferring causes of physical disorders or diseases, providing a category that fits the pattern of a disease, and prescribing an appropriate treatment. *Psychological diagnosis* entails identifying an emotional or behavioral problem and making a statement about the current status of a client. It includes stipulating the possible causes of the individual's emotional, psychological, and behavioral difficulties. It also entails suggesting the appropriate therapeutic techniques to deal with the identified problem and estimating the chances for a successful resolution. *Differential diagnosis* consists of distinguishing one form of psychiatric disorder from another by determining which of two (or more) diseases or disorders with similar symptoms the person is suffering from. The American Psychiatric Association's *Diagnostic and Statistical Manual of Mental Disorders* (*DSM-IV-TR*) is the standard reference for the nomenclature of psychopathology.[5] Publication of the fifth edition, *DSM-5*, is scheduled for May 2013.

A practitioner's view of diagnosis will depend on his or her theoretical orientation, as we have seen. For instance, psychoanalytically oriented therapists tend to favor diagnosis as one way of understanding how past situations contribute to an individual's current dysfunction. Practitioners with a behavioral orientation also favor diagnosis because they emphasize observation and other objective means of appraising both a client's specific symptoms and the factors that have led to the person's malfunctioning. Such an assessment process allows them to employ techniques that are appropriate for a particular disorder and to evaluate the effectiveness of a treatment program. On the other side of the issue are person-centered practitioners, who maintain that diagnosis is not essential for counseling because it tends to pull therapists away from a subjective way of understanding their clients and fosters an external conception about them.

Regardless of your theoretical orientation, it is likely that you will be expected to work within the framework of the *DSM-IV-TR* if you are counseling in a community agency. Even if you are in private practice, you will have to provide a diagnosis on the client's claim form if you accept insurance payments for mental health services. Because you will need to think within the framework of assessing and diagnosing clients, it is essential that you become familiar with the diagnostic categories and the structure of the *DSM-IV-TR*. Most of the guest contributors in this book address their views on diagnosis and demonstrate how they would apply this framework in assessing and treating Ruth.

MY PERSPECTIVE ON ASSESSMENT Assessment, broadly construed, is a legitimate part of therapy. The assessment process does not necessarily have to be completed during the intake interview, however; nor does it have to be a fixed judgment that the therapist makes about the client. This is a time to encourage the client to tell his or her story and to listen not only to the content of the story but to the manner in which the client presents this account. Assessment is a continuing process that focuses on understanding the person. Ideally, assessment is a collaborative effort that is part of the interaction between client and therapist. Both should be involved in discovering the nature of the client's presenting problem, a process that begins with the initial session and continues until therapy ends. In assessing a client, the emphasis is on the client's strengths and inner resources available to address life concerns. Here are some questions that are helpful for a therapist to consider during the early assessment phase:

- What are my immediate and overall reactions to the client?
- What is going on in this person's life at this time?
- What are the client's main assets and liabilities?
- What are his or her resources for change?
- To what degree does this client possess the power to change his or her situation?
- Is this a crisis situation, or is it a long-standing problem?
- What does the client primarily want from therapy, and how can it best be achieved?
- What should be the focus of the sessions?
- What major internal and external factors are contributing to the client's current problems, and what can be done to alleviate them?
- What are the cultural and systemic influences of current behavior?
- In what ways can an understanding of the client's cultural background shed light on developing a plan to deal with the person's problems?
- What are the client's beliefs and experiences pertaining to spirituality? How might these beliefs and experiences be resources that can be drawn upon in dealing with a problem?
- What significant past events appear to be related to the client's present level of functioning?
- What specific family dynamics might be relevant to the client's present struggles and interpersonal relationships?
- On what support systems can the client rely in making changes? Who are the significant people in the client's life?
- What are the prospects for meaningful change, and how will we know when that change has occurred?

As a result of questions such as these, therapists will develop tentative hypotheses, which they can share with their clients as therapy proceeds.

This process of assessment does not have to result in classifying the client under some clinical category. Instead, counselors can describe behavior as they observe it and encourage clients to think about its meaning. In this way assessment becomes a process of thinking about issues *with* the client rather than a mechanical procedure conducted by an expert therapist. From this perspective, assessment and diagnostic thinking are vital to the therapeutic procedures that are selected, and they help practitioners conceptualize a case.

Even if mental health practitioners are required to diagnose clients for administrative or insurance reasons, they are not bound rigidly to that view of their clients. The diagnostic category is merely a framework for viewing and understanding a pattern of symptoms and for making treatment plans. It is not necessary to restrict clients to a label or to treat them in stereotypical ways. It is essential that practitioners be aware of the dangers of labeling and adopt a tentative stance toward diagnosis. As therapy progresses, additional data are bound to emerge that may call for modification of the original diagnosis.

General Guidelines for Assessment

The intake interview typically centers on making an assessment and prescribing an appropriate course of treatment. As you have seen, this assessment may take various forms depending on the practitioner's orientation. For example, Adlerians look for ways in which the family structure has affected the client's development, whereas a psychoanalytic practitioner is interested in intrapsychic conflicts. I have pulled together some guidelines that might be helpful in thinking about how to get significant information and where to proceed with a client after making an initial assessment. Eleven areas that are a basic part of conceptualizing an individual case are discussed here.

1. *Identifying data.* Get details such as name, age, sex, appearance, ethnic background, socioeconomic status, marital status, religious identification, and referral source (who referred the client, and for what purpose).

2. *Presenting problem(s).* What is the chief complaint? This area includes a brief description, in the client's own words, of the immediate problems for which he or she is seeking therapy. The presenting situation includes a description of the problems, how long they have existed, and what has been done to cope with them.

3. *Current living circumstances.* Information to collect here includes marital status and history, family data, recent moves, financial status, legal problems, basic lifestyle conflicts, support systems, and problems in personal relationships.

4. *Psychological analysis and assessment.* What is the client's general psychological state? For example, how does the person view his or her situation, needs, and problems? What is the client's level of maturity? Is there evidence of detrimental influences in the client's life? What are the person's dominant emotions? Is the client excited, anxious, ashamed, or angry? This phase of assessment entails describing the client's ego functioning, including self-concept, self-esteem, memory, orientation, fantasies, ability to tolerate frustration, insight, and motivation to change. The focus is on the client's view of self, including perceived strengths and weaknesses, the person's ideal self, and how the client believes others view him or her. What is the client's level of security? What ability does the person have to see and cope with reality, make decisions, assert self-control and self-direction, and deal with life changes and transitions? Standardized psychological tests of intelligence, personality, aptitudes, and interests may be used.

Another assessment procedure is the *mental-status examination,* which is a structured interview leading to information about the client's psychological level of functioning. This examination focuses on areas such as appearance, behavior, feeling, perception, and thinking. Under the behavior category, for example, the counselor making the assessment will note specific dimensions of behavior, including posture, facial expressions, general body movements, and quality of speech in the interview situation. Under the thinking category it is important to assess factors such as the client's intellectual functioning, orientation, insight, judgment, memory, thought processes, and any disturbances in thinking. The mental-status examination is also used to screen for psychosis.

5. *Psychosocial developmental history.* The focus here is on the developmental and etiological factors relating to the client's present difficulties. Five types can be considered: (1) precipitating factors—for example, maturational or situational stress, school entry, divorce, or death of a parent; (2) predisposing factors—for example, parent–child relationships and other family patterns, personality structure, and hereditary or constitutional factors; (3) contributory factors—for example, a current or past illness or the problems of family members; (4) perpetuating factors—for example, secondary gains such as the sympathy that a sufferer from migraine headaches elicits; and (5) sociocultural factors—that is, customs, traditions, family patterns, and cultural values.

From a developmental perspective these questions could be asked: How well has the client mastered earlier developmental tasks? What are some evidences of conflicts and problems originating in childhood? What were some critical turning points in the individual's life? What were some major crises, and how were they handled? What key choices did the client make, and how are these past decisions related to present functioning? How did the client's relationships within the family influence development? What was it like for the client to be in the family? What are family relationships like now? How are the client's cultural experiences related to his or her personality? This section might conclude with a summary of developmental history, which could include birth and early development, toilet training, patterns of discipline, developmental delays, educational experiences, sexual development, social development, and the influence of religious, cultural, and ethical orientations.

6. *Health and medical history.* What is the client's medical history? What was the date of the client's last consultation with a physician, and what were the results? Is there any noticeable evidence of recent physical trauma or neglect (for example, battering, welt marks, bruises, needle marks, sloppy clothing, sallow complexion)? What is the client's overall state of health? This section should include an assessment of the client's mental health. Has the client been in treatment previously for the present problem? Has there been a prior hospitalization? Has the client been taking medications? If so, obtain a list of the client's medications, dosages, and reason for taking each of the medications. What were the outcomes of previous treatments? Is there any history of emotional illness in the family? It is important to be alert to signs that may indicate an organic basis for a client's problem (such as headaches, sudden changes in personal habits or in personality, and other physical symptoms). Regardless of the therapist's orientation, it is essential to rule out organic causes of physical symptoms before proceeding with psychotherapy.

7. *Adjustment to work.* What work does the client do or expect to do? How satisfied is the client with work? What is the meaning of employment to the

person? Does he or she have future plans? What are the benefits and draw-backs of work? What is the client's work history? Has the person had long-term employment or a history of work problems? What is the balance between work and leisure? What is the quality of the client's leisure time? "Work" is used in the broad sense, whether or not the person receives pay for it. For instance, it would be important to inquire about a woman's satisfaction with her work as a homemaker and mother, even if she is not employed outside the home.

8. *Lethality.* Is the client a danger to self or others? Is he or she thinking about suicide or about hurting someone or something? Does the client have a specific plan either for committing suicide or for harming another person? Does the client have the means available to kill him- or herself? Have there been prior attempts at self-destruction or violent behavior toward others? Is the client willing to make a no-suicide contract as a condition of beginning therapy?

9. *Present human relationships.* This area includes a survey of information per-taining to spouse, siblings, parents, children, friends, colleagues, and other so-cial ties. Included are the person's level of sexual functioning, family beliefs and values, and satisfaction derived from relationships. What are the client's main problems and conflicts with others? How does he or she deal with con-flict? What support does the client get from others?

10. *Client goals.* What does the client hope to accomplish in therapy? What will the client's life look like if the goals are reached? Where would that person like to be one year hence in terms of personal growth, relationships, family, and employment?

11. *Summary and case formulation.* Provide a summary of the client's major de-fenses, core beliefs, and self-definition of current problems, strengths, and lia-bilities, and make an assessment. What are the major recommendations? What is the suggested focus for therapeutic intervention? This formulation might specify the frequency and duration of treatment, the preferred therapeutic ori-entation, and the mode of treatment. The client might be included in the as-sessment process as a collaborator, which tends to set the stage for a shared therapeutic venture.

After the initial assessment of the client is completed, a decision is made whether to refer the person for alternative or additional treatment. Again, it is important to include the client in this decision-making process. If the client is accepted by the therapist, the two can discuss the assessment results. This information can be used in exploring the client's difficulties in thinking, feel-ing, and behaving and in setting treatment goals. Assessment can be linked directly to the therapeutic process, forming a basis for developing methods of evaluating how well the counselor's procedures are working to achieve the cli-ent's goals. Because most work settings require an intake interview, familiarity with these assessment procedures is essential.

Therapeutic Goals

After the initial comprehensive assessment of a client, therapeutic goals need to be established. These goals will vary, depending in part on the practitio-ner's theoretical orientation, the client's situation, and the setting in which the client is being seen. For example, psychoanalytic therapy is primarily an insight approach that aims at regressing clients to very early levels of psychological development so that they can acquire the self-understanding necessary for major character restructuring. It deals extensively with the past, with unconscious dynamics, with transference, and with techniques aimed at changing attitudes and feelings. At the other extreme is reality therapy, which focuses on evaluating current behavior so that the client can develop a realistic plan leading to more effective ways of behaving. Reality therapy is not concerned with exploring the past, with unconscious motivation, with the transference that clients might develop, or with attitudes and feelings. It asks the key question, "What is the client doing now, and what does the client want to be doing differently?" It assumes that the best way to change is by focusing on what one is doing and thinking. If these dimensions change, it is likely that the client's feelings and physiological reactions will also change.

Therapeutic goals are diverse; a few include restructuring personality, finding meaning in life, substituting effective behaviors for maladaptive ones, correcting mistaken beliefs and assumptions, finding exceptions to their problems, reauthoring one's life, discovering what is working and doing more of this, and facilitating individual differentiation from the family system. Given this wide range, it is obvious that the perspectives of the client and the therapist on goals will surely have an impact on the course of therapy and on the therapeutic interventions chosen. Many agencies require that counseling goals be observable, measurable, and realistic.

Despite this diversity of goals, all therapies share some common denominators. To some degree they have the goal of identifying what the client wants and then modifying the person's thoughts, feelings, and behaviors. Although there is common ground, each theoretical orientation focuses on a particular dimension of human experience as a route to changing other facets of personality.[6]

I attempt to integrate goals from most of the major theories by paying attention to changes clients want to make. My early interventions are aimed at helping clients identify specific ways in which they want to be different. Once they have formulated concrete goals, it is possible to utilize a variety of techniques that foster modification of thinking processes, feelings, and ways of behaving.

When counseling culturally diverse client populations, it is important to consider the degree to which the general goals and methods employed are congruent with the cultural background and values of clients. It is essential that both therapist and client recognize their differences in goal orientation. For example, it can be a therapeutic mistake to encourage some clients to be assertive with their parents and tell them exactly what they are thinking and feeling. A client from a Middle Eastern culture might believe it is rude and disrespectful to confront one's parents and that it is inappropriate to bring out conflicts. The therapist who would push such a client to be independent and to deal with conflicts within the family would probably alienate this person.

Therapists must listen to their clients and enter their perceptual world. The process of therapy is best guided by the particular goals and values of each client, not by what the therapist thinks is best. Questions therapists frequently ask of their clients are "Why are you seeking counseling from me?" "What is it that you would like to explore?" and "What is it about yourself or your life situation that you most want to change?" By staying focused on what their clients want, therapists can greatly reduce the danger of imposing their own goals on clients.

Having considered the basic assumptions, views of assessment, and goals of therapy, we now consider a specific case. It is possible to learn a great deal about Ruth's interpersonal style by the manner in which we interact during the assessment process. As you study Ruth's case, look for ways to apply what you have just read to gain a fuller understanding of her.

The Case of Ruth

The themes in Ruth's life are characteristic of those of many clients with whom I have worked. As mentioned earlier, I took typical struggles from a number of clients and compiled a clinical picture of a client I call "Ruth." Ruth's intake form and autobiography, reproduced here, will provide you with much of the information you need to understand and work with her. Each of the theory chapters will provide additional information. As you read the next 13 chapters, refer to this information about Ruth to refresh your memory on some of the details and themes in her life.

In addition to what is presented here, Ruth is also the subject of an interactive self-study program titled *DVD for Integrative Counseling: The Case of Ruth and Lecturettes*. See Session 1 ("Beginning of Counseling") in particular for more information about Ruth.

Ruth's Autobiography

As a part of the intake process, the counselor asked Ruth to bring the autobiography she had written for her counseling class. Although most therapists do not make it a practice to ask their clients to write an autobiography, doing so can be beneficial. It provides clients with a way of reviewing significant life experiences and gives therapists insight into their clients' self-perception. Here is what Ruth wrote:

> Something I've become aware of recently is that I've pretty much lived for others. I've been the one who gives and gives until there is little left to give. I give to my husband, John. I've been the "good wife" and the "good mother" that he expects me to be. I realize that I need John, and I'm afraid he might leave me if I change too much. I've given my all to see that my kids grow up decently, but even though I'm trying my best, I often worry that I haven't done enough. When I look at my life now, I don't like what I see. I don't like who I am, and I certainly don't feel very proud of my body. I'm very overweight, and despite my good intentions to lose weight I just can't seem to succeed. I enjoy eating and often eat too much. My family nagged me as a child, but the more they wanted me to stop, the more I seemed to eat, sometimes to the point of making myself sick. I make resolutions to start an exercise program and stick to a diet, but I've yet to find a way to be successful.
>
> One of the things I do look forward to is becoming a teacher in an elementary school. I think this would make my life more meaningful. I worry a lot

about what will become of me when my kids leave and there is just John and me in that house. I know I should at least get out and get the job as a substitute teacher in a private school that I've wanted (and have an offer for), yet I drag my feet on that one too.

One thing that troubles me is my increasingly frequent feelings of panic. I never remember feeling that bad. Often during the day, when I'm at school, I feel dizzy, almost like fainting, and have difficulty breathing. Sometimes in class I get hot flashes, and then sweat profusely. At times my hands tremble, and I'm afraid that others will notice this. There are times when I wake up at night with my heart beating very fast, in a cold sweat. I feel a sense of doom, but I don't know what over. I get scared over these feelings, which just seem to creep up on me. It makes me think that I might be going crazy.

I worry about death—about my dying—a lot. As a kid I was motivated by fear. Nine years ago I finally broke away from my strong fundamentalist church because I could see that it was not me. A philosophy class in the community college years ago got me to thinking about the values I was taught. When I was 30, I made the break from the fundamentalist religion that I had so closely lived by. I'm now attending a less dogmatic church, yet I still feel pangs of guilt that I am not living by the religion my parents brought me up with. My parents haven't formally disowned me, but in many ways I think they have. I'll never win their approval as long as I stay away from the religion that's so dear to them. But I find it more and more difficult to live by something I don't believe in. The big problem for me is that I so often feel lost and confused, wanting some kind of anchor in my life. I know what I don't believe, but I still have little to replace those values with that I once lived by. I sometimes wonder if I really did discard those values.

As part of my college program I took a course that was an introduction to counseling, and that opened my eyes to a lot of things. One of our guest speakers was a licensed clinical psychologist who talked about the value of counseling for people even though they are not seriously disturbed. I began to consider that maybe I could benefit from getting some counseling. Up until that time I had always thought you had to be mentally ill before going to a psychotherapist. I see that I could work on a lot of things that I've neatly tucked away in my life. Yet even though I think I've almost made the decision to seek therapy, there is still this nagging fear within me. What if I find out things about myself that I don't like? What will I do if I discover an emptiness inside of me? What if I lose John while I'm getting myself together? I so much want magical answers. All my life I've had clear answers to every question. Then nine years ago, when I became a questioner to some extent, I lost those answers.

What I most want from therapy is that the therapist will help me discover the things I need to do in order to change. My fear is that I could settle for a comfortable life that I have now, even though a great part of it drives me nuts. Sure, it's boring and stale, but it's predictable. Then again it's uncomfortable to be where I am. I'm scared to make the wrong decisions and that in doing so I'll ruin not only my life but John's life and the future of my kids. I feel I owe it to them to stay in this marriage. I guess I'm trapped and don't see a way out. Sometimes I wonder if I should turn my life over to God and let Him take over. I so much wish He would take over! I don't know what lies ahead. I'm afraid and excited at the same time.

TABLE 1.1

CLIENT'S INTAKE FORM

AGE	SEX	RACE	MARITAL STATUS	SOCIOECONOMIC STATUS
39	Female	Caucasian	Married	Middle Class

APPEARANCE
Dresses meticulously, is overweight, fidgets constantly with her clothes, avoids eye contact, and speaks rapidly.

LIVING SITUATION
Recently graduated from college as an elementary education major, lives with husband (John, 45) and her children (Rob, 19; Jennifer, 18; Susan, 17; and Adam, 16).

PRESENTING PROBLEM
Client reports pervasive dissatisfaction. She says her life is rather uneventful and predictable, and she feels some panic over reaching the age of 39, wondering where the years have gone. For 2 years she has been troubled with a range of psychosomatic complaints, including sleep disturbances, anxiety, dizziness, heart palpitations, and headaches. At times she has to push herself to leave the house. Client complains that she cries easily over simple matters, often feels depressed, and has a weight problem.

HISTORY OF PRESENTING PROBLEM
Client made her major career as a housewife and mother until her children became adolescents. She then entered college part time and obtained a bachelor's degree. She has recently begun work toward a credential in elementary education. Through her contacts with others at the university she became aware of how she has limited herself, how she has fostered her family's dependence on her, and how frightened she is of branching out from her roles as mother and wife.

Ruth completed a course in introduction to counseling that encouraged her to look at the direction of her own life. As part of the course, Ruth participated in self-awareness groups, had a few individual counseling sessions, and wrote several papers dealing with the turning points in her own life. One of the requirements was to write an extensive autobiography that was based on an application of the principles of the counseling course to her own personal development. This course and her experiences with fellow students in it acted as a catalyst in getting her to take an honest look at her life. Ruth is not clear at this point who she is, apart from being a mother, wife, and student. She realizes that she does not have a good sense of what she wants for herself and that she typically lived up to what others in her life wanted for her. She has decided to seek individual therapy for the following reasons:

• A physician whom she consulted could find no organic or medical basis for her physical symptoms and recommended personal therapy. In her words, her major symptoms are these: "I sometimes feel very panicky, especially at night when I'm trying to sleep. Sometimes I'll wake up and find it difficult to breathe and my heart will be pounding. I toss and turn trying to relax, and instead I feel tense and worry a lot. It's hard for me to turn off my thoughts. Then during the day I'm so tired I can hardly function, and I find that lately I cry very easily when minor things go wrong."

• She is aware that she has lived a very structured and disciplined life, that she has functioned largely by taking care of the home and the needs of her four children and her husband, and that to some degree she is no longer content with this. Yet she reports that she doesn't know what "more than this" is. Although she would like to get more involved professionally, the thought of doing so frightens her. She worries about her right to think and act in her own best interests, she fears not succeeding in the professional world, and she most of all worries about how all this might threaten her family.

• Her children range in age from 16 to 19, and all are now finding more of their satisfactions outside of the family and the home and spending increasing time with their friends. Ruth sees these changes and is concerned about "losing" them. She is having particular problems with her daughter Jennifer, and is at a loss about how to deal with her. In general, Ruth feels very much unappreciated by her children.

• In thinking about her future, Ruth is not sure who or what she wants to become. She would like to develop a sense of herself apart from the expectations of others. She finds herself wondering what she "should" want and what she "should" be doing. Ruth does not find her relationship with her husband, John, satisfactory. He appears to resist her attempts to make changes and prefers that she remain as she was. She is anxious over the prospects of challenging this relationship, fearing that if she does, she might end up alone.

• Lately, Ruth is experiencing more concern over aging.

All of these factors combined have provided the motivation for her to take the necessary steps to initiate individual therapy. The greatest catalyst for her to come for therapy was the increase of her physical symptoms and her anxiety.

PSYCHOSOCIAL HISTORY

Ruth is the oldest of four children. Her father is a fundamentalist minister, and her mother is a housewife. She describes her father as distant, authoritarian, and rigid; her relationship with him was one of unquestioning, fearful adherence to his rules and standards. She remembers her mother as being critical, and she thought she could never do enough to please her. At other times her mother was supportive. The family demonstrated little affection. In many ways Ruth took on the role of caring for her younger brother and sisters, largely in the hope of winning the approval of her parents. When she attempted to have any kind of fun, she encountered her father's disapproval and outright scorn. To a large extent this pattern of taking care of others has extended throughout her entire life.

One critical incident took place when Ruth was 6 years old. She reported: "My father caught me 'playing doctor' with an 8-year-old boy. He lectured me and refused to speak to me for weeks. I felt extremely guilty and ashamed." It appears Ruth carried feelings of guilt into her adolescence and thus repressed her own emerging sexuality.

In her social relationships Ruth had difficulty making and keeping friends. She felt socially isolated from her peers because they viewed her as "weird." Although she wanted the approval of others, she was not willing to compromise her morals for fear of the consequences.

Ruth was not allowed to date until she completed high school; at the age of 19 she married the first person that she dated. She used her mother as a role model by becoming a homemaker.

Diagnostic Impressions of Ruth

While I was revising an earlier edition of this book, I had a telephone call from Michael Nystul, a professor of counseling at New Mexico State University, who told me that he was using *Case Approach to Counseling and Psychotherapy* for one of his courses.

"Dr. Corey," he asked, "what diagnosis would you give Ruth? My students are discussing her case, and they are interested in getting your opinion about her diagnostic category."

"Well," I replied, "I generally don't think in diagnostic terms, so I would be hard pressed to give Ruth a diagnosis."

"But if you *had* to give her a diagnosis," Dr. Nystul insisted, "what would it be?"

We exchanged our views on a possible diagnosis for Ruth. Because several possible diagnoses seemed to fit in her case, I began thinking about the process a practitioner goes through in attempting to identify the most appropriate diagnostic category for a client. I then asked several of my colleagues at the university who were familiar with Ruth's case to suggest a diagnosis. Interestingly, I got a variety of interpretations, each with a good supporting rationale. I also asked some of those who were reviewing this manuscript to give me their impressions of the most appropriate diagnostic category for Ruth. As you might suspect, there were a variety of diagnostic impressions.

At this point you are just beginning to familiarize yourself with Ruth. What would be your provisional diagnosis for Ruth? Justify the diagnosis you select on the basis of the information presented in this chapter. In learning about the various approaches to counseling Ruth, you may find new evidence or emerging patterns of behavior that warrant modifying your original diagnosis. This section deals with diagnostic impressions of Ruth, but this topic is revisited in each of the following 12 theory chapters. I've asked the guest contributors to give their diagnostic impressions of Ruth and to discuss how their views of diagnosis and assessment influence their practice.

Rather than identifying one specific major disorder, I will describe a number of possible provisional diagnoses that *may* be appropriate for Ruth's case. As you review the different theories, consider these diagnostic classifications from the *DSM-IV-TR* to see which category you think best fits the case of Ruth.

🐾 **Adjustment Disorder**   The key feature of adjustment disorder is the development of clinically significant emotional or behavioral symptoms in response to psychosocial stresses. Some stressors may accompany specific developmental events, such as beginning school, becoming a parent, having children leave home, or failing to attain educational or career goals. There is some basis for giving Ruth a diagnosis of adjustment disorder, possibly with anxiety. She is experiencing some key developmental crises. A number of stressors are resulting in symptoms such as nervousness, worry, and fear of separation from major figures in her life. She could also be classified as "adjustment disorder, unspecified," which reflects symptoms such as physical complaints, social withdrawal, or work or academic inhibition.

🔖 Panic Disorder   Individuals who have unexpected panic attacks typically describe their fear as intense and report that they feel as if they are going to die, lose control, or have a heart attack. In general, Ruth presents evidence of an anxiety disorder; specifically, her pattern of symptoms meets the diagnostic criteria for panic attack: palpitations of the heart, sweating, shortness of breath, dizziness, trembling, hot flashes and cold sweats, fear of dying, and fear of losing control or going crazy.

🔖 Dysthymic Disorder   The essential feature of a dysthymic disorder is chronic depression, which occurs for most of the day on more days than not for at least 2 years. Individuals with such a disorder often describe their condition as feeling "down in the dumps." When people experience a depressed mood, they often manifest some of the following symptoms: overeating, insomnia, low energy or fatigue, low self-esteem, difficulty making decisions, and feelings of hopelessness. At times, individuals are self-critical and view themselves as uninteresting or incapable. Ruth appears to fit this picture. She exhibits a long-term depressed mood that is part of her character but not severe enough to be considered major depression. She also manifests dependent personality traits in that she consistently puts the needs of others ahead of her own and has low self-esteem. She exhibits a number of physical complaints but does not indicate any serious physical disease necessitating surgery or other severe medical intervention.

🔖 Identity Problem   Ruth's patterns fit the syndrome of identity problem. The main features of this classification include uncertainty about long-term goals, career choice, friendship patterns, sexual orientation and behavior, moral and religious values, and group loyalties. Affected clients respond to their uncertainty with anxiety and depression and are preoccupied about their lack of a sense of self. These people doubt themselves in everyday situations. One of the most common questions asked by the person with an identity disorder is "Who am I?"

I asked two of the reviewers of *Case Approach to Counseling and Psychotherapy* to provide their diagnostic perspectives on Ruth's case. They are Dr. Michael Nystul, who was introduced earlier, and Dr. Beverly Palmer, professor of psychology at California State University at Dominguez Hills.

DR. NYSTUL'S *DSM-IV-TR* DIAGNOSIS   The three key factors I use to facilitate the process of a differential diagnosis are onset, severity, and duration. Normally, I would explore these three issues within the context of a clinical interview, which would include a mental-status exam. In this instance, I must base my diagnostic impressions on Ruth's autobiography.

The *DSM-IV-TR* provides guidelines for a comprehensive assessment leading to a diagnosis. There are five categories, called axes, in the *DSM-IV-TR* that can be used by clinicians in formulating a treatment plan:

- *Axis I.* Clinical disorders; other conditions that may be a focus of clinical attention
- *Axis II.* Personality disorders; mental retardation

- *Axis III.* General medical conditions
- *Axis IV.* Psychosocial and environmental problems
- *Axis V.* Global assessment of functioning

As I read Ruth's autobiography, the major symptoms that stood out for me were anxiety and depression (Axis I disorders). The primary considerations for a differential diagnosis in this case appear to be an adjustment disorder with mixed anxiety and depressed mood, a panic disorder without agoraphobia, or a dysthymic disorder. For example, Ruth's diagnosis could be an adjustment disorder if (1) her symptoms (anxiety and depression) occurred within 3 months of the stressor and were resolved within 6 months of the termination of the stressor, and (2) her symptoms did not fulfill the criteria for one or more Axis I disorders such as a panic disorder or a dysthymic disorder. If her symptoms fulfilled the criteria for one or more Axis I disorders such as a panic disorder and dysthymic disorder, then those disorders would be recorded on Axis I and adjustment disorder would not be recorded.

Axis I also includes other conditions that are not mental disorders but may be a focus of clinical attention. Some of the "other conditions" that may be appropriate for Ruth include parent–child relational problem, partner relational problem, occupational problem, identity problem, and phase of life problem. I would use the clinical interview to determine if one or more of these "other conditions" would be included in Ruth's *DSM-IV-TR* diagnosis on Axis I.

In terms of Axis II, I would want to rule out a dependent personality disorder. The history suggests "she has fostered her family's dependence on her" and has "pretty much lived for others." If she did not meet the full criteria for a dependent personality disorder, I would record "dependent personality traits" on Axis II if I believed Ruth had prominent maladaptive personality features relating to dependency.

I would record "none" on Axis III (general medical conditions) because the history notes that a physician did not find anything medically wrong with Ruth.

Axis IV requires a listing of the psychosocial and environmental problems Ruth has experienced within the last year (or longer if she had experienced a posttraumatic stress disorder). A stressor that would be included for Ruth is discord with child. (The history suggested Ruth was having significant problems with Jennifer.) If my clinical interview suggested marital discord, that would also be included on Axis IV.

Axis V allows for the determination of Ruth's Global Assessment of Functioning (GAF). Based on *DSM-IV-TR* guidelines, I would estimate her current GAF to be 60, which would indicate that she has moderate symptoms or moderate difficulty in her overall psychological functioning.

DR. PALMER'S *DSM-IV-TR* DIAGNOSIS Ruth's case is difficult to diagnose because she is a person on paper rather than a person in front of me. I prefer to work in a collaborative way with the client so that questions may arise from either of us that yield information to inform the diagnosis. Ruth's nonverbal behavior also may contribute to refining the clinical picture. The *DSM-IV-TR* category of panic disorder without agoraphobia (300.01) is the one most supported by the evidence presented. Ruth experiences unexpected panic attacks and is worried about having additional attacks. The symptoms of a panic attack she experiences are dizziness, heart palpitations, shortness of breath, trembling, sweating, and a fear of going crazy. All of these symptoms occur within a 10-minute period and occur both at school and during the evening when she is trying to sleep. Presently, there is no evidence that she has agoraphobia (anxiety about being in a place from which escape might be difficult, which often causes the person to not want to leave her house). However, I would want to monitor her for agoraphobia because recurrent panic attacks can develop into panic disorder with agoraphobia. Ruth's binge eating puts her in another *DSM-IV-TR* disorder: eating disorder not otherwise specified (307.50)—specifically, binge eating disorder. She reports eating more than she should when she is depressed and being very overweight. She also ate to the point of making herself sick when she was a child, and she has tried exercise and dieting but is unable to stick to either. Thus, it appears that in a discrete period of time Ruth eats an amount of food that is larger than most people would eat and that she experiences a lack of control over eating during these episodes.

Ruth has two other *DSM-IV-TR* conditions: a phase of life problem (V62.89) and an identity problem (313.82). She is concerned about what her life will be like after her children leave home or if she begins a professional job, and these concerns are characterized by the existential therapist as components of a midlife crisis. She is struggling with the identity issues of finding the values she does believe in and who she is apart from the expectations of others. Ruth is also having conflicts with her teenage daughter and with her husband, but it is difficult to determine whether these relational problems are causing clinically significant symptoms or significant impairment in family functioning. Thus, two other *DSM-IV-TR* conditions, a partner relational problem (V61.10) and a parent–child relational problem (V61.20), are probably not warranted from the evidence given.

As important as ruling *in* a particular diagnosis is ruling *out* other possible diagnoses. Ruth mentions several times that she feels "depressed" and that she eats more when she is depressed, yet there are not enough symptoms of depression to diagnose a mood disorder such as dysthymic disorder according to the *DSM-IV-TR*. Ruth does have low self-confidence and she does overeat, but she has had an issue with overeating since childhood and her depressed mood and crying are not present for most of the day almost every day for at least 2 years. Her tiredness during the day may be due to the panic attacks that make it difficult for her to sleep some nights. If she had "depression," she would feel tired even though she had had a good night's sleep, and her insomnia (typically early-morning awakening) would not be due to worrying or panic attacks. Many people use "depression" as a catch-all term to describe their present condition, but dysthymia does not fit this case as well as does an anxiety-based disorder such as panic disorder. The difference between self-diagnosis and a therapist's diagnosis is often in the degree of understanding of the psychological, social, and biological theories that are the foundation of the *DSM-IV-TR* categories. Of course, sometimes beneath the panic attacks and anxiety is a depression that can pop up once the panic attacks are alleviated. Another factor that must be eliminated when making the diagnosis of panic attacks is that there is no substance use or general medical condition (such as hyperthyroidism) that might cause the symptoms Ruth reports. She did have a recent checkup by a physician, which is always a wise recommendation for every therapist to make during the initial assessment.

The *DSM-IV-TR* is a multiaxial system of diagnosis, and so far I have given only Axis I diagnoses. Axis II is used to diagnose personality disorders or personality features that might also be the focus of treatment. Sometimes a person can have only an Axis I or only an Axis II diagnosis, but often a person has diagnoses on both axes, and the two axes influence each other in treatment. In the case of Ruth there is no Axis II diagnosis, although she does show a few dependent personality features. As the behavior therapist says, Ruth has trouble stating her viewpoints clearly, and she often accepts projects in which she does not want to get involved. She admits dragging her feet in getting the substitute schoolteacher job she wants, which may be an indication of the dependent personality trait of having difficulty initiating projects or doing things on her own. Ruth shows only three dependent personality traits, so she does not have the full-blown picture of dependent personality disorder. The therapist also has to be careful that those traits typical of the socialization of a woman Ruth's age and ethnicity are not pathologized into dependent personality disorder.

Axis III is the place to indicate the results of her recent medical consultation and her problem with being overweight. Her physical condition and physical problems interact with her psychological problems reported on Axes I and II, so it is important to record them in this multiaxial system of diagnosis. For example, her being overweight affects her self-esteem, and her self-esteem affects her weight. Also, her panic attacks might be treated by medication as well as by psychological means, so health professionals from all fields need to communicate with one another. This multiaxial system is an ideal way to start this communication.

Axis IV is the place to record any social or environmental factors in Ruth's life. She reports relational problems with her daughter and with her husband, so it is on this axis that these social issues are recorded as problems with her primary support group.

The final axis, Axis V, is used to report Ruth's overall level of functioning. The usual way of recording this is by using the GAF scale. Ruth has some moderate symptoms, such as occasional panic attacks, which cause her to have some difficulty in her functioning at home, so she receives a GAF score of between 51 and 60.

One important axis is missing from the *DSM-IV-TR,* and that is one that records Ruth's strengths. Ruth has many strengths: she has recently pursued higher education successfully, and she has good insight into her present condition as well as a thirst for exploring her future directions. Ruth's strengths will be used in treatment just as much as will her difficulties, so it is important to have a record of them along with the *DSM-IV-TR* system of diagnosis.

This section on diagnostic procedures with Ruth is necessarily brief. I encourage you to consult the *DSM-IV-TR* as a reference tool because it will introduce you to the categories and the labeling system that are part of the assessment and diagnostic process.

What to Look for in the Theory Chapters

The case approach chapters are all structured in a similar way. First, you will read a brief overview of the featured approach. This is followed by one or more sections written by experts in each of the theoretical orientations that illustrate their way of working with Ruth. It is a good practice for counselors to consult with other practitioners at times, for doing so provides them with ideas of other ways to proceed with a client. In working with Ruth, I am using this model of consultation. Background information on Ruth's case was sent to well-known representatives of each approach, and they were asked to answer these questions: "How would you assess Ruth's case?" "On what themes would you probably focus?" "What procedures would you likely use?" and "How would you expect the therapeutic process to unfold?" You can gain much from examining these working models. You can read more about these guest consultants in the "About the Contributors" section at the front of this book.

After the guest contributors' section, I assume the identity of a therapist from the particular orientation being considered, and, staying within the spirit of each specific approach as much as possible, I show you my interpretation and my own style of working with Ruth. In each chapter I give an overview of the particular theory by describing (1) the basic assumptions underlying practice, (2) my initial assessment of Ruth, (3) the goals that will guide our work, and (4) the therapeutic procedures and techniques that are likely to be employed in attaining our goals. A section on the therapeutic process shows samples of our work together. It is illustrated with dialogue between Ruth and me, along with an ongoing process commentary that explains my rationale for the interventions I make and the general direction of her therapy.

There are many differences in therapeutic style among practitioners who share the same theoretical orientation, and there is no "one right way" of practicing any of these theoretical approaches. I encourage you to do your best in assuming each of the separate theoretical perspectives as you follow the case of Ruth. Doing this will help you decide which concepts and techniques you want to incorporate in your own therapeutic style.

Questions for Reflection

1. In looking over the provisional diagnoses described here, what patterns do you see in these assessments taken as a group?
2. Which assessments do you tend to agree with the most? Why? If you do not agree with a particular diagnostic formulation, give your reasons.
3. What are your legal and ethical responsibilities when diagnosing Ruth?
4. What would you ask clients regarding their cultural background as part of the assessment process?
5. Under what circumstances, if any, would you be likely to share your diagnostic impressions with her?

Notes

1. Corey, G., & Haynes, R. (2013). *DVD for integrative counseling: The case of Ruth and lecturettes.* Belmont, CA: Brooks/Cole, Cengage Learning.
2. Corey, G. (2013). *The art of integrative counseling* (3rd ed.). Belmont, CA: Brooks/Cole, Cengage Learning.
3. Corey, G. (2013). *Theory and practice of counseling and psychotherapy* (9th ed.). Belmont, CA: Brooks/Cole, Cengage Learning and this book and have parallel coverage of each of the theories you will be studying. As a basis for understanding the guest contributors' presentations on working with Ruth in the chapters that follow, refer to *Theory and Practice of Counseling and Psychotherapy* for background information on the basic assumptions, key concepts, elements of the therapeutic process, and application and techniques for each of the theories.
4. Three excellent books on the subject of psychotherapy integration are Norcross, J., & Goldfried, M. Eds. (2005). *Handbook of psychotherapy integration* (2nd ed.). New York: Oxford University Press; Stricker, G. (2010). *Psychotherapy integration.* Washington, DC: American Psychological Association; and Stricker, G., & Gold, J., Eds. (2006). *A casebook of psychotherapy integration.* Washington, DC: American Psychological Association.
5. The official guide to a system of classifying psychological disorders is the *Diagnostic and Statistical Manual of Mental Disorders* (4th ed., compiled in 1994, with a Text Revision in 2000), by the American Psychiatric Association. The *DSM-IV-TR* gives specific criteria for classifying emotional and behavioral disturbances and shows the differences among the various disorders.
6. In Session 3 ("Establishing Therapeutic Goals") of *DVD for Integrative Counseling: The Case of Ruth and Lecturettes,* I demonstrate my way of assisting Ruth in formulating her goals, which will provide a direction for her counseling.

CHAPTER TWO

Case Approach to Psychoanalytic Therapy

General Overview of Psychoanalytic Therapy

The main goal of psychoanalytic therapy is to resolve intrapsychic conflicts, toward the end of reconstructing one's basic personality. Analytic therapy is not limited to problem solving and learning new behaviors; there is a deeper probing into the past to develop one's level of self-understanding.

From the psychoanalytic perspective, all techniques are designed to help the client gain insight and bring repressed material to the surface so that it can be dealt with consciously. Major techniques include gathering life-history data, dream analysis, free association, and interpretation and analysis of resistance and transference. Such procedures are aimed at increasing awareness, gaining intellectual and emotional insight, and beginning a working-through process that will lead to the reorganization of personality.

Psychoanalytic clients are ready to terminate their sessions when they and the therapist agree that they have clarified and accepted their emotional problems, have understood the historical roots of their difficulties, and can integrate their awareness of past problems with present relationships. Outcomes of therapy are subjectively evaluated, primarily by the therapist, and to some extent, by the client. The main criteria used to assess outcomes are the client's degree of emotional and cognitive insight and the degree to which he or she has worked through the transference relationship.

Developed by Sigmund Freud, psychoanalytic theory is the foundation for modern-day psychiatry, psychology, and counseling and is the yardstick by which all subsequent therapies have been measured. Every student in the counseling field should be familiar with this approach and how it has evolved into a variety of more contemporary, brief psychodynamic models. The psychoanalytically oriented approach described by Dr. Blau provides a solid base to build on in later chapters.

A Psychoanalytic Therapist's Perspective on Ruth

by William Blau, PhD

Assessment of Ruth

❧ Psychoanalytic Perspective and Overview of Case Material

As a psychoanalytically oriented therapist, I suspect that Ruth's background descriptions of her parents, her siblings, and herself are less than objective. Moreover, I predict that the areas of inaccuracy will turn out to be clues to the core of her personality problems. I anticipate finding that her symptoms (anxiety attacks, overeating, fear of accomplishment, panic over being 39, fear of abandonment, and so forth) can be interpreted as outward manifestations of unconscious conflicts that have their origins in childhood experiences and defensive reactions to these experiences that were necessary to her as a child. I suspect, given her intelligence and motivation, that her current exacerbation of symptoms is related to her recognition of discrepancies between what makes sense to her logically and what seems to drive her emotions and behavior. I hypothesize that Ruth is experiencing a split (a struggle between opposing dimensions of herself). This conflict is between the part of her that wants to change and the other part of her that clings to old patterns that were once necessary and have helped her maintain mental stability all her life. Although some of her defenses seem maladaptive from my perspective, I believe I cannot give her the most effective help unless I can fully understand why her patterns of defense seem necessary to her now and why, once, they were necessary to her psychological survival.

In contrast to some therapeutic practitioners, I am very interested in why Ruth thinks, feels, and behaves as she does. I have no interest in excusing her behavior or condemning others, but I believe her problems can be most fully helped by answering the "why" as well as the "what" questions regarding her life. This fundamental interest in the "whys" of an individual client's experience and behavior is a critical distinction between analytic therapy and other approaches. My proposed treatment is based on the work of Sigmund Freud and those later psychoanalysts whose contributions enhanced, rather than disputed, the core elements of psychoanalytic theory.

Unraveling the dynamics of Ruth's history and filling in the story of her life with newly emerging memories will be an ongoing part of treatment; hence, this aspect of assessment is never complete although it becomes less important in the final phases of treatment.

❧ Assessing Ruth's Suitability for Analytic Therapy

Before establishing a contract to do analytic therapy with Ruth, I need to ascertain whether she is a good candidate for the treatment and whether she has the perseverance and resources to make this approach the treatment of choice. Assessment of her need for analytic therapy would include determining whether she wants and needs to understand the unconscious roots of her neurosis. If simply teaching her about the irrationality of some of her beliefs would lead to significant change, she would probably not need analytic therapy. Didactic, cognitive approaches would suffice. I suspect, however, that Ruth does not consciously know why she reacts in symptomatic ways and that she is repeatedly frustrated when she has been given good advice by others (or by herself) but still finds the old patterns persisting.

Ruth's case history does include a number of factors suggesting that she could be a good candidate for analytic treatment. Her autobiography shows her to be a woman for whom understanding the meaning of her life is important and for whom achieving individuation is a meaningful goal. Her autobiography also shows that she has the ability to look at herself from a somewhat objective perspective. Her need for symptom alleviation is sufficient to provide strong motivation for change, yet her symptoms are not currently incapacitating.

Ruth may expect that her therapist will tell her what to do with her life and take the place of her father and the God of her childhood religion. In contracting with her for treatment, I would let her know that fulfillment of such expectations is not provided by analytic psychotherapy; however, this would by no means end the issue. Despite the formal contract, I anticipate that Ruth will continue to demand that the therapist take charge of her life. This aspect of transference may be of ongoing significance in treatment. On the whole, Ruth is the sort of client for whom analytically oriented psychotherapy might be indicated.

🪶 Diagnosis   Analytic therapy is more clearly indicated for some disorders than for others, and some disorders require extensive modification of technique. But traditional, symptom-based diagnosis is limited in that an individual's ability to form a therapeutic alliance, which is the key issue in assessment for analytic treatment, is largely independent of diagnosis. Moreover, *DSM-IV-TR*[1] diagnoses typically fail to convey the essence of the client or of the client's suffering.

Ruth's reported unhappiness with her life could be her way of expressing symptoms of depression that might be helped by medication in addition to psychotherapy. *DSM-IV-TR* diagnoses can be useful in determining the role of organic factors in Ruth's symptomatology and in deciding if she should be referred for medication. Although she does not appear to meet the criteria for a major depressive disorder, a *DSM-IV-TR* diagnosis of dysthymic disorder should be considered if she is depressed "for most of the day, for more days than not" for a period of at least 2 years. Her panic attacks could be related to a cardiac condition, and her other psychophysiological symptoms could have organic as well as psychodynamic origins. In *DSM-IV-TR* terms, Ruth meets the following diagnostic criteria:

300.01: panic disorder without agoraphobia

313.82: identity problem

Neither of these diagnostic categories, in my opinion, conveys a feeling for Ruth as she is described in her autobiography and intake form. *DSM-IV-TR* diagnoses tend to reify symptom clusters rather than promote understanding of the client as a person or address the etiology of the symptoms. Analytic assessment recognizes that symptoms have underlying causes, and the etiology of a symptom must be addressed if permanent healing is to occur. If the focus of treatment is limited to individual symptoms, symptom substitution may occur, a phenomenon in which the symptom that has been "cured" is replaced by another symptom, just as one addictive behavior may be replaced by another.

Panic attacks are the essential elements of the *panic disorder* diagnosis, and I would consider treating these attacks initially with the cost-effective techniques of psychophysiological counseling and biofeedback rather than psychoanalytic psychotherapy. *DSM-IV-TR* diagnoses of panic disorder are coded as either with or without agoraphobia. I specified "without agoraphobia" because Ruth doesn't describe herself as being unduly afraid to travel or to be in crowds or similar social or confining situations.

The *DSM-IV-TR* category of *identity problem* is descriptive of the contents of Ruth's concerns. However, it is not a "clinical disorder" in *DSM-IV-TR* terms, and it minimizes the intensity of her very real suffering. The real, human Ruth presents a blending of neurotic symptoms and existential concerns.

Ruth's symptoms seem to be at a critical stage and could flower into an eating disorder, a counterphobic impulsive behavior, a generalized anxiety disorder, or a psychosomatic conversion disorder, as well as agoraphobia or a dysthymic disorder as previously discussed. Ruth's difficulties in establishing a sense of self suggest that her individuation is an important goal of treatment. I do not anticipate overtly psychotic symptoms, and her basic reality testing appears sufficiently stable that she can be expected to undergo some degree of regression in the course of treatment without danger of precipitating a psychotic break.

Ruth's history does not include any incidents of suicidal behavior. Nevertheless, risk factors, including possible suicidal ideation and potential danger to others, must be assessed. In some cases, suicidal clients may be treated with analytic therapy, but modifications in technique are necessary.

Key Issues and Themes in Working With Ruth

🦋 Intrapsychic Conflicts and Repression of Childhood Experiences   As a psychoanalytically oriented psychotherapist, I accept the role of detective in ferreting out the secrets of the past that are locked away in Ruth's unconscious. Although I am guided by theory to suspicious content areas, her psyche and the secrets therein are uniquely hers, and it is ultimately she who will know the truth of her life through her own courage and perceptions.

I suspect that the psychosexual aspects of Ruth's relationships with her parents (and possibly her siblings) remain key conflict areas for her, even now. In the classical Freudian model of healthy development, she would have experienced early libidinal attraction to her father, which she would eventually have replaced with normal heterosexual interests in male peers; likewise, her feelings of rivalry with her mother for her father's affection would have been replaced with identification with her mother. In the ideal model, moreover, she would have experienced rebellion against parental constraints, particularly during the developmental period associated with toilet training and also in adolescence.

In reality Ruth appears to have superficially avoided normal rebellion and to have suppressed her sexuality except for adopting a wifely role with the first man she dated. Although she followed the format of using her mother as role model and having children by an acceptable husband, she apparently abdicated in the struggles of sexuality, rebellion, and identification, leaving these conflicts unresolved. Her conscious recollections of her parents are of a rigid, fundamentalist father and a "critical" mother. I would be interested in knowing what these parents were really like, as perceived by Ruth in childhood. How did her father handle his feelings for his children? Did his aloofness mask strongly suppressed incestuous feelings that she intuitively sensed? Were these ever acted out?

A Freudian view of her father's harsh reactions to Ruth's "playing doctor" would emphasize the Oedipus/Electra aspects of this father–daughter encounter. Her father's refusal to speak to her for weeks after this incident suggests jealousy rather than simply moral rejection of childhood sexual activity. This suspicion is supported by the parentally imposed isolation of the children that delayed dating until after high school. Ruth's attempts to win her father's approval by supplanting the role of her mother (in caring for her younger siblings) is also consistent with these Oedipus/Electra dynamics. Ruth internalized her father's overtly negative attitude to sexuality.

If these hypotheses are correct, a theme in therapy will be Ruth's reexperiencing of the sensual aspects of her attachment to her father and his response to her. As she is able to fully remember, accept, and "own" these repressed feelings and fantasies, she will begin to loosen her unconscious attachment to them. She can become open to an adult relationship in which her sexuality is appreciated rather than scorned or distorted.

Although there is no direct evidence of sexual abuse in the case material, the family dynamics are such that there is the possibility of actual incestuous acts by the father, the memories of which have been repressed by Ruth. Even more likely is the pattern wherein the father's incestuous feelings were not overtly acted out but were so intense that he developed defenses of reaction formation and projection, labeling her sexuality (rather than his) as reprehensible. The jealous response of Ruth's mother is consistent with either of the above patterns of paternal behavior, but the mother's response is more pathological (and more pathogenic) if actual abuse occurred.

Oedipus/Electra feelings by both parent and child are considered part of normal development. However, intense conflicts and guilt regarding these feelings or experiences are common in clients seeking counseling or psychotherapy and frequently have their origin in childhood experiences of abuse, the memories of which may or may not have been repressed. Regardless of the details of the actual memories and buried feelings unearthed in therapy, the analytic therapist is alert for indications of psychological traumas in the client's early life, psychic wounds that may be associated with a family *secret* that the client has needed to protect from exposure through suppression, denial, and repression. The probability of a secret being at the heart of Ruth's neurosis is increased by the indication in the case material that she was socially isolated and that her lack of relationships outside the family was enforced by her parents, at least in terms of dating. The entire family may have lived with their unspoken secrets in relative isolation. Although incestuous themes in one form or another are the most common secrets unearthed, other "unthinkable" secrets may be at the center of the repression—hidden mental illness, homosexuality, or alcoholism of a family member are unmentionable secrets in some families.

To what extent is Ruth bringing themes from her family of origin to her present family? She defines her husband only by what he is not (her father) and by his potential to reject her (as her father had rejected her). Does she know the man she married at all, or is he merely a stand-in for the real man in her life? Is her husband's apparent rejection of her attempts at personal growth a facet of his personality, or is he being set up? Her reaction to her daughter Jennifer may very likely be related to her own failure to rebel. Acceptance and nurturance by Ruth of the suppressed child-rebel aspect of herself may well improve her relationship with her daughter.

Symptoms and Psychodynamics

The unconscious is an important determinant of human emotional responses and decision making. This assertion is central to Freudian psychoanalytic theory and has been strongly supported by empirical research.[2]

A psychoanalytic approach views psychological symptoms as active processes that give clues to the client's underlying psychodynamics. Some acute symptoms are valuable in that they alert the client that something is wrong. Other symptoms, particularly when chronic, may be extremely resistant to intervention and may be disabling or even, as in the case of anorexia, threaten the life of the client.

Ruth's symptoms suggest compatibility with psychoanalytically oriented therapy. I would use analytic theory to help Ruth understand the role of anxiety in her life and the methods she uses to control her anxiety. I view Ruth's current existential anxiety as related to these issues: Her early training by her parents clearly made individuation (in the object-relations sense) a very scary proposition for her; hence, any attempt toward individuation is anxiety provoking. She is, therefore, terrified not only of acting impulsively but also of acting independently. She hopes to make her own choices in life but also hopes that her therapist will make her decisions for her.

Ruth's symptom of overeating probably gratifies her need for affection, but a psychoanalytic approach to this symptom would also explore its developmental origin. Oral gratification is the primary focus of libidinal energy in the earliest stage of development. Symptoms associated with this stage can appear if the client suffered deprivation during this period. If this is the case, the adult tends to be fixated on getting the satisfaction never adequately obtained during the childhood stage.

Ruth's weight problem also has psychodynamic meaning. Being overweight may lead to her feeling sexually unattractive and, therefore, less likely to be faced with dealing with her sexuality. Ruth's increasing difficulty in leaving home suggests a fear of meeting others who might threaten the stability of her marriage. This symptom is consistent with the dynamics of her being overweight.

The exacerbation of physical symptoms and anxiety are cited in the background information as being the catalyst for Ruth's seeking therapy at this time. A psychoanalytic approach to these symptoms would explore the "secondary gain" associated with each symptom. A symptom may protect the client from anxiety evoked by both sides of an intrapsychic conflict. For instance, a headache might serve to keep her sexually distant from her husband while also providing a pretext for avoiding social contacts that might threaten the marriage.

Analytic therapy provides a means for treating Ruth's symptoms, but only in the context of broader treatment of her psychological problems. Some symptoms can be treated directly, and at lesser expense, by nonanalytic therapies. When the client desires to obtain insight as well as symptom relief or when the "secondary gain" of the symptom leads to either failure of the direct approach or to the substitution of a new symptom for the old one, analytic therapy is indicated. Ruth gives evidence of multiple symptoms and of a desire to examine her life. Hence, consideration of analytic therapy rather than a symptom-focused behavioral approach is reasonable.

Ruth might also consider the alternative of brief therapy. I consider brief analytic therapy a specialty area in which selected clients opt to focus on highly specific goals. Although it shortens the duration of treatment, it also modifies the therapeutic contract and places stringent demands on client and clinician alike. Brief therapy as a specialty should not be confused with arbitrary restrictions on the length of treatment imposed by managed care. Such restrictions are generally inconsistent with insight-oriented analytic therapy.

Open-ended treatment, in which a third-party payer periodically approves or rejects additional sessions, is incompatible with analytic therapy. Terminating therapy at the whim of an outside agency can be highly deleterious to the client. Such a termination is experienced as abandonment at best, and it may be equated unconsciously with betrayal or even malevolence on the part of the therapist.

Treatment Techniques

🐾 Psychoanalytically Oriented Psychotherapy Versus Psychoanalysis   The treatment approach I propose for Ruth is psychoanalytically oriented psychotherapy rather than psychoanalysis. This choice does not indicate a theoretical disagreement with the methods of classical analysis; psychoanalytic psychotherapy is a form of analytic treatment that has advantages and disadvantages compared with classical psychoanalysis. In classical analysis the analyst adopts a "blank-screen" approach, in which expressions of the real analyst–client relationship are minimized to promote development of the client's transference relationship with the analyst. Transference leads the client to react to the analyst "as if" he or she were a significant person from the client's past life.

Psychoanalytic therapy does *not* require the blank-screen approach, is less frustrating to the patient, allows the therapist more flexibility in technique, is less costly, may be shorter in duration, and provides "support" for the patient's least maladaptive defenses. Hence, it is often the treatment of choice. The drawbacks of analytic psychotherapy as compared with psychoanalysis are directly related to the advantages. The variations in technique lead to a lowering of expectations, as many aspects of the client's personality will remain unanalyzed due to elimination of the blank screen and the consequent intrusion of aspects of the "real" relationship into the "as-if" transference relationship. If, for example, Ruth is in psychoanalysis with me, free-associating from the couch, and she states her belief that I disapprove of some feeling or behavior of hers, I can be reasonably sure that she is reacting to me "as if" I were some other figure in her life. In contrast, if she makes the same assertion in face-to-face psychotherapy, my actual nonverbal behavior (or prior self-disclosure of any sort) may have given her valid clues to my actual (conscious or unconscious) disapproval of her feelings or behavior. I can never know the exact degree to which her response is a transference response as opposed to a response to my real behavior in our real relationship. In psychoanalytically oriented psychotherapy with Ruth, I must keep in mind that every aspect of our interaction will have a mix of real and as-if components. To the degree that I participate in the real relationship by providing support, by giving advice, or by sharing an opinion or personal experience, I am limiting my ability to maintain an analytic stance to the material she presents.

Although significant therapeutic work is possible using this model, I must be very sensitive to the meanings Ruth will attribute to my real interactions with her. If I disapprove of a particular act or intention of hers, for example, I can reasonably expect her to assume that I approve of all her reported acts or intentions to which I have not expressed disapproval. Thus, although I am free to use the real as well as the as-if relationship in making therapeutic interventions, I am not free to vacillate in my therapeutic stance without risk of doing harm.

The Therapeutic Contract   I form as clear a therapeutic contract as possible with Ruth, explaining the goals, costs, and risks of the treatment as well as briefly describing the methods and theory of psychotherapy. As a psychoanalytic therapist, I believe the economics of treatment, both in terms of financial arrangements and also in the investment of time and energy in therapy, cannot be separated from the process and outcomes of therapy. Thus, I make my expectations regarding payment explicit, including the analytic rule that fees are charged for canceled sessions. This contractual clarity regarding fees has therapeutic implications in that Ruth's obligation to me for my services is specified at the outset of treatment. Thereafter, she can feel free of any additional requirement to meet my needs, and I can interpret concerns that she does express about pleasing me or otherwise meeting my needs in terms of the as-if relationship.

A treatment schedule of two or three sessions per week, each session lasting 50 minutes, is typical for psychoanalytically oriented therapy, but many of my clients are seen weekly. Any planned vacations in the next 6 months or so, by either Ruth or me, should be noted, and therapy should not commence shortly before a vacation.

Other aspects of the contract include confidentiality (and its limitations), the degree to which I am available for emergencies or other between-session contacts, and an admonition to generally avoid making major life decisions during the course of treatment. The latter "rule" for clients in analysis is relevant to Ruth. She indicates that she wants a therapist to make decisions for her, and I have some concern about the possibility of her leaping to decisions while experiencing regression in the course of treatment. Unlike some analytically oriented therapists, I make myself available to clients by telephone between sessions. Ruth has some symptoms of depression, and I would encourage her to contact me should these symptoms worsen. With suicidal clients I establish a contract, often in writing, specifying that the client *will* contact me in the event of worsening symptoms.

🔖 Free Association   Free association is a primary technique in psychoanalysis and is the "basic rule" given to clients. As an analytic psychotherapist, I instruct clients to say whatever comes into their minds without censorship and without directing their words toward any particular problem or topic. The material obtained from this free association provides clues to the client's unconscious conflicts. I ask questions based on these clues to bring unconscious thoughts, feelings, and attitudes into conscious awareness. This technique is a form of the Socratic dialectic, in which questioning elicits psychological truths of which the person questioned was unaware. In my therapy with Ruth I emphasize the technique of free association at certain times. However, we have many other verbal interactions, even in the early phases of therapy. I often instruct her to express her associations to her dreams, to elements of her current life, and to memories of her past life, particularly new memories of childhood events that emerge in the course of treatment.

🔖 Dreams, Symptoms, Jokes, and Slips   Dreams are considered the "royal road" to the unconscious, and I encourage Ruth to report her dreams and to associate to them. I conceptualize each of her dreams as having two levels of meaning, the manifest content and the latent meaning. Analytic theory postulates that each dream is a coded message from the unconscious, a message that can be interpreted so as to understand the unconscious wish that initiated the dream and the nature of the repression that forced the wish to be experienced only in disguised form. Hypotheses about the latent meaning of dream symbols can be derived from theory, but the actual interpretation of her dream elements is based on her own unique associations to her dream symbols.

In addition to dreams, the hidden meanings inherent in Ruth's symptoms are subject to analysis. Her presenting symptoms, manifestations of resistance, memories, and spontaneous errors (slips of the tongue) are clues to her underlying dynamics. The wordplay involved in slips of the tongue is meaningful, as may be any intentional joke or pun made or recalled by her in a session.

🔖 Interpretations of Resistance and Content   My initial interpretations are of resistance, and I follow the rule of interpreting the resistance Ruth presents relative to a content area before actually interpreting the content. I recognize that every accurate interpretation is an assault on her defenses, and I know that she will react to the interpretation as a threat to her present adjustment. Hence, in choosing the timing of a particular interpretation, I am guided by her readiness to accept it as well as by my sense of its accuracy. I also follow the general rule that more inferential interpretations should be made in the later stages of therapy after a therapeutic alliance and trust have been established. Early interpretations should be minimally inferential, often only noting a correspondence. For example, commenting to Ruth that she wrote less in her autobiography about her mother than she did about her father is much less inferential than interpreting her overeating as a defense against sexuality.

Many interpretations, particularly in the later stages of therapy, relate to her transference reactions and are geared to helping her work through childhood-based conflicts in the context of her therapeutic relationship with me. This brief dialogue begins with the here and now and ends with an insight about the past:

> RUTH: I worry I'm just hiding in my therapy. It's an indulgence; I should be using your time to fix my problems, not just to talk about anything I like.
>
> THERAPIST: What's being hidden here?
>
> RUTH: That I'm not really working. I tell myself I'm going to a doctor's appointment, but you just listen, and I just play around with my thoughts.
>
> THERAPIST: Is it OK to play here, at your doctor's appointment?
>
> RUTH: Of course not. This is work; we're not playing. You wouldn't see me if I were here to play, Dr. Blau.
>
> THERAPIST: There was a time when your father didn't speak to you for weeks.
>
> RUTH: That was about playing doctor too! Do I still think it's sinful to explore? My dad would be shocked at some of the thoughts I've explored here.
>
> THERAPIST: How would he react?
>
> RUTH: He'd be—Oh, I just remembered how he looked then. He got red in the face and stammered. His brow got sweaty. He punished me for my sin.
>
> THERAPIST: For whose sin?
>
> RUTH: Maybe for his own. I hardly knew anything about sex when he decided I was bad; maybe his thinking about me being sexual made him feel guilty or something.
>
> THERAPIST: But you're the one who got punished.
>
> RUTH: Yeah. I got punished for what he thought and felt, not for what I actually did.

In this example I follow a hunch that Ruth's concern about "playing" at her "doctor's" appointment might have associations to the childhood incident when she was punished for "playing doctor." Her acceptance of this association sets the stage for the final interpretive exchange and insight.

Even the best interpretations are only hypotheses that are presented to the client for consideration. Premature interpretations can be harmful, even if correct. As a therapist, I keep an open mind about the meaning of Ruth's thoughts, feelings, memories, dreams, and fantasies, and I rarely make interpretations about the actuality of past events, imagined or remembered. Although I use my hunches to promote the process of freeing repressed memories, I do not treat my hunches about the past as if they were facts to be imposed on the client's reality. Like other contemporary analytic therapists, I believe there are multiple interpretations that are equally true for each of Ruth's symptoms, dream images, and fantasies. I search for interpretations that convey useful truth, rather than striving for statements of *the* truth about elements of her life.

❧ Transference and Countertransference

Ruth's experience in therapy is both gratifying and frustrating. It is gratifying in that we spend each hour focusing on her life. Her needs, hopes, disappointments, dreams, fantasies, and everything else of importance to her are accepted as meaningful, and she need not share center stage with anyone else. It is her hour, and I listen to everything without criticizing her or demanding that she see anything my way or do anything to please me. My sustained, active attention to and interest in her are different from any other interpersonal interaction. Other people in her life insist on wanting things from her, or they want to criticize her, or at the very least they expect her to be as interested in them as they are in her.

But the sessions are also frustrating. Ruth wants help, and all I seem to do is listen and occasionally ask a question or comment on what she has said. Do I like her? Or am I only pretending to be interested because that's what I am paid for? When, she wonders, will the therapy start helping? When will she find out how to resolve her issues about her marriage and her boring life?

Given this mixture of gratification and frustration, it is not surprising that Ruth begins to see *me* as a source of both of those emotions. Moreover, it is not surprising that she will "transfer" onto me attributes of others in her life who have been sources of gratification and frustration to her. Hence, she begins to react to me as if I were her father, mother, or other significant figure.

The permissiveness of the sessions also allows Ruth to regress—to feel dependent and childlike and to express her thoughts and feelings with little censorship. I take almost all the responsibility for maintaining limits; she need only talk. Her regression is fostered to the degree that I maintain the classic analytic stance, and it is ameliorated to the degree that I interact with her in terms of our real relationship—for example, by expressing empathy.

Ruth's past haunts her present life and interpersonal relationships, and to an even greater degree it haunts her relationship with me. But the distortions projected onto me exist in a controlled interpersonal setting and, therefore, are amenable to interpretation and resolution. The therapeutic session provides a structure in which the nature of her conflicts can be exposed and understood, not only in the sense of intellectual insight but also in the analysis of their actual impact on her perceptions and feelings about me and the therapeutic relationship. My nonjudgmental acceptance of all aspects of Ruth's experience, including her darkest fears and impulses, provides a model from which she can begin to fully accept these parts of herself without condemnation or attachment. I believe such "radical acceptance" is healing, and I also find it a necessary foundation for positive change.

The therapeutic relationship provides gratification and frustration for the therapist as well as for the client. My therapeutic task includes monitoring not only the content of the sessions but also my feelings that grow out of this relationship. There are aspects of Ruth that I like and others that I dislike. I find her dependency both appealing and irritating. I enjoy the positive attributes she projects onto me, and I experience some hurt when she projects negative attributes onto me. Nevertheless, I must minimize indulgence in these reactions and concentrate instead on ensuring that my participation consistently promotes her self-understanding and individuation. Although she is free to demand anything and everything from me, I must deny myself almost all the rewards of a real relationship with her.

Understanding the theory of therapeutic techniques helps me keep my perspective, as does recollection of my own therapy. The therapy I have received is useful to me in understanding the psychotherapeutic experience from the client's point of view, and it helps me understand some of my conflicts that could impair my effectiveness as a therapist. Nevertheless, my adherence to the ideal role is imperfect. To some extent I inadvertently let my feelings and conflicts distort my perceptions of Ruth. My distortions include my projecting onto her attributes of significant figures in my own life; I experience countertransference. Although I can minimize countertransference, it can never be eliminated. Therefore, to minimize the negative impact of my countertransference on Ruth's treatment, I monitor my feelings about her and my reactions toward her, and I periodically discuss my treatment of her, including these feelings, with a trusted colleague. Voluntary consultation about my feelings and interventions is, in my opinion, an effective method for assessing and minimizing deleterious effects of countertransference. If I find myself uncomfortable discussing a particular aspect of Ruth's treatment, I suspect that countertransference is at work. Consultations must be conducted so as to protect her confidentiality; this usually includes her releasing the information and my altering information about her identity during the consultation. Should my countertransference have the potential to negatively affect Ruth's treatment, I would enter therapy myself and would either refer Ruth to a colleague or continue to treat her under supervision.

My scrutiny of my countertransference reactions to Ruth may be of value in helping me understand her; often my unconscious reactions give clues to a client's dynamics and to the reactions that others have to the client. Countertransference can be used in the service of the therapy if it can be understood and controlled. Monitoring my own countertransference feelings serves as a major source of clinical information about the client.

Some aspects of countertransference may be partially inseparable from the conscious motivation of the therapist to engage in the arduous work of psychotherapy. As I work actively with Ruth to break the spell cast on her in her past, I apply my understanding of the nature of the spell and of the "magic" needed to break it. As I engage in this struggle, I run the countertransference risk of becoming invested in the hero role, thereby fostering her dependence and prolonging her regression. But to some extent I have opted for this role by choosing the profession of psychotherapist. Thus, by participating in Ruth's life as the hero she has dreamed of, I am fulfilling my own not-so-unconscious needs. But if I am to stay a hero in the sense of being a good therapist, I must renounce the role of hero to Ruth at precisely the moment in therapy in which I have released her from the past's constricting spell.[3]

Jerry Corey's Work With Ruth From a Psychoanalytic Perspective

If you are using the *DVD for Integrative Counseling: The Case of Ruth and Lecturettes,* refer to Session 10 ("Transference and Countertransference") and compare what I've written here with how I deal with transference and countertransference.

Basic Assumptions

As I work with Ruth within a psychoanalytic framework, the psychosocial perspective of Erik Erikson provides me with a useful conceptual model to understand Ruth's development and the challenges she is presently facing. My work is influenced to some extent by contemporary psychoanalytic trends such as ego psychology, object-relations theory, and relational analysis. To the extent possible, I am applying the conceptual framework of brief psychodynamic therapy with Ruth.

The *psychosocial* theory, developed primarily by Erikson, emphasizes sociocultural influences on the development of personality. It assumes that there is continuity in human development. At the various stages of life, we face the challenge of establishing equilibrium between ourselves and our social world. At each crisis, or turning point, in the life cycle, we can either successfully resolve our conflicts or fail to resolve them. Failure to resolve a conflict at a given stage results in fixation, or the experience of being stuck. It will be difficult for Ruth to master the psychosocial tasks of adulthood if she is psychologically stuck with unresolved conflicts from an earlier period of development. Ruth is not doomed to remain forever the victim of earlier fixations, however. By increasing her self-understanding, Ruth will be able to choose a more meaningful path.

The more recent work in the *psychoanalytic approach* is represented by the writings of Margaret Mahler, Heinz Kohut, and Otto Kernberg, among others. Contemporary psychoanalytic practice emphasizes the origins and transformations of the self, the differentiation between the self and others, the integration of the self with others, and the influence of critical factors in early development on later development. In viewing Ruth's case, I make the assumption that her early development is of critical importance and that her current personality problems are influenced by her experiences in childhood. Borrowing from Kohut's thinking, I surmise that she was psychologically wounded during childhood and that her defensive structure is an attempt to avoid being wounded again. I expect to find an interweaving of old hurts with new wounds. Thus, I pay attention to the consistency between her emotional wounding as a child and those situations that result in pain for her today.

Assessment of Ruth

The assessment process with Ruth is based on her initial sessions, her intake form, and her autobiography. Her relationships with her parents are critically important from a therapeutic standpoint. She describes her father as "distant, authoritarian, and rigid." My hunch is that this view of her father colors how she perceives all men today, that her fear of displeasing her husband is connected to her fear of bringing her father displeasure, and that what she is now striving to get from her husband is related to what she wanted from her father. I expect that she will view me and react to me in many of the same ways she responded to her father. Through this transference relationship with me, Ruth will be able to recognize connecting patterns between her childhood behavior and her current struggles. For example, she is fearful of displeasing her husband, John, for fear he might leave. If he did, there would be a repetition of the pattern of her father's psychological abandonment of her after she had not lived up to his expectations. She does not stand up to John or ask for what she needs out of fear that he will become disgruntled and abandon her. She is defending herself against being wounded by him in some of the same ways that she was wounded by her father.

Viewing Ruth from a *psychosocial perspective* will shed considerable light on the nature of her present psychological problems. Ruth never really developed a basic trust in the world. As an infant, she learned that she could not count on others to provide her with a sense of being wanted and loved. She did not receive affection throughout her early childhood, a deprivation that now makes it difficult for her to feel that she is worthy of affection. The task of early childhood is developing *autonomy*, which is necessary if one is to gain a measure of self-control and any ability to cope with the world. In Ruth's case she grew up fast, was never allowed to be a child, and was expected to take care of her younger brother and sisters. Although she seemed to be "mature" even as a child, in actuality she never became autonomous.

From the *contemporary psychoanalytic perspective*, Ruth will not feel truly independent until she feels properly attached and dependent. This notion means that to be independent she must allow herself to depend on others. Ruth, however, never felt a genuine sense of attachment to her father, whom she perceived as distant, or to her mother, whom she viewed as somewhat rejecting. For Ruth to have developed genuine independence, she would have needed others in her life whom she could count on for emotional support. But this support was absent from her background. During the school-age period she felt inferior in social relationships, was confused about her gender-role identity, and was unwilling to face new challenges. During adolescence she did not experience an identity crisis because she did not ask basic questions of life. Rather than questioning the values that had been taught to her, she compliantly accepted them. In part, she has followed the design established by her parents when she was an adolescent. She was not challenged to make choices for herself or to struggle to find meaning in life. In her adulthood she managed to break away from her fundamentalist religion, yet she could not free herself of her guilt over this act. She is still striving for her father's approval, and she is still operating without a clearly defined set of values to replace the ones she discarded. A major theme of Ruth's life is her concern over how to fill the void that she fears will result when her children leave home.

Psychoanalytic theory provides a useful perspective for understanding the ways in which Ruth is trying to control the anxiety in her life. She feels in control when she takes care of her children, and she does not know what she will do once they leave home. Coupled with this empty-nest syndrome is her ambivalence about leaving the security of the home by choosing a career. This change brings about anxiety because she is struggling with her ability to direct her own life as opposed to defining herself strictly as a servant of others. This anxiety will be a focal point of therapy.

In my work with Ruth I am guided by many of the principles of *brief psycho-dynamic therapy,* including psychodynamic concepts such as the enduring impact of psychosexual, psychosocial, and object relational stages of development; the existence of unconscious processes; reenactment of the client's past emotional issues in relationship to the therapist; and the therapeutic relationship. There is an emphasis on a client's strengths and resources in dealing with real-life issues.

Brief dynamic therapy focuses more on the here and now of the client's life than on the there and then of childhood experiences. Adopting this perspective allows me to think psychodynamically and at the same time to be open to using a variety of techniques from other approaches. It requires me to be more inter-active, directive, and self-disclosing than would be the case if I were practicing within a traditional psychoanalytic framework.

Brief psychodynamic therapy treats specific problems within the limits of a time frame of generally 10 to 25 sessions, so it will be necessary to keep to a circumscribed focus with limited goals when working with Ruth. A central theme or problem area will guide our work, and Ruth will focus on specific personal problems that realistically can be explored within the time we have together. The goal is not to bring about a cure but to foster changes in behavior, thinking, and feeling that will continue to shape Ruth's life long after the end of formal therapy. The ideas presented here are based on Hanna Levenson's contributions to the field of brief psychodynamic therapy. Levenson's book is a most useful resource in gaining a better grasp of the essentials of time-limited psychodynamic therapy.[4]

Goals of Therapy

One of the overall themes of Ruth's therapy is coming to a better understanding of the kinds of relationships she wants to change. Understanding how Ruth's past experiences are still influencing her current relationships is a central topic for exploration in our sessions. From the perspective of brief dynamic therapy, two major goals will guide our work together. I hope to provide Ruth with new experiences, both within herself and in relationships with others. In addition, I expect that Ruth will develop new understandings of how her past is influenc-ing her today, especially in terms of her relationships with others.

Psychodynamic therapy is aimed at promoting integration and ego development. The various parts of Ruth's self that she has denied will become more connected. The ideal type of identity is an autonomous self, which is characterized by self-esteem and self-confidence and is capable of intimacy with others.

Therapeutic Procedures

I expect that I will become a significant figure in her life, for I assume that she will develop strong feelings toward me, both positive and negative. For example, she may relate to me in some of the same ways that she related to her father. Although I do not use a blank-screen model, keeping myself mysterious and hidden, in our work together Ruth is bound to expect me to fulfill some of her unmet needs. She will probably experience again some of the same feelings she had during her childhood. How she views me and reacts to me will be a part of the relational work we do. This transference material is rich with meaning and can provide Ruth with considerable new understandings about herself.

Adopting a brief dynamic therapy perspective implies that we are doing a great deal of work in the here and now. The crux of my therapeutic work with Ruth consists of bringing her past into the present, which is done mainly through exploring the transference relationship. My aim is to do more than merely facilitate recall of past events and insight on her part; instead, I hope that she will see patterns and continuity in her life from her childhood to the present. When she realizes how her past is still operating, significant change is possible, and new options open up for her.

Ruth will come to understand that many of her earlier established patterns of behavior are rewoven in her current life. She learned patterns that afforded her some protection against anxiety, but these old patterns are not serving her well today. Ruth's therapy will provide her with a corrective emotional experience that will allow her to develop new patterns of behavior that are functional.

The Therapeutic Process

ELEMENTS OF THE PROCESS After Ruth has been in therapy for a short time, she grows disenchanted with me. She does not see me as giving enough. She becomes irritated because I am not willing to share anything about my marriage, my relationships with my children, and my personal life. She complains that she is the one doing all the giving and that she is beginning to resent it. Here is a brief sample of a session in which we talk about these feelings.

> RUTH: I want you to be more real with me. It feels uncomfortable for you to know so much about me when I know so little about you.
>
> JERRY: It's that I know a lot more about your life than you know about mine and that you're more vulnerable than I am.
>
> RUTH: You seem professional and somewhat distant from me. You're hard to reach. This is not easy for me to say . . . uhm . . . I suppose I want to know what you really think of me. I'm often left wondering what you're feeling. I work hard at getting your approval, but I'm not sure I have it. I get the feeling that you think I'm weak.

JERRY: I wonder if you have felt this way before?

RUTH: Well, ah . . . you know you remind me of my father. No matter what I did to get his approval, I was never successful. Sometimes that is the way I feel around you.

I am consciously not disclosing much about my reactions to Ruth at this point because she is finally bringing out feelings about me that she avoided in our work thus far. I encourage her to express more about the ways in which she sees me as ungiving and unreachable. It is through this process of exploring some of her persistent reactions to me that she will see more of the connection between her unfulfilled needs from the past and how she is viewing me in this present relationship. At this stage in her therapy Ruth is experiencing some very basic feelings of wanting to be special and wanting proof of it. By exploring her transference reactions toward me, she will eventually gain insight into how she has given her father all the power to affirm her as a person and how she has not learned to give herself the approval she so much wants from him. I am not willing to reassure her because I want to foster the expression of this transference.[5]

PROCESS COMMENTARY I am not working with Ruth from the perspective of classical psychoanalysis. Rather, I am drawing from psychosocial theory and from concepts in the newer psychoanalytic thinking, especially from Kohut's work. I direct much of our therapy to the exploration of Ruth's old issues, her early wounding, and her fears of new wounds. The bruises to her self that she experiences in the here and now trigger memories of her old hurts. Especially in her relationship with me, she is sensitive to rejection and any signs of my disapproval. Therefore, much of our therapeutic effort is aimed at dealing with the ways in which she is now striving for recognition as well as the ways in which she attempted to get recognition in the past. In short, she has a damaged self, and she is susceptible to and fearful of further injury. We discuss her attachments, how she tried to win affection, and the many ways in which she is trying to protect herself from suffering further emotional wounds to a fragile ego.

Ruth begins to realize that her past is important and that old wounds will need to be healed if she is to make the changes in her current relationships that she desires. By coming to a greater understanding of the ways in which Ruth responds to me, she gains increased awareness of some key connections between how she related to significant people in her life. She looks to me in some of the same ways that she looked to her father for approval and for love. I encourage her recollection of feelings associated with these past events so that she can work through the barriers preventing her from functioning as a mature adult.[6]

Some Final Thoughts

The psychodynamic model provides a conceptual framework for understanding an individual's history. Practitioners can learn to *think* psychoanalytically even if they do not *practice* psychoanalytically. Although psychoanalytic techniques may have limited utility for counselors working in many settings, these concepts can help explain the dynamics operating in a diverse range of clients.

Ignoring the influence of the past can result in limited therapeutic gains, and as Ruth's case illustrates, understanding the influence of her past gives Ruth more control over her present behavior.

Questions for Reflection

As you continue working with the therapeutic approaches described in this book, you will have many opportunities to apply the basic assumptions and key concepts of each theory to your own life. Some of these questions for reflection will assist you in becoming involved in a personal way. Other questions are designed to give you some guidance in beginning to work with Ruth. They are intended to help you clarify your reactions to how the consultant and I worked with Ruth from each of the therapeutic perspectives. Select the questions for reflection that most interest you.

1. Dr. Blau emphasizes the importance of understanding the "whys" of a client's experience and behavior. What advantages and disadvantages do you see in this focus?
2. Dr. Blau suggests that the psychosexual aspects of Ruth's relationships with her parents, and possibly her siblings, still represent key conflict areas in her present behavior. In what ways may her early experiences be having a significant impact on her life today? How might you explore these dynamics with her?
3. Do you share the emphasis of this approach on the importance of Ruth's father in her life? How might you go about exploring with her how conflicts with her father are related to some of her present conflicts?
4. What is one of the most significant themes (from the analytic perspective) you would focus on in your sessions with Ruth?
5. In what ways would you encourage Ruth to go back and relive her childhood? How important is delving into the client's early childhood in leading to personality change?
6. What defenses do you see in Ruth? How do you imagine you would work to lessen these defenses?
7. Dr. Blau discusses the importance of both the therapist's real relationship and the as-if relationship with Ruth. How might you differentiate between her transference reactions and her real reactions to you?
8. What role does therapist self-disclosure play in Dr. Blau's and my own approach to counseling Ruth?
9. My work with Ruth uses some contemporary psychoanalytic models and illustrates brief dynamic therapy. What are some ways that psychoanalytic concepts can be applied to a time-limited perspective? How can a here-and-now focus be useful in understanding a client's past?
10. How well does the psychoanalytic/psychodynamic approach fit with your counseling style? What aspects of this approach do you find most useful? Which aspects might you want to modify to fit your personal counseling style?

Notes

See *DVD for Theory and Practice of Counseling and Psychotherapy: The Case of Stan and Lecturettes,* Session 2 ("Psychoanalytic Therapy Applied to the Case of Stan"), for ways of working with Stan's resistance and transference and for my presentation applying psychoanalytic therapy.

1. The source for the *DSM-IV-TR* is as follows: American Psychiatric Association. (2000). *Diagnostic and statistical manual of mental disorders* (4th ed., Text Revision). Washington, DC: Author.

2. For more information on research supporting unconscious determinants of decision making, see Nisbett, R., & Wilson, T. (1977). Telling more than we can know: Verbal reports on mental processes. *Psychological Review, 84*(3), 231–259; Bargh, J., & Ferguson, M. (2000). Beyond behaviorism: On the automaticity of higher mental processes. *Psychological Bulletin, 126*, 925–945.

3. Here Dr. Blau discusses his views of working with Ruth's transference and makes important comments pertaining to his ability and willingness to recognize, monitor, and deal with his own potential countertransference. If you are using the *DVD for Integrative Counseling: The Case of Ruth and Lecturettes,* refer to Session 10 ("Working With Transference and Countertransference") to see my perspective on these issues.

4. For a very clear presentation of the key elements of the process of brief psychodynamic therapy, see Levenson, H. (2010). *Brief dynamic therapy.* Washington, DC: American Psychological Association.

5. If you are using the *DVD for Integrative Counseling: The Case of Ruth and Lecturettes,* refer to Session 10 ("Transference and Countertransference") and compare what I've written here with how I deal with transference and countertransference.

6. For a more detailed treatment of psychoanalytic theory, see Corey, G. (2013). *Theory and practice of counseling and psychotherapy* (9th ed.). Belmont, CA: Brooks/Cole, Cengage Learning. The basic concepts introduced in William Blau's work with Ruth and in my version on psychodynamic work with Ruth are covered comprehensively in Chapter 4 ("Psychoanalytic Therapy").

CHAPTER THREE

Case Approach
to Adlerian Therapy

General Overview of Adlerian Therapy

The Adlerian approach focuses on assisting clients to better understand how they perceive themselves, others, and life and to better appreciate their strengths and assets while avoiding the counterproductive perceptions and behaviors that have led to the development and maintenance of symptomatic behaviors in their lives. Adlerian practitioners are not bound by any set of prescribed techniques. Rather, they may employ a variety of strategies and techniques, sometimes referred to as *technical eclecticism,* that are suited to the unique needs of their clients. The concept of social interest, which is Adler's criterion for mental health, provides further direction for therapeutic interventions and evaluation of the therapy process. *Gemeinschaftsgefuhl,* meaning "a community feeling" in the original German, involves a sense of belonging, of being part of the flow of humankind and connected to one's fellow humans; social interest is enacting this community feeling, and it can be seen in the contributions one makes to society through friendship, occupation, and cooperation with others. People with social interest function on the basis of social equality and mutual worth with others. The important criterion determining the relative health or pathology of any behavior is the issue of its usefulness to others and to the larger social community.

Therapeutic procedures commonly employed by Adlerian therapists to facilitate growth and change include encouragement, confrontation, relabeling, cognitive restructuring, humor, paradoxical interventions, interpretation, homework assignments, and teaching new behavioral skills. Adlerians stress a democratic, collaborative approach to therapy, and the client and therapist typically discuss and decide upon all processes leading up to and including termination. The emphasis on goal alignment provides a common frame of reference from which to assess the outcomes of therapy.

An Adlerian Therapist's Perspective on Ruth

by James Robert Bitter, EdD, and William G. Nicoll, PhD

Introduction

Jerry Corey consulted with us on the case of Ruth and asked for our help conducting a thorough initial interview and developing a summary of impressions based on this initial interview. This initial interview generates a relatively clear picture of the client in relation to what Adler called the *life tasks* of (a) friendship and social relations, (b) work and occupation, and (c) love, intimacy, and sexuality. We also provided a lifestyle assessment, including a summary of the family constellation, a record of early recollections, and an interpretation of Ruth's pattern of basic convictions. We use a modified form of Adlerian counseling that we call *Adlerian brief therapy*.[1]

Lifestyle information is most often collected and interpreted by a single therapist within a professional clinical setting, but it is ideal and our preference to include two therapists and use a technique called *multiple therapy*.[2] The client is initially interviewed by one therapist, who then presents the data to a second therapist. The client experiences social interest in the very structure of therapy. The model of two therapists cooperating in a single effort is often therapeutic in and of itself. In addition, multiple therapy goes a long way toward establishing the therapist as a fellow human being who is working to understand the client—and willing to entertain input from outside sources.

This section provides a detailed and comprehensive assessment of Ruth's early background and her current functioning. We hope you will continue to use this material as you work with her case in other chapters. We begin with our narrative summaries from a general diagnosis and lifestyle assessment.[3] We co-construct these summaries with the client based on an interviewing model delineated in the *Individual Psychology Client Workbook*, which was developed by Robert L. Powers and Jane Griffith.[4] Here, we have provided some minimal data and our initial summaries from our assessment process. We follow these summaries with a process outline of *Adlerian brief therapy* and an example of its application with Ruth.

The Initial Interview

In addition to the information presented in Chapter 1 in Ruth's autobiography and intake interview, Ruth also indicated that she was the oldest of four children who are ordered as follows: Ruth, age 39, living with her husband in California; Jill (–4), age 35, an architect living in Chicago; Amy (–6), age 33, a social worker and homemaker in California; and Steve (–9), age 30, a clerk in a shipping office who still lives at home with Ruth's parents.

Ruth believes she is the one who is most affected by her unhappiness. Her family is kind and understanding. Ruth was a homemaker and mother until her children became adolescents. She then entered college part time and obtained a bachelor's degree. Through her contacts with others at the university, she has become aware of how she has limited herself, how she has fostered her family's dependence on her, and how frightened she is of branching out from her roles as mother and wife. Ruth responded to questions about the three life tasks in the following way.

🔩 Love and Intimacy

"I have had only one relationship. John and I started dating after I graduated from high school. We got married, and we've been together ever since. John says he had been interested in me for a long time before we went out. He had seen me in church. We met formally at a church social. He stayed with me for a whole day. We talked, and he listened to everything I said. He was very attentive. When he walked me home, he asked if we could go to a movie. I said yes, and my parents didn't object. John was strong-minded, knew what he wanted, and had goals and dreams. I liked his dreams, especially since they included me. He was always calm and never seemed to get angry. He's still very patient, the way I think men should be. He's the only man I ever dated, and he has been good to me.

"I think being feminine means that you are nurturing and give a great deal of yourself to others. You must be able to balance family, which is your responsibility, and community. There is always a lot to do. I think being feminine also means that you're attractive to men. I do really well at the first part, but I doubt that I'm attractive to men, especially with my weight.

"John hardly ever complains, but he would probably like to have sex more often. I never really enjoyed sex that much. It's OK, but I don't get in the mood as often as John. If I have any complaint, it's that I would like to make more decisions in the family and even for myself, but I would probably not do very well.

"If I could have anything going better in this area, I would like to feel more feminine and appreciated and loved. I would like to feel comfortable doing things for myself without feeling as if I'm letting John down or worse, losing him."

🔩 Work and Occupation

"I have worked all my life in the home; first, my father's home and now my own home. I have taken care of children and a home since I was a young teenager. I occasionally do volunteer work, but very little, really. There's so much to do with the children and John. What I like most about being a homemaker, or housewife, is when people like what I do for them. Sometimes, though, it feels as if the kids don't even notice. They just expect everything. John notices more. I notice all the things that never get done, especially now that I'm getting my teaching credential. I guess school is my work for the moment. It's still hard, but I like it more than I liked high school. I'm learning a lot, but it takes a lot of time and energy, and I'm way behind at home.

"I want very much to finish my certification as a teacher and to teach in an elementary school, third grade. I want to help students who are struggling."

🔩 Friendship and Community

"I have developed some good friends recently at school. I feel that school has been a turning point for me, both for work and for having people to talk to. My classes have helped me meet people who seem to like me and with whom I feel comfortable, just talking.

"Most of my friends are women, but I don't have very many friends. I maybe have one or two long-term friends, but I have shared more with college friends than I have with my long-term friends. I think people like it that I listen well. I'm interested in what people have to say. I'm not a leader, but I like to be a part of things."

OUR SUMMARY From this information, we developed a summary of our initial impressions. The summary is written in the third person to allow Ruth to stand back from her experience and to see herself through a narrative that puts her life in context and shows its dynamic movement.

Ruth has presented herself for therapy at a potential turning point in her life. She has spent many years doing what she prepared to do early in life. Ruth, the oldest of four children, was drafted into caring for her brother and two sisters at a young age. She used her mother as a role model of a "good home-maker" and continued her work when she married her husband, John. John and Ruth have four children, who are now adolescents. When her children became teenagers, she decided to seek work where she would continue to feel needed. Returning to school, she completed a bachelor's degree and is seeking a teacher's certificate. College and her fellow students opened a whole new world to Ruth. She began to see many new possibilities for herself, including a place in the world as a professional teacher and as a person with many more friends than she has been used to having. She is feeling both excited by the new possibilities and worried about losing the people and world she has known all her life.

Ruth feels pulled by both worlds; she is experiencing a conflict between satisfying her needs in the occupational life task and her needs in the family–intimacy life task. In one world (school), the opportunities seem limitless, exciting, and full of promise—even if new and somewhat overwhelming and risky. In the other world (home), her life is safe, known, familiar, and predictable, and she knows exactly what she needs to do to succeed and to feel safe and secure. She wants both worlds to fit together, but she is not always sure how to make that happen. She also wants to perform *perfectly* in both worlds. Even though part of her knows that the demand for perfection is impossible, she has not let herself off the hook. Mostly, she wants everyone involved to be happy with her and, above all, to avoid displeasing anyone. She wants John to be happy; she wants her children to be happy; she wants her instructors to be happy; she wants her new friends to be happy; and last, and least, she wants herself to be happy. Soon, she may even want her therapist to be happy with her. When she cannot figure out how to make everyone happy, she often finds herself becoming worried, anxious, and depressed. When she doesn't have time to become worried, anxious, or depressed, she settles for dizziness, headaches, heart palpitations, sleeplessness, and other physical disturbances, which act as a message to her family and herself that she needs some rest and needs some care.

Ruth has put everyone else in her life first. She comes from a family in which at least one other child achieved success easily, and she found it hard to please her mother and father. She could not guess what would make them happy, and she feared their disapproval and rejection. The family atmosphere was strict and controlled, and she found her place by caring for children and others in the way that she believed women were supposed to do. It is hard for her to put herself first at this point in life without fearing she will do something wrong, displease her husband and family, and thereby risk losing everything.

Ruth has a well-defined set of goals for therapy:

- Deal with the physical and emotional symptoms that express the conflict and demands she feels in her life.
- Find a balance between seeking what she wants and maintaining what she has.
- Get help with at least one daughter, whose rebellion acts as a constant reminder of "what can happen if Mom is not ever-present and vigilant."
- Discover what she can make of herself and her life with opportunities opening up and time running out. She is, after all, 39 years of age and "losing it" . . . fast!

Ruth's Lifestyle Assessment

🐚 **The Family Constellation**   During a lifestyle assessment, Ruth described her father as devoted to his work. When she was young, he was stern, and he was an authority figure in the community. He was respected and righteous. He was also cool and detached. With Ruth, he was often distant, strict, and ungiving. He was rather aloof from all of the children and insisted on respect. Jill is his favorite child: He likes her accomplishments.

With regard to discipline, he would yell at the children, or he would withdraw from a misbehaving child totally and not talk to the child for weeks. Ruth felt scared and, at times, disowned.

Ruth doesn't know what nationality her dad is, but she knows he is the oldest of four boys, and he came from a religious family. It was assumed early in his life that he would be a minister, and he prepared for it all his life. His family was poor, but always got by, and they were always proud.

Ruth's mother was a hard worker; she rarely complained out loud. She was very proper, always did the right thing, and was quite dignified. She was proud of her role as a minister's wife, and she was self-sacrificing. She would go without so that her husband or the kids could have the things they needed. She would even give up things for herself so that people in the church could have food, clothing, or shelter.

It was very important to Ruth's mother that the children maintain a good image in the church and the community. As unselfish as she could be, she was emotionally ungiving, very serious, not very happy (or so it appeared), and very strict with the children.

She was devoted to seeing that the children grew up right, but she was not personally involved in their lives unless they got in trouble. Her favorite child is Steve. He could do no wrong in her eyes. She did not want any of the children to bring shame on the family, and she wanted all of them to be hard workers.

Ruth's mother is Scots-Irish. She was also poor when she was little. She was the youngest of three girls, and she was the only one to marry. "She always told us how lucky she was to have a Christian life."

Ruth's parents have a stiff and formal relationship. Very little affection was demonstrated, and they rarely laughed. They did not argue: Mother stood behind whatever father said or did. Ruth wanted to make them happy, but it was not an easy task.

Ruth's paternal grandmother took an interest in her. She seemed to understand Ruth, and she often would talk to Ruth and give her good advice. She was the one who first approved of John.

Ruth's description of her siblings can be drawn as follows:

Sibling Array

Ruth (39)	Responsible, hard-working, organized, dedicated, capable, trustworthy, self-critical, undemanding, scared, unable to please either parent.
	Ruth's perspective: I was lonely: I felt useful and needed; I wanted approval from my folks; I was a good girl, and I took care of my sister and brother.
Jill (–4)	Bright, pretty, accomplished, conforming, well- behaved. Got along with Dad; got along fairly well with Mom.
	Ruth's perspective: Jill was the most like me; she was good and was successful at life. Things came more easily to her. She won honors at school.
Amy (–6)	Immature, demanding, the family "troublemaker"; admiring of Ruth, hard-working, independent. In trouble with Dad, and tried to please Mom, without success.
	Ruth's perspective: Amy was the most different from me; she seemed irresponsible by comparison.
Steve (–9)	Pampered, overprotected, in trouble with Dad but protected by Mom. Got Mom's attention. Sensitive, argumentative with Ruth, not too accomplished.
	Ruth's perspective: Steve was also different from me; in Mom, he found a shelter from life.

In Ruth's childhood neighborhood, Ruth and her siblings were mostly absent; she didn't play much. Children from church were sometimes invited to the house, but mostly siblings worked or played with one another, if at all. She didn't have any real friends of either sex: just her brother and sisters.

Ruth was expected to do well in school. It was hard for her. She had to work at it all the time. Even when she worked hard, she sometimes didn't do very well. Math and sciences were the hardest for her. English and history were her best subjects. She liked to read, and that helped. She would get so nervous when she was doing math or science that she couldn't concentrate. The teachers generally liked her (with one or two exceptions), but they always felt that she was not living up to her potential, and that's what they told her parents. She didn't socialize with other kids much. She was quiet and kept to herself. Other kids thought she was "weird."

When Ruth was 6 years old, she reports: "My father caught me 'playing doctor' with an 8-year-old boy. He lectured me and refused to speak to me for weeks. I felt guilty and ashamed." Ruth reached adolescence with minimal information from her mother, father, or peers. She remembers being scared at 12 when menarche occurred. "I didn't know what was happening. My mother gave me the things I needed and a booklet to read." She was not allowed to date until she completed high school; at age 19, she married the first person she dated. "I was lucky to find a good man. All I knew was my mother's version of how to be a good homemaker."

From Ruth's lifestyle information, we were able to co-construct with Ruth a narrative summary of the meaning she attached to her family constellation and family life. This summary constitutes a retelling of Ruth's life story with an emphasis on the meaning and patterns associated with her current life experiences.[5]

🌲 Our Summary

Ruth is the oldest of four children, raised in a family where hard work and perfection were expected; unfortunately, as she learned early in life, hard work was no guarantee that perfection could be achieved. Even after a huge effort, the slightest mistake could lead to a rebuke or a rejection that was deeply felt, leaving her lonely, cautious, and scared. Thus, Ruth approaches life with an emphasis on seeking to always do the "right" thing as she perceives others to define it while guarding against doing anything wrong, displeasing others and thereby inviting their rejection and loss of affection.

Ruth's father set a masculine guiding line that was characterized by a harsh, strict, stern, and angry persona; his every stance was authoritarian, critical, and religiously perfectionistic. Indeed, her father was such a dominant authority in her life that it was easy for her to confuse God-fearing with father-fearing. Ruth was locked in a struggle for approval in which she would never be good enough and her sister Jill could do no wrong. The struggle to please her father gradually settled into strategies for avoiding his displeasure, and fear became the operative motivator in her life.

Ruth's mother set a feminine guiding line that was characterized by a serious devotion to principle, righteousness, duty, and her husband. Her behavior suggested that life was filled with hard work and sacrifice, a burden that women should suffer quietly, with dignity, and without complaint. Although she provided for the children's physical and spiritual needs, she did little to provide relief from the harsh stance that her husband took in the world.

Only Ruth's grandmother provided her with a different role model for womanhood. She demonstrated that it was possible for women to be interested in, involved with, and caring toward others.

The family atmosphere was characterized by formality and stiffness, a rigid consistency and discipline in which frivolity and, indeed, happiness were out of place. The family values included were hard work, perfectionism, and a belief that appearances were extremely important. No crack in the architecture could be tolerated.

🌲 Record of Early Recollections

Within an Adlerian lifestyle assessment, early recollections function as a projective technique. Each individual recounts 6 to 12 early memories that are chosen by the person to reflect images of self, others, the world, and, sometimes, ethical convictions. Early recollections are like little stories with morals (as in Aesop's fables) that serve as meaning-markers in the person's life. As such, early memories always reveal more about the person in the present than they do about the person's past. Indeed, sometimes an early memory is "real" to the person but can easily be shown to be historically inaccurate or even impossible.

To be useful as a projective device, our directions must remain minimal and neutral. We start by asking Ruth to think back to when she was very little (before the age of 9) and to tell us one thing that happened one time. In Ruth's interview, she is able to provide just five early recollections.

1. *Age 3.* "I remember my father yelling at me and then putting me in another room because I was crying. I don't remember why I was crying, but I know I was scared, and after he shouted, I was petrified."

   Most vivid moment: father yelling
   Feeling: scared, petrified

2. *Age 4½.* "I was in church, talking with a boy. My mother gave me dirty looks, and my father, who was conducting the service, gave me a stern lecture when we got home."

   Most vivid moment: the looks parents gave me
   Feeling: scared and confused

3. *Age 6.* "An 8-year-old neighbor boy and I had our clothes off and were 'playing doctor' when my father caught us in my bedroom. He sent the boy home and then told me in a cold and solemn voice that what I had done was very wrong. He did not speak to me for weeks, and I remember feeling very dirty and guilty."

   Most vivid moment: being caught by my father
   Feeling: scared, "bad," and guilty

4. *Age 7.* "I remember my second-grade teacher saying that I was not doing well in school and that I was going to get a bad report card. I tried so hard to do well because I didn't want to bring home bad grades. This teacher didn't like me very much, and I couldn't understand what I had done wrong. I thought I was trying my best. I was scared."

   Most vivid moment: the teacher telling me I was getting a bad report card
   Feeling: scared

5. *Age 8.* "I was in a church play, and I worked for months memorizing my lines. I thought I had them down perfect. My parents came to the play, and for a time I was doing fine, and I was hoping they would like my performance. Then toward the end, I forgot to come in when I was supposed to, and the director had to cue me. My mistake was apparent to my father, who later commented that I had spoiled a rather good performance by my lack of attention. I remember feeling sad and disappointed, because I had so hoped that they would be pleased. And I don't recall my mother saying anything about the play."

   Most vivid moment: father commenting on my mistake
   Feeling: embarrassed

❧ **Our Summary** These memories represent Ruth's convictions as she is now, so we summarize her position and stance in the first person. In many ways, the summary expresses Ruth's commentary on her life experiences.

"I live in a man's world that is often harsh, uncaring, and frightening. Helplessness and emotional expression will not be tolerated in this world and will lead to being separated from it. In a man's world, women must not speak, not even to other men. The rebuke of authority is both immediate and frightening. Men and their world are never available to women. A woman is wrong to want to know about men or explore them. Dabbling in a man's world can lead to banishment and total exile.

"Only achievement counts in the real world. No amount of hard work can make up for a lack of performance. No amount of pleasing can win over someone who is against you. Significant people always find out about mistakes: The most important people always seem to be present when a lack of attention leads to an error that ruins even a good effort. To err in the real world is embarrassingly human; to forgive is against policy."

From this summary, we fashion this list of basic convictions that serve as interfering ideas in Ruth's quest for a rich and fulfilling life:

- The power and importance of men are exaggerated, as is her fear of their disapproval. Pleasing seems to her the best route to safety in a man's world, but it leaves her unsure of her own identity and in constant fear of rejection.
- The inevitability of mistakes and failure is exaggerated and feared; the slightest human errors are to be avoided: 100% is passing, 99% is the start of creeping failure.
- Doing the right thing, being "good," is required just to survive; doing the wrong thing signals impending doom: caution is always warranted in an unpredictable world.
- Murphy's Law governs: what can go wrong will go wrong.
- Hard work is always demanded but will not necessarily produce the desired results or achievements.

Adlerian Brief Therapy With Ruth

Adlerian counseling has evolved substantially over the more than seven decades since Adler's death in 1937. Many different models have borrowed from Adler's Individual Psychology concepts and have been integrated with Adlerian therapy. Even under the umbrella of Adlerian psychotherapy, different approaches to clinical practice currently coexist. Despite differences in style, all Adlerians share a focus on understanding lifestyle, the individual's socially constructed pattern of living, and a commitment to holistic, systemic, and teleological assessments and treatment.[6] We have successfully applied the Adlerian brief therapy model to our work with individuals, couples, and families.[7]

Five points define our therapeutic process: (a) time limitation, (b) focus, (c) counselor directiveness and optimism, (d) symptoms as solutions, and (e) the assignment of behavioral tasks. The two of us (Jim and Bill) differ to some extent on the relative emphases that should be given to a definitive time limitation, counselor directiveness, and the assignment of behavioral tasks. We both agree, however, that *focused work* will tend to keep therapy brief, that nonorganic *symptoms are the client's solution* to a personal problem, and that *motivation modification* is the goal when both directive interventions and behavioral tasks are used.

Integrating a time limitation into therapy reflects the reality that we meet people in the middle of their lives, and we will say "good-bye" to them in the middle of their lives. We enter into a contract with our client that suggests we can make a difference in each other's lives in a relatively short period of time. There is optimism in the contract, a belief in the client's ability to change, grow, and improve her or his life situation. For the time we will be meeting, our focus is on being fully present for our clients. While we do not always define exactly the number and duration of sessions with a client, when we do, we are able to work more quickly, staying focused on desired outcomes.

Clarity of focus and practice is the central element that limits time in therapy. For the Adlerian brief therapist, two goals guide every session. First, the therapist seeks to develop a systemic, holistic understanding of the person in treatment. This is most often accomplished by some form of formal or informal lifestyle assessment process that seeks to elicit individual patterns and motivations and the rules of interaction that govern the individual's idiosyncratic patterns of perceiving, behaving, and coping. Second, the therapist wants to know what the individual wants from therapy: Toward what goals will they work together? Effective work requires that the therapist balance both goals. We ask ourselves recurrently: "Where are we going . . . and with whom?"

The process within sessions often resembles a meeting of minds and hearts. While both of us (Jim and Bill) recognize that "therapeutic relationship" and "client change" are intimately connected, Jim's focus emphasizes relational qualities in therapy (PACE), whereas Bill tends to organize his work around strategies for change (BURP). For a look at how the two of us think about therapist–client interactions, see Table 3.1.

Human beings have goals. They act purposefully and in goal-motivated patterns based on the interpretations they make about self, others, and life (their worldviews). A teleological understanding "makes sense" out of symptoms, patterns of behavior, feelings, convictions, values, and beliefs. A teleological orientation illuminates the client's present and intended future. In this sense, the past is merely a remembered (and often revised) context generated by the person in support of current goals and purposes. Real change, second-order change, always follows from some form of motivation modification, a reorientation of client interpretations regarding the circumstances that brought him or her to therapy.

Adlerian brief therapists want to co-develop (with clients) functional solutions, expand limited choices, and create new possibilities. We want to activate underutilized resources—both internal and external. Actually, it is often possible to accomplish these therapeutic goals in a single session. Whether in one session or 12, making a difference in clients' lives requires the therapist to pay attention to the flow of therapy as well as to the unique understandings that arise from that therapy.

TABLE 3.1 Two Levels of Focus Within Adlerian Brief Therapy

JIM'S FOCUS Jim likes to bring his attention to the rhythm of the therapeutic experience. This reflects his work with Virginia Satir and Erv and Miriam Polster and a focus on experiential therapy.

P*urpose:*
Since every interaction, as well as every thought, feeling, and behavior, has a purpose, what is the purpose of what is happening right at this moment in therapy? What motivates the patterns that make up the person's life? What purpose do feelings serve? What meaning is attached to living?

A*wareness:*
Awareness is the alpha and omega of experience. What awareness does the client enjoy? What experiences are blocked from client awareness? What meaning is lost? What purpose is served? How is awareness related to contact with others?

C*ontact:*
What is the quality of contact between the therapist and the client? What kind of contact does the client make with others in her or his life, with the environment, and with oneself? What purpose is served by the contacts the client makes? How can contact augment client awareness? Which awarenesses would augment contact?

E*xperience:*
What is the quality of life experience the person brings to therapy? Is it a thin life or one thick with meaning? Is it a fascinating or interesting life story? What experience exists between therapist and client? Would an experiment (only one form of experience) lead to a fuller appreciation of life and other experiences available to the person?

BILL'S FOCUS Bill first listens to the "how" of behavior, especially what people do and what they feel. Next, Bill listens for the "what for," or the purpose or functions of behavior. Finally, Bill works with the client to reveal the "whys" of behavior and the rules of interaction.

B*ehavior redescription:*
Clients, and counselors, often adopt the language of pathology, a language of possession: for example, "I am bipolar." "I have an anxiety disorder." By adopting a language of use, we move the client to focusing on behavioral interactions. We ask: When was the last time this occurred? What did you do? How did you feel? Who else was affected? What did they do? How did you respond?

U*nderlying rules:*
Careful attention to the client's answers opens an avenue to the purpose(s) that symptoms may serve. The sequence of behaviors and interactions also begins to suggest the rules the person uses to function in life, to cope, and to maintain stability.

R*eorientation:*
The therapist seeks a cognitive shift in the client's understanding of self and symptoms. Adlerians use tentative disclosures of purpose, reframing of rules and experience, relabeling concepts, paradox, and even humor. The therapist seeks to shift the client's "private logic" to common sense.

P*rescribing behavioral rituals:*
Real change takes place *between* sessions, not *in* sessions. Rituals are regular, repeated actions that reaffirm and maintain new possibilities. We ask: What is the client going to do? What strategies and interventions will encourage the client to take "real" steps in his or her own behalf? How can the therapist use self to align with and augment client functioning?

The Flow of Adlerian Brief Therapy

Figure 3.1 presents a structural map for the flow of therapy that we adapted from Dreikurs's holistic approach to psychotherapy.[8] We use the word *flow* to indicate a fluid and dynamic movement, one that eschews mechanistic steps or stages. Indeed, there is nothing in the arrangement of the flow of the session that cannot be rearranged to fit the needs of the client or the therapy session.

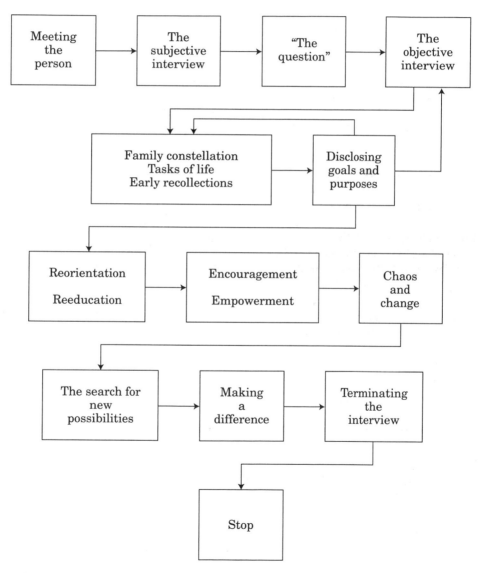

FIGURE 3.1 The Flow of Adlerian Brief Therapy

🌀**Meeting the Person**   The first contact we have with a client may be by phone or through a referral. We recognize that coming to therapy can be challenging, and we want to facilitate a smooth transition. We want the client to feel welcome. While client concerns are often rehearsed and tend to surface quickly, Adlerian brief therapists focus initially on the *client-as-a-person*. Through mutual respect, genuine interest, and even fascination, we hope the client will experience our full presence. This presence, real contact with the client, is supported even in the first few minutes of therapy by the use of our five senses. What the therapist sees, hears, and experiences, perhaps in the touch of a handshake, is especially important.

🌀**The Subjective Interview**   Being fully present provides the client with the support that is needed to tell her or his unique story. Empathy, interest, and fascination enable the therapist to follow the client closely, staying with the next most interesting question or development. This concentration on *the next* brings focus to the interview and encourages a depth of disclosure and understanding between counselor and client. A client who can clearly articulate what is important to her or him has already begun to take some control of self and life. Toward the end of this part of the interview, Adlerian brief therapists ask: "Is there anything else you feel I should know to understand you and your concerns?"

During the subjective interview, motivational and behavioral patterns in the person's life begin to emerge. At first tentatively, Adlerian counselors begin to hypothesize about what works for the client. How do the patterns in a person's life reflect the individual's rules of interaction? How do the patterns and rules directly contribute to maintaining the concerns that are being identified? And in what way might the stated concerns actually be the person's best current solution to life's demands?

🌀**"The Question"**   Based on Dreikurs's[9] formulation of "The Question," Adlerians attempt to differentiate organic symptoms or problems from ones that are psychogenic. Initially phrased by Adler[10] and later reframed by Dreikurs, The Question is: "What would you be doing, what would change, if you didn't have these symptoms or problems?" or "How would your life be different if you didn't have these issues, concerns, or problems?" When the answer is: "Nothing would be different, except the symptoms would be gone," then we suspect the problem is probably physiological or organic—even if it is masquerading as a psychological complaint. When the client indicates that life, work, friendships, or family relations would improve, we immediately suspect that the problem serves the purpose of helping the client retreat from the challenge of these life tasks.

When Ruth was asked "The Question," she said she would be happy at home and at work. She would have a job as an elementary school teacher and would work with a third-grade class. She would have energy for her children's activities and those of her husband, and she would see her family more often. Her answer suggests that she lives in doubt about her worth and value, and she fears possible failure and disapproval when she faces the test of her worth in the real world. Can she make it in the world of work as an elementary school teacher? Does she have a right to work and also be happy at home? Can she ever do enough for her husband and children to feel really loved by them? When Ruth faces these questions, she begins to doubt herself and her abilities, and her symptoms enable her to retreat from the answers she most fears.

✺ The Objective Interview   The objective interview is essentially a lifestyle assessment of the client. We want to create a holistic picture of the individual, including information about when the problem or concern started, precipitating events, medical history, present or past medications, social history, and the reasons the person is seeking therapy. The most important aspects of the objective interview, however, started with the early systemic work of Adler: an investigation of *family constellation;* the *life tasks of friendships, occupation,* and *intimacy*; and *early recollections.*

Each of these areas of investigation will produce life stories that, taken together, yield patterns of living and coping: They "make sense" of the client's concerns. Listening to the client's interpretation of the place she or he holds in the family also helps us understand the client's overall sense of place in the world. The individual's experience of life's demands or tasks allows us to uncover client strengths, perceived weaknesses, and most important, coping styles. Early recollections reveal the person's convictions about self, others, life, the world and, sometimes, even ethical convictions. They also can reveal the client's stance in relation to the therapeutic relationship and the therapist.

✺ Disclosing Goals and Purposes   Adlerians introduce goals and purposes as part of a meaningful dialogue about symptoms, behaviors, feelings, values, and convictions. Most goals and purposes function out of the client's awareness at a non-conscious level. To make goals conscious and explicit is to already change the client's process. Behavior is enacted in social engagements, and assessing the results of social interactions is the surest way to formulate a hypothesis or guess about an individual's motivation. When such disclosures follow from a "clarity of focus" obtained in the subjective and objective interviews, they often elicit a recognition reflex in the person.

✺ Reorientation and Reeducation   Adlerian therapists use the concepts of reorientation and reeducation to emphasize that treatment is an educative process; it is about helping the client to change direction, cope more effectively, and meet life with a new understanding. Rather than merely decreasing or eliminating symptoms, Adlerian brief therapy aims at augmented social-emotional competence and mental health. We want clients to have a sense of belonging and a sense of being valued in their community as an antidote to isolation and withdrawal; we want to increase *community feeling* and *social interest.* While we do not have specific outcomes for therapy in mind before we meet the client, we believe that some general conditions can be identified that are better for human life: to think rationally, to feel fully within the human experience, to greet the world with optimism and hope, to have courage and confidence, to make a contribution, to have a sense of humor, to have friends and to be a true friend, and to be interested in the well-being of others.

❧ Encouragement and Empowerment   Encouragement and empower-ment are the foundation for all change through therapy. Adlerian counselors believe that courage follows from a sense of empowerment, which results from rediscovering the individual's internal and external resources. The discovery of strengths gets one through the difficult times and prepares the way for new possibilities. Functional solutions and real change are the result of facing life's challenges with courage rather than in retreat.

❧ Chaos and Change   Change is seldom easy. It requires the person to move from what is familiar and known to what is unfamiliar and unknown. Disori-entation and chaos are the most common experiences one has when change happens too fast or when the requirements are overwhelming. When a client is in chaos, the therapist must remain steady and focused if she or he is to help the client refocus. Careful and often delicate, small movements are needed dur-ing this time. We remind our clients that they are not alone—and not without strengths. We hold them *only* to decisions that can be implemented immedi-ately, leaving longer-range issues for later.

❧ The Search for New Possibilities   New possibilities tend to emerge rath-er than be created. They are what follows when a tight therapeutic focus is connected to the client in what we call "the relational present," the experience of being together with the therapist. In general, client-generated possibilities are more useful than therapist-generated possibilities because they reinforce a sense of personal strength, courage, and capability in the client. Still, when the relationship has been caring and collaborative throughout, most clients will ac-cept a therapist's suggestions and prescriptions calmly and with hope.

❧ Making a Difference   Adlerian counselors want to make a difference in the lives of their clients. In a single session, that difference may be only a small shift in understanding, a new clarity about patterns or meaning, an emotional realization, or a small experiment designed for more useful interactions. As therapists, we ask ourselves: "If I had only one session to be helpful in this person's life, what would I want to accomplish? And what would they want me to accomplish?" There is never any guarantee that a future session will occur.

❧ Terminating the Interview   Terminating an interview session is merely an interruption of therapy. Of necessity, any therapeutic relationship, no mat-ter how intense the involvement, is time-limited. Each session is followed by separation, the space in which clients may actually enact the new possibilities of their lives. In the beginning, these separations may be only days or a week, but over time, they will evolve into separations of months—or even years. Still, the relationship is always available and reconnection is only a phone call away. In this sense, we do brief, intermittent therapy, and we treat our therapy as a way-station in the ongoing journey through the client's life. The professional counselor–client relationship is never terminated, therefore; it is merely inter-rupted, much like the relationship with one's physician or dentist wherein we find ourselves returning when we require further assistance.

In the case of Ruth, the data for the initial interview and the lifestyle assessment were collected by Jim, her primary therapist. Those data were then presented to and discussed with Bill, while Ruth listened and acted as a collaborating or clarifying agent to the discussion. The two therapists then generated their initial summaries, including the *pattern of basic convictions* and the *interfering ideas.* The session ended with the two therapists listening to Ruth give her initial impressions of the ideas and information contained in the summaries. Written copies of the summaries were sent to her the following day, so that she could read them before the next session.

REVIEWING THE PREVIOUS SESSION Following this multiple therapy session, Ruth met with Jim alone. After they greet each other, they began this discussion.

JIM: What was the last session like for you?

RUTH: I was really amazed. The summaries that you came up with seemed just like me. Then when they came in the mail, I read them, and I wondered if my family knew me as well as I feel the two of you do.

JIM: So what was it like for you to have two therapists instead of one?

RUTH: It was very interesting. I was surprised that the two of you disagree sometimes. I liked the way you disagreed and stayed friends and didn't get mad or anything. That's hard for me. I don't like to disagree with John. [*Pause*] I think I'm afraid he'll get mad at me.

JIM: What does he get mad at you about?

RUTH: I know John pretty well, I guess, and there's not much we disagree about—except my schooling.

JIM: If I were to hazard a guess based on what we learned in the lifestyle assessment, I would guess that there may be quite a lot you have not directly asked your husband—or even your children—because you were concerned about displeasing them. Does that fit you? Do you find yourself "guessing," trying to read their minds so you won't upset them?

RUTH: Yes, I know I do that a lot.

JIM: What did you notice when Bill and I disagreed?

RUTH: Well, the two of you were just fine. You just listened, and then you asked me what I thought.

JIM: Actually, I was quite pleased that you and Bill had come to an understanding that I had missed. If we were all alike in the world, there wouldn't be much use in talking, would there? Do you think John would enjoy hearing your opinion even if it was different from his?

RUTH: Maybe.

JIM: I think you would really like to know what John thinks about your lifestyle summaries, and no amount of guessing is going to be the same as really hearing from him. The worst that might happen is that he wouldn't agree with them.

Here, in a relatively early session, the therapist uses the cooperation and mutual respect modeled in therapy to encourage Ruth to take a small chance with her husband. If she actually asks John to look at her lifestyle summaries and share his opinion with her, there will be some material for the next session whatever his response or her reaction to the response may be.

A SMALL REEDUCATION DURING MULTIPLE THERAPY Near the end of Ruth's counseling experience, she again meets with Bill and Jim together. This time the focus is on her value when she is engaged in meaningful work and when she is not. An early recollection is used to mark change and growth in her therapy.

BILL: Ruth, it's good to see you again. How long has it been? About 2 months or so since I last sat in with the two of you? How have things been going?

RUTH: I think our work together has been very good. We had some sessions that included John, and I really feel that he's supporting me in all of the transitions I'm making. In recent weeks, I walk away from here, and I sometimes wonder if I am doing enough in therapy. Much of what we talk about now seems easier to me than in earlier sessions.

JIM: This is interesting. We haven't really talked about this before. How was it for you when you left here last time?

RUTH: Well, I think we did some good work together in that I learned something about staying with change in my life even when the going gets tough, but it was not actually hard to learn that. I used to leave here wondering if I would ever figure myself out. Last time, I felt, well, I can do what I need to do.

BILL: When I listen to Ruth, Jim, there's an idea that is repeated over and over. It's something like "Anything worth doing requires very hard work. Without the hard work, Ruth may doubt whether she is doing anything worthwhile." Did I get that right, Ruth?

RUTH [*With a look of recognition on her face*]: I think you did. That's been one of my beliefs since childhood.

BILL: Yes, it may have been, but I think we're inviting you to reconsider that notion. It may be a mistaken notion, especially now that you're older and more competent. Things do come easier to people as they gain competence.

RUTH: Maybe I have this therapy thing figured out.

JIM: My experience of you is that you have a lot of things figured out. There's been a lot of progress since you started about 9 months ago.

BILL: Let's try something—another early recollection. Ruth, see if you can think back to a time when you were very young. Something happened one time . . .

RUTH: Very young? Well, I remember something in second grade. Is that OK?

BILL: Yes, that's fine. You were about 7 or 8?

RUTH: Seven, I think. I was asked by a neighbor to help her little girl learn colors because she was in kindergarten. Her mother had colored four squares in the driveway with chalk. I think her name was Jan, the little girl, and we played all afternoon, bouncing a ball from one color to another. Her mother later told my mother that I had made all the difference in the world.

BILL: What stands out about that story. And how did you feel?

RUTH: The look of pride on my mother's face when she told me what Jan's mother had said. I like making a difference in someone's life.

JIM: It's a great memory! There's not an ounce of hard work in it. And it's a great early recollection for a future teacher to have. Can you sense how different this memory is from the ones you reported when you first came to see us?

RUTH: I don't actually even remember the early recollections I gave you originally. Is this one different?

BILL: Very different. I was just looking at them here in your file. I think the next time you get together with Jim, you should go back and review where you were when you started and where you are now.

A change in one's early recollections is not uncommon when change has also happened in one's life. The change may not be dramatic, as in a completely new memory. Sometimes, it is a shift in emphasis: something new stands out, or the client's reaction is different than originally reported. In Ruth's new memory here she is "making a difference" in someone's life (social interest), and she is now focused more on her own competence and experiencing the appreciation of others for her work. This is a significant change in her sense of belonging and a great place for a new teacher to start.

Jerry Corey's Work With Ruth From an Adlerian Perspective

With the detailed information about Ruth derived from the initial interview, the lifestyle assessment, and the sample therapy sessions provided by Drs. Jim Bitter and Bill Nicoll, I will continue counseling Ruth from an Adlerian orientation. In the following section, I demonstrate the Adlerian slant on working with Ruth regarding her mistaken beliefs.

Session 6 ("Cognitive Focus in Counseling") of the *DVD for Integrative Counseling: The Case of Ruth and Lecturettes* illustrates Ruth's striving to live up to expectations and to measure up to perfectionistic standards. I draw upon Adlerian concepts in this particular therapy session with Ruth.

Basic Assumptions

As an Adlerian therapist, I view my work with Ruth as teaching her better ways of meeting the challenges of *life tasks*. One assumption that will guide my interventions with her is that although she has been influenced by her past, she is not necessarily molded by it. This premise of self-determination leaves little room for a client to take the role of a passive victim. I assume that my client has the capacity to influence and create events.

Ruth's childhood experiences are of therapeutic interest to me. They are the foundation and early context for the social factors that contributed to her psychological development. True to the Adlerian spirit, I function as a therapist on the belief that it is not her childhood experiences in themselves that are crucial; rather, it is her *attitude* toward these events. Since these early influences may have led to the development of *faulty beliefs* and assumptions in her style of life, I will explore with her what it was like at home as she was growing up. Our focus will be on understanding and assessing the structure of her family life, known as the *family constellation,* and her *early recollections* (both of which were reported in detail in the previous section by Drs. Bitter and Nicoll).

Because I operate from a phenomenological stance (dealing with the client's subjective perception of reality), I will want to find out how she views the major events and turning points of her life. I assume that she has created a unique style of life that helps to explain the patterns of her behavior. My attention will be on how she has developed her distinctive behaviors in the pursuit of her life goals.

Assessment of Ruth

As is evident from Drs. Bitter and Nicoll's work with Ruth, Adlerian therapists typically use the lifestyle questionnaire in making an initial assessment of the client and in formulating the goals and directions for therapy. This questionnaire gathers information about the client's childhood experiences, especially as they relate to family influences, birth order, relationships of each of the other family members, early memories, and other relevant material that will provide clues about the social forces influencing the client's personality formation. The goal of assessment is to identify the mistaken logic, movement, and motivations represented in the major themes and patterns of the client's life, especially as these are connected to the presenting issue(s). I also identify assets (strengths and internal resources) Ruth has developed that can be drawn on to provide a direction for the course of her therapy. (Drs. Bitter and Nicoll provided an Adlerian lifestyle assessment of Ruth, so I will not repeat that discussion here.)

Goals of Therapy

The four major goals of an Adlerian approach to therapy with Ruth correspond to the four phases of the therapeutic process. These goals are (1) to establish and maintain an effective working relationship with Ruth, (2) to provide a therapeutic climate in which she can come to understand her basic beliefs and feelings about herself, (3) to help her reach insight into her mistaken goals and self-defeating behaviors, and (4) to assist her in developing alternative ways of thinking, feeling, and behaving by encouraging her to translate her insights into action.

Therapeutic Procedures

One of the aims of Ruth's therapy is to challenge her to take risks and make changes. Throughout the entire process, *encouragement* is of the utmost importance. My assumption is that with encouragement Ruth will begin to experience her own inner resources and the power to choose for herself and to direct her own life. By now, Ruth will ideally have challenged her self-limiting assumptions and will be ready to put plans into action. Even though she may regress to old patterns at times, I will ask her to "catch herself" in this process and then continue to experiment with and practice new behavior.

Throughout her therapy, I will use a variety of techniques aimed primarily at challenging her cognitions (beliefs and thinking processes). Adlerians contend that first people think, then feel, and then behave. So, if we want to change behavior and feelings, the best way is to focus on Ruth's mistaken perceptions and faulty beliefs about life and herself.[11]

The Therapeutic Process

The process of Adlerian therapy can be understood by recalling some basic ideas from contemporary psychoanalytic therapy. There is a link between these two approaches, especially on the issue of looking at how early patterns are related to our present personality functioning.

ELEMENTS OF THE PROCESS

🜚 Uncovering a Mistaken Belief Ruth and I have been working together for some time, and she is beginning to see striking parallels between the role she assumed as an adolescent, by becoming the caretaker of her sisters and brother, and her contemporary role as "supermother" to her own children. She has discovered that all of her life she has been laboring under the assumption that if she handled herself unselfishly, she would be rewarded by being acknowledged and feeling a sense of personal fulfillment. As a child she wanted to be loved, accepted, and taken care of emotionally by her father, and she has worked very hard at being the perfect wife and the devoted mother to her own children. In this way, she hopes her husband will love and accept her. Still, she has never really felt appreciated or emotionally nurtured by him, and now she is realizing that she has built her life on a personal mythology: If people loved her, she would be worthwhile and would find happiness through her personal sacrifices.

🜚 Helping Ruth Reach Her Goals At this time in Ruth's therapy, we are exploring some other options open to her. Lately, we have been talking a lot about her goals and about her vision of herself in the years to come. Ruth talks about feeling selfish that she is going to school because this means that she has less time to give at home. Ruth becomes aware that the guilt often stops her from reaching the goals that are meaningful to her. For part of our counseling session, we explore some of Ruth's mistaken notions that get in the way of her doing what she would like to be doing.

> RUTH: I keep feeling I shouldn't be at school and should be at home. John keeps telling me how much he and the kids miss me. If only I could stop feeling guilty.
>
> JERRY: You say that John keeps telling you how much he and the kids miss you. It's really very nice to be missed; but you interpret his meaning to be "Ruth, you should stay at home. You're displeasing everyone."
>
> RUTH: That's true. That's what I think he is saying.

JERRY: Well, it may be a mistaken notion you have. You could check it out. You could ask John what *he* means when he says he misses you. Maybe all he means is that he loves you [*Pause*], and believes that the kids love you too. You could ask.

RUTH: Asking John how he really feels about my school and career and what I'm doing is extremely hard. [*Pause*] He could tell me that he hates my school and career goals, and they're threatening our relationship. But I am willing to give it a try.

I am hoping that Ruth, by confronting a mistaken notion, will find the courage to check a lifelong idea against a current reality. She will be scared, to be sure. Without some fear there is no need for courage. A week passes, and Ruth returns.

RUTH: Guess what? John and I talked. We both cried. He was afraid that I wouldn't need him anymore. Afraid of losing *me*! Can you believe it? But he didn't want me to stop school.

JERRY: I'm very happy for you. How great that a real risk worked out so well for you.

RUTH: When John talked about the kids wanting their mother home, I started to feel guilty all over again. But at least now I notice those times when my guilt stops me, and I'm working at not letting it control me. It's like you said: Guilt is what we "good" people do when we don't feel that we are living up to other people's expectations.

JERRY: Good! At this point in your life, guilt is a habit. Like any habit, it takes time to change it. Right now you're catching yourself when guilt is getting in your way. Eventually I suspect that you will be able to control your guilt instead of it controlling you.

From here we proceed to look at a week of Ruth's time and how she might balance personal needs with the needs of others. Planning special time for her family maintains Ruth's sense of belonging and her real need for social interest without short-circuiting the gift of time her family is giving her for school. It also provides her with a structure by which she can devote her full attention to the tasks or people at hand: quality time in both cases.

PROCESS COMMENTARY My major aim in our sessions is to both encourage and challenge Ruth to consider alternative attitudes, beliefs, goals, and behaviors. By seeing the link between her mistaken beliefs and her current feelings and behaviors, she is able to consider options and change. She takes a big risk in approaching her husband. Given her history with and interpretation of men, she anticipates a harsh, rejecting rebuke. What she gains, however, is an increased sense of her worth and value to this important man in her life. She also gains in courage and confidence.

Once Ruth has made some new decisions and modified her goals, I teach her ways in which to evaluate her own thinking. At those times when she is critical of herself, I provide encouragement. Partly because of my faith in her and my encouragement, she comes closer to experiencing her inner strength. She becomes more honest about what she is doing, and she augments her power to choose for herself instead of merely following the values she uncritically accepted as a child.

A most important ingredient of the final stages of Ruth's therapy is commitment. She is finally persuaded that if she hopes to change, she will have to set specific tasks for herself and then take concrete action. Although she attempts to live up to what she believes is the role of the "good person," she eventually develops increased tolerance for learning by trial and error, and with this she becomes better at "catching herself" when she repeats ineffective behavior.[12]

Some Final Thoughts

A basic premise in the Adlerian approach is that if the therapist can encourage clients to change their thinking, they will then change their feelings and behavior. Applied to Ruth, this means that it is important to work with how she views the world, how she thinks, how she feels, and how she is acting in her world. From my perspective, one of the strengths of the Adlerian approach is its integrative nature. I find that many Adlerian concepts can be applied to understanding a diversity of client populations. This is a holistic approach that encompasses the full spectrum of human experience, and practitioners have great freedom in working with clients in ways that are uniquely suited to their own therapeutic style.

Questions for Reflection

1. As you review the basic features of a lifestyle assessment (family constellation, early recollections, basic convictions, and interfering ideas) of Ruth, what associations do you have with your own childhood experiences?
2. As you think about your own family of origin, what most stands out for you? After reflecting on your early experiences in your family, attempt to come to some conclusions about the ways in which these experiences are operating in your life today.
3. What are three of your earliest recollections? Can you speculate on how these memories might have an impact on the person you are now and how they could be related to your future strivings?
4. List what you consider to be the major "basic mistakes" in your life. Do you have any ideas about how you developed these mistaken perceptions about yourself and about life? How are these perceptions influencing the ways in which you think, feel, and act today?
5. From what you learned about Ruth through the lifestyle assessment, what aspects of her life might you want to give the primary focus? What themes running through her life lend themselves especially well to Adlerian therapy?
6. One of the goals of Adlerian therapy is to increase the client's social interest. Can you think of ways in which you could work with Ruth to help her attain this goal?
7. Ruth describes herself as coming from a middle-class family. They were fundamentalist Christians, and the family values involved doing right, working hard, and living in a way that would reflect well on the family. Considering

this background, how well do Adlerian concepts and therapeutic procedures fit for Ruth? How would the Adlerian approach fit for her if she were an Asian American? Latino? African American? Native American?

8. What major cultural themes do you see in Ruth's case? How would you address these themes using an Adlerian framework?

9. How well does the Adlerian approach fit with your counseling style? What aspects of this approach do you find most useful? Which aspects might you want to modify to fit your personal counseling style?

Notes

See the *DVD for Theory and Practice of Counseling and Psychotherapy: The Case of Stan and Lecturettes,* Session 3 ("Adlerian Therapy Applied to the Case of Stan"), for a demonstration of gathering Stan's early recollections, and for my presentation of ways to apply Adlerian therapy.

1. See the following sources for a full discussion of Adlerian brief therapy: Nicoll, W., Bitter, J. R., Christensen, O. C., & Hawes, C. (2000). Adlerian brief therapy: Strategies and tactics. In J. Carlson & L. Sperry (Eds.), *Brief therapy strategies with individuals and couples* (pp. 220–247). Phoenix: Zeig/Tucker; Sonstegard, M. A., Bitter, J. R., Pelonis-Peneros, P., & Nicoll, W. G. (2001). Adlerian group psychotherapy: A brief therapy approach. *Directions in Clinical and Counseling Psychology, 11*(2), 11–24.

2. Multiple therapy is discussed in Dreikurs, R., Shulman, B. H., & Mosak, H. H. (1982). *Multiple therapy: The use of two therapists with one patient.* Chicago: Alfred Alder Institute.

3. Based on material in Powers, R. L., & Griffith, J. (1987). *Understanding life style: The psycho-clarity process.* Chicago: AIAS; Shulman, B. H., & Mosak, H. H. (1988). *Manual for lifestyle assessment.* Muncie, IN: Accelerated Development.

4. *The Individual Psychology Client Workbook (with supplements),* by Robert L. Powers and Jane Griffith, © 1995 by the Americas Institute of Adlerian Studies, Ltd., 600 North McClurg Court, Suite 2502A, Chicago, IL 60611-3027.

5. For a more complete discussion on this topic, see Disque, J. G., & Bitter, J. R. (1998). Integrating narrative therapy with Adlerian lifestyle assessment: A case study. *Journal of Individual Psychology, 54*(4), 431–450.

6. An excellent overview of Adlerian therapy can be found in Carlson, J., Watts, R. E., & Maniacci, M. (2006). *Adlerian therapy: Theory and practice.* Washington, DC: American Psychological Association.

7. Adlerian brief therapy is dealt with in detail in these two sources: Bitter, J. R., Christensen, O. C., Hawes, C., & Nicoll, W. G. (1998). Adlerian brief therapy with individuals, couples, and families. *Directions in Clinical and Counseling Psychology, 8*(8), 95–112; Bitter, J. R., & Nicoll, W. G. (2000). Adlerian brief therapy with individuals: Process and practice. *Journal of Individual Psychology, 56*(1), 31–44.

8. Dreikurs, R. (1997). Holistic medicine. *Individual Psychology, 53*(2), 127–205.

9. Ibid.

10. Adler, A. (1964). *Problems of neurosis: A book of case histories* (P. Mairet, Ed.). New York: Harper & Row. (Original work published 1929)
11. Here I demonstrate the Adlerian slant on working with Ruth cognitively, especially regarding her mistaken beliefs. Session 6 of the *DVD for Integrative Counseling: The Case of Ruth and Lecturettes* reflects Ruth's striving to live up to expectations and to measure up to perfectionistic standards.
12. In Session 13 ("Evaluation and Termination") of the *DVD for Integrative Counseling: The Case of Ruth and Lecturettes*, I encourage Ruth to make concrete plans regarding where she wants to go now that therapy has ended. For a more detailed treatment of Adlerian theory, see Corey, G. (2013). *Theory and practice of counseling and psychotherapy* (9th ed.). Belmont, CA: Brooks/Cole, Cengage Learning. The basic concepts introduced by Jim Bitter and Bill Nicoll in their assessment of Ruth are covered comprehensively in Chapter 5 ("Adlerian Therapy"). Also see Corey, G. (2013). *Student manual for theory and practice of counseling and psychotherapy* (9th ed.). Belmont, CA: Brooks/Cole, Cengage Learning. This manual contains a lifestyle assessment that you can take as an exercise. Completing the inventory will help you understand the comprehensive approach to assessment of Ruth used in this chapter by Drs. Bitter and Nicoll.

CHAPTER FOUR

Case Approach to Existential Therapy

General Overview of Existential Therapy

The principal goal of existential therapy is to challenge clients to recognize and accept the freedom they have to become the authors of their own lives. Therapists confront clients on ways in which they are avoiding their freedom and the responsibility that accompanies it. This approach places primary emphasis on understanding clients' current experience, not on using therapeutic techniques. Thus, counselors are not bound by any prescribed techniques and can borrow therapeutic strategies from other schools of therapy. Interventions are used in broadening the ways in which clients live in their world and creating meaning from that experience. When techniques are used, they grow out of the here-and-now context of the therapeutic work and are aimed at expanding clients' self-awareness.

The issues of termination and evaluation are typically resolved through an open dialogue between client and therapist. Clients generally make the choice to enter therapy, and it is their choice and responsibility to decide when to leave therapy. If clients continue to rely on the therapist for this answer, they are not yet ready to terminate. However, therapists are given latitude to express their reactions and views about clients' readiness for termination. The choices clients are making and the changes in their perceptions of themselves in their world are the basis for an evaluation of therapeutic outcomes.

An Existential Therapist's Perspective on Ruth
by J. Michael Russell, PhD, PsyD

Introduction

Existential counseling is rooted in existential philosophy. It is a way of thinking about people. It is not a specific method or set of techniques and not even a unified theory, but it draws from a group of philosophers and theorists who stress the idea that we are responsible for the meaning we choose to give to our circumstances. It is based on phenomenology, which means it emphasizes subjective experience. However, unlike some other viewpoints and in common with psychoanalysis, it does not assume that clients know themselves particularly well, and it does not assume that they see very clearly the choices they make. Personal claims about experience are important, but they do not have any decisive and privileged status. On the contrary, from an existentialist perspective all of us are frequently self-deceived and inauthentic about our experience.

Various themes routinely emerge in the counseling process, and some are particularly prominent in how existentialist counselors conceptualize their work. These are typically interconnected and all have to do with choice. One theme is that we all seem anxious about our sense of personal identity. We worry about who we want to be, who we don't want to be, how we are seen by others, and how we see ourselves. The most common pitfall involves trying to regard "who we are" as fixed and finished so we do not have to face our choices. For the most part, who we are will depend on what we do in the future and how much we stick to resolves we make now. Hence, anxiety is a related theme because it alerts us to uncertainty about what we might do. We can also turn this formulation around and consider that we try to pin down our identity to stave off anxiety. So another closely related existential theme is about freedom. People often come to counseling because they would like more freedom. Just as often, clients want less freedom, or less of the sense of responsibility that goes with it.

Existential counseling seeks to enlarge clients' awareness of how they construct meaning in the world in which they live. The goal is for clients to have greater insight into how they think, what they feel, and what they can do. Clients learn what freedom entails and take responsibility for their own circumstances. Existentialism holds that we are responsible for the choices through which we give meaning to the circumstances in which we find ourselves, and these concerns take on particular force in light of the prospect of our own death, and the related experience of loss and isolation that can come with the death of significant others. Existential therapists help clients explore their uncertainty and anxiety about whether they are relating to others in an authentic or inauthentic and self-deceived way.

Assessment of Ruth

Existential issues—such as identity, freedom, and anxiety—practically jump off the pages of Ruth's autobiography. With respect to *identity*, Ruth has defined herself as a superwoman, a good wife and a good mother, faced with the prospect of losing all of these familiar designations as her children mature and begin to leave home. She also seems to identify with her family's view of her as overweight. She identifies with and then distances herself from her parents' religious values. These facets of the identity theme are pretty obvious. On a more subtle level, we can wonder to what extent she brings her panic attacks on herself. Does she tell herself she's prone to panic, and make this a self-fulfilling prophecy?

Ruth presents at least two very different perspectives on *anxiety* as an existential theme. We can see her as anxious because of her quest for identity. However, her efforts to establish a sense of identity may be seen as an attempt to manage a core of anxiety. From the first perspective, she is anxious because she is afraid she won't know who or how to be if she loses her roles as mother and wife or if new professional ambitions don't pan out. Insecurities like these build on some level of her awareness that it was never really possible to be safe and secure. In fact, she acknowledges that she has not always been the perfect mother or perfect wife, and there's enough hesitancy about pursuing a career as a teacher that we know that neither her past performance nor her future aspirations are concrete and fixed certainties.

Ruth is ambivalent about *freedom*. She sought out a form of counseling that is insight-oriented. This suggests that she is interested in exploring options for change. But she also says she wants someone to tell her what to do, and evidently she has had plenty of directive people in her past, including her father.

Virtually all the key existential issues pertain to Ruth, and they are interconnected. She may come to see that identifying herself as a wife and mother could be protecting her from a frightening kind of *isolation*, and a collapse of familiar *meaning*. Her concerns about *death* are likely to be a particularly valuable window for understanding what might be meaningful for her, what choices she has, and how her anxiety has something to teach her.

What about a more formal diagnostic assessment of Ruth? Existentialists are likely to dislike labels generally and to dislike "medical" labels in particular. Up to a point, I agree; however, the same opportunity for using or abusing adjectives arises whether in everyday speech or technical psychological jargon. Whether we say Ruth is "dysthymic" or say she "sometimes gets the blues," the real question is whether our language helps or gets in the way. Should we say she "has a panic disorder" or say she's "really uptight"? Is it "an adjustment disorder" or is she "going through some changes"? If a diagnostic label fits loosely, it may enhance my capacity to understand my client. If it fits precisely, then I had better be open to learning from the experiences of other therapists of various orientations.

Each of the five *DSM* axes can sharpen my thinking about Ruth. I am not a slave to any of this vocabulary but neither do I dismiss it. Axis I considerations tend to highlight conditions that Ruth, herself, would like to overcome. That certainly applies to her panic attacks and her depression. In my view, she tentatively qualifies for "panic attacks without agoraphobia" and for dysthymia. "Adjustment disorder" also fits, and it helps us to focus on specifics in her existential situation. She will experience her symptoms and circumstances as something that happens to her, and it remains to be seen to what extent she may learn to think of them as anything like choices. Surely she can, at least, consider what choices she has about how to deal with them.

I rather like Axis II terminology because I use it to enhance my understanding of a client without taking it so seriously as to try to reduce a person to a "disorder." I don't think Ruth fully meets the criteria for any full-fledged disorder, but I do think that some of the Axis II terms, applied loosely, can help me to understand her. "Dependent personality" fits somewhat. More interesting is "narcissism," not because Ruth shows anything close to a "narcissistic personality disorder" but because self-esteem issues are very relevant to her. About Axis III, the fact that a medical doctor has ruled out relevant medical conditions helps to assure me that insight-oriented psychotherapy may be appropriate for Ruth, but I suspect that further exploration from a medical perspective may be very much in order. A medical or physiological perspective and a meaning or existential perspective are not incompatible, nor does applicability of one pre-empt the value of the other. As for Axes IV and V, assessing situational factors and stressors is part of what any therapist would consider. And, whether we want to admit it or not, all of us in fact make some sort of assessment of how well we think a client is functioning and how well we believe the client might function. I would rate Ruth's stressors as considerable, and I see her as fairly high function-ing even if compromised by the issues and symptoms she brings to therapy.

So far I have addressed existential and diagnostic features of Ruth's case that can be made fairly explicit. In addition, a subtle dimension of assessment goes on all the time and shows up in the nuances of our interactions. Tone of voice, emotionality, eye contact, body language, sense of humor, level of sophis-tication in expression, and how I find myself responding to such traits, all figure into my overall "sizing a person up." For example, suppose my first impressions of Ruth were from her initial phone call in which she says she is "shopping for a therapist." I asked her to tell me more about what she was "shopping for," and she details some of the issues covered in the autobiography she will give me later. But in this telephone exchange there is a voice quality and even a playfulness I would not have picked up on in the autobiography. We set up an initial interview "to see whether we hit it off," with her first saying she wanted to be sure I didn't mind that she was "just shopping." I reply, "How else are you going to find your kind of bargain?" This question might help me better understand her goals. The fact that I find myself phrasing things in a somewhat playful way figures into my overall experience of her.

First impressions are often mistaken, but sometimes they are right on tar-get, and usually there is some useful grain of truth implicit in our spontaneous responses. Putting it in a rather nonclinical way, I like her. I feel comfortable with her, and I think we can work together.

Goals of Counseling

In spite of the fact that I sometimes use the term, I do not like the word "ther-apy." To me it suggests some kind of procedure that is going to happen to the client so that afterward she will be "fixed" or cured. Existential counseling isn't going to make you change. Insight doesn't make you change any more than does looking into a mirror, but it can broaden your options. I think of myself as a consultant in this process. My goal, first and foremost, is to be responsive to Ruth's goals.

THERAPIST: Tell me what you hope to get from having me as your counselor.

RUTH: Well, I'd certainly like to be rid of my panic attacks and not feel anxious. I'd like to lose some weight. I'd like to get a job—something besides being wife and mom. I guess I'd like to simply feel gener-ally better about myself. I hope you can tell me how to do that and how long it's going to take. But I think there's something else that I'm wanting from counseling, and I don't quite know how to say what it is. I know I'm afraid that my life might not go on as usual, but in some ways I'm thinking being too "usual" is my problem! I'm tired of my usual routine, and I'm not sure that it means very much. And there's something that intrigued me about your description of yourself as an existentialist.

THERAPIST: Some of what you want is pretty specific, and you and I could target those objectives and go straight after them. Or, I could refer you to someone who focuses more on specific behavioral objectives. But I think there's also a side to you that your counseling class is tapping into, which is a more general kind of wanting to know yourself better, which is what I would like to offer.

🪷 **Process Commentary**   I do have some goals of my own, but I think of these as being in the service of my client. I would like Ruth to have an enlarged consciousness of herself as the free author of her own meaning, and a broader awareness of her choices. I would like her to develop a greater capacity to tolerate ambiguity, although she prefers what she calls "neat answers." She would like to be rid of her panic attacks, and I want this for her too. But I also want her to retain a certain amount of legitimate "existential anxiety." I think she can get past the incapacitating moments of panic. I would hope the enlarging of her awareness is not simply on an intellectual level, but also comes out in her capacity to feel a greater range of feelings and a broader range of possibilities for action. I think the process of pursuing these goals by means of thinking, feeling, and acting is intrinsically worthwhile, and I also believe she may be in a better position to deal with her options and choices because of this process of consulting with me. I would hope this shows up not only in how she thinks, but also in terms of what she can let herself feel and do within our consulting room and outside as well.

Counseling Process and Technique

There is no specific set of techniques for doing existential counseling. At our first meeting I looked through her autobiography while she read my consent form and description of services. I asked her to tell me more about some of the issues she mentioned in the autobiography, sometimes asking for elaboration, sometimes noting some connection between themes. While I often hint at the existence of choices, I virtually never impose an "existentialist" vocabulary of freedom and responsibility. Toward the end of this first session, after Ruth stated her hopes or goals in counseling, I proposed that we meet twice a week for half-hour sessions.

RUTH: Isn't that kind of unusual?

THERAPIST: You said being usual might be one of your problems.

We talked more about this twice a week idea and how the greater frequency of meetings might fit with her enthusiasm for "really getting into a phase of self-exploration." Half sessions meant half the fee, which she could afford. She liked the experiment. I said, "It's an experiment for me too."

🐾 **Process Commentary**   Why did I say that? One reason is that unpretentious candor is in keeping with an existentialist's way of thinking. The short session idea really was an experiment. I am more self-disclosing than most therapists, and far more self-disclosing than ever would have been advocated in my psychoanalytic training. I hesitate to call that a "technique," although I do hope to be modeling candor and an openness to experimenting with options. I see existential counseling as an encounter between two people, not just one person scrutinizing the other.

Particularly in the early phases of time-indefinite insight-oriented counseling I am careful to not be "preachy" about believing we are all free persons responsible for making choices about the meaning of our circumstances. With exceptions for crisis situations that require immediate action and a shift in attitude, such lectures are generally pointless. My hope is that in the long run the client will attain a deep appreciation of personal responsibility. A prelude to accepting responsibility at a deep level may be first having some time to complain about how unfair the world is.

In our fourth session Ruth reported that she had talked with her father by phone and said nothing about being in counseling. She knew he would not approve. According to her, he "never" approves of anything she does. He certainly would never approve of "existential counseling." Basically, I encourage her to elaborate whenever her emotions are more evident. The bulk of what Ruth said in this meeting portrayed her as the doomed victim of a disapproving father. I certainly did *not* give her a lecture on how she has many choices.

In a subsequent session when Ruth was again bemoaning her critical father, I borrowed from Gestalt therapy the technique of role playing: talking to her father by talking to me, saying in a first-person way some of the things she did not say to her father on the phone. I elected to encourage her to talk directly to me—look me in the eyes—rather than either reporting in an abstract way or "talking to the empty chair." Ordinarily, in long-term work, I hesitate to employ any of these techniques, relying on supportive listening. Perhaps because of the pace of these half-hour sessions, this more "active" style on my part seemed right at the time. If I had consciously entertained a rationale, which I did not, it would involve a couple of objectives. One of these is that I would like Ruth to become more aware of her feelings and more aware of how she has considerable choice in whether or how she enters into what she feels—how she can "get into it." Another is that I'm sure her experience of her father is much more complex than her usual black-and-white portrait of him lets on. Expressing different sides of her in these role plays paves the way, in the long run, for a greater appreciation for ambiguity, complexity, and freedom.

I believe we choose our moods, and I look for opportunities to get a glimpse of how Ruth is making these choices. Ruth started off one session by saying she was depressed. I encourage Ruth to list features of her life that get her down and to elaborate on these, speaking in the most discouraged voice she can muster. I then propose that she now feign a more positive tone of voice and tell me, in an upbeat way, some things she can see about *me* that ought to get *me* down. This proves to be an amusing exercise for her. She becomes almost gleeful in enumerating things like my receding hairline, my worn furniture, and the declining property values around my home-office. Out of nowhere her mood seems to have been transformed!

> THERAPIST: So what I want you to see is how talented you are in rather literally talking yourself into the blues, and how you are able to take on a positive voice as well. I think you have some choice in your moods and feelings. I wonder what you might gain from "depressing yourself."

> RUTH: Well, that's pretty much all I know to talk about when I'm here in a therapy session. I focus on the parts of my life that aren't so good.

> THERAPIST: Understood. But maybe there's a larger truth to this idea that you know how to work yourself into depression. I think you are seeing how you have some options here.

When I do use a technique, it is usually a creative adaptation to unplanned events in which I am seeking to create a meaningful connection between events and themes. For example, I arrived at the seventh session out of breath, barely on time. Ruth talked more about her father, who approves of almost nothing, and her husband, who is supportive of her being in counseling, but with "strings attached." John doesn't like the resulting late dinners.

> RUTH: Approval from men always seems so conditional!

> THERAPIST: Anyone here remind you of a man? [*I like using humor appropriately, and Ruth laughed.*]

> RUTH: Well, you are different. Like the way you were so out of breath, rushing to getting here today. It made me feel you really care.

> THERAPIST: Well, thanks for the compliment. I'm not sure I'm all that unique, but I appreciate your letting me represent some different ways men might be experienced. You know, we've noticed before how ready you are to label yourself. Sometimes you'll say you are "just a mom," or "just a wife," or just someone who will never feel good about herself after so often being put down by Dad. Today I think we are getting a more complete picture not only about the simplified identity you give yourself, but also how you oversimplify other people in your life.

🐦 **Process Commentary**   There are several ingredients in this complex interpretive remark, and they illustrate a subtle promotion of existentialist thinking. It allows Ruth the space for a "positive transference" yet also suggests she is responsible for how she is constructing our relationship. It connects with calling attention to how self-labeling can be self-deceiving. It suggests that these current expressions of attitude are choices and yet have a history. And it moves Ruth toward possible insight into how she renders her world static with her oversimplified labels of herself and others.

As another example of subtly promoting insight into existential responsibility, at a later meeting Ruth was venting anger about her daughter Jennifer, who had ditched school to go to the beach with friends.

RUTH: I can't get over how angry I am at Jennifer for ditching school. She's so irresponsible!

THERAPIST: Well, much as it's important for Jennifer to take school seriously, I wonder whether you are a bit jealous of how much she seems to be sort of a free spirit?

🔆 **Process Commentary** Ruth's exceptionally "responsible" identity as a supermom and superwife is perhaps an evasion of another kind of flight from her responsibility for having made her life safe and "usual," without risk but without meaning and excitement. Jennifer reminds Ruth of something she has been missing.

Time-Limited Counseling

Up to now I have been trying to provide some sense for how I might work with Ruth in the early and middle phases of time-indefinite, insight-oriented existential counseling. As time goes on, I tend to put increasing emphasis on how Ruth and I interact and focus less on past events and people not present in the consulting room or, at least, highlight comparisons between events outside and the "here and now, you and me." There is no way to neatly demarcate what counts as the early phase and what counts as the middle phase of existential counseling because there is no preconceived formula for when counseling should end. I will continue working with Ruth as long as there is vitality to the exchange.

Ruth's situation changed when she was presented with an unexpected opportunity to substitute full time for a teacher who would be taking a lengthy leave. This meant that our meetings would have to end in 8 weeks.

With time-limited existential counseling (and also, with the ending phase of long-term work) I become more active, more directive, and more focused on specific goals. My general objective remains the same, which is to address the client's goals while also promoting an enhanced awareness of one's freedom. What is different is the way specific changes are explored both in seeking solutions to specific problems and in promoting lasting habits of thinking that will plant seeds for continued growth. For example, Ruth's job opportunity came about because I had commented that going to an interview did not obligate her to accept an offer. I phrased this with, "What's holding you back from just having an interview?" This lessened her reluctance to simply *try out* choices and possibilities, and I hope she will generalize learning from this event. To take another example, in these last weeks I renewed a suggestion I had made before—that Ruth get a second medical opinion about her excessive sweating. The previous (male) doctor's opinion seems to have been provided in a somewhat offhand way. The second (female) doctor, a specialist in hyperhidrosis, proposed further evaluation of Ruth's hormone factors. As a result of further tests, Ruth was able to make progress with this physical symptom, and she did so without devaluing the time spent in counseling exploring the emotional significance of this symptom. She was also able to use this as an opportunity to review her habit of putting male (her father's) opinions too highly.

Topics of meaning, loss, and death ran through many of Ruth's sessions, but they took on a particular importance with the transition to a time-limited format.

RUTH: I'd like to be able to leave the door open to seeing you again once this teaching job is over.

THERAPIST: The door is open to our working together again down the road. And I like the way you are looking out for your options. But I also recommend that we not deprive ourselves of experiencing the ending of what we've been doing here. When we choose to avoid the reality of endings, we tend to lose sight of what's meaningful.

RUTH: I can see that. But don't worry. I'll be taking away plenty from our meetings.

THERAPIST: I'm sure you will. But in order to maximize that, I suggest that in these last times we get together we review some of the ground we have covered, and see if we can identify any particular accomplishments you would like to achieve either by the time we wrap up, or some time afterward. To do that, we need to be as specific as we can.

Process Commentary   As mentioned earlier, learning about our choices is not merely a matter of enlarging our thinking. It is also learning how to feel. And it is also experimenting with action. I tend to incorporate a behavioral perspective toward the end of our counseling relationship because I would like Ruth to clarify choices available to her and think about translating these choices into an action plan. I hope these choices will be relevant both to the goals she brought to counseling and to my goal for her of an expanded consciousness of her part in giving meaning to the world she lives in. I asked her to think about some way she might summarize her time in counseling when we meet for the last time. Here, in part, is what she said at that last meeting.

RUTH: I think I've seen something about how eager I was to get myself and everyone else neatly packaged up into familiar labels. I've got a long way to go, but I think I see, for instance, how convenient it was to feel like the victim of my father's harsh judgments, my kids' lack of appreciation for my efforts, and my husband's lack of real supportiveness. I think I came here bemoaning what other people were doing to me, and I'm leaving with more of a sense of being responsible for what I do.

CONCLUDING COMMENTS We do not learn such things once and for all, but Ruth is learning. For a more complete discussion of my views on topics such as the applications of existential theory to counseling practice, interventions and the therapeutic process, using the relationship, and case suggestions, see chapter 7 on existential psychotherapy in *Applying Counseling Theories: An Online, Case-Based Approach* (Rochlen, 2007).[1]

Jerry Corey's Work With Ruth From an Existential Perspective

In the *DVD for Integrative Counseling: The Case of Ruth and Lecturettes,* Session 11 ("Understanding How the Past Influences the Present and the Future"), I demonstrate some ways I utilize existential notions in counseling Ruth. We engage in a role play where Ruth becomes the voice of her church and I take on a new role as Ruth—one in which I have been willing to challenge certain beliefs from church. This segment illustrates how Ruth explores finding new values. In Session 12 ("Working Toward Decisions and Behavioral Changes"), Ruth solidifies the process of making new decisions, which is also an existential concept.

Basic Assumptions

The existential approach to counseling assumes that the relationship the therapist establishes with the client is paramount in determining how successful therapy will be. Therapy is not something that I do to the person (in this case, Ruth); I am not a technical expert who acts on a passive client. I view therapy as a dialogue in the deepest and most genuine sense, an honest exchange between Ruth and me. We will be partners traveling on a journey, and neither of us knows where it will end. She and I may both be changed by the encounter, and she will likely affect me in personal ways. My hope is to understand her world from a subjective viewpoint and, at the same time, to let her know my personal reactions to her in our relationship.

Initial Assessment of Ruth

Ruth appears to be a good candidate for existential therapy. She is willing to question the meaning of life, to question the status quo, and to challenge some of her comfortable patterns. She is facing a number of developmental crises, such as wondering what life is about now that her children are getting ready to leave home. Her anxiety increases as she begins to expand her vision of the choices open to her. The process of raising questions has led to more questions, yet her answers are few. She is grappling with what she wants for herself, apart from her long-standing definition of herself as wife and mother. A major theme is posed by the question "How well am I living life?" One of Ruth's strengths is her willingness to ask such anxiety-producing questions. Another of her assets is her willingness to critically think about her existence. As a result of her examination of her life, she has already made some choices and taken some significant steps. She did diverge from her fundamentalist religion, which she no longer found personally meaningful; she is motivated to change her life; and she has sought out therapy as a way to help her find the paths she wants to travel.

Goals of Therapy

The purpose of existential therapy is not to "cure" people of disorders, nor to simply get rid of symptoms; rather, it is to help them become aware of what they are doing and to encourage them to act to make life-changing decisions. It is aimed at helping people like Ruth get out of their rigid roles and see more clearly the ways in which they have been leading a narrow and restricted existence. Therapy aims at helping clients to reflect upon and understand their existence. The basic purpose of Ruth's therapy is to provide her with the insights necessary to discover, establish, and use the freedom she possesses. In many ways Ruth is blocking her own freedom. My function is to help her recognize her part in creating her life situation, including the distress she feels. I assume that as she sees the ways in which her existence is limited she will take steps toward her liberation. My hope is that she can create a more responsible and meaningful existence.

Therapeutic Procedures

As an existential therapist, I do not rely on a well-developed set of techniques. Therapy is a fluid and creative process, and techniques I may choose arise from what is taking place in the ongoing therapeutic process and our relationship. I focus on certain themes that are part of the human condition, and I emphasize my ability to be fully present with Ruth by challenging her and by sharing my reactions with her as they pertain to our therapeutic relationship. My role is to help Ruth clarify what it is that brought her to me, where she is right now, what it is she wants to change, and what she can do to make these changes happen. I will borrow techniques from several therapies as we explore her thoughts, feelings, and behaviors within the current situations and events of her life.[2]

When we deal with her past, I will encourage Ruth to relate her feelings and thoughts about past events to her present situation. Here are some of the questions I might pursue with her, any of which we might eventually explore in therapy sessions:

- In what ways are you living as fully as you might? How are you limiting yourself?
- To what degree are you living a life outlined by others?
- What choices have you made so far, and how have these choices affected you?
- What are some of the choices you are faced with now? How do you deal with the anxiety that is part of making choices for yourself and accepting personal freedom?
- What changes do you most want to make, and what is preventing you from making them?

In essence, Ruth is about to engage in a process of opening doors to herself. The experience may be frightening, exciting, joyful, depressing, or all of these at times. As she wedges open the closed doors, she will also begin to loosen the deterministic shackles that have kept her psychologically bound. Gradually, as she becomes aware of what she has been and who she is now, she will be better able to decide what kind of future she wants to carve out for herself. Through her therapy she can explore alternatives for translating her visions into real life.

The Therapeutic Process

At this point in her therapy, Ruth is coming to grips more directly with her midlife crisis. She has been talking about values by which she lived in the past that now hold little meaning for her, about her feelings of emptiness, and about her fears of making "wrong" choices. Here are some excerpts from several of our sessions.

ELEMENTS OF THE PROCESS

✿ Helping Ruth Develop New Values   In a later session Ruth initiates her struggles with religion:

RUTH: I left my religion years ago, but I haven't found anything to replace it. I'm hoping you can help me explore this. You have so much more experience, and you seem happy with who you are and what you believe in. On my own I'm afraid I might make the wrong decisions.

JERRY: If I were to give you answers, it would be a way of saying that I don't see you as capable of finding your own way. Maybe a way for you to begin is to ask some questions. I know, for me, one way of finding answers is to raise questions.

RUTH: I know that the religion I was brought up in told me very clearly what was right and wrong. I was taught that once married, always married—and you make the best of the situation. Well, I'm not so willing to accept that now.

JERRY: How is that so?

RUTH: I'm afraid that if I stay in therapy I'll change so much that I'll have little in common with John, and I may eventually leave my marriage.

JERRY: I'm aware that you've somehow decided that your changes will cause the breakup of your marriage. Could it be that your changes might have a positive effect on your relationship?

RUTH: You're right, I haven't thought about it in that way. And I guess I've made the assumption that John won't like my changes. I more often worry that what I'm doing in therapy will eventually make me want to leave him, or he might want to leave me. Sometimes I have an impulse to walk away from my marriage, but I get scared thinking about who I'd be without John in my life.

JERRY: Why not imagine that this did happen, and for a few minutes talk about who you would be without John in your life. Just speak whatever thoughts or images come to your mind, and try not to worry about how they sound.

RUTH: All my life I've had others tell me who and what I should be, and John has picked up where my parents and church left off. I don't know what my life is about apart from being a wife and a mother. What would our kids think if John and I split up? How would it affect them? Would they hate me for what I'd done to the family? I know I'm tired of living the way I am, but I'm scared to death of making any more changes for fear that it will lead to more turmoil. John and the kids liked the "old me" just fine, and they seem upset by the things I've been saying lately.

JERRY: In all that you just said, you didn't allow yourself to really express how you might be different if they were not in your life. It's easier for you to tune in to how the people in your life might be affected by your changes than for you to allow yourself to imagine how you'd be different. It does seem difficult for you to imagine being different. Why not give it another try? Keep the focus on how you want to be different rather than on the reactions your family would have to your changing.

❧ Dealing With Ruth's Anxiety   It is obvious that Ruth has trouble dealing with change. There is immediate anxiety whenever she thinks of being different. She is beginning to see that she has choices, and that others do not have to make her choices for her. Yet she is terrified by this realization, and for a long time it appears that she is immobilized in her therapy. She will not act on the choices available to her. So I go with her feelings of being stuck and explore her anxiety with her. Here is how she describes these feelings.

> RUTH: I often wake up in the middle of the night with the feeling that the walls are closing in on me! I break out in cold sweats, I have trouble breathing, and I can feel my heart pounding. At times I worry that I'll die. I can't sleep, and I get up and pace around.

> JERRY: Ruth, as unpleasant as these feelings are, I hope you learn to pay attention to them. They're telling you that all is not well in your life and that you're ready for change.

I know that Ruth sees anxiety as a negative thing, something she would like to be rid of once and for all. I see her anxiety as the possibility of a new starting point for her. Rather than simply getting rid of these symptoms, she can go deeper into their meaning. I see her anxiety as the result of her increased awareness of her freedom along with her growing sense of responsibility for deciding what kind of life she wants and then taking action to make these changes a reality.

❧ Exploring the Meaning of Death   Eventually we get onto the topic of death and explore its meaning to Ruth.

> RUTH: I've been thinking about what we talked about before—about what I want from life before I die. You know, for so many years I lived in dread of death. I suppose that fear has kept me from looking at death.

> JERRY: Why don't you talk about areas of your life where you don't feel really alive. How often do you feel a sense of excitement about living?

> RUTH: It would be easier for me to tell you of the times I feel half dead! I'm dead to having fun. Sexually I'm dead.

> JERRY: Can you think of some other ways you might be dead?

I am trying to get Ruth to evaluate the quality of her life and to begin to experience her deadness. After some time she admits that she has allowed her spirit to die. Old values have faded, and she has not acquired new ones. Ruth is gaining some awareness that there is more to living than breathing. It is important that she allow herself to recognize her deadness and feel it as a precondition for her rebirth. I operate under the assumption that by really experiencing and expressing the ways in which she feels dead she can begin to focus on how she wants to be alive. Only then is there hope that she can find new ways to live.

PROCESS COMMENTARY Ruth's experience in therapy accentuates the basic assumption that there are no absolute answers outside of herself. She learns that therapy is a gradual process of opening up doors, giving her more potential for choices. She becomes well aware that she cannot evade responsibility for choosing for herself. She learns that she is constantly creating herself by the choices she is making, as well as by the choices she is failing to make. As her therapist, I support her attempts at experimenting with new behaviors in and out of our sessions.

One of my aims is to show Ruth the connection between the choices she is making or failing to make and the anxiety she is experiencing. I do this by asking her to observe herself in various situations throughout the week. Through this self-observation process Ruth gradually sees some specific ways in which her choices are directly contributing to her anxiety. My goal in working with Ruth is not to eliminate her anxiety, but to help her understand what it means. From my perspective, anxiety is a signal that all is not well, that a person is ready for some change in life.

Perhaps the critical aspect of Ruth's therapy is her recognition that she has a choice to make. She can continue to cling to the known and the familiar, or she can push through the uncertainty and anxiety and make some different choices for her future. Ruth chooses to commit herself to therapy.[3]

Some Final Thoughts

Given today's emphasis on brief therapy and time-limited practical strategies aimed at solving immediate problems, some may wonder about the applicability of the existential perspective. Personally, I value the existential emphasis on freedom and responsibility and our capacity to redesign our life by making choices. The existential approach provides a sound philosophical base on which to build a personal therapeutic style because it addresses the core struggles people face. This approach can provide a foundation upon which to design a way of practicing counseling that will help people like Ruth find their own answers to the problems that brought them to therapy.

Questions for Reflection

1. What life experiences have you had that could help you identify with Ruth? Have you shared any of her struggles? How have you dealt with these personal struggles and issues? How are your answers to these questions related to your potential effectiveness as her therapist?
2. What are your general reactions to the ways in which Dr. Russell and I have worked with Ruth? What aspects of both of these styles of counseling might you use? What different themes would you focus on? What different techniques might you use?
3. Compare this approach to working with Ruth with psychoanalytic therapy and Adlerian therapy. What major differences do you see?
4. What are your thoughts about Dr. Russell's view of assessment and diagnosis as applied to Ruth?

5. How would you work with Ruth's fears associated with "opening doors" in her life? Part of her wants to remain as she is, while part of her yearns for change. How would you work with this conflict?

6. Using this approach, how would you deal with Ruth's fears of dying? Do you see any connection between her anxieties and her view of death?

7. What are your thoughts and feelings about death and dying? To what extent do you think you have explored your own anxieties pertaining to death and loss? How would your answer to this question largely determine your effectiveness in counseling a person such as Ruth?

8. What are some of the other existential themes mentioned in this chapter that have personal relevance to your life? How do you react to the question "Can therapists inspire their clients to deal with their existential concerns if they have not been willing to do this in their own lives?"

9. How well does existential therapy fit with your counseling style? What aspects of this approach do you find most useful? Which aspects might you want to modify to fit your personal counseling style?

Notes

See the *DVD for Theory and Practice of Counseling and Psychotherapy: The Case of Stan and Lecturettes,* Session 4, ("Existential Therapy Applied to the Case of Stan"), for an exploration of Stan's anxiety over death and the purpose of his life, and for my presentation of ways that existential therapy can be applied.

1. Russell, J. M. (2007). Existential psychotherapy. In A. B. Rochlen, *Applying counseling theories: An online, case-based approach* (pp. 107–125). Upper Saddle River, NJ: Pearson Prentice Hall.

2. In Session 9 ("An Integrative Focus") of the *DVD for Integrative Counseling: The Case of Ruth and Lecturettes,* I illustrate my existential way of working with Ruth. As an existential therapist, I am free to draw techniques from many therapeutic modalities as an avenue for exploring with Ruth current situations and events of her life.

3. For a more detailed treatment of the existential approach, see Corey, G. (2013). *Theory and practice of counseling and psychotherapy* (9th ed.). Belmont, CA: Brooks/Cole, Cengage Learning; Corey, G. (2013). *Student manual for theory and practice of counseling and psychotherapy* (9th ed.). Belmont, CA: Brooks/Cole, Cengage Learning. The combination of the textbook and manual will flesh out the existential perspective in my work with Ruth demonstrated in this chapter. For a good overview of the existential approach, see Schneider, K., & Krug, O. (2010). *Existential-humanistic therapy.* Washington, DC: American Psychological Association.

Case Approach
to Person-Centered Therapy

General Overview of Person-Centered Therapy

The person-centered approach seeks to provide a climate of understanding and acceptance through the client–therapist relationship that will enable clients to come to terms with aspects of themselves that they have denied or disowned. Other goals are enabling clients to move toward greater openness, trust in themselves, willingness to be a process rather than a finished product, and spontaneity.

Because this approach places primary emphasis on the client–therapist relationship, it specifies few methods. It minimizes directive intervention, interpretation, questioning, probing for information, giving advice, collecting history, and diagnosis. Person-centered therapists maximize active listening, reflection, and clarification. Current formulations of the theory stress the full and active participation of the therapist as a person in the therapeutic relationship. Therapeutic styles may differ in newer versions of the person-centered approach, and counselors have greater freedom to participate in the relationship, to share their reactions, and to challenge clients in a caring way.

In keeping with the spirit of person-centered therapy, it is the client who largely determines when to stop coming for therapy. Likewise, the therapist assumes that clients can be trusted to determine the degree to which therapy has been successful for them. As clients increasingly assume an inner locus of control, they are in the best position to assess the personal meaning of their therapeutic venture.

A Person-Centered Therapist's Perspective on Ruth

by David J. Cain, PhD, ABPP, CGP

Introduction

Assessment and diagnosis are viewed as ongoing processes by the person-centered therapist, not as formal procedures undertaken at the beginning of psychotherapy. The word *diagnose* is derived from a Greek word that means "to know" or "to discover." In my view, therapy is basically a process of self-discovery whose critical components are intrapersonal and interpersonal learning. The therapist's primary function is to facilitate experiential and cognitive learning in the client. Thus, the client's discovery of personal knowledge about self is much more relevant than what the therapist knows about the client or the psychiatric disorder the client is viewed as experiencing.

As a person-centered therapist, I do not undertake any formal assessment with a client unless the client requests it, nor would I attempt to establish a *DSM-IV-TR* diagnosis for the client. In more than 30 years of experience as a psychotherapist, I have found the practice of formal diagnosis to be fraught with more liabilities than assets. Although an extensive discussion of the pros and cons of diagnosis is beyond the scope of this book, some of the most significant limitations can be lightly touched upon here.

First, I have not found that establishing a diagnosis helps much with treatment. The *DSM-IV-TR* system of diagnosis does not provide treatment guidelines. With few exceptions (for example, exposure and cognitive restructuring for anxiety problems), the bulk of psychotherapeutic research has shown that all established approaches have roughly equivalent success with a wide variety of problems.

Second, all diagnostic categories are inevitably reductionist in that they reduce clients and their experiences to a list of symptoms. In reality there is considerable variability among individuals with the same diagnosis.

Third, the uniqueness of each person tends to be lost in the diagnostic process because the emphasis is placed on common characteristics. It is a biological and psychological fact that each person is unique. The act of categorizing tends to constrict the therapist's conceptual understanding of the client and de-emphasizes the importance of individual differences and the complexity of the person.

Fourth, diagnosis overly emphasizes what is wrong with clients and gives relatively little attention to their strengths and resources. Person-centered therapists have a stronger focus on client *growth* and development of personal resources than on problem solving and remediation of psychopathology.

And, finally, a diagnosis is made primarily from an external point of view (that of the clinician) rather than from the internal frame of reference of the client. Clients generally have relatively limited participation in the determination of their diagnosis, even though they are the best authorities on their experience.

I find that dimensions of the person other than diagnostic symptoms are more important in understanding and responding therapeutically to my client. Among the most relevant dimensions are the client's self-concept and world-view; incongruencies between the self-concept, behavior, and experience; the capacity to attend to and process experience, especially affect; learning style and ability to learn from experience; comportment or characteristic manner of living; implicit and explicit personal goals and strivings; a sense of purpose and personal meaning; and the sense of being grounded, whole, and integrated.

In my experience a critical endeavor of the client is the definition ("Who am I?") and redefinition of the self ("Who am I becoming?"). This process is facilitated by the therapist's and client's openness to the client's experience and its personal meaning and is hindered by limited diagnostic formulations of the client's psychopathology. In the optimal case, diagnosis is a continuous process of self-learning in which the client remains receptive to all sources of experience and relevant information. In contrast, diagnostic categorization on the part of therapists may create a false sense of security about what they "know" about the client and limit their creativity and adaptability in responding therapeutically. The danger here is that therapists may begin to interact with a static category rather than an evolving being, thus limiting their range of perceptions and variety of therapeutic responses and, consequently, the client's potential for change. Instead of attempting to identify the client's diagnostic category, two guiding questions that I hold throughout therapy are "What is it like to be you?" and "How are you living?"

The essential purpose of assessment is to enable the client to develop relevant and meaningful personal knowledge, especially knowledge about the "self" and how the self-concept affects behavior. One of the major factors characteristic of person-centered therapy is the responsibility placed on the client for self-direction. Although I may play a significant role in helping the client explore her- or himself, the client is more likely to be affected by, and to put to use, personal experiences and learning that are self-discovered. The excitement and deep satisfaction that come from self-exploration and self-discovery are potent factors that engage the client in the therapeutic process.

In many settings, therapists are required by insurance providers to make a formal diagnosis. The formal diagnosis provided by the person-centered therapist is based on the client's stated problems and constellation of symptoms/complaints. The vast majority of person-centered therapists do not find formal diagnosis valuable in the therapeutic endeavor for the reasons mentioned above, but some may find a diagnosis helpful in making useful distinctions between the problems and experiences described by clients. Useful distinctions between disorders such as autism, obsessive-compulsive, bipolar, eating disorders, substance abuse disorders, phobias, mood disorders, and psychotic disorders help person-centered therapists identify and orient themselves to core concerns experienced by their clients.

Assessment of Ruth

In working with Ruth, I will be especially attentive to how she views her *self*, including aspects that are evident and those that are implicit and unclear but forming. Several components of Ruth's self-concept emerge from her autobiography. In her own words Ruth identifies herself as the "good wife" and the "good mother" that "he [John] expects me to be." Thus, she strongly identifies herself with the roles of wife and mother, but she has defined and attempted to fulfill these roles in the image her husband wishes. By allowing her husband to define what she is and should be (if she is to be accepted), she has abdicated her role and power in defining the person she is and in making personal choices about her life. She has allowed her husband to determine her conditions of worth, and she lives in fear that if she does not live up to his conditions "he might leave me." Ruth's tendency to mold herself for others is a pervasive aspect of her functioning. As she says, "I've pretty much lived for others so far . . . I've been the superwoman who gives and gives." Defining herself as a giving and caretaking person are, of course, aspects of herself in which Ruth takes pride, and understandably so. At the same time, defining herself in this relatively narrow manner limits her view of who she might become.

Until she was 30, Ruth's identity and value system were strongly influenced by the fundamentalist religion of her parents, especially her father. She feared that she would be rejected by her parents if she did not live up to their expectations of who she should be. She states, "They haven't formally disowned me, but in many ways I think they have. I know I'll never win their approval as long as I remain away from the religion that's so dear to them." Ruth is intent on pleasing others, even at the cost of sacrificing her own needs and identity. In a real sense she is selfless, without a clear sense of who she is or can become. Some of the basic questions she is likely to address in therapy are "What do I want?" "What kind of person do I want to be?" "How do I want to live?" "Can I be this person and maintain a good relationship with my husband and family?" and "Can I value myself separately from the views that significant others have of me?"

Other aspects of Ruth's self-concept are more peripheral. An important clue to her self-concept is the view she has of her body and its many symptoms. However she defines herself, it is important to realize that the self is embodied, that it is contained in and functions through a body. Thus, an essential part of her sense of herself has to do with how she sees and feels about her body. At present she views her physical self as overweight and unattractive. In her words, "I don't like what I see. I don't like who I am, and I certainly don't feel proud of my body." Ruth experiences many disturbing bodily symptoms that adversely affect her sense of her physical self. A large part of Ruth's manner of being is dominated by fear, anxiety, panic, and a sense that many daily life events and ongoing concerns are overwhelming. She is afraid that she will die. These fears and anxieties seem to manifest themselves in various forms of bodily symptoms (namely, insomnia, heart palpitations, headache, dizziness, and crying spells). Quite literally, much of Ruth's life is *sickening*—depressed, fearful, constricted, and avoidant.

Although Ruth feels some pride and satisfaction in being a caretaker, this role also results in ambivalence and dissatisfaction. She experiences considerable conflict over who she is, what she believes, and how she is living. By her own admission, she doesn't like who she is, her overweight body, and the fact that her life is devoid of any joyful or meaningful activity apart from her roles as wife and mother.

A potential aspect of her identity is that of a teacher, but she has not yet incorporated this role into her self-structure. She imagines that teaching will be fulfilling, but as yet she places her own desires behind those of her family. Her religious beliefs and values are changing and are in conflict with her earlier fundamentalist views. Other aspects of Ruth's identity will emerge during the course of therapy.

Ruth's future is vague and tentative. She is dimly aware of the person she might become, yet she is fearful that pursuing her interests and needs and developing her own identity will result in her losing her husband and family. But she has not given up. In recent years she has become a "questioner" and holds onto the glimmer of hope that she can "begin to live before it's too late." There is a yearning in Ruth to be more than she is—to expand herself and her life possibilities. She is entering a transitional phase in her life with considerable trepidation.

Key Issues

A key issue with Ruth is the incongruence between the person she is and the selves that are "trying" to emerge, though hesitantly and cautiously. Her incongruence manifests itself in a variety of ways—as cognitive dissonance, in her many physical symptoms, and in anxiety and stress—all of which have the tendency to impel her toward the solution of her discomfort. Her depression and physical symptoms tell her that something is wrong with her life, but fear is her main obstacle to becoming a more autonomous, fuller, and more gratified person. Fear of the loss of her husband's and children's support and love renders her hesitant to move from the safety of her current life, but her dissatisfaction with it and herself are drawing her forward.

Ruth feels somewhat secure in her present life, even though it is boring and unfulfilling in terms of personal growth and meaning. Her capacity to move forward is limited by her lack of trust in her judgment ("I'm scared I'll make the wrong decisions.") and resourcefulness ("I'm trapped and don't see a way out."). As a consequence, she is inclined to look to others (God, husband, her therapist) for guidance and direction.

Paradoxically, Ruth is as much afraid of living as she is of dying. The anticipation of change terrifies her because it threatens the limited security and stability she experiences in her family and current lifestyle. Yet there are hopeful signs. Ruth is restless, dissatisfied, and afraid that her life is slipping by. She has a fragile desire for a better life and a tenuous vision of what she might become. She is "excited and afraid at the same time." If she can listen to the inner voices of her feelings and attend to the distress signals of her body, Ruth will begin to see more clearly who she is and what she wants and, in the process, will begin to find her own voice and path.

Therapeutic Process and Techniques

As I anticipate working with Ruth, my primary focus is on the quality of the relationship I hope to provide for her. My desire is to allow myself to be curious about her and receptive to anything she would like to share about herself and her life. To the best of my ability, I will be fully present and listen carefully to what she says while being sensitive to how she presents herself, including her nonverbal and implicit messages. As much as possible, I hope to leave any preconceptions and hypotheses I may have about her behind and to attend to her with fresh ears and eyes. It is my desire to create a trusting, supportive, safe, and encouraging atmosphere in which Ruth will experience me as genuinely interested and invested in her, sensitive to her feelings, nonjudgmental, and accurately understanding of her expressed and intended meanings. I hope to communicate my belief in her resourcefulness and my optimism about her capacity to learn what she needs to learn and move forward in her life. If I am successful in these endeavors, Ruth will listen to herself, learn from her experiences, and effectively apply her learnings, and in the process, move from an external to an internal locus of control.

Any specific techniques, methods, or responses I use will be dictated by Ruth's therapeutic needs and what best fits her at a given time. I will bring forth for Ruth's consideration any personal and professional resources that may be of value to her. Because I view Ruth as a collaborator in the therapeutic process, I will take my cues from her regarding how I might best respond at the moment. At times I may collaborate more directly with Ruth to determine what might be helpful or check directly with her to ascertain if what I'm doing is helpful, trusting that she knows best how I can serve her at a given time. A variety of therapeutic responses or methods might be employed on Ruth's behalf with her participation in choosing the approaches that she feels might be most helpful. Careful listening and accurate understanding of my client's overt and tacit meanings always precede the introduction of therapeutic techniques or exercises. My basic question in employing any technique is, "Does it fit?"

One important aspect of my role is as a facilitator of learning. Life is constantly teaching us important lessons about ourselves, about others, and about life in general. At times, I view my role as helping my client "learn how to learn." My style of responding to Ruth will reflect my attempt to adapt to her personal learning style, which often can be inferred through observation or discussion.

Finally, I will be myself in the relationship. Thus, Ruth will have a good sense of who I am as a person. Consequently, she will experience my sense of humor, my openness and directness, and my serious and playful sides. She will find that I can be provocative and challenging as well as quietly attentive and gentle as she undertakes her personal journey. I will strive to engage various aspects of myself in a congruent manner intended to be in Ruth's best interests. I anticipate that she will also see the pleasure I feel in working with her and seeing her become the person she wishes to be.

THE BEGINNING PHASE OF THERAPY I anticipate that Ruth will tend to be tentative as therapy begins, perhaps starting with her general sense of dissatisfaction with her life, herself, and her physical symptoms. She may find the relatively nondirective nature of our interaction somewhat of a challenge at first, preferring that I lead her in the "right" direction, ask questions, advise her on what she "should" do, and "push" her to do it. However, I believe she will gradually perceive that my reluctance to direct or advise her is based on my trust in her ability to determine her own direction and find a course of action that fits her. My message is, "This is your life, and you are the author of its future." I am

confident that Ruth will discover that she has more personal str   ⅛
sources than she is aware of at present.

The beginning phase of therapy goes as follows:

THERAPIST: I'm interested in hearing anything you would like to share about yourself—anything that's troubling you—whatever is on your mind.

RUTH: Right now the thing that's bothering me the most is my weight. Whenever I get anxious or depressed, I tend to overeat. Lately I've gained about 10 pounds. I feel fat and dumpy. I hate the way I look.

THERAPIST: You sound angry with yourself for your eating and your appearance.

RUTH: I am. And my husband likes me better when I'm thinner. I've been trying to diet, but I just can't seem to stick with it.

THERAPIST: You're not pleasing your husband or yourself. And I guess you're getting discouraged about whether you're able to lose weight.

RUTH: It's not just losing weight. It's accomplishing anything I set out to do. I just can't seem to follow through. Usually I get off to a good start, but as soon as something goes wrong, I get discouraged.

THERAPIST: And when you get discouraged you . . . ?

RUTH: I start to give up and get depressed.

THERAPIST: And when you get depressed you . . . ?

RUTH: Eat.

THERAPIST: So you eat to ease those feelings?

RUTH: I guess so.

THERAPIST: If your feelings could talk, what might they say?

RUTH: I think they would say "You can't do anything right."

THERAPIST: Pretty harsh words. You start criticizing yourself.

RUTH: I do tend to get down on myself when I start to falter. Sometimes I think I need someone else to push me to accomplish my goals.

THERAPIST: Sometimes you'd just like someone to help push you through the tough times.

RUTH: I'm almost 40 and I'm still not sure what I want to do, much less if I can do it. I'd like to be a teacher, but my husband wants me to stay home and take care of him and the kids. I like being a mother and a wife, but I feel that life is passing me by.

THERAPIST: So there's a sense of urgency in your life. Life is moving on, and although you think you'd like to teach, you don't trust yourself to stick to it or your diet or anything else. And when you have a setback, you get discouraged, criticize yourself, and wish someone else could get you to stick to your goals. To ease the pain you eat. And all this is complicated by your fear that if you do teach you may alienate your husband.

RUTH: That about says it.

⸗**Process Commentary** What quickly emerges are the emotions that impair Ruth's progress. She is fearful that she will fail, becomes angry and self-critical when she does, and then feels depressed and discouraged. She attempts to assuage these feelings by eating, only to find herself dissatisfied by her weight and herself again. Although she seems to like teaching and experiences some success at it, she is not yet certain that this career choice is right. Nor is she willing to take a step that might disrupt her family. As her therapist, I hope to enable her to view her feelings as "friendly" and potentially constructive messages that can help her develop a greater sense of clarity, direction, self-acceptance, and confidence in her endeavors. So we continue.

THERAPIST: So what do you make of all that?

RUTH: I guess I do wish I could depend on someone else to help me when I'm stuck. I've always depended on my parents or John for guidance. I did break away from my church several years ago, but I don't think my parents will ever understand that or accept my beliefs about religion. John couldn't understand why I wanted to finish college and be a teacher. He thinks I should be happy being a homemaker and a mother.

THERAPIST: I guess you long to be understood and supported by your parents and husband, but sometimes they just don't. What makes sense to you doesn't always make sense to them. What you feel may be best for you and what they want for you are often in conflict. Yet you'd still like their approval and backing.

RUTH: I'm such a wimp. Sometimes I think I'll never be able to do what I believe in without worrying about what someone else thinks.

THERAPIST: What is clear is that what people think of you does matter—often a great deal. Then you feel like a wimp when you let others' opinions of you become more important than your own. But you did change your religious convictions, and you did finish college. So you sometimes do finish what you start and do what you really want to do despite others' misgivings.

RUTH: Well, I do feel good about those things. It took me forever to finish college, but I did. And I think I did a pretty good job in my student teaching. I guess there's no reason I should expect them to agree with me. They have their own ideas about what is right.

THERAPIST: And so do you.

RUTH: Yes, I think I do. I'm pretty sure I want to be a teacher.

Ruth's dissatisfaction with her need for approval is becoming evident. When her self-initiated religious changes and completion of college are acknowledged and affirmed by the therapist, Ruth begins to see herself more positively apart from the views of others. She is beginning to recognize that she can give herself the credit she deserves for her accomplishments.

As therapy progresses, Ruth becomes increasingly aware of the incongruence she experiences between the person she is and the person she yearns to be.

It is likely that she will feel guilty about what she perceives as selfishness when she attends more to her own needs, and fearful that her marriage and family will be disrupted. As Ruth expands and modifies her perceptual field, however, she comes to believe that her desires and goals are as deserving of attention as those of her family.

THE MIDDLE PHASE OF THERAPY Ruth may, at some point, wish to bring her husband into her therapy sessions to address the conflict she feels over taking a course of action that displeases him or her children. Whether John is supportive of her change or not, she will have to wrestle with her own conflict about doing what she wants and becoming a more separate, independent person. Her marriage will probably go through a dramatic transition if she pursues her hopes. It may improve as she becomes a fuller person or become more conflicted if her husband is threatened by her development.

The middle phase of therapy highlights these ideas:

RUTH: John and I had another fight last night. He wants me to spend more time with him and the kids and less time with my friends and at the new church I've been attending. I feel a little guilty about being away from home more, but I really like some of the new people I've met.

THERAPIST: You feel torn between allegiances to your family and yourself.

RUTH: Yes. I love my kids and John, and I like taking care of them. But there's more that I want to do. And besides, the kids are old enough now to take care of themselves more. In fact, Rob just moved out last week, and Jennifer has started in a community college. Susan and Adam are involved in lots of activities at the high school. And John is involved in his bowling two nights a week. So it's not as if they need me around all the time.

THERAPIST: As you see that they have lives of their own, it seems that your family needs you less than they did. Or maybe you need them less as you have begun to do more things that are important to you.

RUTH: I think it's a little of both. I got a lot of satisfaction from making sure they were happy—you know, being a good mother and wife. But I realize that sometimes I got too involved and didn't let them do more for themselves because I thought they needed me. Now I kind of like taking more time for myself. The kids are basically OK. Even Jennifer has begun to settle down. She just had to realize that when I said "no" I meant "no," not "maybe." She doesn't always like some of my rules, but she's more accepting of limits.

THERAPIST: Being a good mother and wife was very important to you, but sometimes you become more involved that you need to be. Now you've become clearer about the kind of mother you want to be and that includes setting limits and sticking to them. And you're less worried about how they'll ever survive without you.

RUTH [*laughs*]: Yeah, I must have thought I was supposed to be Mother Teresa or something. Actually, the kids aren't the problem. John is. He's having a hard time accepting the ways I've changed. He's used to having me spend more time with him and do little things for him that I don't have as much time to do now. Sometimes he complains that I'm not as interested in him as I used to be, or he just sulks. I think I've spoiled him, and he's having a hard time adjusting.

THERAPIST: Having a life of your own is risky to you and threatening to John. You seem to be struggling with your feelings about John's reactions to the ways you've changed.

RUTH: I am. But I'm not sure what I feel. Sometimes I think he's acting like a big baby. At other times I feel sorry for him. Or sad.

THERAPIST: What seems to be the main feeling?

RUTH: Kind of sad and annoyed. Doesn't make sense.

THERAPIST: Notice where in your body the feeling seems to be located.

RUTH: Mostly in my stomach.

THERAPIST: Can you describe the sensation in your stomach?

RUTH: Kind of queasy and scared.

THERAPIST: Just pay attention to that feeling for a while. See if there's a word or maybe an image that seems to fit that queasy, scared feeling.

RUTH: It's kind of like the panicky feelings I get sometimes.

THERAPIST: Panicky. Stay with it.

RUTH: It's like the feeling I get when I'm scared that I can't handle something. Sort of being afraid that I'll be overwhelmed.

THERAPIST: Um Hm. Scared. Overwhelmed.

RUTH: What comes to mind is the fight I had with my parents over leaving the church. I knew it was the right thing, but I was terrified of losing their support.

THERAPIST: So it's more like terrified.

RUTH: Like I'm frightened of having to be on my own. Like being abandoned! That's it.

THERAPIST: Abandoned. A sense that you're on your own as you venture out and change, and there's no one there to support you.

RUTH: Exactly. When I left the church, my parents were utterly disapproving of me. Whenever I wanted to do something they disapproved of, they would become distant and sometimes wouldn't even speak to me. It's the same with John. When I'm a good wife and focus my life around him and home, he's happy with me. But when I started doing things that meant a lot to me—like teaching and developing new friends—well, he got sulky and pulled away. So I guess I've been feeling abandoned by him too. It all makes sense.

THERAPIST: So it's fear of being abandoned and not being supported in being yourself.

RUTH: Yes, it's a challenge, and there's a downside to it. But I think I'm ready for it.

🍂 **Process Commentary** Ruth is beginning to become more separate from her family, though she remains involved with them and concerned about their well-being. She is more acceptant and tolerant of the reality that taking care of her needs and desires may, at times, displease other family members. Ruth is also learning to allow her husband and her kids to take care of themselves more.

During the latter segment of this interview, Ruth was encouraged to focus on a feeling that was initially unclear. Using a process called experiential focusing, Ruth was encouraged to pay attention to where and how her feeling manifested itself in her body. Through a series of steps, Ruth was able to clarify the feeling and understand its relationship to her panic states and primary relationships. Such insights as these are often quite powerful because they clarify the way the problem is carried bodily. It's as if the body knows what's wrong in a more profound way than can be articulated verbally. As the problem is processed physically and cognitively, the insight derived has a convincing ring of truth. More important, Ruth has learned a process that will be invaluable in helping her make sense of her feelings by paying attention to them more closely.

You may wonder why I am utilizing the therapeutic technique of experiential focusing, which seems beyond the typical empathic understanding response characteristic of Rogers's therapeutic style. In my view, to be "person-centered" includes doing what best serves the client in a given moment or phase of therapy. In this more pragmatic approach, the practitioner individualizes the therapy as needed while remaining grounded in the core values and beliefs of the person-centered approach. As therapists are freed to use themselves in more varied and creative ways and to incorporate a variety of concepts and response styles from other approaches, clients benefit from therapy tailored to their individual needs. Therapist and client become collaborative partners in the definition of the client's problems, goals, means to achieve those goals, and the development of an optimal therapeutic relationship.

Later in the therapy, Ruth continues to address her marriage and its personal meaning.

RUTH: I sometimes feel a little guilty about taking more time for myself, but John has things to do on his own. And we still spend a lot of time together. It's just that he doesn't think I need him as much as I used to, and I think he feels insecure about this.

THERAPIST: Maybe you don't need him or his approval as much as you used to.

RUTH: Hmm. Well, I'm not sure. I think maybe I used to want him to approve of me more than I do now. And now he seems to want me to need him the way I used to. I think he doesn't feel as important to me as he did. He is important, but for different reasons. Now, I want us to be friends and more like equal partners. Before, he was more like my father—more controlling and demanding. It was as if he didn't think I could do anything without having him to guide me. And I guess I often did let him take charge because I was so terrified of doing things on my own. In my mind he was more the head of the house. Now, I'm a little more confident and . . . well, I guess I don't want to need him like a little girl needs her parents. What I really want is his support and understanding about what's important to me and how I've changed.

THERAPIST: Looks to me like you've changed and grown quite a bit. Earlier in your marriage you wanted and allowed John to take charge more. You felt then that you needed his guidance because you weren't able to make decisions for yourself. And you became extremely anxious when John would withdraw and sulk. Now, as your confidence has grown, you want someone who will offer advice when you ask him but support you in your choices. Instead of a father, you want an equal partner.

RUTH: Yes! That's what I want. I want John to see that I'm different from him and to appreciate me for the person I am. When I want his input on something, I want him to understand that I may or may not do what he suggests. I think he still thinks that when I ask his opinion it means I'll do things his way. No wonder he gets frustrated or hurt sometimes. I think I need to make it clear that his ideas do matter to me but if I don't follow his suggestion it doesn't mean that I don't value him. I just want to do things my own way sometimes.

Ruth is growing stronger and more independent. She is clearer about the kind of relationship she wants with her husband and able to see her husband more objectively. As Ruth has progressed in therapy, she is beginning to see herself in a more positive and differentiated way. She is feeling more power and control in her life and is beginning to become more assertive. More of her satisfaction will be derived from her work and interests apart from, but not excluding, her roles of mother and wife. As she learns to listen to the messages of her feelings and her body, she will identify her needs more clearly and draw on her resources more effectively to satisfy them. Her depression, anxiety, and physical symptoms should diminish as Ruth learns to identify and effectively address the sources of her conflicts. Gradually, she will learn that there is someone in her life on whom she can always depend—herself.

THE FINAL PHASE OF THERAPY Here is a sample dialogue of the final phase of our therapy:

RUTH: Things have settled down a lot with John. Although it's been a difficult adjustment for him, he seems to accept me more the way I am now.

THERAPIST: And how are you now?

RUTH: I think the main thing is that I feel a lot more separate and independent. I still want my family and friends to like me and approve of
what I do, but it's OK if they don't. The main thing is that I feel good
about me, at least most of the time.

THERAPIST: You sure look better—more confident and settled. Your
sense of independence and your ability to trust your decisions have
made you stronger.

RUTH: I am. And I feel pretty good most of the time. Once in a while I'll
get a panicky feeling, but I've learned to pay attention to my feelings,
understand what's troubling me, and deal with it. Last week I was real
anxious about my younger daughter, Susan. I didn't like the guy she's
been going out with, and I told her why. Well, she insisted on seeing
him, and I didn't know what to do. I talked it over with John, and we
decided to let her continue to see this guy as long as we knew where
she was and she made curfew. I think the main thing that helped me
was realizing that she has pretty good judgment.

THERAPIST: Sounds like you've learned to trust your feelings and your
judgment and to tolerate your anxiety about Susan because you trust
her judgment. Maybe you haven't done such a bad job as a parent. You
and John also seem to be working together more as parents—more as
partners.

RUTH: Believe me, it hasn't been easy. It's still hard to sleep until I hear
that door open when she comes home, but nothing awful has happened so far. As for John and me, most of the time we work out our
differences. We still fight occasionally, but I don't worry anymore that
he'll leave me. Even when I get stubborn about something he dis-
agrees with, he tries to see my point of view. And sometimes we just
agree to disagree.

THERAPIST: You've found that you can tolerate your anxieties much
better than you thought you could. It seems, too, that you and John
can deal with your differences without them becoming fatal.

RUTH: You know, I actually think he likes me better the way I am now.
I may be harder to live with in some ways, but I'm not so dependent
and scared. I'm more fun now, and John likes that. I like myself a lot
better too.

THERAPIST: You've become more of the person you've been struggling
to be. There's a lot to like in you.

🌀**Process Commentary**   Ruth now views others' acceptance and liking
as desirable though not necessary to her well-being. More important, she has
learned to like herself and feel at peace with who she is. She is more confident
about herself as a wife and mother and is more able to tolerate the inevitable
anxieties of parenting.

The process of person-centered therapy can be conceived of as a rebirth of
the self, with the therapist serving as midwife. Many clients who seek therapy

are conflicted about who they are and how they are living. Their sense of self lacks clarity and is often viewed in terms of important roles (namely, daughter, mother, wife, student) that are largely defined by their culture and significant others. To the degree that we buy into these roles, we tend to move away from and lose a sense of our natural inclinations and tendency to actualize our potential in a manner consistent with our true selves. In an attempt to find acceptance and approval and avoid conflict with others, especially with those most important to us, we try to bend and shape ourselves in a manner that often leaves us feeling incongruent, dissatisfied, conflicted, and at odds with ourselves and with others. Self-acceptance is usually a critical step in growth.

Person-centered therapy, as is evident in Ruth's case, provides the client with an opportunity to experience one's self and life in a clearer, more differentiated, and grounded manner. This process is assisted enormously by the therapist's ability to capture the essence of the client's experience, especially the person's current view of self, worldview, and explicit and implicit needs, goals, and strivings. The therapist helps the client recognize that his or her experiences are the basis for critical learning and the creation of personal knowledge, meaning, and choice about how one might live and who one might become. One of the critical processes of therapy is enabling clients to develop confidence in their perceptions, judgments, and sense of knowing. Because both affective and cognitive ways of knowing have strengths and limitations, a goal of person-centered therapy is to enable clients to draw effectively from both ways of knowing. When their knowledge of feelings is congruent with their cognitive knowledge, clients will usually experience a sense of clarity, peace, and confidence in their learning. The cognitive and affective realms have been integrated, and they feel freer to act on their learning.

As Ruth became clearer about what she wanted in her life—as mother, wife, and individual—and began to re-create and accept herself, she also realized that this choice required that she stand up for herself and sometimes take a position that not all others would like, support, or approve. The therapist's genuine acceptance and affirmation help Ruth free herself from beliefs and feelings about how she "should" live. I believe Ruth learned to face life's most basic challenge: to be herself and find a way to live with others that allows her to maintain self-respect and integrity while accepting the reality that being herself will sometimes bring conflict with others.

Concluding Comments

A misconception about person-centered psychotherapy is that it is inevitably long-term therapy. It is not. In fact, like many therapeutic approaches, person-centered therapy is often effective in 10 sessions or less, and many clients have benefited from a single session. Therapies that are directive are thought to be briefer because they employ more teaching and guiding techniques. Such therapies assume that the therapist knows how to help the client relieve symptoms rapidly. In my view, such approaches fail to appreciate fully and draw from the resources and inherent wisdom in clients. Both personal and therapeutic experiences have convinced me that feeling understood and accepted by important others is conducive to our well-being. Regardless of one's therapeutic approach, the desire to hear our clients and to enter into their experiential world is almost inevitably helpful and never harmful.

Although it may take a bit longer to help Ruth tap her own resources, find her own direction, and learn how to move forward, "slower may be faster." As Ruth learns how to process her experiences more effectively, she also develops attitudes and skills that can enable her to become more self-sufficient. The confidence Ruth gains from learning to trust her own experiences and decision-making capacity enables her to feel more grounded, centered, and optimistic.

In concluding, I would like to offer some thoughts about the trajectory of the person-centered therapist's development. When graduate students first learn person-centered therapy, conversations with clients may bog down or go in circles, recycling the same issues without any apparent insight or movement. The therapist's empathic responding often remains superficial and sometimes becomes repetitive, which results in lack of progress because no deeper understanding of clients' experiences take place. Beginning therapists soon recognize and acknowledge they are not as good at listening as they previously thought and that responding with accurate and incisive empathy is much more challenging than it seems.

As therapists become more sophisticated in their precise use of language in empathic responding, and especially in their focus on and effective processing of clients' feelings, clients see themselves more clearly, locate the core meanings in their experiences, and begin to see the implications for more effective living. With accumulating experience, person-centered therapists increasingly understand that the responsibility for change rests primarily with their clients, and they focus on creating an optimal relational and learning environment in which clients can tap their own resources for constructive change. In brief, person-centered therapists are less invested in effecting client movement directly than in enabling their clients to make changes that they have chosen freely based on their desire to live in a more effective and satisfying manner.[1]

Jerry Corey's Work With Ruth From a Person-Centered Perspective

David Cain views the therapeutic relationship as the core of the therapeutic process. In the *DVD for Integrative Counseling: The Case of Ruth and Lecturettes* I provide a concrete illustration of how I view the therapeutic relationship as the foundation for our work together. See Session 1 ("Beginning of Counseling"), Session 2 ("The Therapeutic Relationship"), and Session 3 ("Establishing Therapeutic Goals)" for a demonstration of these principles as they pertain to the person-centered approach.

Basic Assumptions

From a person-centered perspective I view counseling as being directed at more than merely solving problems and giving information. It is primarily aimed at helping clients tap their inner resources so they can better deal with their problems, both current and future. In Ruth's case, I think I can best accomplish this goal by creating a climate that is threat free, one in which she will feel fully accepted by me. I work on the assumption that my clients have the capacity to lead the way in our sessions and that they can profit without my directive intervention. I assume that three attributes on my part are critical to release Ruth's growth force: genuineness, positive regard, and empathy. If I genuinely experience these attitudes toward her and successfully communicate them, chances are that Ruth will decrease her defensive ways and move toward becoming her true self, the person she is capable of becoming. Therapy is not so much a matter of my doing something to Ruth as it is establishing a relationship that she can use to engage in self-exploration and ultimately find her own way.

Assessment of Ruth

In talking to Ruth I can see that she is disappointed with where she is in life and that she is not being herself around her friends or family. Her therapy is based on this concern.

As I review Ruth's autobiography, I see her wondering: "How can I discover my real self? How can I become the person I would like to become? How can I shed my expected social roles and become myself?" My aim is to create an atmosphere in which she can freely, without judgment and evaluation, express whatever she is feeling. If she can experience this freedom to be whatever she is in this moment, she will begin to drop her masks and to reconsider her roles.

Goals of Therapy

My basic goal is to create a therapeutic climate that will help Ruth discover the kind of person she is, apart from being what others have expected her to be. When her facades come down as a result of the therapeutic process, four characteristics will likely become evident: (1) her openness to experience, (2) a greater degree of trust in herself, (3) her internal source of evaluation, and (4) her willingness to live more spontaneously. These characteristics constitute the basic goals of person-centered therapy.

Therapeutic Procedures

When clients begin therapy, they tend to look to the therapist to provide direction and answers. They often have rigid beliefs and attitudes, a sense of being out of touch with their feelings, a basic sense of distrust in themselves, and a tendency to externalize problems. As therapy progresses, they begin to express fears, anxiety, guilt, shame, anger, and other feelings that they have deemed too negative to incorporate into their self-structure. Eventually, they are able to distort less, express feelings previously out of awareness, and move in a direction of being more open to all of their experience. They can be in contact, moment by moment, with what they are feeling, with less need to distort or deny this experience.

The Therapeutic Process

ELEMENTS OF THE PROCESS During the early stages of her therapy, Ruth does not share her feelings but talks instead about externals. To a large degree she perceives her problems as being outside of herself. Somehow, if her father would change, if her husband's attitude would change, and if her children would present fewer problems, she would be all right. During one of our early sessions, she wonders whether I will be able to really understand her and help her if she does share her feelings.

❧ Exploring Our Relationship

Ruth lets me know how difficult it is for her to talk personally to me, and she tells me that it's especially uncomfortable for her to talk with me because I'm a man. I feel encouraged because she is willing to talk to me about her reservations and her present feelings toward me.[2]

RUTH: I'm careful about what I say around you. It's important that I feel understood, and sometimes I wonder if you can really understand the struggles I'm having as a woman.

JERRY: I appreciate your willingness to let me know what it's like for you to attempt to trust me. I hope that you won't censor what you say around me, and I very much want to understand you. Perhaps you could tell me more about your doubts about my ability to understand you as a woman.

RUTH: It's not what you've said so far, but I'm fearful that I have to be careful around you. I'm not sure how you might judge me or react to me.

JERRY: I'd like the chance to relate to you as a person, so I hope you'll let me know when you feel judged or not understood by me.

RUTH: It's not easy for me to talk about myself to any man; all of this is so new to me.

JERRY: What is it that you think I'd have a hard time understanding about you as a woman? You might want to talk more about what makes it difficult to talk to me.

RUTH: So far, no man has ever been willing to really listen to me. I've tried so hard to please my father and then to please John. I wonder if you can understand how I depended so much on my father, and now on John, to give me a feeling that I'm worthwhile as a woman.

JERRY: Even though I'm not a woman, I still know what it feels like to want to be understood and accepted, and I know what it's like to look to others to get this kind of confirmation.

It is important that we pursue what gets in the way of Ruth's trust in me. As long as she is willing to talk about what she is thinking and feeling while we are together in the sessions, we have a direction to follow. Staying with the immediacy of the relationship will inevitably open up other channels of fruitful exploration.

❧ Exploring Ruth's Marital Problems

In a later session Ruth brings up her marital difficulties. She explores her mistrust of her own decisions and her search outside of herself for the answers to her problems.

RUTH: I wonder what to do about my marriage. I'd like to have some time to myself, but what might happen to our family if I made major changes and nobody liked those changes?

JERRY: You wonder what would happen if you expressed your true feelings, especially if your family didn't appreciate your changes.

RUTH: Yes, I guess I do stop myself because I don't want to hurt my family.

JERRY: If you ask for what you want, others are liable to get hurt, and there's no room in your life to think both about what's good for others and what's good for yourself.

RUTH: I really didn't realize that it had to be either them or me. It's just that at 39 I'm just now thinking about who I am. Perhaps it's too late for me to question what I have in my relationships.

JERRY: Well, I don't know that there's a given time when we should ask such questions. I feel excited for you and respect you for asking these questions now.

RUTH: What I know is that my life has been very structured up to this point, and now all this questioning is unsettling to me and is making me anxious. I wonder if I want to give up my predictable life and face the unknown. I get anxious thinking about how my husband and kids will be if I keep making changes. What if they don't like my changes and it upsets them?

JERRY: I'm touched by what you're saying, and I remember some of my own struggles in facing uncertainty. When you say you're anxious, it would help me to understand you better if you could tell me some of the times or situations in which you feel this anxiety.

RUTH: Sometimes I feel anxious when I think about my relationship with John. I'm beginning to see things I don't like, but I'm afraid to tell him about my dissatisfactions lest he get angry.

JERRY: Would you be willing to tell me some of the specific dissatisfactions you have with John?

Ruth then proceeds to talk about some of the difficulties she is experiencing with her husband. I encourage her to share with me some of the impulses that frighten her. I am providing a safe atmosphere for her to express this new awareness without reacting judgmentally to her. I also give her some of my personal reactions to what she is telling me. Then I ask her if she talks very often with John in the way she is talking to me. I am receptive to her and wonder out loud whether he could also be open to her if she spoke this way with him. We end the session with my encouraging her to approach him and say some of the things to him that she has discussed in this session.

PROCESS COMMENTARY We proceed with how Ruth's fear of others' anger keeps her from asking for what she really wants in her life. She then begins to seek answers from me, not trusting that she knows what is best for her. Ruth thinks I have the experience and wisdom to provide her with at least some answers. She continues to press for answers to what she should do about her marriage. It is as though she is treating me as an authority who has the power to fix things in her life. She grows very impatient with my unwillingness to give her answers. As she puts it, she is convinced that she needs my "validation and approval" if she is to move ahead.

We return to an exploration of Ruth's feelings toward me for not giving her more confirmation and not providing reassurance that she will make correct decisions. She tells me that if I really cared I would give her more direction and do more than I am doing. She tells me that all I ever do is listen, that she wants and expects more. I reassure Ruth that I do care about her struggle, but I am convinced that she will be able to find better answers within herself than any I could provide.

Ruth continues to risk sharing more of her feelings with me, and with my encouragement she also begins to be more open with her family. Gradually, she becomes more willing to think about her own approval. She demands less of herself by way of being a fixed product, such as the "perfect person," and allows herself to open up to new experiences, including challenging some of her beliefs and perceptions. Slowly, she is showing signs of accepting that the answers to her life situation are not to be found in some outside authority but inside herself.[3]

Some Final Thoughts

A principal strength of the person-centered approach is its emphasis on truly listening to and deeply understanding the client's world from his or her internal frame of reference. As is clear from both of our presentations, the quality of the therapeutic relationship is critical in Ruth's therapy. Empathy is the cornerstone of this approach, and it is a necessary foundation upon which every theory rests. The ability to listen to the client and to understand his or her world is basic to creating and maintaining a working alliance, and practitioners with diverse theoretical perspectives can benefit by attending to these qualities. The philosophy and principles of the person-centered approach permeate the practice of many therapists, regardless of their theoretical orientation.

Questions for Reflection

1. Knowing what you do of Ruth, how would it be for you to develop a therapeutic relationship with her? Is there anything that might get in your way? If so, how do you think you would deal with this obstacle? To what degree do you think you could understand her subjective world?
2. Dr. Cain indicates that he would not undertake any formal assessment or attempt to establish a *DSM-IV-TR* diagnosis for a client unless the client requested it. In working with Ruth, he emphasizes her self-assessment and her own definition of her problems. What are your thoughts about excluding formal assessment strategies before engaging in a therapeutic relationship? Do you believe Ruth is able to make a valid self-assessment?

If you do not support formal diagnosis, what would you do if the agency where you work requires that you provide a diagnosis as part of your treatment plan?

3. Dr. Cain says, "If she can listen to the inner voices of her feelings and attend to the distress signals of her body, Ruth will begin to see more clearly who she is and what she wants and, in the process, will begin to find her own voice and path." To what degree do you agree with this assumption? How does your answer influence the way you would work with Ruth?

4. In the therapeutic relationship with Ruth, Dr. Cain's interventions were based mainly on listening and accurately responding to what she says. He did not make directive interventions but attempted to stay with her subjective experiencing. What kind of progress do you see Ruth making with this approach?

5. Ruth confronted me with her doubts about my ability to understand her as a woman. Do you think she would do better to see a female therapist? Would you recommend that I suggest a referral to a woman, especially since she brought up her concerns about my being a man? Do you think a male therapist would have a difficult time understanding her world and her struggles as a woman?

6. Ruth mentioned that it was especially difficult to trust a man and that she felt judged by men. How could you work with this theme therapeutically from a person-centered perspective?

7. With both this approach and existential therapy, the client–therapist relationship is central, and the focus is on clients' choosing their way in life. Do you agree that Ruth has this potential for directing her life and making wise choices? Would you be inclined to let her select the topics for exploration, or might you suggest topics? Would you be more directive than either Dr. Cain or I was?

8. How well does the person-centered approach fit with your counseling style? What aspects of this approach do you find most useful? Which aspects might you want to modify to fit your personal counseling style?

Notes

See the *DVD for Theory and Practice of Counseling and Psychotherapy: The Case of Stan and Lecturettes*, Session 5 ("Person-Centered Therapy Applied to the Case of Stan"), for an exploration of the immediacy of the therapeutic relationship and for my presentation of ways I might apply person-centered therapy.

1. For a foundation for understanding David Cain's work with Ruth from a person-centered perspective, see Cain, D. (2010). *Person-centered psychotherapies.* Washington, DC: American Psychological Association.

2. In this section of my work with Ruth, I encourage her to explore our relationship, especially her reservations about talking about herself. What I describe here is similar to what is depicted in the *DVD for Integrative*

Counseling: The Case of Ruth and Lecturettes, Session 2 ("The Therapeutic Relationship"). What are some ways that I am attempting to build trust with Ruth?

3. For a more detailed treatment of the person-centered approach, see chapter 7 ("Person-Centered Therapy") in Corey, G. (2013). *Theory and practice of counseling and psychotherapy* (9th ed.). Belmont, CA: Brooks/Cole, Cengage Learning.

CHAPTER SIX

Case Approach to Gestalt Therapy

General Overview of Gestalt Therapy

The goal of the Gestalt approach is to enhance awareness of here-and-now experiencing. This process of attending to present experience tends to provide the direction therapy takes; following the client's flow of awareness can lead in many directions.

Gestalt therapists seek a dialogue with their clients and employ experiments to sharpen and highlight their present and ongoing experiencing. Out of this dialogue experiments are created that deepen clients' exploration of what becomes salient for them. Experiments always grow out of the phenomenological context of the therapeutic relationship, and they are done collaboratively with the client and the therapist. Clients may engage in role playing by performing all of the various parts and polarities, thus gaining greater awareness of inner conflicts. Some examples of experiments include creating a dialogue with conflicting parts of oneself, exaggeration, focusing on body messages, reexperiencing past unfinished situations in the here and now, and working with dreams.

Clients are ready to terminate therapy when they become increasingly aware of what they are thinking, feeling, and doing in the present moment. When they have recognized and worked through their unfinished business, they are ready to continue therapy on their own. As with the other experiential therapies (existential and person-centered), the evaluation of therapeutic outcomes is rooted in clients' subjective experiences and perceptions about the changes that have occurred.

A Gestalt Therapist's Perspective on Ruth

by Jon Frew, PhD, ABPP

Introduction

Gestalt therapy is practiced with a theoretical foundation grounded in field theory, phenomenology, and dialogue. Individuals are inseparable from the environments they inhabit. Gestalt therapists are interested in the ongoing relationship between the individual and the environment (also referred to as the "field"). Phenomenology involves seeking an understanding based on what is comprehensible through the senses rather than on interpretations or meanings defined objectively by the observer. The therapist encourages the client to describe his or her experience and to attend to moment-to-moment awareness of elements of the field. The emphasis is on the subjective world as the client perceives it.

Gestalt therapy has adopted Martin Buber's dialogical philosophy of relationship to capture the spirit of the I/Thou relationship between therapist and client.[1] The healing that occurs in psychotherapy is a result of the quality of the meeting that occurs between client and therapist. Practicing in a dialogical manner, Gestalt therapists attempt to be fully present, convey to the client that they comprehend and accept the other's experience, and vigilantly attend to the impact of each of their interventions.

The goal of Gestalt therapy is, quite simply, the restoration of awareness. The essential method involves following the aspects of the client's experience of self and of environment that become figural or salient. Gestalt therapists will selectively bring aspects of their own moment-to-moment experience, what is figural for them, into contact with the client. In Gestalt therapy, we are not trying to get anywhere or make something in particular happen. Rather, our work is designed to heighten the client's awareness of the present moments as they unfold. Change occurs through attention to what is, not by striving toward preordained objectives.[2]

Assessment of Ruth

Gestalt therapy emphasizes healthy functioning and does not use the language of "pathology," or "normal" and "abnormal." Instead, individuals are viewed as having the capacity to self-regulate in their dealings with the various environments they encounter throughout life. Contact with the environment can be satisfying or interrupted in a variety of ways. The Gestalt therapist's assessment involves examining the process that occurs as the individual interacts with the environment.

Instead of a *DSM-IV-TR* diagnosis, the Gestalt therapist assesses to determine a "functional diagnosis." The need–fulfillment cycle is one model used to assess a client's level of functioning in two primary and related areas: to what degree is the client aware of self and environment, and can the client move into contact with aspects of the environment in ways that meet needs, achieve self-regulation, and promote growth and change? The need–fulfillment model outlines a "cycle of experience," which begins with physical or emotional sensations and proceeds through awareness (a sharpened sense of meaning), excitement, action, and toward contact with the environment. A functional diagnosis allows the Gestalt therapist to assist clients to understand exactly how they experience interruptions in the natural process of need identification and fulfillment. This is eminently more useful to clients than telling them they are depressed or have an adjustment disorder.

Assessment is an ongoing process embedded in the dialogue between client and therapist, not something separate from or occurring before the therapy itself. Gestalt therapists assess in two ways. First, hypotheses are formed as the therapist listens to clients talk about their lives outside the therapy session. For example, from Ruth's autobiography we learn that she is frequently flooded with powerful sensations (panic, dizziness) that do not lead to a sharpened awareness that could move Ruth into contact with her environment. Instead, she translates her sensations into worry patterns about dying or losing control, and that cycle of experience ends without closure. The panic attacks continue because Ruth is unable to move from the sensation level into some type of action (for example, talking about her anxiety with another) and contact. Ruth also sets goals in her life, such as losing weight or getting a job, but does not engage in actions to reach those goals. She imagines that if she were different she would be happier, or in Gestalt therapy terms "be in more satisfying contact with the environment."

The second and primary way the Gestalt therapist assesses clients' level of awareness and contacting style is by attending to how clients are in contact with the therapist in the therapy session itself. Clients' diminished awareness and ways of making or interrupting contact will become manifest in the relationship with the therapist. The therapy relationship becomes a key vehicle for clients to learn more about how they experience themselves and how they can bring that awareness into contact with the therapist.

Gestalt therapy is practiced in both brief and longer-term contexts. The client's functional diagnosis can be determined relatively quickly through history taking and attending to the client's level of awareness and the quality of contact made in the therapeutic relationship. In a brief therapy model, the therapist supports the client's understanding of his or her characteristic ways of diminishing awareness and contact. Clients can do homework assignments between sessions and continue to examine their own awareness and contacting processes after the therapy is complete. In long-term therapy, outdated patterns of contacting are examined, and clients learn to shift their awareness with more intensive and sustained support from the Gestalt therapist.

Key Issues and Themes

From her autobiography, certain key issues emerge about how Ruth makes contact with her environment. For much of her life Ruth has concentrated on what others want or expect her to be. Operating in that mode, Ruth does not pay attention to what she wants from others. The payoff for Ruth in living for others has been the avoidance of conflict and a certain kind of security . . . others do not leave. She fears change in general and attending to her own wants and desires in particular. She engages in contact through "confluence" or through blending with others. She has already lost her parents. She fears that any expression of her needs and wants could drive her husband away.

These points are drawn from her autobiographical information and must be viewed purely as hunches until the therapy with Ruth begins. The themes we will actually work with must arise in the session, within the dialogue between Ruth and the therapist, not from clever interpretations in the therapist's head.

Therapeutic Interventions

Gestalt therapy proceeds by watching and listening to clients as they describe their experience as they sit with you during a therapy session. Assessment, "diagnoses," and identification of themes and issues follow from practicing in a phenomenological and dialogic way. In this dialogue with Ruth, my goals are to assist Ruth in identifying a "figure" or an experience that becomes salient for her, to heighten her awareness of that experience, and to explore how she might make contact with me about that figure of interest.

> THERAPIST: What are you aware of, Ruth, as we begin today?
>
> RUTH: Recently I've become aware that I live for others. I give and give until there is little left to give.
>
> THERAPIST: How is it for you to give so much?
>
> RUTH: Exhausting and frustrating. The expectations and demands of my husband and children never end, and I never feel like I am doing enough.
>
> THERAPIST: What do you notice as you tell me this?
>
> RUTH: I don't understand your question.
>
> THERAPIST: You have been telling me about how much you give to others and how tiring that is. What are you experiencing right now?
>
> RUTH: Well, I'm not tired.
>
> THERAPIST: Take a minute and check in with yourself.
>
> RUTH [*After a minute*]: I realize I don't do this very often.
>
> THERAPIST: What are you discovering?
>
> RUTH: I feel a little nervous, but it's different from the anxiety and panic I usually feel.
>
> THERAPIST: Pay attention to the nervousness and tell me what you can about it.
>
> RUTH: My stomach is fluttering, and I have lots of energy in my legs and arms. I did some theatre in college, and this feels like those moments before I would go on stage.
>
> THERAPIST: From your description and the way you look right now, it sounds like you might be excited.
>
> RUTH: Yeah, that fits—excited and apprehensive. I realize I don't know exactly what will happen next.
>
> THERAPIST: You are looking at me very intently. Are you aware of that?
>
> RUTH: I am now. [*Fidgets in her chair and looks away*] Do you have any ideas about how I can stop giving so much?
>
> THERAPIST: I don't have any idea about that at this moment, Ruth. Tell me what you are aware of now.
>
> RUTH: When you pointed out how I was looking at you, I got scared.
>
> THERAPIST: Scared?

RUTH: Yeah, a wave of anxiety came over me.

THERAPIST: And now?

RUTH: Now I am having trouble looking at you. It's more comfortable to look out the window.

THERAPIST: Would you be willing to try an experiment?

RUTH: Sure, if you think it would help. What should I do?

THERAPIST: You agree to experiment without any information about what I have in mind?

RUTH: Sounds like me. I agree to a lot before I know what I'm getting into. To be honest, I'm not sure I want to experiment. What would be the objectives of this experiment?

THERAPIST: Experiments in Gestalt therapy don't have any particular preset goals. The purpose would be to help you learn more about yourself.

RUTH: Actually, I like the idea of not having a goal. I never seem to reach the ones I set in my life. OK, what do you have in mind?

THERAPIST: The experiment would be to alternate back and forth between eye contact with me and looking away . . . to see what happens for you in each mode.

RUTH: That sounds easy enough. I would like to try it. [*Ruth spends more time looking away from the therapist at first but gradually increases time in eye contact.*]

THERAPIST [*After several minutes*]: So what do you notice?

RUTH: Looking away is easier, more comfortable. When I look at you, the anxiety returns.

THERAPIST: You are looking at me now. How is this for you?

RUTH: Like I said, I feel anxious, edgy. [*She pauses, takes a deep breath.*] Actually, right now I feel lost and confused. I get this feeling a lot.

THERAPIST: Finish this sentence for me. Right now I'm lost and confused because _____.

RUTH: . . . because I know you must want something from me, but I don't know what it is. I know how to be a good mother and wife, but it's not clear what I should do here.

THERAPIST: I saw something shift in your expression. Did you notice that too?

RUTH: Yeah, the feeling has changed.

THERAPIST: What's going on now?

RUTH [*With a look of mild surprise*]: I'm frustrated. No, that's not all of it. I'm angry. [*She smiles.*]

THERAPIST: You seem amused by that.

RUTH: It's different. I never get angry except at myself.

THERAPIST: And this time?

RUTH: I'm angry at you.

THERAPIST: Will you say that again, and look at me when you do?

RUTH: Another experiment? OK, I'll try. I'm angry at you for not telling me what you want from me.

THERAPIST: What happens as you say that to me?

RUTH: I feel good, energized, and even powerful. [*Ruth sits silently, looking relaxed and content; then she looks away and begins to fidget.*]

THERAPIST: Where did you go?

RUTH: Images of my husband and father came in. I'm angry at them too. I don't know exactly what they want from me either. [*Ruth's expression changes again; she is quiet and tears begin.*]

THERAPIST: What's happening now?

RUTH: I'm so caught up in giving to others that I don't have a clue about what I want. I wouldn't even know where to start to find out.

THERAPIST: We could start here. Is there anything you want from me now?

RUTH: [*Ruth takes a few moments to consider my question.*] When I started therapy with you, I wanted you to tell me what I should do.

THERAPIST: And now?

RUTH: I want you to be interested in how I feel and the things I think about.

THERAPIST: Look at me again Ruth. What do you see?

RUTH: I see a kind face. I see interest, even concern and care. It's very comfortable for me now to have this eye contact.

🐾 **Process Commentary** Experienced basketball players talk about "letting the game come to them." They use this phrase in contrast to "forcing the action" or "trying to make something happen." Practicing Gestalt therapy in a dialogic, phenomenological way is very similar. Therapists take their time, follow their clients' lead, and let the dialogue unfold without rushing or pushing for results.

I began the session by inviting Ruth to check in with herself as she talked about issues in her life. That intervention brings her into the present moment and brings her to the awareness that she rarely attends to her immediate experience. The next several interchanges follow a cycle of experience as Ruth identifies a sensation that leads to an awareness and a sense of excitement about what will happen next.

A contact boundary "event" occurs at this point that is a key theme in Ruth's life. Instead of carrying on into action and contact that would be anchored in what Ruth wants, she scans the field (the environment) to ascertain what is wanted from her at that moment. When I point out how intently she is looking at me, her anxiety level increases, and she deflects by changing the subject.

I suggest an experiment. Notice how the experiment emerges "organically" from the moment-to-moment dialogue between us. She was already looking at me and looking away. The experiment simply allows us to explore that behavior more intentionally. As Ruth experiments with eye contact, the figure or theme of our session comes into sharper focus. When she looks at me, she experiences a set of uncomfortable feelings that are tied to an assumption that I want something from her (and she doesn't know how to find out what it is).

Ruth's assumption that I want something from her could be conceptualized as a projection, one of the boundary phenomena delineated in Gestalt theory. Often a Gestalt therapist would respond to this projection by suggesting that Ruth "own" her own experience. Ruth might then say, "OK, I want something from you." At this point in the session, however, Ruth does not have a sufficient level of awareness of her wants to make that statement genuinely. She might "fake it," though, by doing what she is told. Another tactic that I did not choose was to clarify the process between us by saying that I did not want anything from her. Instead, I stayed with Ruth's ongoing experience. As she perceived me as wanting something from her, what was that like for her?

Supporting Ruth by not challenging her perception of me as wanting something from her led her to another awareness. She was angry at me for not being clear about what I wanted. In the next experiment, she directed her anger outward, which is a departure for Ruth from her pattern of self-criticism. Telling me she was angry seemed to complete a cycle of experience (there are many in any therapy session). Ruth acted on the environment, and her contact with me led to a momentary sense of contentment. As that figure reached completion, another emerged. Ruth realized that she doesn't attend to what she wants. Invited to do that as we end the session, she identifies a specific want—my interest in her—and through eye contact sees accurately (without projection) that I am interested.

Like all of us, Ruth has characteristic ways of organizing and making meaning out of her moment-to-moment experience of both herself and her environment. These ways of making sense out of experience are frequently shaped more by past experiences than by present needs and opportunities. The present moment is accessed through awareness, which is explored through the therapist's active interest in Ruth's ongoing experience.

As Ruth attended to herself and to contact with the therapist, one of her characteristic ways of perceiving relationships surfaced almost immediately. She saw the therapist as wanting something from her. As the session progressed, that figure eventually shifted to what she wanted from the therapist. This session demonstrates how change occurs through attention to "what is" and how the exact nature of change cannot be aimed for or predicted by a Gestalt therapist.

What Ruth perceives others to want from her and what she wants from others is a key theme, and I believe it will reappear in future sessions. Ruth's inclination to reflexively (with limited awareness) attempt to discern the needs and expectations of others began years earlier as a creative adjustment. It was Ruth's solution to a set of conditions in her environment in which her options were limited. Currently, her relationships with her husband, children, and college professors replicate those same conditions.

As my therapy relationship with Ruth proceeds, I continue to encourage her to be aware of her moment-to-moment experience. Present awareness, by definition, will counter her tendency to operate on automatic pilot in relation to me and others. Ruth will continue to learn, as she did in this session, how to more accurately assess the present situation. Eventually, Ruth will be aware of her own needs as well as the needs of others.

Jerry Corey's Work With Ruth From a Gestalt Perspective

In my version of Gestalt work with Ruth, I watch for cues from Ruth about what she is experiencing in the here and now. By attending to what she is expressing both verbally and nonverbally, I suggest experiments during our sessions. In the *DVD for Integrative Counseling: The Case of Ruth and Lecturettes*, Session 7 ("Emotive Focus in Counseling"), I demonstrate how I create experiments to heighten Ruth's awareness. In this particular session I employ a Gestalt experiment, asking Ruth to talk to me as if I were John. During this experiment, Ruth becomes quite emotional. You will see ways of exploring emotional material and integrating this work into a cognitive framework as well.

Basic Assumptions

Approaching Ruth as a Gestalt therapist, I assume that she can deal effectively with her life problems, especially if she becomes fully aware of what is happening in and around her. My central task as her therapist is to help her fully experience her being in the here and now by first realizing how she is preventing herself from feeling and experiencing in the present. My approach is basically noninterpretive. I will ask Ruth to provide her own interpretations of her experiences. I expect her to participate in experiments, which consist of trying new ways of relating and responding.

I operate under the assumption that it is useful to invite clients to work in the present as much as possible. A basic premise of Gestalt therapy is that by experiencing conflicts directly, instead of merely talking about them, clients will expand their own level of awareness and integrate the fragmented and unknown parts of their personality.

Assessment of Ruth

Ruth has never learned that it is acceptable to have and to express feelings. True, she does feel a good deal of guilt, but she rarely expresses the resentment that she likely feels. Any person who is as devoted to others as she is probably feels some resentment at not having received the appreciation she believes is due her. Ruth does not allow herself to get angry with her father, who has punished her by withholding his affection and approval. She does not experience much anger toward John, despite the fact that here again she does not feel recognized. The same is true for both her sons and daughters. Ruth has made a lifetime career out of giving and doing for her family. She maintains that she gets little in return, yet she rarely expresses how this arrangement affects her. It appears that Ruth is keeping all of these feelings locked inside herself, and this is getting in the way of her feeling free. A lot of Ruth's energy is going into blocking her experience of threatening feelings, sensations, and thoughts. Our therapy will encourage her to express her moment-by-moment experience so that her energy is freed up for creative pursuits instead of being spent on growth-inhibiting defenses.

Goals of Therapy

My goal is to provide a context in which Ruth can expand her awareness of what is going on within herself and also how she interacts with others. With awareness, Ruth will be able to recognize denied aspects of herself and proceed toward the reintegration of the many facets within herself. Therapy will provide the necessary intervention to help her gain awareness of what she is thinking, feeling, and doing in the present. As Ruth comes to recognize and experience blocks to maturity, she can begin experimenting with different ways of being.

Therapeutic Procedures

I draw heavily on interventions aimed at intensifying here-and-now experiencing. These techniques are designed to help Ruth focus on what is going on within her body and to accentuate whatever she may be feeling. In this sense I am active in my sessions with Ruth. However, I take my cues from her, largely by paying attention to what she is saying and not saying. It is essential that I work within the context of what emerges for Ruth as we talk with each other rather than imposing my agenda of what I think Ruth should explore. From the cues I pick up from Ruth, I suggest experiments that enable her to heighten whatever she is experiencing.

Some of the experiments that Ruth might carry out may entail giving expression to unexpressed body movements or gestures, or they may involve talking in a different tone of voice. I may ask her to experiment with rehearsing out loud those thoughts that are racing through her—ones she usually keeps to herself. Ruth will be invited to try new behavior and see what these experiments can teach her. If Ruth learns how to pay attention to whatever it is she is experiencing at any moment, this awareness itself can lead to change.

JERRY: Ruth, as we sit here, what are you aware of?

RUTH: I'm having a hard time knowing what I want to talk about today. There are so many things going on, and I want to cover everything. I'm impatient and want to get to work.

JERRY: I can appreciate wanting to do a lot in a short time. Let me suggest that you sit for a few moments and listen to yourself. What is it that you'd most want for this hour?

RUTH: I just keep feeling guilty over all that I haven't been, especially as a mother. Right now I'm feeling pretty sad because of all the mistakes I've made with my kids.

JERRY: Does any child stand out for you?

RUTH: Jennifer! She's on my mind a lot. No matter what I try, nothing seems to work. I read books on parenting and that doesn't help. I just feel guilty!

JERRY: Ruth, rather than telling me about how guilty you feel over not having been the mother you think you should have been to Jennifer, how about simply listing all the ways that you feel this guilt?

RUTH: Oh, that's easy—there are so many ways! I feel guilty because I haven't been understanding enough, because I've been too easy on her and haven't set limits, because I've been away at college when she needed me during her difficult years. And in some ways I feel responsible for the problems she is faced with—I could go on!

JERRY: So go on. Say more. Make the list as long as you can. [*I am encouraging her to say aloud and unrehearsed many of the things she tells herself endlessly in her head. She continues to speak of her guilt.*]

RUTH [*Letting out a deep sigh*]: There! That's it!

JERRY: And what is that sigh about?

RUTH: Just relief, I suppose. I feel a little better. I just had a flash. You know, I resent Jennifer for expecting me to be the perfect mother. After all, I've gone out of my way for all of my kids. But Jennifer never gives me a clue that I do anything right for her.

JERRY: And what is it like for you to acknowledge that you resent the expectation that you have to be the perfect mother?

RUTH: Well, now I'm feeling guilty again that I have such negative feelings!

I am aware that Ruth is not going to rid herself forever of her guilt. If she does not let her guilt control her, however, she can make room for other feelings. Based on Ruth's bringing up her resentment, which I suspect is related to her guilt, I propose the following experiment:

JERRY: If you're willing to go further, I'd like you to repeat your list of guilts, only this time say "I resent you for . . ." instead of "I feel guilty over . . ."

RUTH: But I don't feel resentment—it's the guilt!

JERRY: I know, but would you be willing to go ahead with the experiment and see what happens?

RUTH [*After some hesitation and discussion of the value of doing this*]: I resent you for expecting me to always be understanding of you. I resent you for demanding so much of my time. I resent you for all the trouble you got yourself into and the nights of sleep I lost over this. I resent you for making me feel guilty. I resent you for not understanding me. I resent you for expecting affection but not giving me any.

My rationale for asking Ruth to convert her list of guilts into a list of resentments is that doing so may help her direct her anger to the sources where it belongs, rather than inward. She has so much guilt partly because she directs her anger toward herself, and this keeps her distant from some people who are significant to her. Ruth becomes more and more energetic with her expression of resentments.

JERRY: Ruth, let me sit in for Jennifer for a bit. Continue talking to me, and tell me the ways in which you resent me.

RUTH [*Becoming more emotional and expressive*]: It's hard for me to talk to you. You and I haven't really talked in such a long time. [*Tears well up in her eyes.*] I give and give, and all you do is take and take. There's no end to it!

JERRY: Tell Jennifer what you want from her.

RUTH [*Pausing and then, with a burst of energy, shouting*]: I want to be more like you! I'm envious of you. I wish I could be as daring and as alive as you. Wow, I'm surprised at what I just said.

JERRY: Keep talking to Jennifer, and tell her more about how you're feeling right now.

With Ruth's heightened emotionality she is able to say some things to Jennifer that she has never said. She leaves this session with some new insights: her feelings of guilt are more often feelings of resentment; her anger toward Jennifer is based on envy and jealousy; and the things she dislikes about Jennifer are some of the things she would like for herself.

EXPLORING THE POLARITIES WITHIN RUTH In later sessions Ruth brings up the many ways she feels pulled in different directions. What emerges for her is all the expectations that her parents had for her and the many expectations others still have for her. She reports that she doesn't always want to be the "perfect person." She resents having to be so good and never being allowed to have fun. As she talks, she becomes aware of the polarities within her that seem incompatible. We continue working with some of the splits within Ruth's personality. My aim is not to get rid of her feelings but to let her experience them and learn to integrate all the factions of her personality. She will not get rid of one side of her personality that she does not like by attempting to deny it, but she can learn to recognize the side that controls her by expressing it.

RUTH: For so many years I had to be the perfect minister's daughter. I lost myself in being the proper "good girl." I'd like to be more spontaneous and playful and not worry constantly about what other people would think. Sometimes when I'm being silly, I hear this voice in my head that tells me to be proper. It's as if there are two of me: one that's all proper and prim and the other that wants to be footloose and free.

JERRY: Which side do you feel most right now, the proper side or the uninhibited side?

RUTH: Well, the proper and conservative side is surely the stronger in me.

JERRY: I have an idea of an experiment that I'd like you to try. Are you willing?

> RUTH: OK, I'm ready to work.

> JERRY: Here are a couple of chairs. I'd like you to sit in this chair here and be the proper side of you. Talk to the uninhibited side, which is sitting in this other chair.

> RUTH: I wish you would grow up! You should act like an adult and stop being a silly kid. If I listened to you, I'd really be in trouble now. You're so impulsive and demanding.

> JERRY: OK, how about changing and sitting in the chair over here and speaking from your daring side? What does she have to say to the proper side over there?

> RUTH: It's about time you let your hair down and had some fun. You're so cautious! Sure, you're safe, but you're also a very, very dull person. I know you'd like to be me more often.

> JERRY: Change chairs again, talking back to the daring side.

> RUTH: Well I'd rather be safe than sorry! [Her face flushes]

> JERRY: And what do you want to say back to your proper side?

> RUTH [Changing chairs]: That's just your trouble. Always be safe! And where is this getting you? You'll die being safe and secure.

This exchange of chairs goes on for some time. Becoming her daring side is much more uncomfortable for Ruth. After a while she lets herself get into the daring side and chides the prude sitting across from her. She accuses her of letting life slip by, points out how she is just like her mother, and tells her how her being so proper stops her from having any fun. This experiment shows Ruth the difference between thinking about conflicts and actually letting herself experience those conflicts. She sees more clearly that she is being pulled in many directions, that she is a complex person, and that she will not get rid of feelings by pretending that they don't exist. Gradually, she experiences more freedom in accepting the different parts within her, without the need to cut out certain parts of her.

A DIALOGUE WITH RUTH'S FATHER In another session Ruth brings up how it was for her as a child, especially in relation to her cold and ungiving father. I ask her not merely to report what happened but also to bring her father into the room now and talk to him as she did as a child. She goes back to a past event and relives it—the time at 6 years old when she was reprimanded by her father for "playing doctor" with a friend. She begins by saying how scared she was then and how she did not know what to say to him after he had caught her in sexual play. So I encourage her to stay with her scared feelings and to tell her father all the things that she was feeling then but did not say. Then I say to Ruth:

> JERRY: Tell your father how you wish he had acted with you. [As Ruth talks to her father, she strokes her left hand with her right hand. At a later point I hand her a pillow.] Let yourself be the father you wished you

had, and talk to little Ruth. The pillow is you, and you are your father. Talk to little Ruth.

RUTH: [*This brings up intense feelings, and for a long time she says nothing. She sits silently, holding "Ruth" and caressing her lovingly. Eventually, some words follow.*] Ruth, I have always loved you, and you have always been special to me. It has just been hard for me to show what I feel. I wanted to let you know how much you mattered to me, but I didn't know how.[3]

PROCESS COMMENTARY During the time that Ruth is doing her work, I pay attention to what she is communicating nonverbally. For example, she describes her heart, saying it feels as if it wants to break; the knots in her stomach; the tension in her neck and shoulders; the tightness in her head; her clenched fists; the tears in her eyes; and the smile across her lips. At appropriate moments I call her attention to her body and teach her how to pay attention to what she is experiencing in her body. At different times I ask her to try the experiment of "becoming" her breaking heart (or any other bodily sensation) and giving that part of her body "voice."

Ruth exhibits some reluctance to getting involved in these Gestalt experiments, but after challenging herself and overcoming her feelings of looking foolish, she is generally amazed at what comes out of these procedures. Ruth does not need interpretations from me as her therapist. Without my interpretations she begins to discover for herself how some of her past experiences are related to her present feelings of being stuck in so many ways. By paying attention on a moment-to-moment basis to whatever she is experiencing, Ruth is able to see the meaning for herself.

Ruth's awareness is, by itself, a powerful catalyst for her change. Before she can hope to be different in any respect, she first has to be aware of how she is. The focus of much of her work is on *what* she is experiencing at any given moment, as well as *how*. Thus, when she mentions being anxious, she focuses on *how* this anxiety is manifested in a knot in her stomach or a headache. I focus her on here-and-now experiencing and away from thinking about *why*. Asking why would remove Ruth from her feelings. Another key focus is on dealing with unfinished business. Business from the past does seek completion, and it persists in Ruth's present until she faces and deals with feelings that she has not previously expressed.

Some Final Thoughts

A theme that emerges repeatedly in Ruth's work is how material comes alive when she brings an experience into the present. She does not merely intellectualize about her problems, nor does she engage in much talking about events. Participating in experiments intensifies whatever Ruth is experiencing. When she does bring a past event into the present by allowing herself to reexperience that event, it often provides her with valuable insights. I especially value bringing all of a client's struggles into the present and creating experiments to enable the client to better understand a problem. Gestalt therapy is a lively way to assist clients in creating new directions for themselves.

Questions for Reflection

1. Dr. Frew describes an assessment process that grows out of an I/Thou dialogue between Ruth and her therapist. What do you think of this approach to assessment?

2. Dr. Frew maintains that in Gestalt therapy the interventions are based on observing and listening to what is in the client's present awareness. He takes his time, follows Ruth's lead, and lets the dialogue unfold without rushing or pushing for results. What are your thoughts about using this approach when designing therapeutic interventions?

3. Gestalt interventions are useful in working with the splits and polarities within a person. As you can see, Ruth has problems because she is not able to reconcile or integrate polarities: dependent versus independent, giving to others versus asking and receiving, and the need for security versus the need to leave secure ways and create new ways of being. Are you aware of struggling with any of Ruth's polarities in your life now?

4. Can you think of some ways to blend the cognitive focus of Adlerian therapy with the emotional themes that are likely to emerge through Gestalt work with Ruth? Provide a few examples of how you could work with her feelings and cognitions by combining concepts and methods from the two approaches.

5. What main differences do you see between the way Dr. Frew worked with Ruth (as a Gestalt therapist) and the way Dr. Cain worked with her (as a person-centered therapist)? What about the differences in the way I counseled Ruth from these two perspectives?

6. Think about Ruth as being from each of the following ethnic and cultural backgrounds: Native American, African American, Latino, and Asian American. How might you tailor Gestalt experiments in working with her if she were a member of each of these groups? What are some of the advantages and disadvantages of drawing on concepts and interventions from Gestalt therapy in working with cultural themes in her life?

7. What specific areas of unfinished business are most evident to you as you read about Ruth? Do any of her unexpressed feelings bring to awareness any of your own business from the past? What potential unresolved areas in your own life might interfere with your ability to work effectively with Ruth? How might you deal with these feelings if they came up as you were counseling her?

8. How well does Gestalt therapy fit with your counseling style? What aspects of this approach do you find most useful? Which aspects might you want to modify to fit your personal counseling style?

Notes

See the *DVD for Theory and Practice of Counseling and Psychotherapy: The Case of Stan and Lecturettes,* Session 6 ("Gestalt Therapy Applied to the Case of Stan"), which deals with Stan reporting a dream in Gestalt fashion and his exploration of the personal meaning of his dream, and for my presentation of ways that Gestalt therapy can be applied.

1. For a discussion of the dialogical philosophy of relationship, see Buber, M. (1970). *I and thou.* New York: Scribner's.
2. For a more detailed discussion of the key concepts of Gestalt therapy, see Corey, G. (2013). *Theory and practice of counseling and psychotherapy* (9th ed.). Belmont, CA: Brooks/Cole, Cengage Learning. Chapter 8 ("Gestalt Therapy") outlines the basic elements of the therapeutic process.
3. The *DVD for Integrative Counseling: The Case of Ruth and Lecturettes* has a vivid illustration of the power of Gestalt experiments. In Session 11 ("Understanding How the Past Influences the Present and the Future"), Ruth symbolically talks to her father. I ask her to bring the past event to life by talking directly to her father as the scared 6-year-old child.

Case Approach
to Behavior Therapy

General Overview of Behavior Therapy

The main goal of behavior therapy is to eliminate clients' maladaptive behavior patterns and replace them with more constructive ones. Therapists identify thought patterns that lead to behavioral problems and then teach new ways of thinking that are designed to change the clients' ways of acting.

Some of the main behavioral techniques are systematic desensitization, in vivo exposure, relaxation methods, reinforcement, modeling, social skills training, self-management programs, mindfulness and acceptance approaches, behavioral rehearsal, coaching, and other multimodal techniques. Assessment and diagnosis are done at the outset to determine a treatment plan. "What," "how," and "when" questions are used (but not "why" questions).

This approach has the advantage of specifying clear and concrete behavioral goals that can be monitored and measured. Empirically supported techniques are selected to deal with specific problems, and assessment and treatment occur simultaneously. Because therapy begins with an assessment of baseline data, the degree of progress can be evaluated by comparing clients' behavior on a given dimension at any point in the therapy with the baseline data. Clients are frequently challenged to answer the question, "Is what we are doing in here helping you make the changes you desire?" With this information, clients are in the best position to determine when they are ready to terminate. Evidence-based practice is best conceived of in a broad way and includes clinician expertise, the best available research, and evaluating the client's characteristics, culture, and preferences. Even in behavior therapy, the therapeutic relationship is of central importance and critical to outcome.

A Multimodal Behavior Therapist's Perspective on Ruth

by Arnold A. Lazarus, PhD, ABPP

Introduction

Multimodal therapy is a broad-based, systematic, and comprehensive approach to behavior therapy that calls for technical eclecticism (that is, the use of effective techniques regardless of their point of origin). The multimodal orientation assumes that clients are usually troubled by a multitude of specific problems, which should be dealt with using a wide range of specific techniques. Whenever feasible, therapists should select empirically supported treatments of choice for specific disorders. The comprehensive assessment, or therapeutic modus operandi, attends to each area of a client's BASIC I.D. (B = behavior, A = affect, S = sensation, I = imagery, C = cognition, I = interpersonal relationships, and D = drugs and biological factors). Discrete and interactive problems throughout each of the foregoing modalities are identified, and appropriate techniques are selected to deal with each difficulty. A genuine and empathic client–therapist relationship provides the soil that enables the techniques to take root.

Multimodal Assessment of Ruth

In Ruth's case more than three dozen specific and interrelated problems can be identified using the diagnostic, treatment-oriented BASIC I.D. methodology:

Behavior: fidgeting, avoidance of eye contact, and rapid speaking; poor sleep pattern; tendency to cry easily; overeating; various avoidance behaviors

Affect: anxiety; panic (especially in class and at night when trying to sleep); depression; fears of criticism and rejection; pangs of religious guilt; trapped feelings; self-abnegation

Sensation: dizziness; palpitations; fatigue and boredom; headaches; tendency to deny, reject, or suppress her sexuality; overeating to the point of nausea

Imagery: ongoing negative parental messages; residual images of hellfire and brimstone; unfavorable body image and poor self-image; view of herself as aging and losing her looks; inability to visualize herself in a professional role

Cognition: self-identity questions ("Who and what am I?"); worrying thoughts (death and dying); doubts about her right to succeed professionally; categorical imperatives ("shoulds," "oughts," and "musts"); search for new values; self-denigration

Interpersonal relationships: unassertiveness (especially putting the needs of others before her own); fostering her family's dependence on her; limited pleasure outside her role as mother and wife; problems with children; unsatisfactory relationship with her husband (yet fear of losing him); looking to the therapist for direction; still seeking parental approval

Drugs and biological factors: overweight; lack of an exercise program; various physical complaints for which medical examinations reveal no organic pathology.

In some cases, medication is essential, and the help of a psychopharmacologist is then requested. I kept a careful watch on Ruth's depression as we began our work, but it seemed that antidepressant medication was unnecessary. My own bias is to avoid medication except where it is clearly indicated.

Like Jerry Corey, I typically don't think in diagnostic labels or terms. Indeed, a multimodal clinician sees the range of problems across the BASIC I.D. as the "diagnosis." Nevertheless, practitioners are often required to provide a DSM-IV-TR multiaxial diagnosis if they want to receive third-party insurance reimbursement. I would diagnose Ruth as follows:

Axis I: 300.01 Panic without agoraphobia

309.28 Adjustment disorder with mixed anxiety and depressed mood

300.40 Dysthymic disorder

V 61.1 Partner relational problem

Axis II: None

Axis III: Somatic symptoms (medical conditions ruled out)

Axis IV: Family relationship issues, especially with eldest daughter

Axis V: (GAF score) 57

Selecting Techniques and Strategies

The goal of multimodal therapy is not to eliminate each and every identified problem. Rather, after establishing rapport with Ruth and developing a sound therapeutic alliance, I would select several key issues in concert with her. Given the fact that she is generally tense, agitated, restless, and anxious, one of the first antidotes might be the use of relaxation training. Some people respond with paradoxical increases in tension when practicing relaxation, and it is necessary to determine what particular type of relaxation will suit an individual client (for example, direct muscular tension–relaxation contrasts, autogenic training, meditation, positive mental imagery, diaphragmatic breathing, or a combination of methods). I have no reason to believe Ruth would not respond to deep muscle relaxation, positive imagery, and self-calming statements.

The next pivotal area is her unassertiveness and self-entitlements. I will employ behavior rehearsal and role playing. Our sessions will also explore her right to be professional and successful. Cognitive restructuring will address her categorical imperatives and will endeavor to reduce the "shoulds," "oughts," and "musts" she inflicts on herself. Imagery techniques may be given prominence, and her homework assignment may include using a particular image over and over until she feels in control of the situation. For example, I may ask Ruth to picture herself going back in a time machine so that she can meet herself as a little girl and provide her alter ego with reassurance about the religious guilts her father imposed.

THERAPIST: Can you visualize yourself stepping into a time machine and traveling back in time to meet up with yourself as a very young child?

RUTH: OK, I think I can do that.

THERAPIST: How far back in time would you like to travel? At what age would you wish to meet up with your alter ego, your much younger self?

RUTH: I see myself as a 10-year-old child.

THERAPIST: The special time machine and you are now journeying back into the past. [*Pause*] Now, please imagine yourself stepping out of the machine, and there you see a little girl. It is you, Little Ruth, at 10 years of age. She looks up at you but does not realize that she is looking at her adult self. But this Little Ruth senses something very special about you, and she will pay close attention to whatever you say to her. [*Pause*] Picture yourself giving Little Ruth a hug. [*Pause*] Now, what would you like to tell her about your father's preachings?

RUTH: [*Big Ruth tells Little Ruth that her father is thoroughly misguided and not to heed the religious guilt he is imposing on her.*]

Most people resonate with this imagery and, with considerable emotion, they narrate the supportive, corrective, reparative, and encouraging points they would share with their alter ego. If they do not spontaneously go there, the therapist will prompt them in this direction. After 5 or 10 minutes (depending on how engrossed they remain in the image) clients are asked to reenter the time machine and go forward until they step out into the present. Many people have found this to be a robust and helpful procedure, and it can be practiced at home several times a day as well as in therapy sessions. The active mechanism behind this procedure is presumed to be a form of desensitization and cognitive restructuring.

If Ruth and her husband agree to it, some marital counseling (and possibly some sex therapy) may be recommended, followed by some family therapy sessions aimed at enhancing the interpersonal climate in the home. Indeed, if Ruth becomes a more relaxed, confident, assertive person, John and her children may need help to cope with her new behaviors. Moreover, I can try to circumvent any attempts at "sabotage" by John or the children.

As a part of the assessment process, I ask Ruth to fill out the 15-page Multimodal Life History Inventory.[1] This process enables me to detect a wide range of problems throughout the BASIC I.D. The following dialogue ensues:

THERAPIST: On page 12 of the questionnaire, you wrote "no" to the question "Do you eat three well-balanced meals each day?" and also to the question "Do you get regular physical exercise?" And on page 15, you wrote that you frequently drink coffee, overeat, eat junk foods, and have weight problems.

RUTH: Maybe I should go on a diet again.

THERAPIST: Well, the problem with going on a diet is that people soon come off it and gain weight, perhaps even more weight than they lost. I think the goal is to develop sensible eating patterns. To begin with,

I have a list of foods a nutritionist gave me, stuff that we should avoid eating or cut down on. [*The list contains mainly foods with a high fat content, especially those with saturated fats, as well as foods with a high sugar content.*] For starters, would you be willing to take it home and see how many of these items you can cut out of your diet?

RUTH: Certainly.

THERAPIST: I wonder if we could make a pact?

RUTH: About what?

THERAPIST: That you would agree to take a brisk 1- to 2-mile walk at least three times a week.

RUTH: I can do that.

THERAPIST: By the way, there's an excellent diet center in your neighborhood. They have a program in which they train people to understand food contents and to easily calculate the amount of fiber and calories you require. They also run support groups. It's often easier to develop new eating habits when you're part of a group instead of trying to do it on your own.

RUTH: Yes, I know the place you mean. I've often thought of going there. Do you really think it would be a good idea?

THERAPIST: Yes, I really do.

If Ruth feels up to it, I will teach her sensible eating habits and suggest that she begin a weight reduction program and an exercise regimen. Referral to a local diet center may be a useful adjunct.

Therapy Sessions With Ruth

After I draw up Ruth's Modality Profile (BASIC I.D. chart), the clinical dialogue proceeds as follows:

THERAPIST: I've made a list, under seven separate headings, of what your main problems seem to be. For example, under behavior I have the following: fidgeting, avoidance of eye contact, rapid speaking, poor sleep pattern, tendency to cry easily, overeating, and various avoidance behaviors.

RUTH: That's what I do; they're all correct. [*Pause*] But I'm not exactly sure what you mean by "various avoidance behaviors."

THERAPIST: Well, it seems to me that you often avoid doing things that you'd like to do; instead, you do what you think others expect of you. You avoid following through on your plans to exercise and to observe good eating habits. You avoid making certain decisions.

RUTH: I see what you mean. I guess I'm a pretty hopeless case. I'm so weak and panicky, such a basic coward, that I can't seem to make up my mind about anything these days.

THERAPIST: One thing you seem to be very good at and never avoid is putting yourself down. You sure won't feel helpless if you start taking emotional risks and if you're willing to speak your mind. What does that sound like to you?

RUTH: Are you asking me if I'd like to be more outgoing and less afraid?

THERAPIST: That's a good way of putting it. What do you think would happen if you changed in that regard?

RUTH: I'm not sure, but I certainly don't think my father would approve.

THERAPIST: And how about your husband?

RUTH [*Looking downcast*]: I see what you're getting at.

THERAPIST: Would you agree that you first tended to march to your father's drum and then handed most of the control over to your husband? [*Ruth is nodding affirmatively.*] Well, I think it's high time you become the architect and designer of your own life.

Ruth does not feel overwhelmed, so I discuss the other items on her Modality Profile. If she had shown signs of concern ("Oh my God! I have so many problems!"), I would have targeted only the most salient items and helped her work toward their mitigation or elimination.

Whenever feasible, I select data-based methods of treatment. Thus, in dealing with her panic attacks, I first explain the physiology of panic and the fight-or-flight response. Emphasis is placed on the distinction between adaptive and maladaptive anxiety. For example, anxiety is helpful when it prompts Ruth to study for an exam, but it is maladaptive when its intensity undermines her performance. Her anxiety reactions are examined in terms of their behavioral consequences; secondary affective responses (such as fear of fear); sensory reactions; the images, or mental pictures, they generate; their cognitive components; and their interpersonal effects. In each instance I apply specific strategies. Behaviorally, for example, I encourage her to stop avoiding situations and instead to confront them. In the cognitive modality, she is enjoined to challenge thoughts like "I must be going crazy!" or "I'm going to die!" and to replace them with these self-statements: "My doctor confirmed that I'm physically healthy." "Being anxious won't make me crazy!" Because so many people who suffer from panic tend to over breathe (hyperventilate), I teach Ruth how to breathe more slowly and to use her diaphragm, thereby dampening her physical symptoms.

A Conjoint Session With Ruth and John

The treatment trajectory depends mainly on Ruth's readiness for change (for example, her willingness to take risks, be assertive, and challenge her dysfunctional thoughts) and the extent to which her husband is invested in keeping her subservient. John feels threatened by Ruth when she starts expressing and fulfilling herself, and conjoint sessions are essential to persuade him that he will be better off in the long run with a wife who feels personally satisfied rather than bitter, frustrated, and bored. Thus I suggest to her that she encourage John to attend at least one therapy session with her. I tell her that I intend to go out of my way to bond with John so as to gain his compliance. In this connection, I have the following dialogue with Ruth and John:

THERAPIST [*Addressing John*]: Thank you for agreeing to meet with me. As you know, I've been trying to help Ruth overcome various fears and anxieties, and I believe she has made considerable headway. But now we're at a point where I need your input and assistance. I wonder if we can start by hearing your views on the subject.

JOHN [*Glancing at Ruth*]: What do you want to know?

THERAPIST: Quite a number of things. I'd like to know how you view her therapy, whether you think it was or is necessary, and if you think she has been helped. I'd like to hear your complaints about Ruth—after all, no marriage is perfect.

JOHN [*Addressing Ruth*]: Can I be perfectly honest?

RUTH: John, that's why we're here.

THERAPIST: Please be completely frank and above board.

JOHN: What do I call you?

THERAPIST: Let's not be formal or stuffy. Call me Arnold.

JOHN: Well, Arnold, the way I see it is that Ruth has bitten off more than she can chew. Things were pretty good until she decided to go to college. I don't think she can manage a career and a home. It's putting too much pressure on her. I mean, you know, I think if you take things away from the family, everyone suffers. It's not as if she needs to work for the money. Heck, I've always made enough to support my family.

THERAPIST: That's very important. Have things changed for the worse inside the family since Ruth started studying? Has she neglected you and the kids? Is the family suffering?

JOHN: Well, not exactly. I mean, Ruth's always been a good wife and a devoted mother. But [*Pause*] I don't quite know how to put it. [*Pause*]

THERAPIST: Perhaps you're reacting to a feeling inside of yourself that there's the potential for some sort of penalty or withdrawal . . . that something will be taken away from you.

JOHN: Yeah, maybe.

THERAPIST: You're facing a turning point that many families encounter. The job of mothering is virtually done. Let's see. Your four children are now 19, 18, 17, and 16 years old. So the energy Ruth had to expend in taking care of them in the past must be replaced by something else. Now that the kids are almost grown up, she has more time on her hands. Her full-time homemaking has now become a part-time activity. As Ruth approaches 40, it seems that she needs to become more than a wife and mother. However, I am guessing that it might be a mistake for her to do anything that would damage or undermine her relationship with you and the children. Is that right?

JOHN [*Smiling*]: You can say that again!

THERAPIST: Well, if she works as an elementary schoolteacher, the time that she used to devote to caring for your kids would be put to constructive use. But if she just hung around at home, you'd soon have a bitter, resentful, and frustrated woman on your hands. What would she do with all that free time except become a royal pain in the neck? Does that make sense?

JOHN: I guess I see what you're getting at.

THERAPIST: Besides, let's face it. Even though you make good money, with four kids to put through college, a bit of extra cash won't hurt. [*Talking to Ruth*] I hope you don't mind too much that John and I have been talking about you as if you weren't in the room. I meant no disrespect, but I really wanted to touch base with him.

RUTH: No, I understand. May I ask something?

THERAPIST [*Paradoxically*]: Only if you get down on bended knee.

RUTH [*Smiling*]: The 6-year-old strikes again! [*Turning to John*] John, have I ever neglected you or the children?

JOHN: Like I said, you've been a good wife and mother.

THERAPIST: Now the question is whether you can continue being a good wife and mother and also become a good teacher.

A follow-up session with Ruth after the conjoint meeting commences as follows:

THERAPIST: I'm curious to know if our threesome meeting seemed to have any positive effects. What do you think we accomplished?

RUTH: It's hard to tell. I mean, John came away saying that you made sense, which I think is a very good sign. He seemed quite comfortable with you.

THERAPIST: Well, I hope that the "sense" I made adds up to getting him to realize that if you don't work, but function as a full-time home-maker now that the children have grown up, it will be to everyone's detriment. I want you, from time to time, to underscore that point. We need John to become fully aware that there's a positive payoff, a defi-nite advantage for him if you work, and that it's in no way a reflection of his earning capacity. As I told him, the extra money will be useful, but it's not essential. Can you gently but firmly make those points over and over?

RUTH: I think that's what's needed for John to feel OK about it.

THERAPIST: And you? Do you feel OK about it? You've expressed quite a bit of conflict over this issue.

RUTH: I'm still afraid of many things, and I'm still not entirely confident that I can succeed.

THERAPIST: Well, should we look into this now?

RUTH: Susan—she's my 17-year-old—has me a little upset over an inci-dent that occurred. Can we discuss this first?

THERAPIST: Sure.

Concluding Comments

The initial objective was to gain permission from John for Ruth to pursue a career. If John seemed motivated to enter couples therapy with a view to improving their marriage—really getting to know and appreciate each other, enhancing their levels of general and sexual communication—this would be all to the good. It would not surprise me if he also elected to seek personal therapy for some of his insecurities. As a multimodal therapist, I would expect to encounter no difficulties in treating Ruth individually, Ruth and John as a couple, and John as an individual.

The multimodal approach assumes that lasting treatment outcomes require combining various techniques, strategies, and modalities. A multimodal therapist works with individuals, couples, and families as needed. The approach is pragmatic and empirical. It offers a consistent framework for diagnosing problems within and among each vector of personality. The overall emphasis is on fitting the treatment to the client by addressing factors such as the client's expectancies, readiness for change, and motivation. The therapist's style (for example, degree of directiveness and supportiveness) varies according to the needs of the client and the situation. Above all, flexibility and thoroughness are strongly emphasized. I very much believe in "bibliotherapy" and would urge Ruth to read my user-friendly self-help book, *The 60-Second Shrink: 101 Strategies for Staying Sane in a Crazy World*. I might also give her a copy of my book, *Marital Myths Revisited: A Fresh Look at Two Dozen Mistaken Beliefs About Marriage*, as a gift.[2]

Most therapists would probably find Ruth capable of being helped and relatively easy to treat. Unlike some clients with severe personality disturbances, she displays no excessive hostility, no intense self-destructive tendencies, and no undue "resistance," and her interpersonal style appears to be collaborative rather than belligerent or contentious. Nevertheless, if one treats only two or three modalities (which is what most nonmultimodal counselors address), several important problems and deficits may be glossed over or ignored, thereby leaving her with untreated complaints that could have been resolved and with a propensity to relapse (for example, revert back to her timid, conflicted, anxious, depressed, and unfulfilled modus vivendi).

In this era, when brief therapy is the order of the day, instead of focusing or dwelling on one or two so-called pivotal issues (which is what many time-limited counselors attempt to do), multimodal therapists address one major problem from each dimension of the BASIC I.D.[3] In Ruth's case, if we had only 6 to 10 sessions in which to work, the following issues might be selected:

Behavior: Address her avoidance response.

Affect: Implement anxiety-management techniques.

Sensation: Teach her self-calming relaxation methods.

Imagery: Use positive self-visualizations.

Cognition: Try to eliminate categorical imperatives ("shoulds," "oughts," and "musts").

Interpersonal relationships: Administer assertiveness training.

Drugs and biology: Recommend a sensible nutrition and exercise program.

The multimodal maxim is that breadth is often more important than depth. The clinician who sinks one or two deep shafts is likely to bypass a host of other issues. It is wiser to address as broad an array of problems as time permits. Through a "ripple effect," a change in one modality tends to generalize to others, but the greater the number of discrete problems that can be overcome, the more profound the eventual outcome is likely to be.[4]

Another Behavior Therapist's Perspective on Ruth

by Sherry Cormier, PhD

Introduction

Behavior therapy initially focused on techniques of systematic desensitization based on classical conditioning and reinforcement strategies based on operant learning. These are still classics in this approach, but behavior therapy has evolved to now include such interventions as cognitive change strategies (see Chapter 8), skills training, exposure therapies, self-management strategies, and mindfulness/acceptance interventions. The more recent evolution of behavior therapy has been both broad and comprehensive. The multimodal approach, described by Dr. Lazarus earlier in this chapter, is as relevant to behavior therapy today as it was when he introduced it to the world some 45 years ago. Contemporary behavior therapy is often integrative in nature, as you will see in my work with Ruth. Here I describe some basic features of behavior therapy today, and how I would apply these concepts to Ruth.

Basic Features of Behavior Therapy

The fundamental characteristics of behavior therapy include the following:

1. Behavior is not just something we can see, such as an overt action, but also includes internal processes: cognitions, images, beliefs, schemas, and emotions. The hallmark of what constitutes behavior is *something that can be operationally defined.* For example, if a client says to me, "I am depressed," we would work together to better understand what that means. For one client, "I am depressed" may mean the client cannot get out of bed in the morning and feels sad. For another client, "I am depressed" may mean the client cries most of the time and feels irritable around other people.

2. Behavior is *learned,* at least for the most part. Neuroscience increasingly shows how behavior is affected by various parts of the brain and by each person's neural wiring, some of which is genetic, but much of human behavior occurs through learning. Although some parts of the brain and hardwiring are associated with what we know as depression, like other behaviors, depression is learned as the person interacts with the environment.

3. Behavior therapy relies on *evidence.* The approach is characterized by results and data. Pragmatically, this means that all aspects of counseling, from the therapy relationship, to the assessment process, to the change intervention process, are based as much as possible on basic scientific evidence.

Quantifiable results are important as well for each client: Does the client change? In what direction? How much? An important feature of the behavioral approach is the careful use of assessment, measurement, and outcome evaluation with each client.

4. Behavior therapy recognizes the importance of the individual, the individual's environment, and the interaction between the person and his or her environment in facilitating change. Attention in the therapy process is given not only to the client but also to the *context* in which the client lives. This includes both cultural and environmental variables, which often have a strong impact on the client's issues.

Behavior analysis, sometimes referred to as a functional or ABC analysis, is an important aspect of behavior therapy. The therapist strives to select an identified issue and determine empirically what environmental conditions are related to the issue, what conditions are preventing its resolution, and what strengths and resources are available for its resolution. Any *behavior* (B) is preceded and followed by other events. Behavioral therapists call contributing events that precede the problem behavior *antecedents* (A) and contributing events that follow the problem behavior *consequences* (C). Antecedents are situational and internal events that are responsible for the behavior occurring in the first place; consequences are situational and internal events that strengthen or weaken a behavior, which influences whether the behavior is likely to occur again. Not everything that precedes or follows a problem behavior maintains it. The behavior analysis helps identify which antecedents and consequences are most likely to be influencing the problem behavior. By pinpointing the events co-occurring with the beginning of the problem; identifying what the client thinks, feels, and does during the problem; and finally pinpointing the events that follow the problem, the behavior therapist can develop functional hypotheses and diagnoses that guide treatment planning. You will see a sample of behavioral analysis in my work with Ruth.

The Process of Behavior Therapy

The general processes involved in behavior therapy include the following:

- Establish a therapeutic relationship
- Assess problems and issues within a contextual framework
- Identify and define targets of change (outcome goals)
- Select and implement evidence-based intervention strategies
- Monitor and evaluate progress toward goals
- Prepare for referral, termination, relapse prevention, and follow-up

Although I describe these as discrete phases of behavior therapy, in actual practice the phases overlap. For example, the therapeutic relationship remains as much a factor during the middle or end stages of counseling as it is at the beginning of counseling.

Establish a Therapeutic Relationship   Behavior therapists emphasize the importance of the therapeutic relationship. It is considered necessary, but not sufficient, to effect therapeutic change in most instances. Behavior therapists recognize that *all* counseling is interpersonal, or between people. As a result, good relationship skills are a must, not an option!

◈ Assess Client Problems and Issues Within a Contextual Framework I conduct a thorough individual assessment with each client I see. Behavioral assessment is *multilevel, multicultural,* and *multimethod*. This involves assessing clients on many dimensions, such as the BASIC I.D. described by Dr. Lazarus and the behavioral analysis assessment I described previously. These dimensions consider not only the individual client but also the context and environmental variables related to the client's issues. For example, if a client says, "I feel way too stressed in my life right now," we would explore what visible behaviors such as hypervigilance, nail-biting, and increase or decrease in appetite are associated with the client's stress picture, as well as internal behaviors such as how the client is feeling and what the client is thinking about during times of being stressed. In addition, I explore the client's strengths: How is the client coping with the stress? What things in the client's life are going well? What kinds of supports and resources does the client have? I also look for events in the client's environment that both cue and maintain the stress symptoms. The goal is to ascertain the function of problematic behaviors so that effective treatment procedures can be selected.

I conduct a cultural assessment with each client because I believe that counseling is not only interpersonal but also multicultural. I use the ADDRESSING model of Pamela Hays[5] to assess the following cultural influences for each client:

- Age and generational influences
- Developmental and acquired influences
- Disabilities
- Religious and spiritual orientation
- Ethnicity
- Socioeconomic status
- Sexual orientation
- Indigenous heritage
- National origin
- Gender

My goal is to help the client articulate ways in which cultural influences may contribute to the problem. This is another way to consider the role of context and environment in assessing client issues. For example, a client may say, "A big part of what makes up stress in my life is that I am a minority person in my work setting, and I don't think people there get me. I feel quite alone at work." This framework also takes into account developmental factors such as the particular life stage of the client and the client's social and developmental history.

I also use a range of other assessment methods, including the SCID (Structured Clinical Interview for DMS-IV-TR disorders),[6] because DSM diagnoses often are required for third-party reimbursement. Sometimes I conduct a mini–mental status exam along with a thorough intake and history assessment interview. Supplemental assessment tools such as a genogram or social network map can be helpful, and standardized instruments such as the Outcome

Questionnaire (OQ-45)[7] supplements the client's self-report. In addition, I use other standardized instruments that are linked to the client's presenting issues. Why? A cardinal feature of behavior therapy is wanting to know and evaluate how well the change interventions are working and what kind of progress the client is making toward the stated goals. These various assessment methods help to do just that! And the eventual effectiveness, or lack thereof, of an intervention I use with a client confirms or disconfirms the functional diagnoses I have made about the client.

🐦 Identify and Define Targets of Change (Outcome Goals)
Behavior therapists spend a lot of time doing a thorough assessment with their clients. Part of the rationale for this is to allow clients to identify and define relevant targets of change or outcome goals. The client and I explore in a collaborative way what he or she would like to happen as a result of our work together. These outcome goals are a direct reflection of the results of our assessment. Outcome goals help to specify what behaviors, thoughts, and feelings a client wants to change.

🐦 Select and Implement Evidence-Based Intervention Strategies
The goal-setting process is important in behavior therapy because it helps determine how to best help clients get the results they want. Therapy is like a journey—if I know I want to get from point A to point B, there are usually several routes to go. Some routes may be longer or shorter and may have certain pros and cons—eventually we pick the route that best suits our needs. After clients determine their goals, the therapist may suggest various routes clients can take to attain their goals, but all routes are evidence-based. That is, change interventions are selected based on available literature, data, and evidence that support the use of that intervention or combination of interventions to help clients achieve particular goals. Exploring for the best possible interventions can be likened to doing a Map Quest search for our journey. A client who is stressed mostly at work because of social and cultural isolation may find culturally relevant stress management interventions useful. These interventions would not only promote individual coping for stress but also address the more systemic issues of lack of support in a culturally challenging work environment.

🐦 Monitor and Evaluate Progress Toward Goals
As clients work with various interventions, therapists are both monitoring and evaluating the progress being made toward the identified target of change. In behavior therapy, repeated evaluations are important. Often I ask clients to self-monitor aspects of their actions, thoughts, or feelings throughout the therapy process. For example, I might ask the client who experiences stress to monitor the daily level of stress on a 1–10 scale and to list things that seem to make the stress better or worse. Also, I follow up with diagnostic- and assessment-oriented questions at various points in the counseling process and repeat the use of standardized instruments such as the OQ-45 at various points. These tools help me to develop information about whether the client is being helped, and to what extent, by what we are doing together. If the data suggest little or no progress is being made, then a route change is indicated.

❧ Preparation for Termination, Relapse Prevention, and Follow-Up   An important feature of behavior therapy is *self-efficacy*,[8] which means clients have confidence in their own abilities to manage and sustain change. Evaluating self-efficacy is part of the termination preparation for clients who are ready to go solo. At the same time, I talk with clients about relapse prevention—the notion that individual and environmental roadblocks may come up that pose particular challenges—and tell clients that follow-up is important to me and that I will check in with them about 6 months after we have had a termination session to see how they are doing.

Application of the Behavioral Approach with Ruth

❧ Establishing the Therapy Relationship and Beginning Assessment   As Ruth's counselor, I am first interested in creating a connection with Ruth. I find therapeutic work to be more effective when my clients feel some sort of connection with me, so I am looking for ways Ruth and I can connect. For example, even though I grew up in a very liberal family, I am also a "PK," or "preacher's kid." What about Ruth can I empathically understand? I understand the pull women feel to put the needs of their families first. I am concerned about showing positive regard for Ruth, especially given the context of her critical family of origin and her current self-loathing. Finally, I am interested in modeling congruence for her as she learns to develop her own sense of congruence about her life and about what matters to her. These aspects of relationship building, which are derived from person-centered therapy, all have a strong evidence base in the literature.[9]

❧ Assessing Ruth's Concerns and Contexts   Ruth and I engage in a period of psychoeducation in which we explore her feelings and experiences about counseling. I attempt to dispel any myths, such as that counseling is a magical cure that works overnight. We discuss the work and processes of change and related ethical issues about confidentiality, informed consent, and privacy. I provide Ruth with written documents describing these ethical issues. I explain the process of therapy and describe something about my approach to assessment. I conduct a thorough intake interview using the ADDRESSING framework to obtain information about her cultural history and influences as well, and in Ruth's case I use the SCID-DSM-IV to help me develop reliable Axis I clinical diagnoses. I note the strong influence of Ruth's religious faith and the strong influence of her gender identification. I also note the potential influence of her age and developmental status (approaching midlife or age 40), and although I note she is married, I am careful not to make any initial assumptions about her sexual orientation. Ruth and I then engage in a behaviorally oriented clinical interview in which she and I work together to understand the functional relationships among the issues that brought her to counseling.

Here is a portion of that interview:

THERAPIST: Ruth, from what you have been telling me, part of what brings you into the counseling room are your feelings of panic, which you describe as intensifying over the last 2 years. Can you tell me a little more about this panic? What do you experience when you have these panicky feelings?

RUTH: Well, I really notice my breath. I feel anxious, and then it feels like it is very hard to breathe. I also get very flushed and feel hot, and sometimes I sweat so much that I think someone else may notice this too. I also often feel lightheaded, almost dizzy, I guess. Sometimes my body feels shaky and my heart starts beating so fast.

THERAPIST: That is such a great description of your panicky feelings. Do you *feel* anything else when this happens other than just panicky?

RUTH: Well, come to think about it, I often now wake up in the night with panic, and I feel some sense of impending doom.

THERAPIST: OK. When you have these feelings, can you identify what you might be thinking about?

RUTH: Oh yeah, I think a lot of it has to do with guilt over my parenting, which I don't think has been that great. I have thoughts about losing people, about either my own dying or having people I love die. I worry about something bad happening to them. At the same time, I worry that something is wrong with me.

THERAPIST: Ruth, I am really impressed with how clearly you are able to describe what your experience of this panic is! Often, when people do experience panic, they feel as if they are going crazy or even dying. In fact, it is really these bodily sensations you are noticing. These sensations become associated with a heightened sense of threat or danger and then you kind of feel panicked about that too! All in all, it makes for some challenging experiences that I imagine feel quite uncomfortable for you. Have you noticed whether these panicky feelings occur randomly or at certain times or in certain places?

RUTH: Actually, my panic attacks seemed to start about 2 years ago when I went to college. I was an older student, about 37 at the time, and I felt out of place. I would often experience anxiety when I was in class. Sometimes I think that is why I am afraid to take a substitute teaching job I have been offered, because I am worried that I will be panicky in front of the kids and maybe even have to leave the classroom.

THERAPIST: Wow. You are even able to link the panicky feelings with your reluctance to take this teaching job. What a great connection you are making. Now that you have completed your degree, have the panic attacks lessened or stopped, or are they still ongoing, and if so, when?

RUTH: It's interesting. Now, when I get panic attacks, it is mostly at night. I wake up with them.

THERAPIST: OK. How has this affected your sleep? You did mention earlier feeling fairly fatigued during the daytime and noticing some lack of energy.

RUTH: Well, once this happens during the night, I tend to stay awake for a while. I guess I obsess over things. Then I do feel tired during the day. Maybe that is another reason I am overweight. I eat because I feel so tired, and it makes me feel better to eat. I would like to join a gym, but I just don't know if I have the energy to go workout. Maybe it would be a big waste of money.

THERAPIST: OK, Ruth, you have told me a great deal there. One concern is about staying awake and dwelling on things. When this happens, what kinds of things are going through your mind?

RUTH: Mainly things I feel guilty about. I was raised strictly. My father is a preacher at a fundamentalist church, and about 9 years ago I decided that wasn't me, so I broke from that denomination. I still go to church regularly, but it is not the church of my parents. Then I worry about not having done a good enough job with my kids. Two of them are ready to leave home. I have some conflict with my eldest daughter, Jennifer, who is now 18. My relationship with my husband does not feel that great to me. We have lost our closeness. I feel isolated and alone much of the time. And other than wanting to be an elementary school teacher, I don't know what I want to do in life.

THERAPIST: I have the sense you have been holding on to some of these things a lot and have not found a good listener for your concerns. I hope that is one of the things that can happen with me. What kind of a social support system do you have outside of your family and church?

RUTH: Well, not much of one. I am sort of disengaged from my parents, although I am pretty close to my younger brothers and sisters because I helped raise them. I don't really have a lot of friends of my own.

THERAPIST: Do you have any hobbies or activities or clubs or groups you belong to or anything like that?

RUTH: Not really now. I used to write poetry in high school, but then I got married at 19 and was pregnant at 20, and then the kids came along really quickly, and I was very absorbed in all of that.

THERAPIST: I have a couple more questions about the panicky feelings, and then we can wrap up for today. How often do you have the panic, say, in a day or night, and when it happens, how long does it last?

RUTH: I wake up at least once a night, sometimes twice; again, more so now at night rather than during the day because I am not in class anymore. When I was in class, I could get these attacks as often as three or four times a day. During the day the panic attacks last about a minute. The night ones are not as often, but seem to last longer, maybe an hour, perhaps because it is dark and quiet and my mind gets so active.

Process Commentary

After completing the behavioral assessment interview, I give Ruth an opportunity to complete the OQ-45, which assesses for symptom distress, interpersonal relations, and social role. I also use the Anxiety Sensitivity Index (ASI), which helps to discriminate between panic disorder and other kinds of anxiety disorders.[10] I explain to Ruth that these measures help me get more quantitative information about her general level of distress and about her panic. I also explain that I will be asking her to complete these same two measures again at successive points during the counseling process. I ensure that any client presenting with panic has a complete medical evaluation, and Ruth's medical findings are negative. Finally, I ask Ruth to keep a self-monitoring log in which she observes and notes triggers for her panic attacks between sessions, rating her panic level on a 1–10 scale, and describing the symptoms, thoughts, and behaviors she experienced during the panic. I explain to Ruth how important collecting this information is and that I will be asking her to do more self-monitoring at later points in the therapy process as well. Self-monitoring is an evidence-based behavioral intervention that is part of a larger intervention process known as self-management or self-directed change. Self-monitoring is used by behavior therapists to help gather information for the behavioral analysis and to help formulate functional diagnoses and hypotheses about the client's issues.

My Conceptualization of Ruth's Presenting Issues and Concerns   Based on my assessment, I would give Ruth the following DMS-IV-TR multiaxial diagnoses:

Axis I: 300.01 Panic without agoraphobia
       313.82 Identity problem
       V62.89 Phase of life problem

Axis II: none

Axis III: medical conditions ruled out, although weight gain, sleep disturbances, and somatic symptoms associated with panic noted

Axis IV: relationship issues with parents, husband, children, especially eldest daughter; lack of social support

Axis V: (GAF score) 55

Conceptualizing Ruth's Case   I see three issues for Ruth: identity, stage or phase of life, and panic. From Ruth's perspective, the bottom is dropping out of her life. Her former identity and clearly defined roles of wife and mother no longer seem as useful or necessary. She does not know who she is if she is not useful or important as a mother and a wife. She has not yet made the transition to other roles in her life that may be purposeful or meaningful to her. This is augmented by her concurrent phase of life issue. She is nearing 40 and anticipating an empty nest when her children leave home. Her relationship with her spouse has become less vital. I think her panic attacks, which began 2 years ago, are related to both the identity and phase of life issues. Often people who have never had panic attacks begin having them when they undergo some significant change or life transition, or when they experience a significant loss.

My behavioral analysis of Ruth's panic attacks based on the various assessment methods employed is as follows:

Topography: rapid heartbeat, shortness of breath, sweating, feeling very hot, feeling shaky; average is once or twice, currently usually at night, upon abrupt awakening, these last for a hour or so while she tries to get back to sleep

Situational antecedents: classroom experiences (which are almost nonexistent now) and being asleep at night (nocturnal panic)

Internal antecedents: heart palpitations, lightheadedness and dizziness, faint feelings, worries about death and dying, thoughts of not being a good enough daughter, wife, or mother

Misappraisals: fear that something is radically wrong with her for feeling this way, that she is going crazy and that others, especially in the classroom, will notice the shakiness and think something is wrong with her

Behavioral reactions: escape behaviors such as avoiding taking a substitute teaching job due to the prior classroom episodes, and having difficulty "turning off her mind" at night in order to go back to sleep

Consequences: daytime fatigue that prevents her from working out or exercising and also promotes overeating, and staying at home more and feeling as though she has to push herself to leave the house; not following up on obtaining a job in her degree field; no social support network; headaches, feels blue, and has some daytime crying spells

Personal and environmental strengths: strong faith perspective, good communication and awareness skills (as evidenced in the behavioral interview), the capacity to write poetry, and relatively good relationships with her siblings

I share my conceptualization with Ruth as psychoeducation, which is an important tool in behavior therapy. Also, because I believe therapy is a shared, collaborative process, I want Ruth's perspective on how I see things as well.

🐾 Identification and Definition of Goals   Assuming Ruth and I agree on the conceptualization of her issues, we then identify and define targets of change or outcome goals. These represent what Ruth seeks from counseling.

THERAPIST: Ruth, since we have talked rather extensively about your issues and how they are connected and how they affect you and your life, let's discuss today how you would like your life to be different as a result of counseling. What changes would you like to see happen in your life?

RUTH: To be truthful, I am not quite sure. I guess I was hoping you could tell me what to change.

THERAPIST: Change is a very personal thing. The reason I am bringing this into the room today is to make sure what we do in counseling together is useful and relevant to you. Let me ask you this in a different way. Suppose a distant relative you haven't seen for a while sees you after you finish your counseling. What would be different then from the way things are now?

RUTH: Well, for one thing, eventually I would like to be employed outside the home as some sort of an elementary school teacher. Also,

I would like to have a much closer relationship with my husband than I do now. I guess related to all this is just having some greater sense of direction for my life. Finally, I think I would just like to feel more peaceful about things, not to be so guilt ridden and worried about things in the past, and less panicky. If these can happen, I feel like I would have some kind of a life I don't have now.

THERAPIST: You have really identified some very specific changes you would like to make: getting a paid job outside the home, improving your relationship with your husband, having a greater sense of direction for your life, feeling less worried and panicky, and being more peaceful. Can you rank these changes in the order of their importance to you?

RUTH: They are all important to me, but I guess if I could feel more peaceful and less worried and anxious then some of the other things might be easier to tackle after that. These panic episodes I have at night and the ones I used to have in class are distressing to me.

THERAPIST: Once again, Ruth, you are demonstrating such important insights. I concur with your take on that. I think that is a great place for us to start, and I would like to move forward with your participation in defining this particular goal more concretely. We will talk about possible action steps we can take together to help you reduce your worry and panic and increase your peacefulness. How does this sound to you?

⚡ Selecting and Implementing Evidence-Based Interventions and Evaluating Progress Toward Goals

I now have an idea of how and where to start working with Ruth on our action plan. Ruth has a number of treatment goals; she has prioritized them as reducing her worry and panic symptoms first and increasing a sense of direction for her life next. I describe each of Ruth's goals and the intervention strategies I recommend in the following sample treatment plan. For additional information about these interventions, see *Interviewing and Change Strategies for Helpers*.[11]

Goal One: Panic Reduction

Ruth and I begin by stating the goal for panic reduction and reviewing the ways in which we will measure progress toward this goal: her scores on the Anxiety Sensitivity Index (ASI) and the Outcome Questionnaire (OQ-45), as well as her daily self-monitoring of the intensity, frequency, and duration of the panic episodes she experiences. The measures of efficacy are important because they allow me to ascertain whether and how well the interventions are working with Ruth. When one intervention does not work well, it is time to try another. Not every intervention works equally well for all clients, as many variables can affect effectiveness. Next, Ruth and I discuss possible interventions to deal with her panic attacks including progressive muscle relaxation, cognitive restructuring, and interoceptive exposure. Providing a rationale for the interventions, describing their role in panic reduction, and obtaining Ruth's agreement are important at this point in the therapy process.

Progressive Muscle Relaxation I begin this phase of counseling with a relaxation intervention in which I teach Ruth the fundamentals of progressive muscle relaxation (PMR), an evidence-based intervention that helps her discriminate between sensations of tensing and then relaxing various muscle groups in her body. I like to start this early on because it will provide Ruth with an increased sense of mastery and control, which has been missing from her experience given the panic episodes. I assign Ruth homework to practice PMR on her own on a daily basis between counseling sessions. After the PMR, I readminister the ASI and the OQ-45 and ask Ruth to continue self-monitoring the intensity, frequency, and duration of panic.

Cognitive Restructuring PMR has been useful in reducing Ruth's experience of panic, and I next introduce cognitive restructuring (CR). Sometimes also referred to as "cognitive replacement," this intervention has its roots in the elimination of distorted or invalid inferences, disputation of self-defeating thoughts or beliefs, and the development of new, more adaptive coping thoughts and self-statements. In working with panic, CR is useful because it helps to target Ruth's misappraisals of her bodily sensations that lead her to believe she is going crazy or dying. CR is not a primary intervention for decreasing her panic directly but helps her correct her distorted thinking, thereby helping panic to eventually subside. After teaching Ruth the elements of CR in the sessions, I give her a homework log that she uses between sessions to self-observe and record the following categories when she is experiencing panic/worry and bodily sensations of panic: Date/Time, Situation, Automatic Thought, Emotion, Adaptive Response, and Outcome.[12] Subsequently, Ruth takes the ASI and the OQ-45 again and continues to self-monitor the intensity, frequency, and duration of her panic.

Interoceptive Exposure Next I introduce interoceptive exposure, a standard, evidence-based component of treatment for panic today. Interoceptive exposure is particularly useful in outpatient settings and is designed to intentionally induce the feared physical sensations enough times and with enough duration to help Ruth disconfirm her misappraisals of the bodily sensations of panic and to help her extinguish conditioned anxiety responses. Implementation of interoceptive exposure occurs using a graduated hierarchy of a standard set of activities. As Ruth goes through this exposure, she learns that these distressing sensations in and of themselves are not really harmful and that the accompanying anxiety they engender can be tolerated. After each activity in the exposure, I repeat the PMR and CR. I also ask Ruth to practice each interoceptive exposure activity we have done in the session as homework. At the conclusion of interoceptive exposure, I ask Ruth to take the ASI and the OQ-45 again, and I examine these scores along with her self-monitoring data to ascertain her progress toward her goal. Once I have reviewed the data, I may refer Ruth to her physician because a serotonergic drug can enhance recovery from panic.

Goal Two: Identity, Phase of Life, and Unemployment

Now that Ruth has made some progress toward her first goal, we begin interventions designed to help her with her second goal, which addresses the role identity confusion and unemployment issue. I recommend bibliotherapy for Ruth, and I particularly suggest two books: *A Woman's Book of Life* (Borysenko)[13] and *Cognitive Behavior Therapy: Basics and Beyond* (Beck).[14] Bibliotherapy is cost-effective for the client because it introduces Ruth to concepts that would take a lot of time to teach during counseling sessions. In addition, bibliotherapy for suitable clients can make the therapy conversations much richer.

Bibliotherapy and Group and Social Support Interventions   In *A Woman's Book of Life* Ruth learns about the concept of codependence and how her excessive caretaking of her husband and children have stunted her own growth and development. While she is reading this book, I recommend that she participate in a Codependents Anonymous group, which reinforces the new learning and provides her with an opportunity to increase her social support network of other adults outside of the home and family setting. I use the framework in *Cognitive Behavior Therapy: Basics and Beyond* to help Ruth explore and understand from a developmental point of view the particular challenges such as rebalancing priorities, revisiting intimate relationships, and emotional healing work that are faced by women in her late-thirties age group.

Shaping and Self-Efficacy   As we integrate these concepts into counseling, I use shaping (successive approximations toward a desired outcome) to help Ruth identify and develop ways in which she can utilize her teaching degree for pay outside the home. We start with small steps in which she might do some voluntary or paid tutoring of a particular student or two and work up to gradually getting paid employment as first a substitute or part-time teacher and later acquiring a full-time teaching position. Shaping is a behavioral tool that helps clients build self-efficacy. I readminister the OQ-45 and, as an additional efficacy measure, I ask Ruth to self-monitor the number of social support networks she uses and her employment-related activities and hours.

Preparation for Referral, Termination, Relapse Prevention, and Follow-Up   Ruth's final issue involves marital dissatisfaction. Again, noting her life developmental stage as part of my cultural assessment, I remember that divorce rates peak at about age 30 for women but continue at a high rate during this decade. I refer Ruth and her husband to several competent couples counselors, whom they can select among. This referral involves preparation and psychoeducation on my part to help Ruth understand the reason for the referral and the role marital counseling might play in her overall treatment progress. I see Ruth and her husband conjointly for one session as Dr. Lazarus did, but I am very clear with both of them that Ruth's husband is a collateral rather than a client: that is, he is there to assist in the assessment and treatment of Ruth. Ruth's husband signs a separate consent form indicating the limits of this role and the limits to my relationship with him. I would not take on Ruth and her husband as marital clients while I am also counseling Ruth individually because the goals of marital and individual counseling sometimes conflict, and this can create issues in the therapeutic relationship with my individual client.

Once the efficacy measures suggest that Ruth is well on her way to achieving her goals, I introduce the topic of termination for Ruth, as she has not already hinted at it herself, which many clients do. I emphasize self-efficacy, giving Ruth important credit and confidence for the changes she has made, and I discuss relapse prevention. I explain that the process of change is not always linear and external and that internal stressors may cause shifts in a backward direction. As Ruth prepares for termination from counseling, she and I together identify potentially high-risk situations for relapse from her goals, reinforce coping skills she has learned to work with such situations, and focus once more on issues of life balance and self-care.

Concluding Commentary

I practice behavior therapy within the context of a person-centered, feminist, and multicultural/ecological mind-set. Behavior therapy requires training, dedication, expertise, and due diligence, but the results that can be achieved are very rewarding. I receive a great deal of satisfaction from seeing a client like Ruth make changes to create a more fulfilling life for herself. I recognize that behavior therapy has many specific features and interventions that have contributed to Ruth's progress, but I am equally aware of the contribution to change of more "common factors" such as the healing therapeutic relationship that Ruth and I have experienced together.

Jerry Corey's Work With Ruth From a Behavioral Perspective

In the *DVD for Integrative Counseling: The Case of Ruth and Lecturettes,* Session 8 ("Behavioral Focus in Counseling"), I demonstrate a behavioral way to assist Ruth in developing an exercise program. It is crucial that Ruth make her own decisions about specific behavioral goals she wants to pursue. This applies to my attempts to work with her in developing methods of relaxation, practicing assertive skills, and designing an exercise plan.

Basic Assumption

A basic assumption of the behavioral approach is that therapy is best conducted in a systematic manner. Although behavior therapy includes a variety of principles and therapeutic procedures, its common denominator is a commitment to objectivity and evaluation.

Assessment of Ruth

I very much like beginning with a general assessment of a client's current functioning. This assessment begins with the intake session and continues during the next session if necessary.

Ruth and I come up with two problem areas on which she wants to focus. First, she feels tense to the point of panic much of the time and wants to learn ways to relax. Second, from the standpoint of her interpersonal relationships, she does not have the skills to ask for what she wants from others, she has trouble expressing her viewpoints clearly, and she often accepts projects she does not want to get involved in.

Goals of Therapy

The general goal of behavior therapy is to create new conditions for learning. I view Ruth's problems as related to faulty learning. The assumption underlying our therapy is that learning experiences can ameliorate problem behaviors. Much of our therapy will involve correcting faulty cognitions, acquiring social and interpersonal skills, and learning techniques of self-management so that she can become her own therapist. Based on my initial assessment of her and on another session in which she and I discuss the matter of setting concrete and objective goals, we establish the following goals to guide the therapeutic process:

- Learn and practice methods of relaxation
- Learn to manage stress effectively
- Learn assertion training principles and skills

Therapeutic Procedures

Behavior therapy is a pragmatic approach, and I am concerned that the treatment procedures be effective. I will draw on various cognitive and behavioral techniques to help Ruth reach her stated goals. If she does not make progress, I must assume much of the responsibility because it is my task to select appropriate treatment procedures and use them well. As a behavior therapist, I am continually evaluating the results of the therapeutic process to determine which approaches are working. Ruth's feedback in this area is important. I will ask her to keep records of her daily behavior, and I will encourage her to become active to accomplish her goals, including working outside the session.

Our therapy will be relatively brief, for my main function is to teach Ruth skills she can use in solving her problems and living more effectively. My ultimate goal is to teach her to become her own therapist. This I will do through a variety of psychoeducational methods that she can practice in daily living. For example, to manage her stress more effectively, I suggest that she read Jon Kabat-Zinn's book, *Full Catastrophe Living: Using the Wisdom of Your Body and Mind to Face Stress, Pain, and Illness.*[15] I also encourage her to purchase Kabat-Zinn's audiotapes as a way for her to practice mindfulness-based stress reduction.

The Therapeutic Process

ELEMENTS OF THE PROCESS The therapeutic process begins with gathering baseline data on the specific goals Ruth has selected. In her case much of the therapy will consist of learning how to effectively manage stress and how to be assertive in situations calling for this behavior.

Learning Stress Management Techniques Ruth indicates that one of her priorities is to cope with tensions more effectively. I ask her to list all the specific areas that she finds stressful, and I discuss with her how her own expectations and her self-talk are contributing to her stress. We then develop a program to reduce unnecessary strain and to deal more effectively with the inevitable stresses of daily life.

RUTH: You asked me what I find stressful. There are so many things. I feel as if I'm always rushing and never accomplishing what I should. I feel pressured much of the time.

JERRY: List some specific situations that bring on stress. Then maybe we can come up with some strategies for alleviating it.

RUTH: Trying to keep up with my schoolwork and with the many demands at home at the same time. Dealing with Jennifer's anger and defiance. Trying to live up to John's expectations. Getting involved in way too many community activities and projects and then not having time to complete them. Feeling pressured to complete my education. Worrying that I won't be able to find a good teaching job once I get my credential.

JERRY: I can see why you feel overwhelmed. We can't address all of them at once. I'd like to hear more about what being in these stressful situations is like for you. Tell me about one of these situations, and describe what you feel in your body, what you're thinking at the time, and what you actually do in these times of stress. [*I want to get a concrete sense of how she experiences her stress, what factors bring it about, and how she attempts to cope with it.*]

RUTH: Well, I often feel that I wear many hats—I just have so many roles to perform, and there's never enough time to do all that's needed. I lie awake at night and ruminate about the things I should be doing. It's hard for me to go to sleep, and then I wake up in the morning feeling tired. Then it's even harder for me to face the day.

JERRY: Earlier you mentioned that you have panic attacks, especially at night. I'd like to teach you some simple ways to use the relaxation response just before you go into a full-scale attack. You'll need to identify the cues that appear before a panic attack. I'd then like to teach you some simple and effective relaxation methods. Instead of wasting time lying there trying to sleep, you could practice a few exercises. It's important that you practice these self-relaxation exercises every day, for 20 minutes.

RUTH: I'm afraid I won't do it successfully.

JERRY: That depends on how you approach it.

We talk at some length because I am afraid Ruth will make this practice a chore rather than something she can do for herself and enjoy. She finally sees that it does not have to be a task that she does perfectly but is a means of making life easier for her. I teach her how to concentrate on her breathing and how to do some visualization techniques, such as imagining a very pleasant and peaceful scene. Then, following the guidelines described in Herbert Benson's book, *The Relaxation Response,* I provide her with these instructions:[16]

JERRY: Find a quiet and calm environment with as few distractions
as possible. Sit comfortably in a chair and adopt a passive attitude.
Rather than worry about performing the technique, simply let go of all
thoughts. Repeating a mantra, such as the word "om," is helpful. With
your eyes closed, deeply relax all your muscles, beginning with your
feet and progressing up to your face. Relax and breathe.

A week later, Ruth reports on how difficult it was to let go and relax.

RUTH: I didn't do well at all. I did practice every day, and it wasn't as difficult as I thought. But it's hard for me to find a quiet place to relax. I
was called to the phone several times, and then another time my kids
wanted me for something. Even when I wasn't disturbed, I found my
mind wandering, and it was hard to just get into the sensations of feeling tension and relaxation in my body.

JERRY: I hope you won't give up. This is a skill, and like any skill it will
take time to learn. But it's essential that you block off 20 minutes in a
quiet place without disturbances to practice.

Ruth and I discuss how difficult it is for her to have this time for herself.
I reinforce the point that this is also an opportunity to practice asking others
for what she wants and seeing to it that she gets it. Thus she can work toward
another of her goals: being able to ask for what she wants.

Learning How to Say No   Ruth tells me that she gives to everyone but
finds it difficult to ask anything for herself. We have been working on the latter
issue, with some success. Ruth informs me that she does not know how to say
no to people when they ask her to get involved in a project, especially if they tell
her that they need her. She wants to talk about her father, especially the ways
in which she thinks he has caused her lack of assertiveness. I ask her to recall
a recent time when she found it difficult to say no and to describe that scene.

RUTH: Last week my son Adam came to me late at night to type his term
paper. I didn't feel like it at all because I had had a long and hard day,
and besides, it was almost midnight. At first I told him I wasn't going
to do it. Then he got huffy, and I finally gave in. What could I do?

JERRY: You could have done many things. Can you come up with some
alternatives?

I want Ruth to search for alternative behaviors to saying yes when it is clear
that she wants to say no. She does come up with other strategies, and we talk
about the possible consequences of each approach. Then I suggest some behavioral role playing. First, I play the role of Adam, and she tries several approaches
other than giving in and typing the paper. Her performance is a bit weak, so
I suggest that she play Adam's role, and I demonstrate at least another alternative. I want to demonstrate, by direct modeling, some behaviors she does not
use, and I hope that she will practice them.

As the weeks progress, there are many opportunities for Ruth to practice a
few of the assertive skills she is learning. Then she runs into a stumbling block.

A PTA group wants her to be its president. Although she enjoys her membership in the group, she is sure that she does not want the responsibilities involved in being the president. In her session she says she doesn't know how to turn the group down, especially since no one else seems available.

We again work on this problem by using role-playing techniques. I play the role of the people pressuring her to accept the presidency, and I use every trick I know, including her guilt. I tell her how efficient she is, how we are counting on her, how we know that she won't let us down, and so on. We stop at critical points and talk about the hesitation in her voice, the guilty look on her face, and her habit of giving reasons to justify her position. I also talk with her about what her body posture is communicating. Then we systematically work on each element of her presentation. Paying attention to her choice of words, her quality of voice, and her style of delivery, we study how she might persuasively say no without feeling guilty later. As a homework assignment, I ask her to read selected chapters of the book *Your Perfect Right*, by Alberti and Emmons.[17] There are useful ideas in this book that she can think about and practice between our sessions.

The next week we talk about what she has learned in the book, and we do some cognitive work. I especially talk with her about what she tells herself in these situations that gets her into trouble. In addition to these cognitive techniques, I continue to teach Ruth assertive behaviors by using role playing, behavioral rehearsals, coaching, and practice.

PROCESS COMMENTARY In this approach Ruth is clearly the person who decides what she wants to work on and what she wants to change. She makes progress toward her self-defined goals because she is willing to become actively involved in challenging her assumptions and in carrying out behavioral exercises, both in the sessions and in her daily life. For example, she is disciplined enough to practice the relaxation exercises she has learned from her reading and our sessions. She learns how to ask for what she wants and to refuse those requests that she does not want to meet, not only by making resolutions but also by regularly keeping a record of the social situations in which she was not as assertive as she would have liked to be. She takes risks by practicing in everyday situations those assertive skills she has acquired in our therapy sessions. Although I help her learn how to change, she is the one who actually chooses to apply these skills, thus making change possible.

Some Final Thoughts

One of the strengths of the behavioral approach is the comprehensive assessment of clients (as in Dr. Lazarus's multimodal approach), which assists clients in identifying personal goals and helps therapists conceptualize an appropriate treatment plan to help clients reach their goals. Behavior therapy precisely specifies goals, target behaviors, and therapy procedures—all defined in unambiguous and measurable terms. This specificity enables assessment, treatment, and evaluation strategies to be linked into a comprehensive plan. Behavioral practitioners often develop techniques and strategies from diverse theoretical viewpoints, yet these methods have some empirical support. As can be seen in Dr. Cormier's work with Ruth, behavior therapists follow the progress of their clients through the ongoing collection of data before, during, and after all interventions. Such a systematic approach provides both the clinician and the client with continuous feedback about therapeutic progress. Practitioners from any orientation can profit from drawing on behavioral interventions and incorporating them in their clinical practice.

Questions for Reflection

1. What are your thoughts about Dr. Lazarus's multimodal approach to assessment as a way to begin therapy? How does Dr. Cormier's approach to assessment differ from Lazarus's?
2. What are some of the features you like best about Dr. Lazarus's approach? About Dr. Cormier's approach? About my approach in working with Ruth? What are some of the basic similarities in these three behavioral approaches? What are some basic differences? How might you have proceeded differently, still working within this model, in terms of what you know about Ruth?
3. What is your reaction to my attempt to get Ruth out of therapy as fast as possible so that she can apply self-management skills on her own? What skills can you think of to teach her so that she can be more self-directed?
4. What are your reactions to the manner in which Dr. Lazarus conducted the conjoint session with Ruth and John? If you were conducting such a behaviorally oriented session, what homework might you suggest to them as a couple? Do you have any suggestions for specific behavioral assignments for each individual?
5. Dr. Cormier prepares Ruth for referral, termination, relapse prevention, and follow-up. What can you learn from this that you could apply to your work with a client?
6. Dr. Cormier suggests homework assignments for Ruth and encourages her to monitor her progress with out-of-session assignments. What is one example of homework you might suggest to Ruth? If Ruth told you she had not kept her agreement in completing her assignments, how would you go forward?
7. In her work with Ruth, Dr. Cormier selects and uses evidence-based interventions and evaluates Ruth's progress. What can you learn about evidence-based practices that you can apply to working with clients, whether or not you are a behavior therapist?
8. How would you evaluate Ruth's progress if you were her behavioral therapist?
9. Using other behavioral techniques, show how you might proceed with Ruth if you were working with her. Use whatever you know about her so far and what you know about behavior therapy approaches to show in what directions you would move with her.
10. How well does the behavioral approach fit with your counseling style? What aspects of this approach do you find most useful? Which aspects might you want to modify to fit your personal counseling style?

Notes

See the *DVD for Theory and Practice of Counseling and Psychotherapy: The Case of Stan and Lecturettes*, Session 7 ("Behavior Therapy Applied to the Case of Stan"), which provides an illustration of how homework and behavioral rehearsals can be used to promote assertive behavior, and for my presentation of ways that behavior therapy can be applied.

1. For detailed information on the Multimodal Life History Inventory, see Lazarus, A. A., & Lazarus, C. N. (2005). The multimodal life-history inventory. In G. P. Koocher, J. C. Norcross, & S. S. Hill III (Eds.), *Psychologists' desk reference* (2nd ed., pp. 16–23). Oxford: Oxford University Press. This is a comprehensive inventory that allows for an assessment of a wide range of problems throughout the BASIC I.D.
2. See Lazarus, A. A., & Lazarus, C. N. (1997). *The 60-second shrink: 101 strategies for staying sane in a crazy world.* Atascadero, CA: Impact Publishers; see also Lazarus, A. A. (2001). *Marital myths revisited: A fresh look at two dozen mistaken beliefs about marriage.* Atascadero, CA: Impact Publishers.
3. For a more detailed description of the BASIC I.D., see Lazarus, A. A. (1997). *Brief but comprehensive psychotherapy: The multimodal way.* New York: Springer.
4. For an overview of multimodal therapy, see Corey, G. (2013). *Theory and practice of counseling and psychotherapy* (9th ed.). Belmont, CA: Brooks/Cole, Cengage Learning. Chapter 9 ("Behavior Therapy") describes the unique features of multimodal therapy as an assessment and treatment approach.
5. Hayes, P. (2001). *Addressing cultural complexities in practice: A framework for clinicians and counselors.* Washington, DC: American Psychological Association.
6. Spitzer, M. B., Gibbon, R. L. M., & Williams, J. B. W. (1997). *Structured clinical interview for Axis I disorders.* New York: New York State Psychiatric Institute.
7. Lambert, M., Hansen, N., Umphress, V., Lunnen, K., Okiishi, J., Burlingame, et al. (1996). *Administration and scoring manual for the outcome questionnaire (OQ45.2).* Wilmington, DE: American Professional Credentialing Services.
8. Bandura, A. (1997). *Self-efficacy: The exercise of self-control.* New York: Freeman.
9. Norcross, J. C. (2011). *Psychotherapy relationships that work: Evidence-based responsiveness* (2nd ed.). New York: Oxford University Press.
10. Reiss, S., Peterson, R., Gursky, D., & McNally, R. (1986). Anxiety sensitivity, anxiety frequency, and the prediction of fearfulness. *Behaviour Research and Therapy, 24,* 1–8.
11. Cormier, S., Nurius, P. S., & Osborn, C. J. (2013). *Interviewing strategies for helpers:* (7th ed.). Belmont, CA: Brooks/Cole, Cengage Learning.
12. Mellody, P. (1989). *Facing codependence.* San Francisco, CA: HarperSan Francisco.
13. Borysenko, J. (1996). *A woman's book of life: The biology, psychology, and spirituality of the feminine life cycle.* New York: Riverhead Books.
14. Beck, J. S. (2011). *Cognitive behavior therapy: Basics and beyond* (2nd ed.) New York: Guilford Press.

15. Refer to Kabat-Zinn, J. (1990). *Full catastrophe living: Using the wisdom of your body and mind to face stress, pain, and illness.* New York: Dell. This is a practical guide to mindfulness meditation and healing.

16. Refer to Benson, H. (1976). *The relaxation response.* New York: Avon. This is a readable and useful guide to developing simple meditative and other relaxation procedures.

17. Refer to Alberti, R. E, & Emmons, M. L. (2008). *Your perfect right: A guide to assertive behavior* (9th ed.). San Luis Obispo, CA: Impact Publishers. Therapy clients will learn about the principles and techniques of assertion training from this popular book.

CHAPTER EIGHT

Case Approach
to Cognitive
Behavior Therapy

General Overview of Cognitive Behavioral Approaches

Traditional behavior therapy has broadened and largely moved in the direction of cognitive behavior therapy and Eastern approaches such as mindfulness and acceptance. Cognitive behavior therapy (CBT), which combines both cognitive and behavioral principles and methods in a short-term treatment approach, has generated more empirical research than any other approach to psychotherapy.

Albert Ellis's rational emotive behavior therapy (REBT) was one of the earliest cognitive behavioral approaches and continues to be utilized by cognitive behavioral therapists today. Around the same time as Ellis was developing REBT, Aaron Beck was designing his cognitive therapy. Cognitive therapy (CT) has a number of similarities to both rational emotive behavior therapy and behavior therapy. These therapeutic approaches are active, directive, structured, time-limited, present-centered, problem-oriented, collaborative, and driven by research. Cognitive therapy (CT) perceives psychological problems as stemming from commonplace processes such as faulty thinking, making incorrect inferences on the basis of inadequate or incorrect information, and failing to distinguish between fantasy and reality. Like REBT, cognitive therapy emphasizes recognizing and changing negative thoughts and maladaptive beliefs. Thus both REBT and CT are psychoeducational models of therapy.

Cognitive therapy and the cognitive behavioral approaches are quite diverse, but they do share these attributes: (1) a collaborative relationship between client and therapist, (2) the assumption that psychological problems are mainly a function of disturbances in cognitive processes, (3) a focus on changing cognitions to produce desired changes in affect and behavior, (4) a present-centered and time-limited focus, (5) an emphasis on the client's responsibility for assuming an active role in the therapy process, and (6) making use of a variety of cognitive and behavioral strategies to bring about change.

The goal of cognitive behavior therapy is to eliminate clients' self-defeating outlooks on life and assist them in acquiring more tolerant and rational views. Clients are taught how they incorporated self-defeating beliefs, how they are maintaining this faulty thinking, what they can do to undermine such thinking, and how they can teach themselves new ways of thinking that will lead to changes in their ways of behaving and feeling.

Typically, REBT practitioners use a variety of cognitive, affective, and behavioral techniques. Procedures are designed to get clients to critically examine present beliefs and behavior. Cognitive methods include disputing faulty beliefs, carrying out cognitive homework, and changing one's language and thinking patterns. Emotive techniques include role playing, REBT imagery, and shame-attacking exercises. A wide range of active and practical behavioral procedures are used to get clients to be specific and committed to doing the hard work required by therapy. Cognitive behavioral approaches insist on client participation in homework assignments both during and outside the therapeutic sessions. Individuals will rarely change a self-defeating belief unless they are willing to act consistently against it.

Clients are ready to terminate when they no longer badger themselves with "shoulds," "oughts," and "musts," replace their faulty and self-destructive beliefs with rational and constructive ones, and translate those beliefs into behavioral change. Therapeutic outcomes can be evaluated by looking at the specific cognitive, affective, and behavioral changes demonstrated by the client.

A Rational Emotive Behavior Therapist's Perspective on Ruth

by Albert Ellis, PhD, ABPP

Introduction

REBT assumes that people like Ruth do not get disturbed by the unrealistic and illogical standards they learned (from their family and culture) during their childhood. Rather, they largely disturb themselves by the dogmatic, rigid "musts" and commands they creatively construct about these standards and values and about the unfortunate events that occur in their lives. Ruth is a good case in point. She has accepted some of the fundamentalist ideas of her parents, which many fundamentalist-reared children adopt without becoming disturbed. But Ruth rigidly insists that she has to follow them while simultaneously demanding that she must be herself and lead a self-fulfilling, independent existence. She could easily disturb herself with either of these contradictory commands. By devoutly holding both of them, she is really in trouble! As REBT shows, transmuting any legitimate goals and preferences into absolutist "musts" usually leads to self-denigration, rage, or self-pity. Ruth seems to have all of these disturbed feelings.[1]

Assessment of Ruth

Ruth has a number of goals and desires that most therapies, including REBT, would consider legitimate and healthy: the desire to have a stable marriage; to care for her family members; to be thinner and more attractive; to keep her parents' approval; to be a competent teacher; and to discover what she really wants to do in life and largely follow her personal bents. Even though some of these desires are somewhat contradictory, they would probably not get her into serious trouble if she held them as preferences because she could then make some compromises.

Ruth could choose to be *somewhat* devoted to her husband and children, and even to her parents, but also be determined to pursue a teaching career and to follow her own nonfundamentalist religious views and practices. She would then fail to lead a *perfectly* conflict-free and happy life but would hardly be in great turmoil. However, like practically all humans, Ruth has a strong (and probably partly innate) tendency to "sacredize" these important values. From early childhood onward, she rigidly concluded: "Because I want my parents' approval, I completely need it!" "Because I love my children, I have to be thoroughly devoted to them!" "Because I enjoy thinking for myself and doing my own thing, I have to do so at practically all times!" "Because I'd like to be thinner and more attractive, I've got to be!"

With grandiose, perfectionist fiats like these, Ruth's reasonable, often achievable, goals and standards are transmuted into absolutist "musts." She thereby almost inevitably *makes* herself—that's right, makes herself—panicked, depressed, indecisive, and often inert. Furthermore, when she sees that she feels emotionally upset and is not acting in her best interests, she irrationally upsets herself about that. She strongly—and foolishly—tells herself "I must not be panicked" instead of "I wish I were not panicking myself, but I am. Now how do I unpanic myself?" She then feels panicked about her panic. And she rigidly insists, "I have to be decisive and do my own thing." Then she feels like a worm about her worminess! This self-castigation about her symptoms makes her even more disturbed and less able to see exactly what she is thinking and doing to create these symptoms. As a rational emotive behavior therapist, I assess Ruth's problems and her belief system about these problems as follows.

Ruth asks certain questions that lead to practical problems:

- How much shall I do for others, and how much for myself?
- How can I exercise and keep on a diet?
- How can I be a teacher and still get along well with my husband?
- How can I get along with my parents and still not follow their fundamentalist views?
- How can I benefit from therapy and live with the things I may discover about myself when undergoing it?
- How can I be myself and not harm my husband and kids?

Ruth could sensibly answer these questions by telling herself these things:

- If I do more things for myself, people may not like me as much as I want them to. Too bad!

- Exercising and dieting are really difficult. But being fat and ugly is even more difficult.
- If I get a teaching job, I may antagonize my husband. But I can stand that and still be happy.
- My parents will never like my giving up fundamentalism, and that's sad. But it's not awful.
- If I find out unpleasant things about myself in therapy, that'll be tough. But I can also benefit from that discovery.
- Being myself at the expense of my husband and kids is somewhat selfish. But I have a right to a reasonable degree of self-interest.

Instead, Ruth holds these irrational beliefs that lead to unhealthy feelings of anxiety and depression and to self-defeating behaviors of indecision and inertia:

- I must not do more things for myself and dare not antagonize others.
- Exercise and dieting are too hard and shouldn't be that hard!
- If my husband hates my getting a teaching job, that would be awful!
- I can't stand my parents criticizing me if I give up fundamentalism.
- I would be a thoroughly rotten person if therapy revealed bad things about me!
- I must never be selfish, for if I am, I'm worthless.

Ruth also holds certain irrational beliefs that lead to secondary disturbances (panic about panic, depression about depression):

- I must not be panicked!
- It's terrible if I'm depressed.
- I'm no good because I'm indecisive.

Key Issues and Themes

The key issues in most disturbed feelings and behaviors that I will look for are (1) self-deprecation, stemming from the irrational belief that "I must perform well and be approved of by significant others"; (2) the irrational insistence that "you [other people] must treat me kindly and considerately"; and (3) the irrational idea that "the conditions under which I live have to be comfortable and easy."

Ruth seems to have the first of these irrational beliefs because she keeps demanding that she be giving and lovable, that she be thin and beautiful, that she be a good daughter, that her "badness" not be uncovered in therapy, and that she make only good and proper decisions. With these perfectionist commands, she leads a self-deprecating, anxious existence. She also seems to have some unacknowledged irrational beliefs that her husband absolutely must not expect her to be herself, thus making her angry at him.

Finally, Ruth has low frustration tolerance and self-pity, resulting not from her desires but from her dire needs to lose weight without going to the trouble of dieting and exercising, to have a guarantee that she won't die, to have the security of marriage even though she has a boring relationship with her husband, to be sure that therapy will be comfortable, and to need a magical, God-will-take-care-of-me solution to her problems.

Because Ruth strongly holds the three basic irrational ideas (dogmatic "musts") that REBT finds at the root of most disturbances and because some of her demands—like those that she be herself *and* be quite self-sacrificial—are quite contradictory, I imagine that she will be a difficult customer and will require intensive therapy. Within a few sessions, however, she may be able to understand some of her *musts* and *demands* and start reducing them. Because she has already taken some big risks and worked at changing herself, I predict a good prognosis despite her strong tendency to create self-defeating beliefs.

Applying Therapeutic Techniques

REBT invariably includes a number of cognitive, emotive, and behavioral methods.[2] As I work with Ruth, I use these main methods.

ꙮ Cognitive Techniques of REBT

I show Ruth how to discover her rational preferences and distinguish them from her irrational "musts" and demands. Then I teach her how to scientifically dispute these demands and change them back into appropriate preferences. I encourage her to create some rational coping statements and inculcate them many times into her philosophy; for example, "I want to be a caring mother and wife, but I also have the right to care for myself." I help her do REBT *"referenting"*—that is, making a list of the disadvantages of overeating and nondieting and thinking about them several times a day. I also have her do reframing to see that losing some of her husband's and children's love has its good as well as its bad sides. I encourage her to use some of REBT's psychoeducational adjuncts: books, pamphlets, cassettes, lectures, and workshops. I show her the advantages of teaching REBT to others, such as to her husband, children, and pupils, so that she will better learn it herself. I discuss with her the advantages of creating for herself a vital, absorbing interest in some long-range project, such as helping other people guiltlessly give up their parental fundamentalist teachings.

Here is one way I may work with Ruth to implement the cognitive technique of helping her dispute her irrational beliefs.

RUTH: Because I love my children, I have to be thoroughly devoted to them.

THERAPIST: That's an interesting conclusion, but how does it follow from the observation, which I assume is true, that you really do love your children?

RUTH: Well, isn't it right and ethical to be kind and helpful to one's children?

THERAPIST: Of course it is. You brought them into the world without them asking to be born, and you'd be quite unethical and irresponsible if you didn't devote considerable time and energy to them. But why must you be ethical? What law of the universe says you always have to be?

RUTH: My own law says so—and that of many other people.

THERAPIST: Fine. But why do you have to always keep your own laws? Actually, do you?

RUTH: Well, no. Not always.

THERAPIST: And do other people always keep their ow
ture's laws?

RUTH: No, not always.

THERAPIST: So obviously, although it's highly desirable
you to care for your children, is it absolutely necessary that you do so?

RUTH: No, I guess not.

THERAPIST: But it still is highly desirable. What is the difference between something being preferable and desirable and being utterly
necessary?

RUTH: I see. Quite a difference!

THERAPIST: Right. And no matter how much you love them, do you
always have to be completely devoted to them?

RUTH: You're questioning my desire to be completely devoted?

THERAPIST: Yes, I am. How realistic would complete devotion be?

RUTH: Thoroughly unrealistic. I need time for other important things.

THERAPIST: So your dire need to be completely devoted to your children and also to your husband doesn't stem from your love for them,
doesn't follow from any law of the universe, and is impractical and
unrealistic. If you strongly believe you absolutely must be completely
devoted to your children, what results will you probably get?

RUTH: I'll feel very anxious about doing what I supposedly must do and
depressed in case I don't.

THERAPIST: Yes, your *mus*turbation probably won't work.

I can have this kind of active, directive dialogue with Ruth in one of her early
sessions and try to start her quickly on a new way of thinking about her
demandingness.

🐾 Emotive Techniques of REBT I will recommend that Ruth use some of
the main emotive, evocative, and dramatic methods that I have found effective
in REBT, such as these:

- She can forcefully and powerfully tell herself rational coping statements:
  "I do not (definitely not) need my parents' approval, though I would certainly prefer to have it!"
- She can tape a rigorous debate with herself, in which she actively disputes
  one of her irrational "musts." Then she can listen to her disputation and
  have some of her friends listen to it to see not only if its content is good
  but also if she is forceful enough.
- She can do rational emotive imagery, by imagining one of the worst things
  that could happen to her—for example, her father strongly berating her for
  her nonfundamentalist views. Then she can work on her feelings so that she
  first gets in touch with the horror and self-downing she unhealthily feels
  and then changes it to the healthy negative feelings of sorrow and regret.

can do some of the famous REBT shame-attacking exercises, whereby
~~~e publicly does something she considers shameful, foolish, or ridiculous
and works on herself not to feel ashamed and self-damning while doing it.

- She can learn to receive unconditional acceptance from me, no matter
  how badly she is behaving in and out of therapy. I can show her how to
  always—yes, always—accept herself, whether or not she does well.
- We can do role playing, where I play her irate father and she plays herself,
  to see how she can cope with his severe criticism. In the course of it we
  stop the role playing from time to time to see what she is telling herself to
  make herself anxious or depressed while reacting to my role-playing her
  father's criticism.
- We can practice reverse role playing, where I stick rigidly to some of her
  irrational beliefs and encourage her to argue me out of them.
- She can use humor to rip up her irrational beliefs, especially singing to
  herself some of my rational humorous songs.

In this session with Ruth, I use one of the emotive techniques of REBT.

THERAPIST: We've been disputing your irrational belief that because
you love your children you have to be completely devoted to them. You
could also use one of our popular emotional techniques, rational emotive imagery. Would you like me to show you how to use this exercise?

RUTH: Yes, I would.

THERAPIST: OK, close your eyes—just easily close them. Now vividly
imagine one of the worst things that could happen to you. Imagine
that you're not thoroughly devoted to your children—in fact, that
you're somewhat neglecting them. Vividly imagine that they're complaining about this and that your husband and your mother are also
chiding you severely for this neglect. Can you vividly imagine this
happening?

RUTH: Definitely. I can clearly picture it.

THERAPIST: Good. Now, how do you honestly feel in your gut and in
your heart? What is your honest feeling?

RUTH: Very guilty. Depressed. Self-critical.

THERAPIST: Good. Really get in touch with those negative feelings. Feel
them. Strongly feel them!

RUTH: I really feel them. Quite strongly.

THERAPIST: Good. Now, keeping the same image—don't change
it—make yourself feel only sorry and disappointed about what's
happening but not guilty, not depressed, not self-downing. Only
sorry and disappointed, which are healthy and appropriate negative
feelings, instead of guilty, depressed, and self-downing, which are
unhealthy negative feelings. You control your feelings, so you can
change them. So let me know when you're only feeling sorry and
disappointed.

RUTH: I'm having a hard time getting there.

THERAPIST: Yes, I know. But you can do it. You can definitely change your feelings. Anyone can.

RUTH [*After a pause of 2 minutes*]: I changed them.

THERAPIST: And now you feel only sorry and disappointed, not guilty or depressed?

RUTH: Yes, I do.

THERAPIST: Good! How did you change your feelings? What did you do to change them?

RUTH: I told myself "It's too bad that my children, my husband, and my mother are chiding me for neglecting the children, but I'm not sure I am being neglectful. Even if I am, that's bad, that's wrong of me, but that behavior doesn't make me a rotten person. I'll try to be less neglectful, while not being overly devoted to my children. But if I'm still criticized, it's just too bad—not the end of the world. I can take this criticism and still have a good life."

THERAPIST: Excellent! Now what I'd like to see you do is to help yourself by repeating this exercise every day for the next 20 or 30 days. Remember, it only took you about 2 minutes to change your unhealthy feelings of guilt and depression to healthy negative feelings of disappointment. So repeat this every day, using the same excellent coping statement you used this time or using several other similar coping statements that will occur to you if you keep doing this rational emotive imagery. If you do this, I think you'll see at the end of 10, 20, or 30 days, when you imagine this bad event with your children happening or when some other unfortunate activating event actually does occur, that you'll tend to feel automatically—yes, automatically—sorry and disappointed about your actions, but not damning your total self for doing this.

RUTH: You think that will really help me?

THERAPIST: Yes, I'm fairly sure it will. So will you try it to help yourself?

RUTH: Yes, I will.

THERAPIST: Great. Now, if you stop doing this exercise because you think it's too hard to continue it or something like that, you can always challenge your irrational belief that it must be easy and that you shouldn't have to do it to improve. You can also use reinforcement methods to encourage yourself to keep doing it.

RUTH: How do I do that?

THERAPIST: Very simply. What, for example, do you enjoy doing that you do practically every day of the week?

RUTH: Uh, reading.

THERAPIST: Fine. No reading, then, for the next 20 or 30 days, until after you do rational emotive imagery for the day and change your feelings of guilt and depression to those of disappointment. Is that OK?

RUTH: Yes, that's OK.

THERAPIST: And if that doesn't work, though it probably will, you can enact a penalty when you don't practice your rational emotive imagery.

RUTH: A penalty?

THERAPIST: Yes. For example, what do you hate doing—some task or chore that you usually avoid doing because you don't like it?

RUTH: Well, uh, cleaning the toilet.

THERAPIST: Good. If, during the next 30 days, your bedtime arrives and you haven't done your rational emotive imagery exercise, you can make yourself clean your toilet for an hour.

RUTH: That would work! I'm sure I'll do the exercise every day.

THERAPIST: Fine!

Rational emotive imagery, like several other REBT emotive techniques, can be taught to clients like Ruth and given as homework assignments, thus making therapy effective in a relatively brief period of time.

❧ Behavioral Techniques of REBT
As with virtually all REBT clients, I use several behavioral methods with Ruth, including these:

- I show her how to select and perform in vivo desensitization assignments, such as registering for education courses despite her anxiety about her family's disapproval.
- I encourage her to do what she is afraid to do—for example, to talk to her husband about her career goals many times until she loses her irrational fears of his disapproval.
- I encourage her to reinforce herself with some enjoyable pursuits, such as reading or music, only after she has completed her difficult-to-do homework. And if she is truly lax about doing it, I urge her sometimes to penalize (but never damn) herself with an unpleasant chore, such as getting up an hour earlier than usual.
- I plan with her and supervise her carrying out practical goals, such as arranging for help with her household tasks.
- If she starts getting over her emotional hang-ups but has skill deficiencies, I help her acquire missing skills, such as assertiveness, communicating well, or decision making.

All of these behavioral methods of REBT can be given as homework assignments to be used between sessions and checked on during the following session. Therefore, the length of therapy can be appreciably shortened for clients who do their homework and are monitored by the therapist.

In one session I show Ruth how to use one of REBT's action-oriented techniques.

RUTH: How will I deal with my panic and, as you say, my panic about panicking?

THERAPIST: Good question. First, let's deal with your panic about your panic. Because of this secondary symptom, you often avoid situations where you might panic, even though it would be good to participate in them. Right?

RUTH: Yes. I especially avoid seeing or talking to my father, who's critical of my handling of the children and almost everything else. So I rarely call him, and when he calls, I get my family members to say I'm out when I'm really not.

THERAPIST: That's a good example. When avoiding these calls, what are you telling yourself?

RUTH: If he criticizes me, I'll panic, and that would be awful!

THERAPIST: Right. But every time you avoid speaking to your father, you reinforce your anxiety about talking to him and being criticized. You tell yourself, "If I speak to him, I'll be very anxious." So you increase your anxiety!

RUTH: You're right about that. Whenever I even think of talking to him, I panic.

THERAPIST: So the first thing you can do is to say to yourself, many times and very strongly, "Panicking is very uncomfortable, but it is not horrible. It's only inconvenient."

RUTH: That will cure me?

THERAPIST: Not exactly, but it will help a lot. In addition, deliberately arrange to talk to your father more. Do, as we say in REBT, what you're afraid of doing. Act, as well as think, against your phobia of panicking.

RUTH: But won't that make me panic more?

THERAPIST: It may at first. But if you keep doing what you're terrifying yourself about—talking to your critical father—and convince yourself at the same time that your panic is only inconvenient, not awful, you will significantly decrease your panic about your panicking.

RUTH: Will my original panic about my father's criticism decrease too?

THERAPIST: Most likely it will, and it may even disappear completely. For you were originally panicked about his criticism but then made yourself so panicked about your panic that this secondary symptom became more important than your primary one and actually helped keep it alive. So if you surrender the panic about panic, your original horror of criticism may well disappear too. If it doesn't, just go back to disputing, which we previously discussed, the irrational belief that criticism makes you a rotten person and that you can't stand it.

RUTH: So I'd better think and act against my panic?

THERAPIST: Yes, think and act against your original panic and your panic reaction over your panic.

RUTH: Sounds good. I'll try it.

PROCESS COMMENTARY As can be seen in these typical excerpts, rational emotive behavior therapists have collaborative, Socratic dialogues with their clients and try to help them think, feel, and behave against their disturbances and, as they do so, to gain positive growth and self-fulfillment in accordance with their self-chosen goals, values, and purposes.

In using any or all of these REBT techniques with Ruth, I do not merely try to help her ameliorate her presenting symptoms (panic, guilt, and indecisiveness) but also try to help her make a profound philosophical change. The goals are for her to acknowledge her own construction of her emotional problems, to minimize her other related symptoms, and to maintain her therapeutic progress. By the time my therapy with Ruth ends, I expect that she will have strongly internalized and kept regularly using the three main insights of REBT:

1. "I mainly emotionally and behaviorally upset myself about unfortunate conditions in my life, and I largely do so by constructing rigid 'musts' and commands about these conditions."
2. "No matter when I originally started to upset myself and no matter who encouraged me do so, I'm now disturbed because of my present *must*urbatory beliefs."
3. "To change my irrational thinking, my unhealthy feelings, and my dysfunctional behaviors, I'd better give up all magical solutions and keep working and practicing—yes, keep working and practicing—for the rest of my life."

Much of Ruth's main problem is learning to be "herself" and at the same time to resist conforming too much to social rules that tell her that she must be a "good woman," must be a "thin woman," and must be a "good fundamentalist." Although she theoretically has the right to avoid following these social rules, she will tend to feel guilty, and she will tend to get into some amount of trouble with her family of origin and her current family if she decides to "truly" be herself. By using REBT and trying to follow her strong preferences without turning them into absolutist demands, she can probably determine how to largely be herself and at the same time largely, but not completely, avoid antagonizing her parents, her husband, and her children. REBT encourages her to lead a balanced life in these respects. But in being an individual, she will have to select the kind of balance she desires and accept the consequences of her own choices.

After working with Ruth for several sessions, I would say that she definitely has a panic disorder and is also dysthymic. I see her as someone with a personality disorder rather than as a "nice neurotic." She is very troubled and conflicted, but she has the ability and, I hope, the determination to work through her main problems. I enjoy working with clients like Ruth because I find them to be quite open to help. If she is willing to put REBT concepts into practice, she has a good chance to change. She has already chosen not to follow some of the rigid rules of her family and her culture and is healthily sorry about the difficulties her rebellion entails. If I can help her continue to be sorry and regretful but to give up her severe guilt and self-deprecation about her rebelliousness, I think she will keep choosing her own pathways and not only she but also her close family members will considerably benefit. I sincerely hope so.[3]

A Cognitive Behavioral Approach to Family Therapy With Ruth

by Frank M. Dattilio, PhD, ABPP

Introduction

In the previous selection Albert Ellis demonstrates how he applied REBT, a form of cognitive behavior therapy, to individual therapy with Ruth. I have been influenced greatly by my former mentors, Aaron T. Beck, who pioneered cognitive therapy, and the late Joseph Wolpe, the father of behavior therapy. In addition to conducting individual therapy in my private practice, I have been heavily involved in developing applications of the cognitive behavioral approach to couples and families.

The basic theory of CBT contends that family members largely create their own world by the phenomenological view they take of what happens to them. The focus of therapy is on how particular problems of family members affect their well-being as a unit. Throughout the course of therapy, family members are treated as individuals, against the backdrop of the systems approach to family therapy. Each of the members subscribes to his or her own specific set of beliefs and expectations. The role of the family therapist is to help members come to the realization that illogical or irrational beliefs and distortions contribute significantly to their emotional distress as well as interactional conflicts and the impact that this has on the system as a whole.

Basic Concepts and Assumptions

Consistent with systems theory, the CBT approach to families includes the premise that members of a family simultaneously influence one another. Consequently, a behavior of one family member influences behaviors, cognitions, and emotions in other members, which, in turn, elicit cognitions, behaviors, and emotions in response. As this process continues to cycle, the volatility of the family dynamics sometimes escalates, rendering members vulnerable to a negative spiral of conflict. As the number of family members involved increases, so does the complexity of the dynamics, adding more fuel to the escalation process.

Some of the more recent CBT approaches place heavy emphasis on *schema*, or what has otherwise been defined as a set of core beliefs.[4] As this concept is applied to family treatment, the therapeutic intervention is based on the assumptions with which family members interpret and evaluate one another and the emotions and behaviors that arise in response to these cognitions. Just as individuals maintain their own basic schemata about themselves, their world, and their future, they also maintain schemata about families. Through my clinical work I have found that emphasis should be placed both on these cognitions among individual family members and on what can be termed the family schema. This consists of beliefs held jointly by the family that have formed as a result of years of integrated interaction among members. An example of such a belief in Ruth's family of origin might be that "It is unacceptable to talk about feelings and emotions openly." Not only is this an unwritten rule, it is also a strong belief or schema among family members.

These schemata have a major impact on how an individual thinks, feels, and behaves within the family setting and also contribute to the development of rules and family patterns. An example in Ruth's present family is that emotions and feelings should only be discussed selectively. Therefore, when it is understood that the father is the head of the household, all decisions regarding the family may be suspended until he has the final word. This pattern may disempower the mother in disciplining the children, and they may perceive her, in effect, as another sibling.

The family schema is very important when conducting family therapy. It also contains standards about how spousal relationships should work, what problems should be expected in marriage and how they should be handled, what is involved in building and maintaining a healthy family, what responsibilities each family member should have, what consequences should be associated with failure to meet responsibilities or to fulfill roles, and what costs and benefits each individual should expect to have as a consequence of being in a marriage.

It is important to remember that the family schema is shaped by the family of origin of each partner in a relationship as well as by environmental influences such as the media and peer relationships. Beliefs funneled down from the family of origin may be either conscious or unconscious, and they contribute to a joint or blended schema that leads to the development of the current family schema (see Figure 8.1 for a diagram of Ruth's family schemata).

When mixed with family member's individual thoughts, perceptions of their environment, and life experiences, the family schema contributes to the development of the family belief system. The family schema is subject to change as major events occur (death, divorce) and also continues to evolve over the course of ordinary day-to-day experience.

As this schema begins to form, distortions may develop, contributing to family dysfunction. Ten of the more common distortions found with both couples and families are listed here:

1. *Arbitrary inference.* A conclusion is made by family members in the absence of supporting substantiating evidence. For example, one of Ruth's teenage children who returns home half an hour after his curfew is judged by the family as having been "up to no good."
2. *Selective abstraction.* Information is taken out of context: certain details are highlighted, and other important information is ignored. John fails to answer Adam's greeting the first thing in the morning, and Adam concludes, "Dad must be angry at me."
3. *Overgeneralization.* An isolated incident or two are allowed to serve as a representation of similar situations everywhere, related or unrelated. Because John and the kids have left food out from time to time, Ruth develops the belief that her family is wasteful and takes everything, including her, for granted.

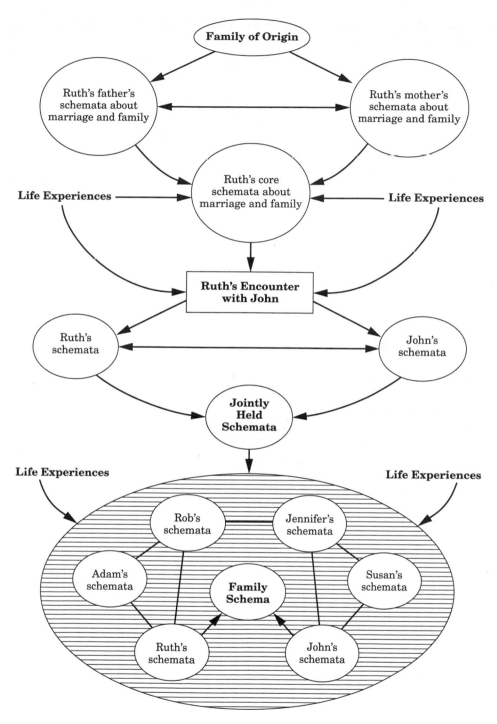

FIGURE 8.1 Ruth's Family Schemata

4. *Magnification and minimization.* A case or circumstance is perceived in greater or lesser light than is appropriate. John demands that the children wash their hands before eating, but he fails to do so himself. When confronted by the children, he minimizes it by saying, "Well, I don't miss very often—so I'm excused."

5. *Personalization.* External events are attributed to oneself when insufficient evidence exists to render a conclusion. Jennifer blames herself for her parents' repeated arguments, saying, "Maybe I never should have been born."

6. *Dichotomous thinking.* Experiences are codified as all or nothing, a complete success or a total failure. After repeated incidences in which Adam becomes involved in trouble at school, John and Ruth conclude, "We failed as disciplinarians."

7. *Labeling and mislabeling.* Imperfections and mistakes made in the past are allowed to serve as a stereotype of all future behaviors. Ruth and John failed to follow through on their word on one occasion and are consequently regarded by the children as being unreliable.

8. *Tunnel vision.* Family members sometimes see only what they want to see or what fits their current state of mind. John holds onto the rigid belief that the man is the "head of the household" because this is the way he perceived a father to be when he was growing up.

9. *Biased explanations.* In a polarized way of thinking that family members develop during times of distress, they assume that another member has an ulterior motive. John and the children distrust Ruth because she does not always admit to depressive thoughts when she indeed is experiencing them.

10. *Mind reading.* A family member has the magical gift of being able to know what others are thinking without the aid of verbal communication. Ruth anticipates that the family views her as a failure because she is unable to stand up for herself and demand what she wants.

These distortions become key targets in family therapy. Much of the intervention in therapy involves helping family members identify these distortions and then gather evidence to aid in reconstructing their thinking. It may also include practicing alternative patterns of behavioral interaction and dealing with their negative attributions.[5]

Cognitive behavioral theory operates on a set of assumptions that Schwebel and Fine feel are central.[6] Here is a modified version of these assumptions:

Assumption 1. All members of a family seek to maintain their environment to fulfill their needs and wants. They attempt to understand their environment and how they can function most effectively in it, even if it sometimes means testing the boundaries. (For example, Adam may exceed his curfew by half an hour.) As family members gather data about how the family operates, they use this information to guide their behaviors and to aid in building and refining family-related cognitions. This leads to the development of an individual's construct of family life and family relationships. In Adam's case, he may begin to develop the concept that he can stretch the limits and not be chastised, thus inferring that rules may be broken.

Assumption 2. Individual members' cognitions affect virtually every aspect of family life. Five categories of cognitive variables determine these cognitions: (1) selective attention (John and Ruth's focus on the children's negative behaviors), (2) attributions (Ruth's explanations for why the children act up), (3) expectations (John's expectation that Ruth and the children will do as he asks without question), (4) assumptions (Adam's view that life is not fair), and (5) standards (Jennifer's thoughts about how the world should be).

Assumption 3. Certain "obstacles" to satisfaction lie within individual family members' cognitions (for example, Ruth's rigid view of the role of a wife and mother).

Assumption 4. Unless family members become more aware of their family-related cognitions and how these cognitions affect them in certain situations, they will not be able to identify areas that cause distress and replace them with healthy interaction.

Assessment of Ruth

My differential *DSM-IV-TR* diagnosis of Ruth would probably include the following:

Axis I: (61.1) partner relational problem; (300.40) dysthymic disorder secondary to identity problem; (300.21) panic disorder without agoraphobia

Axis II: (301.6) dependent personality disorder; (313. 2) identity problem

Axis III: exogenous obesity

Axis IV: problems related to social environment

Axis V: GAF = 60 (on admission)

A family history is conducted to ascertain pertinent information about Ruth's family of origin. Although in most cases the family approach, like other modalities of family therapy, prefers to avoid "identifying a patient" and instead takes a balanced approach to dealing with family dysfunction, there are exceptions. It appears that this case is one. Ruth has already initiated individual psychotherapy, and it was decided to include her family as well. In a sense, therefore, she has already been designated as the "identified patient," and family treatment can initially center on her issues. However, typically, the CBT approach follows along much of the lines as the systems approach and prefers to consider the family as a whole as the identified patient.[7] Given Ruth's history and background, I elected to work on gaining a better understanding of her family of origin by having her invite members in for several visits. This will certainly lead toward developing a good grasp of her core schemata about herself and family life and will possibly provide me with insight into the development of her thinking style. Traditionally this should only involve Ruth, her parents, and any siblings. No other extended family members are invited—most importantly, her husband.

This session is exclusively designed for Ruth and the therapist to better understand the thinking styles of her origin and also to clear up any areas of conflict that remain from her past. If all were amenable, we could meet for three to five sessions of 2 hours each, focusing on the family schema and particularly on her emancipation from certain thinking styles that are deleterious to her. Although this is the ideal situation, such meetings are not always successful.

Ruth's family-of-origin meeting, which only included Ruth's biological parents, proved unsuccessful. Ruth's father, a very rigid man, decided to leave the family session abruptly, stating that he didn't believe in "this sort of stuff." Ruth's mother, being a rather passive individual, complied with her husband's demands to leave and maintained the basic family schema involving power and control.

Initial Session With Ruth's Current Family

Because cognitive behavior family therapists attempt to identify both distorted schemata and maladaptive behavior patterns within the family dynamics, the next order of business in Ruth's case is to meet with her entire (immediate) family. As a result of the little that had been gathered from her family of origin and a separate interview with John, I now have some foundation for understanding the diverse philosophies that exist in each of their family backgrounds and can develop some insight into what schemata may have trickled down into the immediate family dynamics and affected Ruth's family schema.

During the initial family therapy session, I may ask various members of the family to describe their perceptions of the family and how things operate at home. It is often best to start with the youngest child and work up to the parents, so that the younger children are not influenced by what is said by their older siblings. As you will see in the excerpt from the initial session, I aim directly at ascertaining a solid understanding of the individual perceptions of the family and then attempt to conceptualize a joint consensus of the family schema. Once this is accomplished, the next step is to begin to educate the family in how the cognitive behavioral model of therapy works and then to begin to collaboratively identify cognitive distortions and erroneous thinking patterns that lead to maladaptive behavior patterns and dysfunction in the family.

> THERAPIST: I appreciate everyone coming in today. The aim of this meeting is to address some of the problems that exist in our family and explore some ways that may improve the way we interact with one another. Does that sound reasonable to everyone? [*Three members nod reticently in affirmation.*]
>
> JENNIFER: It doesn't to me! I think this sucks, and I don't want to be here.
>
> THERAPIST: So why did you agree to come?
>
> JENNIFER: I didn't. I was forced by my parents.
>
> THERAPIST: Listen, Jennifer, I want you to know that I never expect people to come here against their will. So if you feel so inclined, you are welcome to leave, provided that your parents and the rest of the family don't object. [*Pause*]
>
> JENNIFER: Well, so what do I do? Just leave now?
>
> THERAPIST: Yes, I suppose you could.

JENNIFER: So where do I go?

THERAPIST: I don't know. That's for you to decide.

JENNIFER: Well, that's dumb. I'm not going to just sit outside in the car—bored!

THERAPIST: OK, you're certainly welcome to stay if you choose, but I'm actually interested in hearing why you don't want to be here, particularly if being here would help the family.

JENNIFER: Because this is all bull, and it's not my problem—it's Mom's. She just makes it everyone else's problem.

THERAPIST: Really? Does anyone else view things the same way Jennifer does? [*Brief pause*]

JOHN: No, I don't, totally. I think we all have some issues here that need to be discussed besides Mom, but Mom does have her problems.

THERAPIST: Anyone else have an opinion?

ROB: Yes, I'd like to say something. I think our family definitely has some problems in the way we think sometimes. Everyone is, like, all over the place, and there's no sense of . . . how would you say . . .

THERAPIST: Family unity?

ROB: Yeah! Sort of. I mean, like, Dad is sort of off in his own world—no offense, Dad—and Mom is doing her thing and trying to do for everyone else. It's sort of crazy.

THERAPIST: So, I'm hearing you say that things at home are somewhat chaotic at times, and you're uncomfortable with it?

ROB: Yes, but not at times. A lot of the time.

THERAPIST: OK! That's one perception. I'd also like to get back to something that Jennifer said about how Mom makes her problems everyone else's. Does that seem to be true for everyone here? Are we all in agreement with Jen's statement?

JOHN: No, I'm having a problem with Jennifer's statement. You know, Ruth and Jennifer really lock horns, and Jennifer will often take every opportunity she can to blame her mother, or anyone else for that matter—except, of course, herself.

THERAPIST: John, in addition to your concerns about Jennifer, you sound as though you're a bit protective of your wife.

JOHN: Well sure, but that's also the way I really see it.

THERAPIST: OK, but is there any agreement with any of what the kids are saying?

JOHN: Yeah, maybe some. I mean, look, Ruth has her problems, and we all know that. She's had a really rough upbringing, so I sort of see our roles as being to support her and not to give her a hard time.

THERAPIST: It seems to me that this is somewhat how your family has functioned for a long time until recently.

JENNIFER: Yeah! Until I screwed everything up, right? Right, Mom? That's it—say it.

RUTH [*Begins to sob*]: Oh, Jennifer, stop!

ADAM: I think Jennifer's problem is that she wants to grow up, and Mom won't let her. That's why she's mad at Mom and sort of miserable with everybody.

SUSAN: I sort of agree. I can see Mom starting to do a little of the same with me.

JOHN: What? Do what?

SUSAN: Uh-oh! Now I'm in deep shit! I opened my big mouth. [*Everyone chuckles*]

THERAPIST: No, that's OK, Susan. Say what you feel. The rule of therapy here is that we enjoy the freedom to say what's on our mind without fear of retribution.

SUSAN: Well, she's starting to be kind of overprotective with me the way she has with Jen.

JENNIFER: Yeah, and it's only with the girls. She's not like that so much with Adam and Rob.

THERAPIST: Ruth, how do you respond to everything you're hearing here today?

RUTH: Well, if I have to be honest, I guess it's true to some degree, but it's hard to listen to.

THERAPIST: OK, so you're protective of the girls, John is protective of you, and who is protective of Rob, Adam, and Dad?

ROB: Rob, Adam, and Dad. [*Everyone laughs*]

THERAPIST: Ah-ha! So the men take care of the men. That's interesting! Protecting one another appears to be a very important theme in your family.

JOHN: Well sure, you've seen that with both mine and Ruth's family.

THERAPIST: So I guess it would be fair to say, in a way, that this belief system was carried down to your family here [*Everyone agrees*]. We've just identified what's called a family schema or a core belief—that we protect each other in certain ways that sometimes differ. What belief exists in your family that calls for this behavior as opposed to the idea of everyone protecting themselves? [*Pause*]

SUSAN: Is it bad that we do this?

THERAPIST: Well, not necessarily, but the manner in which it has evolved in your family patterns here has caused some uneasiness. But let me get an answer to my question, because I think this is very important. [*Pause*]

JOHN: Well, I guess as the father, I feel the blame for some of it. While I support Ruth, I've kind of dumped on her by not taking more of an active role with the kids.

THERAPIST: Yes, and as a result of Ruth's upbringing, she has felt compelled to assume all of the responsibility for the family, perhaps in part to compensate for you. So there are several family-held distortions, as well as individual distortions about ourselves.

ADAM: What do you mean, distortions?

THERAPIST: Good question, Adam. Let me explain.

I then explain and review the cognitive distortions listed earlier in this chapter in a clear manner that the family members can understand, often using specific examples from their family.

THERAPIST: Let's try to identify some of the distortions together.

ROB: I have one that Mom does big-time.

THERAPIST: OK, let's hear it.

ROB: Well, it's the arbitration thing you said.

THERAPIST: Arbitrary inference?

ROB: Yeah, I guess that's it. Well, like if we're out past curfew, she freaks and starts accusing us of being up to no good, like we're guilty until proven innocent.

THERAPIST: Well, that's one that you may perceive Mom as doing, but do any of the other family members engage in the same distortion?

ADAM: Yeah, Jen does!

JENNIFER: Do not!

ADAM: Yes, you do.

SUSAN: Yes, you do, Jen. You're just like Mom in that way.

THERAPIST: Look, guys, we're just trying to identify cognitive distortions that you all engage in from time to time. This not meant to be an antagonizing session. Also, you want to identify those distortions that you engage in yourselves as well as those that you witness with other family members.

JOHN: OK, I have one about myself. I sometimes find myself thinking much the way Ruth's father does, and I get annoyed when my decisions are questioned—as much as I hate to admit it. I guess I view compliance by the other members of my family as a gesture of respect, yet I tend to dump a lot onto Ruth.

At this point I have attempted identify some of the family's standards and schemata and also to highlight cognitive distortions. At the same time the family members are being oriented to the cognitive model in a subtle but clear way in which they will eventually be able to apply some of the techniques to themselves. The next step after identifying these distortions will be to teach them how to begin to question and weigh the evidence that supports the internal statements that they make to themselves and to challenge any erroneously based assumptions.

THERAPIST: All right, that's a good one, John. So one of your beliefs that you're choosing to identify as being based on a distortion is that "the boss is never questioned, or it's disrespectful." In a sense, it's a matter of "do as I say, not as I do." That's a standard that you have established based on your belief?

JOHN: Yeah, I guess. Boy, that sounds horrible when someone else actually says it in those terms.

THERAPIST: Well, don't worry so much about that, John. Let's just analyze it for a moment and see if we can challenge some of the basic tenets of that belief. Now, do you have any idea why you view things in that manner—that the man should be the boss and his requests or decisions should go unquestioned?

JOHN: Well, I know that I was closer to my father than I was to my mother. I also think that Ruthie's father had something to do with it early on. When we were first married he used to . . . sort of . . . drill me.

THERAPIST: Drill you?

JOHN: Yeah, you know, like take me aside and give me his lecture about how I need to act as the man of the house and family. Also, well, this may sound odd, but I kind of get the impression that this was sort of the way Ruthie was more comfortable with also, you know—like she kind of . . . oh, I forget the word you guys use all the time. It's a popular term . . .

THERAPIST: Enabled it?

JOHN: Yeah, yeah, enabled. That's it. She enabled me to be that way, subtly, I guess.

THERAPIST: I see. So, do you believe that you may enable Ruth as well with certain things, and perhaps you both enable the children?

RUTH AND JOHN [*In unison*]: Yes! Definitely.

THERAPIST: Might this be tied to the schema of taking care of one another? How does this all relate?

ROB: Well, I was thinking about that for a while when you were talking to Dad, and I think we're like a pack of wolves that sort of just look out for one another casually, and if one of us is in need, somebody will step in. But we never talk about it openly otherwise.

THERAPIST [*This was an interesting metaphor because wolves are animals that clearly tend to be protective of one another yet certainly are capable of protecting themselves as well.*]: OK, but how does this cause conflict?

ROB: I'm not sure.

SUSAN: I think that maybe the conflict comes when one person has one expectation and the other has a different expectation and it's never communicated. We just sort of . . . uh . . .

THERAPIST: Mind-read.

SUSAN: Yeah.

THERAPIST: OK, that's another distortion.

ADAM: Wow, we're one distorted family—cool! [*Everyone laughs*]

THERAPIST: Well, yes, you have your distortions, but all families do. It's not so unusual!

RUTH [*In jest*]: I don't know. When I listen to it all, it makes us sound as if we're the Adams family. [*Everyone laughs*]

THERAPIST: Good, Ruth! That was funny!

Here I am attempting to bolster some family cohesion through levity and at the same time trying to understand the family dynamics and how each member thinks and perceives various situations. Next, I will slowly introduce the idea of restructuring some of the thinking styles to bring about change.

THERAPIST: I think it might be important for us to take a look at some of the distortions you frequently engage in, now that you have identified a few of them, and see whether we may be able to challenge them, particularly those that interfere the most with your family dynamics. For example, John, would you be willing to volunteer so that I can demonstrate?

JOHN: Sure.

THERAPIST: You said, as I recall, that one of your beliefs is that as the father and one of the heads of the household "the boss is never questioned, or it would demonstrate disrespect"—something to that effect.

JOHN: Right.

THERAPIST: OK, now how well do you believe this statement can be substantiated?

JOHN: I don't know. It's just something I've come to know.

THERAPIST: So there's no substantiating evidence that renders it a sound principle. It's merely conjecture. So is it possible that it might be based on erroneous information?

JOHN: Possibly.

THERAPIST: Well, what do you know about the effect of this principle? In other words, what results have you received from it thus far?

JOHN: Well, not too good. In fact, no one obeys it, and I'm sort of scoffed at by my kids for believing it.

THERAPIST: All right, so perhaps you're seeing more evidence that says that it's not so effective than evidence supporting its use. So maybe it needs some modification, and you don't have to abandon the principle completely. I mean, respect is important, but to expect that no one will ever question what you say or do may be a bit unreasonable.

JOHN: Yeah, I see your point. But then how do I get it out of my head? I mean, it's ingrained there pretty heavily.

THERAPIST: Good question. Cognitive therapy can utilize a number of homework assignments. The basic theory contends that you must practice challenging negative self-statements, or what we call automatic thoughts, just as much as you have been using them in the past. One way to do this is by writing the corrected statement out each time you experience a negative self-statement, or in this case, a cognitive distortion. So, I'd like you to take a piece of paper and write across the top several headings, drawing a vertical line down the side of each to make columns like this:

Situation or Event	Automatic Thought	Cognitive Distortion	Emotion	Challenging Self-Statement	Alternative Response

Then, each time a situation occurs when you have a negative automatic thought, write it down. Starting with the left-hand column, record the situation or event in which you had the thought, and in the next column put exactly what the thought was. Next, attempt to identify what type of distortion you are engaging in and the emotional response that accompanies it. Then try to challenge that thought or belief by weighing the evidence that exists in favor of it. After that, write down an alternative response, using any new information you may have gathered. Does that make sense to you?

JOHN: Yes, but could we run through it once so that I'm sure I have it right?

THERAPIST: Certainly. Let's try an example.

JOHN: Something happened last week with Adam when he came in a little past curfew, and I said something about his being 5 minutes late. He started to, well, what I call challenge my authority by attempting to minimize what he had done, saying it had only been 5 minutes and was no big deal.

THERAPIST: So let's get everything down on paper.

Situation or Event	*Automatic Thought*	*Cognitive Distortion*
Adam arrives home 5 minutes late for curfew.	"He's defying me. He doesn't respect my position. If I don't chastise him, I'll be a lousy father."	Arbitrary inference Dichotomous thinking Personalization

Emotions	*Challenging Self-Statement*	*Alternative Response*
Upset Angry	"Just because he comes home 5 minutes beyond his curfew doesn't mean that it's aimed directly at me. It also doesn't mean that he's intending to defy me."	"I could talk to him about it rather than jumping to conclusions and punishing him. Perhaps he just honestly lost track of time."

THERAPIST: That's excellent. Do you all see how we attempt to restructure some of our thinking?

ROB: Yeah, but what if Adam was really defying Dad? I mean, how do we know that it's correct?

THERAPIST: Good question, Rob. We gather information to support our alternative beliefs, and so one of the things that your dad could do is, as he said on the sheet, talk to Adam about what his intentions were in arriving home late. This could be applied to all of you at one time or the other as you recognize yourselves engaging in distorted thinking. We want to begin to examine your mode of thought and really question the validity of what you tell yourselves. This may make a monumental difference in how you interact.

From this point I begin to monitor the family members in challenging their belief statements in the fashion just demonstrated. During this process, feelings and emotions are also addressed, as well as communication skills and problem-solving strategies. Regular homework assignments are also employed to aid family members in learning to challenge their distorted thoughts more spontaneously. Eventually, I will walk each family member through this specific technique to ensure its correct use. In addition, the use of behavioral techniques, such as the reassignment of family members' roles and responsibilities, becomes an integral part of the treatment regime in this particular case. Also, homework assignments are essential in facilitating change in the process of treatment.[8] The general concept behind this is that with the change and modification of dysfunctional thinking and behaviors there will be less family conflict.

Jerry Corey's Work With Ruth From a Cognitive Behavioral Perspective

In the *DVD for Integrative Counseling: The Case of Ruth and Lecturettes* I work with Ruth from a cognitive behavioral perspective in a number of therapy sessions. Refer to the three sessions in which I demonstrate my way of working with Ruth from a cognitive, emotive, and behavioral focus (Sessions 6, 7, and 8). See also Session 9 ("Integrative Perspective"), which illustrates the interactive nature of working with Ruth on thinking, feeling, and doing levels.

Basic Assumptions

In this section I combine elements from Ellis's rational emotive behavior therapy (REBT) and Beck's cognitive therapy (CT) in an integrative approach for my work with Ruth.[9] Beck's cognitive therapy shares with REBT an active, directive, time-limited, person-centered, structured approach. I draw on a range of cognitive, emotive, and behavioral techniques to demonstrate to my clients that they contribute to their own emotional disturbances by the faulty beliefs they have acquired. As a cognitive behavior therapist, I operate on the assumption that events or situations in life do not cause problematic emotions such as guilt, depression, and hostility. Rather, it is mainly our *evaluation* (or interpretation) of the event and the *beliefs* we hold about these events that get us into trouble.

Initial Assessment of Ruth

As I review Ruth's intake form and her autobiography, it becomes evident that her beliefs are contributing to the majority of her problems. She has uncritically accepted certain values, many of which rely on guilt as a main motivation to control behavior. She is not making clear decisions based on self-derived values; rather, she is listening to intimidating voices in her head that tell her what she should do.

Ruth has an underlying dysfunctional belief that she must be perfect in all that she attempts. If she is not perfect, in her mind, there are dire consequences. She is continually judging her performances, and she is bound to think poorly of herself because of her unrealistically high standards. Indeed, there is a judge sitting on her shoulder and whispering in her ear. What I hope to teach Ruth are practical ways to talk back to this judge, to learn a new self-dialogue, and to help her reevaluate her experiences as she changes her behavior. This will be the focus of my therapy with her.

Goals of the Therapy

The basic goal of cognitive behavior therapy is to assist clients in learning how to replace self-defeating beliefs with constructive beliefs. To accomplish this goal, I will teach Ruth the A-B-C model of personality. This model, which is different from the behavioral ABC paradigm, is based on several premises of REBT: A (the activating event) does not cause C (the emotional consequences); rather, it is mainly B (Ruth's belief about the activating event) that is the source of her problems.

I assist Ruth in formulating the goals for her therapy. During the initial session, she indicates that she does not want to act out the rest of her life according to her parents' design. Establishing a therapeutic contract with Ruth as a way to structure our working relationship is a way to reach agreed-upon goals.

Therapeutic Procedures

In working with Ruth as a cognitive behavior therapist, I employ a directive and action-oriented approach. Functioning as a teacher, I focus on what she can learn that will lead to changes in the way she is thinking, feeling, and behaving. Drawing on Beck's ideas from CT, I intend to focus on the inaccurate conclusions Ruth has reached by teaching her to look for the evidence that supports or contradicts her views and hypotheses. She will frequently hear the question "Where is the evidence for_____?" Through the use of open-ended questions and a Socratic dialogue, I will try to teach Ruth ways to systematically detect errors in her reasoning that result in faulty assumptions and misconceptions (*cognitive distortions*). After she has recognized her cognitive distortions, I will encourage her to carry out a range of homework activities, to keep a record of what she is doing and thinking, and to form alternative interpretations to replace her faulty assumptions. I will also ask Ruth to read literature from a cognitive behavioral perspective as an adjunct to her therapy sessions. Eventually, through a process of *guided discovery*, I expect her to acquire insights into the link between her thinking and the ways she feels and acts. I also expect her to learn a range of specific coping skills to deal with current and future problems.

In working with Ruth, I attempt to integrate the cognitive and affective (feeling) dimensions. Although I emphasize the cognitive aspects of therapy, I believe that changing entails actually experiencing feelings. However, experiencing feelings alone is not enough to bring about a substantive change in behavior. Much of our therapy will focus on examining Ruth's current behavior and trying on new ways of behaving both during the therapy hour and in her daily life.

The Therapeutic Process
ELEMENTS OF THE PROCESS

🍃 **Working With Ruth's Faulty Beliefs** To assist Ruth in achieving a constructive set of beliefs and acquiring a self-enhancing internal dialogue, I perform several tasks as her therapist. First of all, I challenge her to evaluate the self-defeating beliefs she originally accepted without questioning. I also urge her to work toward giving up her faulty beliefs and then to incorporate functional beliefs that will work for her. Throughout the therapeutic process, I actively teach her that self-condemnation is the basis of many of her emotional problems, that it is possible for her to stop critically judging herself, and that with hard work, including behavioral homework assignments, she can greatly reduce many of her dysfunctional notions.

Ruth's *real* work, then, consists of doing homework in everyday situations and bringing the results into our sessions for discussion and evaluation. I am concerned that she not only recognize her self-defeating thought patterns but also take steps to critically evaluate and change them.

We explore how Ruth's fear of failing stops her from doing so many things. She then says that she would love to square dance but has not because she is afraid of being clumsy and looking like a jerk. She would love to ski but avoids it for fear that she will fall on the "bunny hill." I am working with Ruth on her evaluation of events and her prediction that she will fail. I want her to see that even if she fails she can still learn to cope with the outcomes.

We continue for a couple of months, with Ruth agreeing to do some reading and also carrying out increasingly difficult homework assignments. Gradually she works up to more risky homework assignments, and she does risk looking foolish several times, only to find that her fantasies were much worse than the results. She gives her speech, and it is humorous and spontaneous. This gives her an increased sense of confidence to tackle some other difficult areas she has been avoiding.

🍃 **Dealing With Ruth's Beliefs About Herself as a Mother** Ruth is feeling very guilty about failing one of her daughters. Jennifer is having troubles at school. Ruth is concerned that Jennifer is "going off the deep end." Ruth partially blames herself for Jennifer's problems, telling herself that she must do better than her own mother.

> RUTH: I don't want Jennifer to suffer the way I did. But in so many ways I know I'm critical of her, just as my mother was of me at that age.
>
> JERRY: What are you telling yourself when you think of this?

I want Ruth to see that her self-defeating thoughts are getting her depressed and keeping her feeling guilty. My hope is that she will see that the key to eliminating needless anxiety and guilt lies in modifying her thinking.

RUTH: I feel guilty that I didn't help Jennifer enough with her schoolwork. If I had tutored her, she would be doing well in school.

JERRY: Do you see how your line of thinking gets you into trouble? What about Jennifer's role in creating and maintaining her own problems?

RUTH: Yes, but I've made many mistakes. Now I'm trying to make up for them so she can change.

JERRY: You might have made some mistakes with her, but that doesn't mean it will be the ruination of her. Can you see that if you do so much for her and make yourself totally responsible for her, she doesn't have to take responsibility?

I am attempting to get Ruth to dispute her destructive thinking. She has continued this pattern for so long that she now automatically blames herself, and then guilt follows.

RUTH: Well, I try to think differently, but I just keep coming back to these old thoughts. What can I say to myself?

JERRY: When Jennifer does something wrong, who gets blamed?

RUTH: Me, most of the time.

JERRY: And those times that Jennifer does well, who gets credit?

RUTH: Not me. I dwell so much on what she's not doing that I don't often see what she does right.

JERRY: How is it that you're so quick to place blame on yourself and just as quick to discount any part you have in Jennifer's accomplishments?

RUTH: Because problems occupy my mind, and I keep thinking that I should have been better with her.

JERRY: I hope that you can begin to be kinder to yourself. Consider saying to yourself something like this: "Even though I've made mistakes in the past and will probably continue making mistakes, that doesn't mean I've ruined Jennifer or will. It doesn't mean I'm the same kind of mother to her that mine was to me."

RUTH: That sounds pretty good. . . . If only I could say those things and mean them, and feel them!

JERRY: Well, if you keep disputing your own thinking and learn to substitute constructive self-statements, you're likely to be able to say and mean these things—and you'll probably feel different too.

PROCESS COMMENTARY My major focus with Ruth is on her thinking. Only by learning to apply rigorous self-challenging methods will she succeed in freeing herself from the defeatist thinking that led to her problems. I place value on behavioral homework assignments that put her in situations where she is forced to confront her faulty beliefs and her self-limiting behavior. I also consistently challenge Ruth to question her basic assumption of needing the approval of others to feel adequate.

Some Final Thoughts

The cognitive behavioral approaches enjoy considerable popularity in various mental health and community agency settings. Its specificity, task orientation, emphasis on objectivity, collaborative spirit, focus on cognition and behavior, action orientation, present focus, attention to brief interventions, and problem-solving orientation are extremely useful in working with diverse client populations. A unifying aspect in the practice of CBT is the emphasis given to replacing maladaptive cognitions, behaviors, and emotions with more adaptive ones. This emphasis is illustrated by the assessments of Ruth by both Dr. Ellis and Dr. Dattilio.

Questions for Reflection

1. What advantages do you see to the manner in which Dr. Ellis drew on cognitive, emotive, and behavioral techniques in working with Ruth's dysfunctional beliefs? Any disadvantages?
2. Assume that you suggested a technique to Ruth (such as keeping a journal or reading self-help books) and she refused, telling you that what you are asking was too much to expect. What might you say to her?
3. What common faulty beliefs do you share with Ruth, if any? To what degree have you challenged your own self-defeating thinking? How do you think this would affect your ability to work with her?
4. Working with Ruth in an active, directive, and challenging manner could raise some ethical issues, especially if you attempted to impose your values by suggesting what she should value. As you review Dr. Ellis's, Dr. Dattilio's, and my work with Ruth, do you have any concerns that any of us are imposing our values on Ruth?
5. Dr. Dattilio focused on Ruth's family schemata, including beliefs from her family of origin and those in her current family. What uses can you see in working with family schemata? What are some advantages of using a cognitive behavioral approach in counseling couples? Any disadvantages?
6. What might you do if Ruth came from a background where her "musts," "oughts," and "shoulds" arose out of her cultural conditioning? What if she insisted that she felt guilty when she dared to question her upbringing and that in her culture doing so was frowned upon?
7. In the example of my work with Ruth as a cognitive behavior therapist, I blended some of the concepts and techniques of Ellis (REBT) and Beck (CT). What are some aspects of REBT and CT that you might combine?
8. What ideas do you have for using cognitive behavior concepts and procedures in conjunction with Gestalt techniques? Can you think of examples in Ruth's case where you could use Gestalt techniques in working with her self-defeating thinking?
9. How well do the cognitive behavioral approaches fit with your counseling style? What aspects of CBT do you find most useful? Which aspects might you want to modify to fit your personal counseling style?

Notes

See the *DVD for Theory and Practice of Counseling and Psychotherapy: The Case of Stan and Lecturettes*, Session 8 ("Cognitive Behavior Therapy Applied to the Case of Stan"), for a demonstration of exploring Stan's faulty beliefs through the use of role reversal and cognitive restructuring techniques and for my presentation of ways that cognitive behavior therapy can be applied.

1. For a more detailed discussion of the basic assumptions, key concepts, and practical applications of rational emotive behavior therapy, see Corey, G. (2013). *Theory and practice of counseling and psychotherapy* (9th ed.). Belmont, CA: Brooks/Cole, Cengage Learning. Chapter 10 ("Cognitive Behavior Therapy") outlines the basic elements of Albert Ellis's REBT, Aaron and Judy Beck's cognitive therapy, and Donald Meichenbaum's cognitive behavior modification.

2. For a discussion of the cognitive, emotive, and behavioral techniques typically employed by rational emotive behavioral practitioners, see Ellis, A. (2001). *Overcoming destructive beliefs, feelings, and behaviors.* Amherst, NY: Prometheus Books.

3. For useful self-help books that present a straightforward approach to REBT based on homework assignments and self-questioning, see Ellis, A. (2001). *Feeling better, getting better, staying better.* Atascadero, CA: Impact Publications; and Ellis, A., & Harper, R. (1997). *A guide to rational living.* Hollywood, CA: Wilshire.

4. See Dattilio, F. M. (2005). Restructuring family schemas: A cognitive-behavioral perspective. *Journal of Marital and Family Therapy, 31*(1), 15–30.

5. See Dattilio, F. M. (2010). *Cognitive-behavior therapy with couples and families: A comprehensive guide for clinicians.* New York: Guilford Press.

6. See Schwebel, A. I., & Fine, M. A. (1994). *Understanding and helping families: A cognitive-behavioral approach.* Hillsdale, NJ: Erlbaum. Modifications made with permission of the authors.

7. See Dattilio, F. M. (1993). Cognitive techniques with couples and families, *The Family Journal, 1*(1), 51–65; Dattilio, F. M. (2000). Cognitive-behavioral strategies. In J. Carlson & L. Sperry (Eds.), *Brief therapy with individuals and couples* (pp. 33–70). Phoenix, AZ: Zeig, Tucker & Theisen; and Dattilio, F. M. (2001). Cognitive-behavior family therapy: Contemporary myths and misconceptions. *Contemporary Family Therapy, 23*(1), 3–18.

8. See Dattilio, F. M. (2002). Homework assignments in couple and family therapy. *Journal of Clinical Psychology, 58*(5), 535–547; Dattilio, F. M., L'Abate, L., & Deane, F. (2005). Homework for families In N. Kazantzis, F. P. Dean, K. R. Ronan & L. L. L'Abate (Eds.), *Using homework assignments in cognitive-behavior therapy* (pp. 357–404). New York: Brunner-Routledge.

9. I do not repeat too much detail about the cognitive behavioral approaches, so it would be helpful to review the perspectives of Dr. Ellis and Dr. Dattilio in this chapter.

CHAPTER NINE

Case Approach
to Reality Therapy

General Overview of Reality Therapy

Reality therapy was first developed by William Glasser for use in a mental hospital and a correctional institution in the 1950s and 1960s. It has enjoyed a gradual but steady growth in acceptance and application and is used in individual, group, and family counseling as well as in school classrooms today. Robert Wubbolding expanded its use to management and supervision and has taught reality therapy in Korea, Japan, India, Kuwait, Singapore, and throughout Europe. It is also taught and practiced in Australia, South Africa, and Colombia, South America. Because the ideas are universal, they are applicable worldwide.

The goal of reality therapy is to help clients get reconnected with the people—both old and new—they have chosen to include in their quality worlds and to teach clients choice theory. A main therapeutic goal is to help clients improve the significant relationships in their lives. Therapists help individuals find more effective ways of meeting their needs for belonging, power, freedom, and fun. Clients are challenged to make an assessment of their current behavior to determine whether what they are doing and thinking is getting them what they want from life.

Reality therapy is active, directive, psychoeducational, and didactic. At the center of the process is the *therapeutic alliance*, the relationship between therapist and client. The therapist assists clients in making plans to change specific behaviors that they determine are not working for them. Skillful questioning and a variety of behavioral methods are used to encourage clients to evaluate what they are doing. If clients decide that their present behavior is not effective, they develop a specific plan for change and make a commitment to follow through.

When clients are more effectively fulfilling their wants and needs and when they have gained (or regained) control of their world, they are ready to leave counseling. This approach has the advantage of being anchored in a specific plan for change, which allows for objective evaluation of outcomes.

A Reality Therapist's Perspective on Ruth
by William Glasser, MD

Introduction

Before showing how I would work with Ruth, I want to provide a brief introduction to a few key concepts of reality therapy. I continue to believe we choose all of our significant behaviors in an attempt to find happiness. Barring extreme poverty, physical illness, and the ravages of old age—none of which are chosen—when we are unhappy enough to seek therapy, I believe it is because we do not have satisfying relationships. All of our chosen ineffective behaviors—neurosis, psychosomatic disease, and psychosis—are our self-destructive attempts to improve a present relationship or find a better one. Therefore, as you will see in the case of Ruth, reality therapy focuses on finding the unsatisfying present relationship.

We do not focus on the past because relationship problems exist in the present and must be solved in the present. We do not focus on symptoms because they are always chosen to deal with the present unsatisfying relationship. Symptoms will disappear when that relationship is improved. In contrast to most theoretical orientations, I believe that although we may be the product of our past we are not victims of our past unless we choose to be so. Approaching a client this way drastically shortens therapy because it quickly gets to the core of the problem, which is a present problematic relationship.[1]

Assessment of Ruth

From my perspective, psychological symptoms are chosen behaviors. For that reason, I use verb forms rather than nouns to describe Ruth's choices. For example, you will see that I use "panicking" instead of "panic" to describe her symptoms. A panic disorder would be a consistent choosing of panicking behaviors as exemplified by Ruth. She will be taught to say, "I am choosing to depress" or "I am depressing" instead of saying, "I am depressed" or "I am suffering from depression." This way of describing symptoms or disorders makes sense when you understand choice theory.

As Ruth presents herself, it is obvious that she has not been able to satisfy her basic needs except her need for survival. She does not feel that she has love, power, fun, or freedom in her life, and her choices of anxietying, panicking, and psychosomaticizing are her ways of expressing her extreme frustration. These symptoms are Ruth's way of saying, "Help me!"

Key Issues and Themes

First of all, Ruth needs someone who will listen to her and not criticize her for what she says. She may, however, present her story and continually ask for criticism by saying things like, "It's wrong for me to complain; I have so much; I'm acting like a baby." My most important task as her therapist is to listen to her, to not get tied into her self-criticism, and to tell her that she has a right to express herself without criticism.

It is important for Ruth to learn about her basic needs. She needs to work on her marriage and improve the relationship with her husband. I ask over and over, "How does your being miserable help you or anyone else?" Although Ruth can be kind to her parents and others when she talks to them, it is important that she tell them firmly that she is going to do what she believes is right for her life.

I would encourage Ruth in her choice to go to work, although I would discuss with her the choice to become an elementary schoolteacher. This is a very giving role, and she may not do well at this now. It may be good for her to work among adults and to be appreciated for her adult qualities by her peers.

If Ruth wants to talk about weight, diet, or symptoms, I will listen but I will not encourage her to explore these topics. My approach is focused on her getting out of the house and finding a satisfying place in the adult world. If it is satisfying enough, her complaints and symptoms will be lessened, but she will still have to work on her relationship with her husband.

Ruth's finances will be discussed. What she earns for the first several years might be spent on herself and on enjoyable activities with her husband and children. I would encourage Ruth not to save her money, give it to charity, or spend it on necessities unless that is what she really wants to do. Instead, I will constantly encourage her to do what is right for her, not what is right for others or "good" for the world. Ruth needs to learn to think about herself more often.

From the first session I will bring up her relationship with her husband in order to guide her to take the initiative and do something she believes will improve her marriage. Following choice theory and reality therapy, she can only control her own life; she cannot control her husband's life. If John is willing to come in for marriage counseling, I will see them together.

Therapeutic Techniques

It is important that I be uncritical and accepting and teach Ruth to be accepting of herself. In fact, I may say to her, "You are choosing your actions and only you can change what you are doing. You can't change anyone else." I will give Ruth my *Choice Theory.*[2] book to read. Because reality therapy emphasizes psychoeducation, we will discuss ideas from the book in each session. This information, coupled with a good client–therapist relationship, should help her get the most from counseling.

As much as possible, humor in the sessions will be helpful. Ruth is overdue for a laugh or two, and laughter will allow her to let go of her psychosomatic symptoms more quickly than anything else she can do. In therapy sessions I will emphasize her good points, which are many, and at each session she will discuss her successes and her current sources of prideful accomplishments. Moreover, it will be good for Ruth to consider the idea of developing a social life in which she will find satisfactory interactions with others.

Ruth can be encouraged to apply the ideas of choice theory to her children. I will ask her what she thinks she needs to do to get along with her daughter Jennifer, and I will advise her to stop telling her daughter what to do and to stop criticizing her. Instead, Ruth might go out with her daughter for a good time, tell her she likes her the way she is, and say, jokingly, that she should not model herself after an unhappy mother, only a happy mother.

I can teach Ruth that it is her life and that it is up to her, not anyone else, to make what she wants of it. Whenever she says that she can't do something, I ask her why she can't, then ask her to give all the reasons why she could do it, and compare the two sets of reasons. Ruth needs freedom from her self-imposed prison, and we will discuss who can let her out. If Ruth is locked in, it is because she won't open the door. My goal is to help her unlock the prison door.

A Sample Session With Ruth

I keep the sessions as light as I can. Ruth needs to learn to take her problems less seriously so it will be easier for her to convince herself that she can make better choices. Here is how I guide the therapy after about a month.

RUTH: It was really bad last night, all horrible feelings.

THERAPIST [*Interrupting*]: The sweats, the palpitations, and the fear of impending doom are all part of your midnight misery, Ruth. If you've learned anything in your 39 years, it's how to panic. Now is the time to make a change.

RUTH: How can you talk like that? Do you really believe I'm choosing this panic, that I enjoy these attacks? How can I possibly be choosing them? They come on while I'm sleeping, and they wake me up.

THERAPIST: Tell me, if you're not choosing them, who is? You've read about choice theory. You choose all you do, just as I do, and just as everyone does. Of course, you're not enjoying this choice but—I know this is hard to believe—to you it's better than anything else you could choose in the middle of the night.

RUTH: You're crazy! It's not better or worse, it's what I do as I sleep. Don't you listen to me? I'm asleep; it wakes me up.

THERAPIST [*Not rising to the bait of arguing with her but continuing on*]: Suppose I called you in the middle of the night and woke you up before you woke up with your choice to panic. In fact, let's do it right now. Pretend you're sleeping, and I give you a call.

RUTH: I'm getting afraid to go to sleep, even to go to bed. The attacks are excruciating. You don't have any idea of how bad they are. If you had one you wouldn't be sitting there so smugly telling me I'm choosing this misery.

THERAPIST: If you want to be able to make better choices while you're asleep at night, you've got to learn to make better choices in the daytime. But, c'mon, let me call and wake you up. Will you do it, or do you have a better idea?

RUTH: Of course I don't have a better idea. If I did, would I be here listening to this nonsense? Go ahead and call me.

THERAPIST: OK, ring, ring!

RUTH: Hello, who is it? What time is it?

THERAPIST: It's me, Dr. Glasser. I got to thinking about you and your problems, and I decided to call you. Can we talk for a few minutes?

RUTH: I'm sleepy. Couldn't it wait until morning?

THERAPIST: Just one question—one, OK?

RUTH: OK, OK, I'm up now, so I might as well talk. What do you want to know?

THERAPIST: I want to know what you were thinking about tonight when you went to bed. Tell me as much as you remember.

RUTH: What I always think about—that my life is all messed up, and it's not getting better. I'm in a rut. There's nothing going on in my marriage, my body looks just awful, and my whole day is horrible. I can understand why people drink and take drugs if they feel the way I do all the time. What more is there to tell you? It's what I tell you every time we talk. That's what I think about, my awful day and my miserable life. What's the sense of repeating it now? What good will it do?

THERAPIST: If I call you tomorrow night, do you think the story will be the same?

RUTH: Of course it'll be the same. It's been the same for the last 10 years.

THERAPIST: No, it hasn't. It's different now.

RUTH: What are you talking about? How is it different?

THERAPIST: The panicking is new, and seeing me is even newer. That's different, a lot different.

RUTH: Yeah, it's even worse than it was. At least I didn't have the panic. And you're no bargain either. I never thought of it that way. Maybe if I get rid of you I'll get rid of the panic.

THERAPIST: If you want to quit, I won't try to stop you.

RUTH: Well, you don't seem to be doing me much good.

THERAPIST: You don't seem to be doing yourself much good either. Why don't you choose to do something for yourself? Do you want to keep going to bed afraid you're going to wake up scared to death and then come here and blame me because I'm not doing anything to help you? How's that going to help you?

RUTH: What can I do?

THERAPIST: You do a lot all day long, but you just don't do anything for yourself. Tomorrow, even if you have what you call a panic attack, don't tell me about it. It's your choice, and I can't do a thing about it. All I can help you do is have a better day and do some different things than you've been doing. Do you want to start tomorrow, start changing the way you live, or do you want to choose to go on as you are?

RUTH [*Softening now. She's been listening. The middle-of-the-night-call technique is getting her attention.*]: But how can I?

THERAPIST [*With emphasis*]: How can you not? Why keep waiting? I know you're afraid. We're all afraid to try new things because they might not work out. Let's stop wasting time and start right now to make a plan for you to do something for you. You won't hurt anyone if you start to take care of yourself. If you begin feeling better, you'll be doing your whole family a favor.

After this, we make a plan to do something that, for a change, will satisfy Ruth's needs, and we're on our way.

🌿 **Process Commentary**   I dare not wait much longer than a month to confront Ruth's resistance. She's not a weak person; it takes a lot of strength to panic as she has. But if I don't do this, and if I let her control me with her panicking as she has been trying to control everyone else, she won't change. To gain a sense of control, she has been willing to choose the suffering she complains about. We all do it once in a while; it's just that she does it a lot. I need to intervene, for that's my job as a therapist. From my experience, her prognosis is very good if she's treated this way. Once she begins to put the energy into taking effective control of her life that she puts into panicking, she will make rapid progress.

I can't tell how long therapy will take. But if we focus on the marital relationship, do not pay attention to the symptoms, teach her that the only person's behavior she can control is her own, get her to put her energy into getting closer to her husband and children, and get her to find a satisfying job, it might not take much more than 10 initial sessions. After that I might see her once a month to keep her on course.

Another Reality Therapist's Perspective on Ruth

by Robert E. Wubbolding, EdD

Introduction

I will present several examples of interventions that typify the practice of reality therapy. These dialogues include specific tools that can be implemented when using reality therapy. It is not my intention to imply that if the therapist merely asks a few questions the client will automatically make a rapid or dramatic change. The dialogues represent samples of the most important interventions, which are made repeatedly and rephrased in dozens of ways throughout the process of counseling.

As you will see in my work with Ruth, assessment and treatment are linked during all the phases of counseling. This assessment is done largely through Ruth's exploration of questions I raise pertaining to her subjective world. Although I do not emphasize formal diagnosis, I do place considerable value on ongoing assessment. In addition, the work of any professional person should fit the standard practice of that profession. Diagnostic labeling best serves as a communication tool among professionals, not as a tool for stereotyping individuals or for rigidly expecting clients to conform to a set of behaviors described in the diagnostic criteria.

🌿 **Setting the Stage for Therapy**   Because of the importance of informed consent, at the beginning of the first session, or as soon as is appropriate, I review with Ruth all pertinent details related to professional disclosure: my credentials, the nature and principles of reality therapy, confidentiality and its limits, her rights and responsibilities, and the general goals of counseling. I emphasize the common formulation used in reality therapy: "my job, your job, our job." "My job" is to function as an ethical professional who recognizes his limitations. "Your job" is to keep the scheduled appointments and to disclose as much as you choose. "Our job" is to work for changes in your life that will result in increased happiness (need satisfaction). I emphasize that if Ruth is willing to work hard, this therapy will indeed be brief.

ᐓ Exploring Ruth's Expectations

I then explore with Ruth the thoughts she had when she decided to come for counseling and the thoughts she had today before her first visit. She describes her uncertainties, her hesitancy, and her sense of failure. I encourage her to discuss her fears about counseling and about "opening Pandora's box" and becoming overwhelmed with what she might find. With empathic listening I begin to form a relationship with her. I show confidence that she can make progress, on one condition—that she is willing to work at feeling better. If she will expend some effort, she can gain a sense of control, which is now lacking.

One of my goals in the first session is to help Ruth relax about her problems. Our conversation goes like this:

THERAPIST: What thoughts went through your mind when you came here today?

RUTH: I was afraid and apprehensive. I have wondered what would happen. I often feel pain and am upset.

THERAPIST: How have you tried to fight off your pain, anxiety, fears, and overall upsetness?

RUTH: I have expended a great deal of energy to purge myself of my misery.

THERAPIST: And has this relentless effort paid off for you?

RUTH: When my efforts have not been successful, I have renewed them with more intensity and vigor.

THERAPIST: Tell me about the result of fighting your worries.

RUTH: Well, I must admit that attacking my fears has not yet worked.

THERAPIST: If this approach is not working for you, I encourage you to think in terms of the opposite approach. Since fighting your fears does not help, now may be the time to admit to yourself, at least for a while, that you will continue to be upset. Could you consider embracing your problems? After all you've been through, it is no wonder you're upset. Who wouldn't be?

Presenting this alternative approach to clients often helps them to feel more confident in themselves. They realize that they are normal or at least are handling their problems in a normal way. For Ruth, my hope is that she will begin to consider that her fear, anxiety, and overall upsetness are reactions to her problems, but not the problem itself. If she can see these reactions as normal, she has a good chance of managing them in the future.

Using Metaphors At this point I introduce two metaphors for Ruth's consideration: the backpack and the fork in the road. These metaphors can help Ruth externalize her problem and thus gain a sense of control over it. The metaphor of the backpack implies that she is carrying unnecessary weights or baggage that she can gradually discard. The fork in the road metaphor is an effective and concrete tool for helping Ruth realize that she can proceed step by step on a more satisfying journey. She can either travel "misery boulevard" or "happiness highway."

Exploring Ruth's Quality World In the initial session and in subsequent sessions, we spend a lot of time exploring her "quality world" as it relates to counseling. She goes into detail about the statement that what she wants most from therapy is to be told "what I have to do and be pushed to do it, so that I can begin to live before it's too late." I again make a significant point that she already has a tremendous advantage: even now she believes she can do something, and she wants to begin to live. I ask her to define what it means for her to "live." She describes her feeling of being a doormat at home, being overweight, being lonely and isolated, and being spiritually alienated. As she describes her pain, I express excitement that she is able to put it into words and point out that being able to articulate this pain is a major step on the happiness highway.[3]

Because Ruth referred to her feelings of depression and powerlessness, I ask how depressed and powerless she feels. Does she feel bad enough to take her own life? Has she tried to harm herself previously? Does she have a plan and a means to carry it out? Is there anyone in her environment who would help her if she feels the urge to injure herself accidently or on purpose? If I judge that Ruth (or any client) is seriously considering suicide, I am obligated to take action to prevent it. However, in this case, Ruth affirms that she is not suicidal and that she will not injure herself in any way.

RUTH: To be honest, I am upset that I need to seek professional help and that I can't work out my problems on my own.

THERAPIST: I would be surprised if you weren't upset about seeking outside help. It's a healthy way to feel. But you deserve to be congratulated for taking this first big step. It must have taken courage to try a new pathway.

RUTH: Well, I never thought of it as a big step.

THERAPIST: Tell me about how you believe counseling might help you and whether you think things can improve in a short time.

RUTH: I came because I think it will help me feel better and get a different perspective.

THERAPIST: I've read your history, and we've talked here for a while, and I believe you could feel better. I make no guarantees, but I think a better life is possible. And I base that thought not on an idle wish but on several pieces of specific information: You have taken a step along a new highway by coming here and by opening the backpack. You also have at least some belief that your life can be better. Moreover, you've already set a goal: to keep living. And finally, you're very open about what hurts. In other words, you can describe your pain.

RUTH: So there's hope.

THERAPIST: I agree. There is hope. I also believe you can feel at least a little better quickly, on one condition.

RUTH: What is that condition?

THERAPIST: That you're willing to put forth some effort, even hard work, as you take steps along happiness highway. And this work, strange as it sounds, means less effort in fighting off the pain.

RUTH: I'm willing to do that.

Working With Ruth's Depression

There are times when Ruth resists my optimistic attitude and my emphasis on her positive steps, insisting that they are minor successes and that she sometimes feels depressed. I decide to use paradoxical techniques with Ruth. At first I ask Ruth to schedule some time for choosing to depress herself, perhaps 10 minutes every other day. I ask her to describe in detail what she can do to make the situation worse. She enjoys this discussion and laughs heartily as she goes into detail about how she can criticize herself publicly, procrastinate even more over her plans, increase her guilt, and exaggerate her fear of death. She comes to see how such ineffective thinking holds her back from a happier and need-satisfying life and keeps her on misery boulevard. But most important, she learns through this upside-down logic that if she can make her life more miserable she can also make it more enjoyable. It is important to reemphasize that I have determined early on that she is not suicidal or depressed to the point of being incapacitated. In such cases, paradoxical techniques are to be avoided.

I then encourage Ruth to describe what she wants that she is not getting and to say what she actually is getting from her husband, from each of her children, from her religion, from school, and, most important, from herself. (She has already described what she wants from me.) This exploration takes more than one session. She gradually develops more specific goals or wants related to her family, social life, self (for example, weight), professional life, and the spiritual aspect of her life (a much-neglected area in the counseling profession).

Exploring What Ruth Wants

An exploration of one aspect of Ruth's wants as they relate to her family—more specifically, her husband—is illustrated in this dialogue.

THERAPIST: You've described your relationship with your husband. Describe how you would like the relationship to be. To put it another way, talk about what you want from him that you're not getting.

RUTH: I want him to be understanding.

THERAPIST: Could you be more specific about what you want that you're not getting?

RUTH: He takes me for granted. He only wants me to be a mother for his children. He's always busy at work and doesn't think of me as an independent person. And, you know, sometimes I think he's right.

THERAPIST: But you still want him to feel something different.

RUTH: I would like him to appreciate me, to like me, to be friendly.

THERAPIST: I wonder what would be different if he appreciated you.

RUTH: He would show me more attention.

THERAPIST: Ruth, if he showed you attention tonight, what would you do?

RUTH: I'd be friendly. If he would share something about himself, I'd realize that he has confidence in me and has some feelings for me.

THERAPIST: It seems to me you're saying that a better relationship with him is very appealing to you.

RUTH: Of course.

THERAPIST: I think you've established a goal for your counseling. We'll be talking about what you can do to make the situation better for yourself.

In this dialogue Ruth has defined one want or goal. Using similar questions and exploratory comments, I help her clarify her wants as they relate to her children, religion, school, and other aspects of her life. The emphasis in formulating such goals is on helping her state her own role in the desired outcome.

During these early sessions Ruth also defines what she can control and what she cannot control. I assist her in evaluating whether she can "force" others to change and how much control she can exert over her past history. I gradually help her come to believe her life will be happier if she focuses on changing her own behavior in small increments by removing a few weights from her backpack.[4]

THERAPIST: You've defined what you want for yourself regarding your husband, children, and school. You've said that you want to feel that your life has some spiritual purpose—that it has lasting value. Would you describe the components of your life process that you have control of and what is beyond your control, especially what happiness highway is like for you?

RUTH: I can tell you better what's on misery boulevard: trying to force my husband to change, trying unsuccessfully to lose weight, failing to see some purpose to my life, night terrors, cold sweats, the pain I feel, little professional identity, and hardly a life of my own.

THERAPIST: Can you really change any of these—the people or things on the list?

RUTH: I'm not sure. I'm so confused.

THERAPIST: Let's take them one by one. How about forcing your husband to be the kind of person you want him to be?

RUTH: No, I've tried for years.

THERAPIST: Have your efforts gotten the result you wanted?

RUTH: No.

THERAPIST: Tell me about the weight situation.

RUTH: I've lost and gained it back so many times.

THERAPIST: You have lost weight! So you know how to reduce your pounds, and you've succeeded many times.

RUTH: Well, I haven't looked at it as a success. It seems to me that regaining weight is a failure.

THERAPIST: But you have succeeded many times. You've taken charge of your eating for extended periods.

RUTH: I suppose you're right.

THERAPIST: What about gaining a sense of purpose—what I would call a sense of importance—that you are somebody, that you are worthwhile? How much control do you have over specific plans to formulate this ideal and to work toward it?

RUTH: Well, the way you put it makes it sound as if I could do it and as if I do have some control.

THERAPIST: Ruth, in my counseling I try to translate my clients' ideas into actions—actions that they can take to fulfill their needs.

RUTH: I want to go down that highway. How do I begin?

THERAPIST: By taking small steps—one at a time. But let's not rush. In fact, I'd suggest that you not make any radical or extensive changes until we talk some more.

Process Commentary   I also ask Ruth to decide on her level of commitment. She is obviously not at the basic level: "I don't want to be here." For some parts of her life such as her weight, she may be at the second level: "I would like the outcome, but not the effort." "I'll try," the third level, is probably characteristic of much of her life. But I want to help her see her efforts to lose weight as successes. And so I lead her to the fourth and fifth levels: "I'll do my best" and "I'll do whatever it takes." If clients are willing to be open and work hard, they can benefit in a short time from reality therapy.

The real benefit in utilizing this system is not "the words" but "the music." This questioning format, often discouraged in counselor training programs, along with comments that encourage self-exploration, helps Ruth develop an internal perceived locus of control and realize that she has choices. She then gains a profound belief that life can be better, that she can feel better, and that she has more control than she ever dreamed of. It should be clear that reality therapy involves more than superficial planning and problem solving.

The underlying principle is that when Ruth improves her relationships, her pain will lessen and she will be happier. I will help her in the areas of her relationship with her husband, career, and education. I will help her cope with her overweight problem. Our work will be guided by the general goal of Ruth gaining increased acceptance of herself as both an imperfect and a worthwhile human being.

Helping Ruth Evaluate What She Is Doing

Interspersed throughout the entire process are dozens of questions and requests for self-exploration related to self-evaluation: "Did your specific activities yesterday help you to the degree that you had hoped for?" "Tell me about your realistically attainable wants." "Is what you want really good for you?" More specifically, "Is your boring but comfortable life what you truly want?" "Is it good for you now?" "What would you be doing differently if you were the type of person you wanted to be?" "Talk about how you are getting closer to your husband and children. Describe the closeness you and your family feel for each other." We pick up the dialogue in a subsequent session.

THERAPIST: Let's focus on one aspect of what you have referred to as a source of great pain, which is your relationship with your husband. You mentioned in previous sessions that he ignores you, takes you for granted, and talks only minimally to you. I gather that you want this situation to change.[5]

RUTH: I sure do.

THERAPIST: And you've also decided that your own actions are the only ones that are within your control.

RUTH: Yes.

THERAPIST: Now I want to go over some important questions about the choices you've been making and what you've been doing in the relationship.

RUTH: OK.

THERAPIST: Tell me what happened last night. Describe exactly what you did last night from the time your husband came in to the time you went to bed.

RUTH: [*She describes the entire evening in detail. I help her to be precise.*]

THERAPIST: What did you want from him at that time?

RUTH: [*She describes what she would have liked from him.*]

THERAPIST: What could you say differently tonight from what you said last night?

RUTH: I'll say, "Hello, how was your day?" and give him a hug. Then I'll say, "Let's read the mail and then fix supper together."

THERAPIST: Sounds good. So you'll take charge of the only part of the relationship that's within your ability to control.

RUTH: Yes, my own actions.

THERAPIST: Now let's suppose he doesn't respond the way you would like. What then?

RUTH: Well, I could tell myself: "I've done what I can do, and there's no guarantee that he'll change. I choose to feel satisfaction at having made better choices than those I've made in the past."

THERAPIST: And, if you make this kind of effort, there is a good chance that the relationship will improve. You will be taking another step along happiness highway.

⚘Process Commentary In this session I put emphasis on helping Ruth evaluate her own behavior rather than her husband's actions. By my manner of conversation, I indirectly reminded her that she has control only of her own actions and that if she takes action she will feel that she is doing her part. She then made short-range, attainable plans that have a high likelihood of success. In subsequent sessions she explores other choices—that is, her other unmet needs and their accompanying ineffective and effective behaviors as well as her perceptions regarding the inner sense of control she has gained and still wants to gain. We continue to use the metaphors of gradually discarding the weights from her backpack and traveling along happiness highway.

I encourage Ruth to make more attainable special plans to fulfill her need for fun. I select fun because it is the most obvious unmet need, the one she is most likely to be able to meet more effectively, and the easiest to work on. In view of the fact that she has said she wants to lose weight permanently, I encourage her to join a support group such as Weight Watchers. I suggest that she get to know the students in her classes and organize study groups. This will give her a sense of belonging and help her fulfill her need for power or achievement. I suggest that she replace ineffective self-talk with positive affirmations built on choice theory.

I ask Ruth to read 10 minutes a day (if she wants to) on a topic that is spiritually uplifting. A good starter is *A Set of Directions for Putting and Keeping Yourself Together*.[6] To be avoided is anything that encourages guilt, fear, or self-deprecation. She has expressed a deep need for "an anchor," and to neglect this part of her life would be unfortunate. She can at least be referred to a sensible clergyman who understands reality therapy.

Overall, I help her fulfill her needs for belonging and power and fun more effectively. This is accomplished by use of the "WDEP" system, a detailed process that can be summarized briefly using these four letters: **W** = determining wants, including level of commitment and perceived locus of control; **D** = examining the total behavior, including exploring what she is doing, thinking, and feeling; **E** = assisting her to make her own inner self-evaluations, especially regarding her wants and behaviors; and finally, **P** = helping her develop positive and realistic plans aimed at fulfilling her needs in ways that are different from previous choices. This system is sometimes erroneously referred to as "the questioning process," but it is a much broader exploration.

I feel confident in applying reality therapy with Ruth. I also feel challenged by the multitude of Ruth's problems, but my knowledge of choice theory helps me to see that when she changes any behavior the good feeling and success generalize. Thus I am confident that picking any symptom to work on will lead Ruth to increased satisfaction with her entire life. Her obvious high level of motivation and minimal resistance facilitate relatively steady and visible progress toward the fulfillment of her wants (goals).

Jerry Corey's Work With Ruth From a Reality Therapy Perspective

Introduction

Reality therapy is active, directive, practical, and cognitive behavioral in focus. As a reality therapist, I see my task as helping clients clarify their wants and perceptions, evaluate them, and then make plans to bring about change. My basic job is establishing a personal relationship with my clients that will give them the impetus to make an honest evaluation of how well their current behavior is working for them. In the *DVD for Integrative Counseling: The Case of Ruth and Lecturettes,* Session 8 ("Behavioral Focus in Counseling"), you will note ways that I attempt to assist Ruth in specifying concrete behaviors that she will target for change.

Assessment of Ruth

Rather than focusing on Ruth's deficits, problems, and failures, I am interested in looking at her assets, accomplishments, and successes. Initially I ask her questions such as these: "What do you want? How might your life be different if you had what you wanted now? What do you consider to be your major strengths? What qualities do you most like about yourself? What have you done that you are proud of? What resources can you build on?" From Ruth's autobiography and intake form, I know that she has several strengths and inner resources. Now she needs to develop a clear plan for attaining her personal objectives.

Goals of Therapy

Ruth's present behavior is not working as well as it might. She is unproductively dwelling on unfortunate events from her past, and she is paying too much attention to feelings of guilt and anxiety and not enough to those things she is doing that create these feelings. In short, she is making herself anxious and guilty by what she is doing. I try to direct her attention toward these actions because they are the most easily controlled part of her life. I continue challenging her to make an honest assessment of how well her current behavior is getting her what she wants. Then we collaboratively make plans to bring about the changes she desires.

Therapeutic Procedures

I expect Ruth to make a commitment to carry out her plans. If she hopes to change, *action* is necessary. It is essential that she stick with her commitment to change and not blame others for the way she is or give excuses for not meeting her commitments. To facilitate this, we will develop a therapeutic contract that spells out what she wants from therapy as well as the means by which she will attain her goals. If Ruth says that she is depressed, I will discuss with her what she is *doing* when she is depressed rather than focusing on *why* she is feeling sad.

The Therapeutic Process

Ruth's therapeutic journey consists of my applying the procedures of reality therapy to help her meet her goals. Although the principles may sound simple, they must be adapted creatively to the therapeutic process. Although these principles are applied progressively in stages, they should not be thought of as discrete and rigid categories. Each stage builds on the previous stage, there is a considerable degree of interdependence among these principles, and taken together they contribute to the total process that is reality therapy. This process weaves together two components: the counseling environment and specific procedures that lead to changes in behavior.

ELEMENTS OF THE PROCESS

☙ Establishing the Relationship   During our initial sessions, my main concern is to create a climate that will be conducive to Ruth's learning about herself. The core of the counseling environment consists of a personal involvement with the client, which must be woven into the fabric of the therapeutic process from beginning to end.

In some of our early sessions, Ruth wants to talk about occasions when she experienced failure in her childhood and youth. However, I do not encourage her to focus on the past with the emotional overtones of negative experiences because I do not want to reinforce her in continuing this pattern.

☙ Challenging Ruth to Evaluate Her Behavior   After getting a picture of how Ruth sees her world, I encourage her to try something different—to take a hard look at what she is doing and see if her present behavior is working for her. Questions that I pose to her are: "What are the things you've done today?" "What did you do this past week?" "Do you like what you're doing now?" "Are there some things you would like to be doing differently?" "What are some of the things that stop you from doing what you say you want to do?" Although I do not bombard her with these questions one after another, the early sessions are geared to getting Ruth to consider this line of questioning. Rather than looking at her past or focusing on her attitudes, beliefs, thoughts, and feelings, I want her to know that we will be zeroing in on what she is doing today and what she will do tomorrow.

My assumption is that Ruth will make changes once she assesses how what she is doing is affecting her overall happiness. Here is a brief excerpt from a session.

> RUTH: So, what do you think I'm doing wrong? There are times I want to give up because I don't know what to do differently. [*She very much wants me to make an evaluation for her.*]

> JERRY: You know how important it is for you to be the one who makes a judgment about your own behavior. It's your job to decide for yourself what is and isn't working. I can't tell you what you "should" do. [*For me to simply tell her that some of her present ways are ineffective will not be of much value to her.*]

RUTH: Well, I do want to go out and get some practice with interviews for part-time or substitute teaching. But I keep telling myself that I'm so busy I just don't have time to set up these interviews.

JERRY: And is that something you'd like to change? [*My line of questioning is to ascertain how much she wants what she says she wants. I am attempting to assess her level of commitment.*]

RUTH: Yes, I want to change it. I want to be able to arrange for these interviews and then feel confident enough to have what it takes to get a part-time job.

We look at how Ruth stops herself (not why) and explore ways she might begin to change behavior that she calls "sitting back and waiting to see what happens." She says that she does not like her passivity and that she would like to do more initiating. One of the factors we talk about is how she lets her family get in the way of her doing some of these things she says she wants to do.

🌱 Planning and Action   Ruth describes a few ineffective behaviors, including procrastinating in arranging for job interviews; sitting at home feeling depressed and anxious and then increasing these feelings by not doing anything different; allowing her 19-year-old son, Rob, to come home after squandering money and then taking care of him; allowing her daughter Jennifer to control her life by her acting out; and continually taking on projects that she does not want to get involved in. Knowing that we cannot work on all fronts at once, I ask her what areas she wants to do something about.

We develop plans to set clear limits with Ruth's family. She has a pattern of doing things for her children and then resenting them and winding up feeling taken advantage of. Part of her plan calls for sitting down with each of her children and redefining their relationship. I suggest that it would be a good idea to have at least one session with her family. The idea both excites and frightens her. Yet she actually surprises herself when she is successful in getting John and her four children to come in for a 2-hour session of family therapy. At this session we mainly negotiate some changes in roles after Ruth has told each family member specific changes she would like and has been striving for. One of her sons and one of her daughters are not at all excited about some of the proposed changes, and they want to know what is wrong with the way things are. What I had in mind when I suggested this family session was to give Ruth an opportunity to ask for what she wants and to witness her negotiating for these changes. The session helps me see how she relates to her family, and it helps her ask for what is important to her.

PROCESS COMMENTARY   Functioning within the spirit of reality therapy, I do not tell Ruth what she should change but encourage her to examine her wants and determine her level of commitment to change. Once she makes an evaluation about what she is actually doing, she can take some significant steps toward making changes for herself. She has a tendency to complain about feeling victimized and controlled, and my intention is to help her see how her behavior actually contributes to this perceived helplessness. In our sessions, we focus on what Ruth does from the time she wakes up to the time she goes to bed. Through a self-observation process, Ruth gradually assumes more responsibility for her actions. She sees that what she does has a lot to do with the way she feels.

Once Ruth becomes clearer about certain patterns of her behavior, I encourage her to develop a specific plan of action that can lead to the changes she desires. Broad and idealistic plans are bound to fail, so we work on a concrete plan for change that she is willing to commit herself to. Through this process, Ruth learns how to evaluate her own behavior and how to adjust her plans to experience success.[7]

Some Final Thoughts

With both Dr. Glasser's and Dr. Wubbolding's approach to counseling Ruth, it is clear that insight and awareness are not enough; Ruth needed to make a self-evaluation. Once she decided she wanted to change a behavior, it was essential for her to develop a plan of action and make a commitment to following through with her plans. The existential foundation of choice theory is a major strength of this approach. The essence of reality therapy is learning how to make better and more effective choices to gain more effective control. People take charge of their lives rather than being the victim of circumstances beyond their control.

Questions for Reflection

1. Dr. Glasser contends, "Although I believe we may be the product of our past, we are not victims of our past unless we choose to be so. Approaching a client this way drastically shortens therapy because it quickly gets to the core of the problem." What do you think of this viewpoint?
2. Dr. Glasser states, "All of our chosen ineffective behaviors—neurosis, psychosomatic disease, and psychosis—are our self-destructive attempts to improve a present relationship or find a better one." What are your reactions to this statement?
3. Dr. Glasser could be said to have a no-nonsense approach. What are your thoughts about the kind of advice he suggested for Ruth?
4. Both Dr. Glasser and Dr. Wubbolding seem very directive in pointing out the themes Ruth should explore, and they also are fairly directive in suggesting what she should do outside of the sessions. What are your reactions to this stance? As Ruth's counselor, would you be inclined to bring up topics for her to explore if she did not specifically mention them? Why or why not?
5. Do you have any concerns that reality therapy could be practiced in such a way that the therapist would impose his or her values on the client? Do you see this as potentially happening with the way Dr. Glasser, Dr. Wubbolding, or I worked with Ruth?
6. Dr. Wubbolding uses frequent questioning to help Ruth clarify what she wants. What are some of his questions that you most like? Why? He also uses metaphors, such as "highway to happiness." What value do you see in using metaphors in counseling?
7. What differences do you see in the various styles and applications of reality therapy as practiced by Dr. Glasser and Dr. Wubbolding with Ruth?

8. Apply the procedures of reality therapy to what you know of Ruth. Systematically show how you would get her to focus on what she is doing, on making an evaluation of her behavior, and on helping her formulate realistic plans.

9. Assume that you are a client in reality therapy. What do you think this experience would be like for you? How would you describe your current behavior? Can you come up with a plan for changing a particular behavior you really want to change?

10. How would you generalize the use of the WDEP system to other issues: anxiety, anger, antisocial behaviors such as defiance, resistance, career counseling, or personal growth issues?

11. How well does reality therapy fit with your counseling style? What aspects of this approach do you find most useful? Which aspects might you want to modify to fit your personal counseling style?

Notes

See the *DVD for Theory and Practice of Counseling and Psychotherapy: The Case of Stan* and Lecturettes, Session 9 ("Reality Therapy Applied to the Case of Stan"), for an illustration of assisting Stan in designing an action plan and for my presentation of ways that reality therapy can be applied.

1. For a more complete discussion of Dr. Glasser's latest thinking on how choice theory applies to the practice of counseling, see Glasser, W. (2001). *Counseling with choice theory: The new reality therapy.* New York: HarperCollins.

2. Glasser, W. (1998). *Choice theory: A new psychology of personal freedom.* New York: HarperCollins.

3. For a more detailed treatment of Dr. Wubbolding's perspective on applying reality therapy, see Wubbolding, R. (2000). *Reality therapy for the 21st century.* Philadelphia, PA: Brunner Routledge (Taylor & Francis). See also Wubbolding, R. (2011). *Reality therapy.* Washington DC: American Psychological Association.

4. Rather than have Ruth become overwhelmed by attempting to make sweeping changes in her life, Dr. Wubbolding suggests that Ruth select small aspects of her behavior that she can change.

5. Dr. Wubbolding uses skillful questioning as a way to help Ruth evaluate what she is doing.

6. See Wubbolding, R., & Brickell, J. (2001). *A set of directions for putting and keeping yourself together.* Minneapolis, MN: Educational Media Corporation. This is a practical and positive self-help book based on the concepts of reality therapy.

7. For an overview of the basic concepts of reality therapy, see Corey, G. (2013). *Theory and practice of counseling and psychotherapy* (9th ed.). Belmont, CA: Brooks/Cole, Cengage Learning. Chapter 11 ("Reality Therapy") describes the WDEP system that both Dr. Wubbolding and I refer to in our work with Ruth. This chapter also contains a comprehensive discussion of Dr. Glasser's formulation of choice theory and reality therapy.

CHAPTER TEN

Case Approach to Feminist Therapy

General Overview of Feminist Therapy

Feminist theory originated in response to the feminist and civil rights movements of the 1960s and focused on affirming the voices of women. The theory encompasses a broader perspective today, valuing marginalized voices of both men and women. The major goal of feminist therapy is empowerment; clients strive for a sense of self-acceptance, self-confidence, self-esteem, joy, and self-actualization. Other therapy goals include enhancing the quality of interpersonal relationships, assisting both women and men to make decisions regarding role performances, and helping clients to come to an understanding of the cultural, social, and political systems' influence on their current situation. Clients can expect more than adjustment or simple problem-solving strategies; they need to be prepared for major shifts in their way of viewing the world around them, changes in the way in which they perceive themselves, and transformed interpersonal relationships.

Feminist therapists carry out a range of information-giving and teaching functions. By focusing on external structures, they attempt to free clients from a "blaming the victim" stance. They are free to use techniques from many other therapy orientations, and they often employ techniques such as reframing and relabeling, bibliotherapy, advocacy, power intervention, social action, and gender-role analysis and intervention.

Feminist therapists emphasize the teaching aspects of therapy and strive to create a collaborative way of working with clients. Emphasis is placed on the demystification of the therapy process and on providing a context wherein informed consent can occur. The egalitarian relationship developed in the sessions serves as a model for relationship building outside of therapy. Clients decide when they want to terminate, which usually occurs when clients feel an increased sense of personal identity and empowerment.

A Feminist Therapist's Perspective on Ruth

by Kathy M. Evans, PhD, Susan R. Seem, PhD,
and Elizabeth A. Kincade, PhD[1]

Introduction

Feminist therapy is unique among counseling and psychotherapy theories in that therapists view the "personal as the political," challenging a basic assumption of psychological thinking that distress is personal and due to individual pathology. This pioneering approach recognizes that individuals are embedded in their social and cultural contexts and that lasting psychological change must address these contextual issues as well as individual issues. Feminist therapy emerged from three aspects of the women's liberation movement of the 1960s: consciousness-raising groups, battered women shelters, and the anti-rape movement. Eschewing patriarchal structures that foster a "father knows best" attitude, women met and worked together to change personal, political, social, and cultural beliefs and values about women and their roles.

Feminist therapists work to change the dominant culture's structure and power that is harmful to individual clients, and they have had a profound effect on the field of counseling and psychology, especially with regard to gender bias and gender-role stereotyping. As a result, there have been significant changes in how the profession views diagnosis, case conceptualization, and treatment. For feminist therapists there is no lasting individual change without social change.

It is important to note that awareness of women as an oppressed group developed from the privileged class of women, who for the most part were White, middle class, and educated. Contemporary feminist therapy recognizes that privilege harms all individuals, both the oppressed and the oppressor. Therapy now focuses on all forms of oppression—racism, homophobia, ageism, classism, and ableism—for both women and men, in addition to sexism and the effect of multiple oppressions on people.

Current feminist therapy more closely resembles existential and humanistic modes of therapy than the evidence-based or empirically validated approaches. Feminist therapy techniques are grounded in empiricism but emphasize the relational intersections in therapy, including those of the client and the greater societal context. This emphasis influences the treatment choices made by feminist practitioners.[2]

Approaches to Feminist Therapy

Feminism holds that gender inequity exists and that this is a source of oppression to individuals and societies. In addition, this oppression is painful and harmful. This inequality is based in power, and for the most part the power balance is in favor of men. Furthermore, feminist philosophy seeks to answer the question, "What is the source of gender oppression?" How one answers this question largely determines how one uses interventions with clients. Various feminist philosophies answer this question differently.

At one end of the continuum is the belief that oppression is due to patriarchy, or male domination. In this model, enduring change requires political and social action rather than merely individual change. At the other end of the continuum is the belief that oppression is largely caused by socialization, our internalized individual and self-replicating cultural beliefs. Within this model, individual change *is* possible and necessary as this forces societal beliefs and positions to change.

Although there are philosophical differences among feminist practitioners, the basic tenets and beliefs of feminist therapy are the same. Therapist and client work together to understand and remove the psychological, sociopolitical, and cultural factors that result in client distress. Feminist therapy holds two overarching goals. The immediate goal is to relieve an individual client's distress. The ultimate goal is to alleviate sociopolitical oppression. This long-term goal requires feminist therapists to consider social change as a part of the therapeutic process.

Initial Assessment and Evaluation

Although none of the three of us takes a single approach to feminist therapy, we agreed that we would each discuss Ruth's case from a different point of view based on the question "What is the basis of gender oppression?" Susan presents the radical feminist perspective that patriarchy is the source of oppression. Kathy presents the liberal perspective that oppression is due to undervaluing women's unique ways of being in the world. Elizabeth takes the socialist perspective that the core of oppression is a complicated blend of economic philosophy and gender disparity. We discuss our theoretical and therapeutic differences in conceptualizing Ruth's case when appropriate. When we agree, we present one point of view. The final dialogue with Ruth is a combination of our three approaches.

Traditional Diagnosis and Assessment   As traditionally practiced, diagnostic systems such as the *DSM-IV-TR* reflect the dominant culture's definitions of pathology and health. Many feminist therapists avoid using these diagnostic systems. However, if we were to use a formal diagnostic system to diagnose Ruth as part of her assessment, we would use the *DSM-IV-TR* with knowledge of its major weaknesses and the context in which it was written.[3]

Clinical bias or subjectivity play a role in diagnosis, and descriptors in the current DSM minimize cultural context. Misdiagnosis and blaming the victim may occur when sociopolitical factors are minimized or ignored. Few diagnostic labels identify the source of the client's problem as being due to the environment. Institutional and societal oppression affect the level of stress a person experiences on a day-to-day basis and can influence behavior. Labeling responses to bias, prejudice, or stereotyped behavior as a mental illness contributes to the system of oppression feminist therapists are trying to change. In addition, diagnostic labeling can disempower the client, leaving the perception that change is not within the client's control.

Feminist Assessment and Evaluation   Historically, feminist therapists eschewed diagnosis because they could not formally diagnose internalized oppression. However, a feminist sensitivity to diagnosis can result in the use of formal diagnostic systems without replicating patriarchal assumptions and attitudes. Diagnosis, as traditionally practiced, is an act of power that exacerbates the power imbalance between counselor and client. In contrast, feminist assessment and diagnosis require a cooperative and phenomenological approach.

After reviewing the summary of Ruth's intake interview and her autobiography, all three of us agreed that our work with Ruth would examine the multifaceted social, political, and economic context of her life. This examination would move beyond understanding Ruth within her family and seek to comprehend her personal relationships within the context of the larger society.

Ruth's exposure to sexism and other forms of oppression constitute an insidious long-term trauma. Our evaluation of Ruth consists of listening for connections between the personal and the political in her story. We work to understand Ruth as a gendered being who, because she identifies and is identified as a woman, is assigned a subordinate status by the dominant male-oriented culture. Thus we use gender and power as categories of analysis for Ruth and her life experience. This type of analysis creates avenues for the exploration of gender-role concerns and issues of power without punishing Ruth for participation in her socialization process and subordinate societal status.

Ruth's people pleasing, living for others, difficulty acting on her own behalf, being a superwoman, and being a good wife and good mother are viewed as evidence of her acceptance of her traditional female gender-role socialization and her second-class status. These are not viewed as behavioral indications of pathology or dependency. Ruth's symptoms of panic are viewed as a result of role conflict. Women are often forced to choose between their own growth as individuals and traditional female gender-role behavior. This choice results in internal conflict that may surface as anxiety. Ruth expresses her awareness of living for others and feeling obligated to stay in her marriage. She communicates her acute awareness of dissatisfaction with her life as it is but also clearly articulates her fear of change. Ruth's symptoms of panic, her feelings of conflict, and her identity confusion are viewed as coping strategies for or adaptations to surviving oppression, discrimination, and gender-role stereotyping. Her symptoms also might be a protest against her oppression. Ruth's behaviors and feelings are adaptive rather than pathological, and we would not give her a diagnostic label at this time.

We also look closely at Ruth's anger because feelings of powerlessness often lead to feelings of rage. Women are not supposed to have legitimate power in patriarchal societies, and they often feel powerless. Patriarchal norms do not support and often punish direct expression of female anger, so women have learned to convert anger into symptoms that are acceptable, such as those associated with depression. Based on this assumption, we explore with Ruth her feelings about being powerless. We encourage Ruth to express her anger at her treatment as a woman. We view anger as potential positive energy and help Ruth use this energy to take either individual or social action to obtain power in her life.

We differ in our assessment work with Ruth in that Susan, working from a radical feminist perspective, pays particular attention to the meaning and presence of female gender-role compliance and noncompliance for Ruth, including past and current rewards and penalties. She examines with Ruth how her second-class status as a woman influences her psychological distress. One focus of assessment, therefore, is to identify how Ruth has internalized oppressive sociocultural forces. Kathy adds to this perspective by helping Ruth identify her stage of feminist identity development and assessing such things as anger, self-examination, acceptance, and role confusion. As a socialist feminist, Elizabeth addresses the economic issues of monetary payment and the sociopolitical implications of a *DSM-IV-TR* diagnosis.

Any assessment is done in collaboration with Ruth, and we encourage Ruth to ask questions or pose alternative options. If, as a result of our assessment, a formal label is given, the diagnosis and its possible consequences are discussed with Ruth. In that discussion we share with Ruth the process by which we arrived at such a formal diagnosis. Also, Ruth will share in decisions about how this information is used.

The Therapeutic Relationship

All therapy demands a firm relational foundation, otherwise client changes tend to be ephemeral or superficial. The necessary conditions for feminist therapy are the establishment of an egalitarian relationship and a deep and thorough understanding of Ruth's story, or the narrative of her experience.

❧ Establishing and Modeling Egalitarian Relationships An egalitarian relationship is essential if Ruth is to achieve a sense of her own power. It is important to work with Ruth to remove artificial power boundaries in the counseling relationship. Feminist counselors consider the first contact with clients as an interview: an opportunity for counselor and client to get to know each other and make a mutual decision about whether or not they will work together. Feminist therapists work to demystify counseling. To that end, we ask Ruth why she is seeking counseling and what she wants to gain from it. We share with her that we are feminist therapists who approach counseling from a feminist perspective and explain what this means without jargon, with respect for Ruth's intelligence.

In addition, since Ruth has little experience with mutually satisfying relationships in which she is viewed as an equal participant, it is important that Ruth experience and learn how to establish egalitarian relationships in her own life. Thus it is important to model an egalitarian relationship in the counseling relationship. This modeling begins with the first session. Ruth is invited to actively participate in the assessment process, in the contracting of counseling, and in setting counseling goals. Further, feminist therapy has the goal of helping Ruth develop interdependence in relationships and enabling her to develop skills to negotiate her needs and wants in relationships.

Kathy, working from her perspective as a liberal, African American feminist therapist, acknowledges the power differential between Ruth and herself, which is based in American conceptions of race. By seeking help from Kathy, the balance of power between Kathy and Ruth shifts so that it is more equal in that Ruth (a White woman with supposedly more power in our society) needs Kathy's help (which gives Kathy more power). Kathy would explore Ruth's experiences with people of color and would tell Ruth about herself as a professional and a little about her perspectives regarding their commonalities as women in society. She would let Ruth know that if she wishes to see a counselor more similar to herself she understands.

Elizabeth, examining the case from the socialist feminist perspective also focuses on power but does so by acknowledging that clients pay for counseling and that this interferes with establishing an egalitarian relationship. In addition, as a socialist feminist she is aware of how titles are used to take power away from people. Those we call by a title usually hold economic power or social status different from our own.

All three of us hold that self-disclosure, when it is in service to Ruth, is a very powerful and important part of establishing and maintaining an egalitarian relationship. We share with Ruth our belief that although we possess expertise in counseling techniques and psychological theory, Ruth has her own specialized knowledge—she is the expert in her life and experiences.

🌀 Understanding Ruth's Story   It is important that Ruth's story is accepted and validated by her therapist. Feminist therapy embraces values that may conflict with some of Ruth's cultural and religious values, and we accept this. We do not lecture Ruth about oppression; rather, we guide her through an exploration of her life experiences that involve oppression. We tell Ruth that we believe each woman experiences her gender, race, ethnicity, and culture differently, and we listen for evidence of all these factors in Ruth's story.

Further, we help Ruth understand herself in relation to her sociopolitical context. Part of understanding Ruth's story and educating her about the complex sources of her distress entails knowing her beliefs, thoughts, and feelings about being a White, 39-year-old, middle-class woman who comes from a fundamentalist religious background. We provide Ruth with information about women in general, and we self-disclose about our own beliefs and experiences when appropriate. In addition, we engage in self-examination of our own strengths and limitations, biases and prejudices, and worldview regarding this client.

Interventions and Therapy Goals

One of the goals of feminist therapy is empowerment for the client; feminist therapists assume that clients will leave counseling empowered to act on their own. When and how they do this is a collaborative effort between therapist and client. This means that the therapist and client are aware of changing needs in the therapeutic relationship and negotiate for more or fewer sessions when mutually agreed upon. Short-term interventions, such as assertion training, cognitive restructuring, and short-term dynamic models are woven into feminist therapy practice.

Goals for counseling are devised collaboratively. Feminist therapists educate their clients about the theory and process of feminist therapy, which empowers clients to make informed choices about therapy. Therapy is demystified, and clients are taught therapeutic skills. Feminist therapists model egalitarian behaviors that will help clients negotiate relationships within and outside of counseling.

Despite ideological differences in conceptualizing women's oppression, the three of us use these interventions with our clients and believe these specific interventions would be useful with Ruth. These interventions are (a) gender-role and power analysis, (b) increasing assertiveness, (c) bibliotherapy, (d) reframing Ruth's concerns and symptoms, and (e) social and political action.

🌿 Gender-Role and Power Analysis   Gender-role analysis is used to increase Ruth's insight about how societal gender-role expectations adversely affect women and how women and men are socialized differently. Ruth needs to examine the gender-role messages (verbal, nonverbal, and modeled) she has experienced in her lifetime from society as a whole, from her family of origin, and from her religion. As a result, Ruth learns that her conflicts about her life and identity are due to the fact that she wants to step outside her traditionally defined female gender role. Ruth identifies the positive and negative consequences of following or rejecting those gender-role messages. She gains awareness about her strengths and how and why these may not be valued in a patriarchal society.

We help Ruth recognize and value her strengths, some of which are part of her learned gender role. These strengths include her ability to nurture and to balance a multitude of roles and a willingness to question the values and beliefs she was taught. Through therapy Ruth learns how she has internalized certain gender-role messages in conscious and unconscious ways. She is supported in developing a woman-identified sense of femininity rather than a male-identified one. Ruth is encouraged to acquire a full range of behaviors that are freely chosen rather than prescribed by gender-role stereotypes.

Working from the radical feminist stance, Susan explores with Ruth several definitions of power, resulting in a definition that best fits her. Together, Ruth and Susan explore the kinds of power to which Ruth has access. Ruth has always been encouraged to exert her power in indirect and helpless ways rather than in direct and competent ways. In therapy with Susan, Ruth is encouraged to change her internalized messages about her use of power and to freely explore various ways she can use her power.

Kathy's perspective differs somewhat. As a liberal feminist therapist, her goal is for Ruth to examine her changing relationships with her husband and children, her parents, and her relationship with God. Kathy seeks to assist Ruth in realigning the balance of power in her familial relationships so that she can develop her own female style of self without subservience.

Elizabeth believes Ruth underestimates her power and is, perhaps, afraid of it. This is shown through Ruth's fears that her choices will destroy her family. As women, we are not trained to accept power or to admit that we have any. It might well be that Ruth's problems with her daughter are a manifestation of the loss of the only power she has been "allowed" to have within her dominant culture. In addition, as a socialist feminist therapist with an awareness of the economic exploitation of women, Elizabeth wonders aloud with Ruth why she is considering substitute teaching (a role that traditionally exploits married women) and has not sought to become a full-time teacher. Elizabeth explores with Ruth whether she does not pursue full-time teaching because she fears the responsibility and freedom of her own classroom.

🌿 Increasing Assertiveness   Assertiveness training has been a part of feminist therapy since its inception. For women, assertiveness is frequently equated

with aggression, and young girls do not learn how to stand up for their rights as human beings. Assertiveness training seeks to teach women how they can assert their own rights, without being aggressive. Because of the goals Ruth has set for herself, we are inclined to work with her on being more assertive.

Our conceptualization of Ruth is that she feels confused and guilty when she wants to step out of her prescribed gender role. Part of the goal of counseling is to help Ruth define a sense of self without taking a subservient role. Group therapy allows members to interact with others in a cooperative manner while at the same time learning new ways of being. An assertiveness group for women is indicated for Ruth. In this group she will learn that she is not alone and that being assertive does not mean she will alienate others. She will learn new skills and be able to help other women as well as receive help from others in the group.

Bibliotherapy

An important goal of feminist therapy is to help Ruth begin to understand how her own situation is connected with the common experience of all women. To that end, bibliotherapy helps Ruth understand that her personal pain is not unique to her and that many women experience similar struggles. It is important that Ruth has an opportunity to discuss her reactions to the readings during counseling sessions and to explore how they apply to her life.

We suggest two types of readings to Ruth. The first are readings from mental health professionals who write about issues similar to hers. The next are essays and fiction by women who have explored and experienced concerns similar to hers. For example, readings in White female experience and in feminist Christianity can help Ruth retain the essence of her faith yet at the same time be more comfortable with the changes she may decide to make in her life. We suggest to Ruth several writers who explore the juxtaposition of Christianity and feminism and describe feminist and Christian ethics. These readings will help to create a sense of connection and possibilities for Ruth without overtly threatening her status quo. As feminist therapists who have benefited from the struggles and experiences of other women, we share with Ruth that reading about the lives and works of others has been a source of strength and learning for us.

Reframing Ruth's Concerns and Symptoms

Feminist therapists believe many of the symptoms clients bring to counseling are symptoms of living in a culture that values male experiences over female experiences. Although all people are harmed by living in a male-dominated culture, women have learned to view their experiences negatively, and Ruth is no exception. She obviously sees her symptoms as signs of weakness and believes something is innately wrong with her. Feminist therapists view Ruth's symptoms as indicative of the stress between cultural and personal conflicts. This reframing, however, does not negate her actual symptoms. Consequently, we work with Ruth to teach her how to gain control of her symptoms through cognitive and behavioral techniques such as stress and relaxation management, thought stopping, and positive self-statements. The techniques chosen do not necessarily come from feminist theory. Techniques should be matched to the needs of the client and thus could come from any theoretical perspective. In addition, even though Ruth comes to an understanding that the cause of her problems lies within society and cultural mores, she is not absolved from taking responsibility for making changes in her life.

As a radical feminist therapist, Susan views many of the symptoms women bring to counseling as passive forms of female rebellion against femininity as defined by the patriarchy. She reframes Ruth's distress with her role in life and her family. She sees Ruth's panic symptoms as ways Ruth is trying to communicate to herself her desire to step outside the constricted traditional female gender role. Susan explores with Ruth the possibility of suppressed rage being manifested in symptoms that allow her to still be feminine yet also revolt against male-defined femininity. Ruth is encouraged to acknowledge and express her anger. Her feelings and thoughts are reframed as evidence of her revolt against being placed in a subservient role, which no long brings her satisfaction. Susan engages in a dialogue with Ruth about the ways in which she wants to define herself as mother and wife that might meet her need to be interdependent and nonsubservient.

The liberal feminist perspective seeks to help women understand the value in women's gender roles and works toward creating a society that values men's and women's strengths equally. Kathy works with Ruth on reframing her experience as a woman in American society and as a cultural being. Together, Kathy and Ruth explore the centuries of cultural and religious mandates regarding women and the inequities of the traditional system of marriage and family. They look at Ruth's family system and how expectations for her to stay at home may keep her from realizing the true value of herself, her skills, and her assets. Interventions include asking Ruth to listen to and identify those internalized negative messages from her parents and church that continue to be replayed in her head and cause most of her conflicts. They engage in reframing or replacing these internalized messages with ones that fit with her current circumstances.

Elizabeth chooses to focus on Ruth's strengths. Ruth is managing a family and is juggling various roles. Together they work to identify and honor her strengths. She is asked to do some simple homework consisting of two lists: things she values about herself and things she does not value. This gives Ruth and Elizabeth a starting point for focusing on what Ruth views as important in her therapy. It helps identify what she has been taught to value and not value about herself. Negative beliefs can then be gently confronted through self-disclosure, assigning readings, and presenting her with conflicting evidence of her own behavior. For instance, Elizabeth congratulates Ruth on having raised a daughter who can stand up for herself and make her own choices, even when she knows that this will displease others.

❧ Taking Social and Political Action

A primary goal of feminist therapy with Ruth is to help her understand how her distress as an individual woman is connected to women as a cultural group. Consequently, we are interested in sharing with Ruth our involvement in social action geared toward changing the oppressive and painful features of society that do not value women and their work. We encourage Ruth to engage in social action to reduce her sense of isolation, to help use her anger constructively and feel better about herself, and to effect some change on the structures of society.

It could be useful for Ruth to engage in some sort of collective work focused on women's oppression. Social action is a way of refocusing and reframing anger. We often tell clients who doubt the usefulness of anger, or who fear their own strong emotions, that such emotions can be positive. If it were not for anger, women's shelters would not exist. If women had not been angry, sexual abuse would not have been addressed, and people would be in pain and more children abused. This puts social action in perspective. For Ruth, being involved in social action would be a way of healing past pains. We might suggest that she volunteer at the local women's shelter either on the hot line or as a support person. Being a support person would allow her to use her nurturing skills to help other women. This, in turn, would help her feel more competent. This is a potent therapeutic modality for both societal and individual change.

Glimpses of Ruth's Therapy

🌾 Establishing and Nurturing the Egalitarian Relationship   This is the beginning of the first session. The therapist's focus on power in the relationship reinforces trust building. This discussion models a healthy relationship between peers, values Ruth's life experience, and allows Ruth to begin making healthy decisions for herself.

THERAPIST: You mentioned that this is your first time in counseling. Would it help you if I tell you a little about myself and about the process of counseling?

RUTH: Yeah. I guess so. I really don't know what to expect. It's a big step for me to admit that things aren't going right. Before I came in today I thought I would just ask you to tell me what to do, but now I don't know. I'm confused about what I want. Is that all right?

THERAPIST: I agree that it is scary and confusing when you realize that you can't solve all your problems yourself. I know this from personal experience. I can't tell you what to do because I haven't lived your life, but I do think that together we will be able to work out a counseling plan for you. I have found with other people who are anxious about counseling that a good place to start is for me to tell you how I work with my clients. Then you can tell me a bit more about why you are here, and we can talk about how we can go about counseling and what will work best for you. How does that sound?

RUTH: You mean I don't have to do all the talking right away?

THERAPIST: No. Not right now. The way I see counseling is that it's the two of us working together to find out what is best for you. You are the expert in your life. I am the expert in counseling. I work from a feminist perspective. This means two things. First, I will work hard to understand your concerns from your perspective. I value your knowledge about yourself and your difficulties. Second, I bring a social and political perspective to my understanding of you and your life. I believe the causes of the problems many women bring to counseling are external. In general women are not valued by our society, and this creates psychological distress.

RUTH [*Looking perplexed and somewhat dubious*]: I'm not sure I understand.

THERAPIST: I understand this sounds confusing at first. After all, if women are not valued, wouldn't you have noticed? I believe that you have noticed, and that is part of what your pain is about, even if you haven't recognized it yet. For example, you mentioned a concern about your weight when we first talked. Look at current fashion magazines and ask yourself who decides what looks good and if it really does look good. Then ask yourself what happens to those of us who don't fit the model. I believe that what happens when we don't fit the ideal is that we feel bad about ourselves.

RUTH: I never thought that my concerns might be connected to being a woman. That's something I'm going to have to think about because all I know is that I feel scared and anxious and worried all the time about what I'm going to do, and I think something is wrong with me.

THERAPIST: Yes, I agree. It is scary to be here. I am not surprised that you're anxious.

RUTH: Also, I don't know if I feel comfortable working with someone who is a feminist. I know my husband will not be happy because he is always putting down feminists.

THERAPIST: That's an important concern for you. It sounds like your husband is important to you, and you don't want to upset him. I am wondering, however, if you can share with me some more of your concerns about working with a feminist counselor?

RUTH: I am afraid you will tell me that all my problems are because of my husband and that all I need to do is divorce him and leave my kids. Don't feminists believe that men are the cause of all problems?

THERAPIST: For the most part, individual men are not the problem, but the fact that our culture places men first might be. With regard to feminism, I can't speak for all feminist therapists, but only for myself. I encourage clients to take responsibility for making changes that will help them feel better about themselves. I will work with you to help you figure out what is best for you.

RUTH: So you're a feminist therapist because of your belief that a lot of women's problems are caused by the way women are treated and valued? But you won't force your beliefs on me?

THERAPIST: No, I won't.

RUTH: OK, I guess I am willing to work with you.

THERAPIST: You don't sound sure.

RUTH: Yes, I am. Well, not exactly sure. I know my father says that feminists are the cause of the destruction of the family.

THERAPIST: It sounds like you have two concerns. One is about doing what the important people in your life think is right, and the other is that you are concerned that feminism might harm you and interfere with your relationships with those people. Does that sound right to you?

RUTH: Maybe I do want to figure myself out without others telling me what to do or how to be. This is new for me.

THERAPIST: You are telling me very clearly that you do not want to be influenced in ways that don't fit with who you are.

RUTH: Yes. I want to be able to figure out what I believe without others telling me what to believe.

THERAPIST: I think your desire to figure things out for yourself is a strength. Let me propose this: How about if we work together for four sessions. That way you can get a feel for me and how I work. We will set aside our fourth session to discuss whether or not you are feeling that I am hearing, understanding, and helping you.

RUTH: So I could leave if I wanted to?

THERAPIST: Yes. Although if you leave, I would like us to be able to talk about why so I can understand your decision.

RUTH: I like that.

THERAPIST: All right, it sounds like we have developed our first plan—together.

ꙮ Power and Gender-Role Analysis in Family Relationships
This is Ruth's fifth session. It occurs after the therapeutic relationship has been established and Ruth and the therapist have negotiated 10 more sessions. This section reflects a melding of therapeutic influences. Elizabeth, influenced by cognitive approaches, and Susan, influenced by psychodynamic theory, collaborated on the response. Thus Ruth is both challenged to confront dysfunctional beliefs and helped to explore emotions and relationships. This section highlights how feminist therapists integrate different styles and perspectives into their repertoire of counseling skills.

RUTH: I am so glad I am here today. I just need to talk to you.

THERAPIST: It sounds like something has come up for you. Last week you said you were learning to manage stress better and your episodes of panic seemed to have subsided.

RUTH: Oh, but this is different [*Pauses and looks somewhat less excited*]. My church has its own school. They know I have my Bachelor's in Education now. They want to hire me full time. How can I do that? I would be away from home all day. Even when I was going to school I was still only gone part time. Will my family think I am a lousy mother because I won't be at home? I am not even a certified teacher yet. What should I do?

THERAPIST: Wow, this sounds like something you are really split about. On one hand you would like to continue as you always have and not have change in your life; on the other hand you have been working toward this change for many years.

RUTH: Yeah. That's the funny thing. I didn't just go to college without a goal. I actually knew that I wanted to teach. I knew that someday it would be real. But, now that it is, I don't know what to do.

THERAPIST: The school must like you and respect you if they want to hire you for the fall.

RUTH: I have been tutoring and volunteering on and off ever since I changed churches. I like the kids and the teachers. I just thought I was lucky because they let me volunteer, but I guess I must have done well.

THERAPIST: So, what stops you from accepting the position?

RUTH: John and the kids. You know, John keeps telling me he wants me back like I was before I went back to college. Last week I asked him to pick up the two younger children from band practice at school while I went to a committee meeting. He told me that he couldn't and then was sarcastic. He said, "Maybe you'd like it better if I divorced you. Then you could go to meetings all the time."

THERAPIST: Are you afraid to accept the position because John talks about divorce?

RUTH: Yeah. He plays the divorce card frequently.

THERAPIST: And it sounds like you back down from doing what you want to do when John plays the divorce card.

RUTH [*Thinks a bit*]: I guess you could see it that way. But he does have the upper hand. I don't want to lose him and the kids. I don't really dislike my life, but I'm just not satisfied. I don't know. Now I'm confused all over again.

THERAPIST: Let's talk about your relationship with John. I think this might help you figure out what to do about the job offer.

RUTH: OK. I think you might be right. It is my fears about my family that are confusing me. I never imagined myself as a working mother. I know I really want to teach, but I am afraid that if I take the full-time job, it won't be good for my family.

THERAPIST: This is a concern many women have. It's hard not to feel selfish when you choose something you really want. We women are told that if we do anything for ourselves, someone else will suffer.

RUTH: I want the family together. That's probably what I am doing wrong here. By pursuing the job I am pulling the family apart. You're right. I am being selfish and my family will suffer.

THERAPIST: That certainly is a piece of what John is telling you. Traditionally this is what women do in our society. It is our job to keep the family together. This gives John a lot of power.

RUTH: I hadn't thought about it like that.

THERAPIST: Your life is changing a great deal right now, and there is much uncertainty. Your kids are getting ready to move on with their own lives in a few years, so they are less invested. John implies that a divorce would be OK with him.

RUTH [*With anger toward the therapist*]: John would be lost without me! He still can't do the laundry. I know that's funny—and you'd probably call it stereotypical—but I have done everything for him. If he left me, he'd fall apart.

THERAPIST: Take a moment and feel this emotion you are expressing. What would you name it?

RUTH [*Thinks for a moment*]: Anger. I am angry with you for suggesting that John would leave me. I know he wouldn't!

THERAPIST [*Nodding in agreement*]: You are right. I don't know John, but I do know that you could easily convince me that John has more invested in this relationship. What does that mean?

RUTH: That I don't have to be afraid that he would leave me?

THERAPIST: Yes. If he has more invested in the relationship, you have more power.

RUTH: Power is scary.

THERAPIST: You are a powerful woman. You passionately care for your family and for your chosen profession.

RUTH: What do I do about the job?

THERAPIST: What do you want to do?

RUTH: I think I want the job, but if John forbids me from taking it, I won't be able to. After all, this is a job in the church school, and the church expects me to obey my husband.

THERAPIST: That does make for quite a conflict. Do you know that John would exercise his power like that—using your religious beliefs?

RUTH: I don't know. I do think John wants us to stay together, and he may think using the religious card instead of the divorce card might change my mind. You say I have power and I'm feeling more like I do, but I don't know what I should do with it.

THERAPIST: You might consider using your power in the relationship to help John change and do the right thing for you and for your family. Your interest in teaching is an extension of being a good and caring parent. In addition, you will be setting a good model for children to follow. This is just another part of being a parent.

❧ Working With Body Image/Acceptance
This is Ruth's eighth session. The therapist helps Ruth question the cultural definition of weight and age.

RUTH: I know it sounds silly, but I just feel old, fat, and ugly these days. I don't even try to diet anymore because it never works. Because I have trouble sleeping, I have dark circles under my eyes. I look like hell.

THERAPIST: You're pretty disgusted with yourself.

RUTH: Oh, I just can't stand myself anymore. I gave my full-length mirror to the girls. They are slim and trim and young; they like looking at themselves.

THERAPIST: They look more like how an attractive woman should look.

RUTH: Yeah, they are beautiful. What I wouldn't do to have their bodies right now!

THERAPIST: You know, it seems like even though we get better in so many ways as we get older, in our society the only way we are appreciated and valued is for how we look.

RUTH: You know, you're right, and it's not fair. I do think I have a lot to offer, even if I'm not thin and young.

THERAPIST: You certainly do, but you came in here today saying that you felt old, fat, and ugly—that you look like hell. I know this is important to you because you usually don't use strong language to describe your feelings.

RUTH [*Smiles slightly*]: It sometimes seems that I feel better about one thing and then worse about something else. I guess this morning I was only thinking about how I looked in the mirror and not about how valuable a person I am. One really doesn't have anything to do with the other, does it?

THERAPIST: No. But that's the way we are trained to think. And if a woman looks like hell, she feels like hell because she is devalued in our society. Ruth, what do you like about yourself?

RUTH: I like that I am a loving and caring person, that I am a good mother most of the time, and that I usually get things done. I'm proud of finishing my degree and finally having taken some action on the job front.

THERAPIST: And what don't you like?

RUTH: That I struggle with my daughter, that I eat and can't stop, and that I'm so fat that I'm unattractive.

THERAPIST: We've talked about your relationship with your daughter a great deal, but we haven't really talked about your weight [*Ruth nods*]. Maybe being overweight is serving some other purpose. Maybe being fat is a way you are able to get people to recognize your strengths and protect yourself from being ogled by men. Your fat is a way of using your power. Can you think of an example of this in your life?

RUTH [*Looks dubious but thinks*]: Well, where I am teaching some of the college boys help out. They make really disgusting comments about the college girls who volunteer. I get embarrassed for the college girls when this happens. I am sort of glad that they don't even seem to notice me [*Ruth pauses*]. You know, I never thought about how I might use my fat to get what I want or even to get respect. That's an interesting idea.

THERAPIST: Our bodies are the single most powerful asset we have in our society. We all use that power a little differently, but we often use that power to get what we want—even if we are not completely aware of it.

RUTH: It seems really manipulative to me, and I don't want to be manipulative.

THERAPIST: You want to become powerful in other ways.

RUTH: Absolutely.

THERAPIST: The way I see it you can do a couple of things to help with this problem. Let me share my ideas, and you see how they fit for you.

RUTH: OK.

THERAPIST: You might try to adjust your thinking about your weight by discovering ways in which being fat affords you power in your relationships and begin to love yourself just the way you are.

RUTH: That won't be easy.

THERAPIST: I know. It wasn't easy for me either. The hardest thing I did was to actually get a full-length mirror in my bathroom. I forced myself to look at my body and learn to love it.

RUTH: How?

THERAPIST: First you discover what you like and admire about your physical self. Then you look at the areas you are indifferent toward. Then think about what those areas do for you. For example, my legs support me when I stand. They get me where I am going and help me run from trouble.

RUTH: So you just looked at your body and started to think about how each part contributes to your life instead of how fat and ugly it is [*Ruth smiles*].

THERAPIST: That's pretty much it.

RUTH: And it worked?

THERAPIST: It worked for me. I don't know if it will work for you. You're the expert on you.

PROCESS COMMENTARY Western culture is unmerciful to women regarding expectations for physicality. We are bombarded daily with images of women considered to be perfect. Not conforming to this iconic image can severely affect self-esteem because women in our society are judged by how they look, not by what they can do. Ruth has been socialized to believe that food is comforting, and, in fact, it may be the only comfort she has when presented with emotions that women are not encouraged to express. Stuffing her emotions to conform with cultural expectations reinforces her position of powerlessness. As a result, Ruth has developed a body size that is unacceptable to that same culture. She is left in the untenable position of being punished for the only solution she could find to comply with cultural mandates. The goal of feminist therapy is to assist Ruth in discovering ways to love her body. Ruth's relationship with food is also reframed as seeking comfort, and we will help Ruth discover other ways to get her needs met.

The work regarding weight issues is aimed at increasing self-esteem and personal power, emphasizing Ruth's strengths, and increasing her repertoire of coping behaviors. We might refer her to a feminist nutrition counselor and to a weight loss support group with an empowerment focus rather than a strict weight loss focus. It is important that Ruth be referred to adjunct modalities that support her emerging sense of self. Ruth needs to be empowered to accept and celebrate her body, her mind, and her life.

Jerry Corey's Work With Ruth From a Feminist Perspective

Introduction

The *DVD for Integrative Counseling: The Case of Ruth and Lecturettes* is especially useful as a demonstration of interventions I make with Ruth that illustrate some principles and procedures of feminist therapy. In Session 1 ("Beginning of Counseling") I demonstrate ways to engage Ruth as an active partner in the therapeutic venture. Session 2 ("The Therapeutic Relationship") highlights the importance of creating a good working relationship and demystifying the therapy process. In Session 3 ("Establishing Therapeutic Goals") I show how I work collaboratively with Ruth in formulating clear and personal goals that will guide the course of therapy. Clearly, Ruth is the expert on her own life and my job is to assist her in attaining the goals we jointly identify as a focus of therapy. In Session 4 ("Understanding and Addressing Diversity") Ruth brings up gender differences, but she also mentions our differences in religion, education, culture, and socialization. Together we explore how any of our differences might affect our therapeutic task. Talking about how our differences might affect Ruth's ability to get the most from her therapy can be fertile ground for establishing a trusting working relationship. Such open exploration is essential if therapy is to be effective.

Basic Assumptions

The basic assumptions, goals of therapy, and therapy strategies of feminist therapy have been spelled out in detail earlier in this chapter by Drs. Evans, Seem, and Kincade. In my description of counseling Ruth from a feminist perspective, I emphasize how I would enlist her as a collaborator. I'll also describe working with Ruth and John in conjoint counseling. In working with Ruth from a feminist perspective, it is essential that the interventions I make be done within the context of her social and cultural world, and that I attend to the environmental factors that are contributing to the problems that bring Ruth to therapy.

Assessment of Ruth

I strive to include Ruth in the assessment and treatment phase. Collaborating with Ruth in all aspects of her therapy will provide a rich therapeutic experience. I am not eager to give Ruth a diagnosis, for I don't see how a diagnostic category will assist her in formulating a picture of what she wants from therapy. Assessment will be an ongoing process in which the two of us will consider what is the most appropriate focus of our work together.

Goals of Therapy

Functioning within a feminist therapy model, my primary goal is to intervene with Ruth in ways that increase the chances of her recognizing, claiming, and embracing her personal power. After the first few sessions, Ruth and I begin the process of establishing these goals to guide the therapy process:

- Trusting her own intuition rather than relying on outside experts
- Learning that taking care of herself is as important as taking care of others
- Accepting her body rather than punishing herself for not having the perfect body
- Identifying internalized gender-role messages and replacing them with her own constructive beliefs
- Acquiring skills to bring about changes at home and school
- Defining for herself the kind of relationship she wants with her husband and her children

Therapeutic Procedures

I spend time talking with Ruth about how therapy works, and I enlist her as an active partner in our relationship. As a part of the informed consent process, we discuss ways of getting the most from the therapy process, clarifying expectations, identifying Ruth's goals, and working toward a contract that will guide her therapeutic journey. This educational process assists Ruth in being an informed client and is the basis for evaluating how useful the therapy is in terms of reaching her personal goals.

The Therapeutic Process

ELEMENTS OF THE PROCESS Ruth says that she loves reading, and she is very open to reading selected books on topics that are directly pertinent to therapy issues. As a supplement to our sessions, I encourage Ruth to keep a journal and talk with her about bibliotherapy. Ruth and I explore a range of possibilities for extending the therapeutic value of our sessions. She also agrees to join a women's support group that is available through the Women's Center at her college. Although at first she was reluctant to take the time for herself to join this group, she is finding that she can identify with other women in her group. Ruth is able to bring her experiences in her support group, her reading, and her journal writing into her therapy sessions.

⚘ The Therapeutic Relationship Guided by the principle that the therapeutic relationship should be egalitarian, I take three steps to reduce the power differential between us. First, I monitor the ways I might misuse my power in the professional relationship, such as by diagnosing unnecessarily, by giving advice too freely, by hiding behind an "expert" role, or by minimizing the impact of the power imbalance between Ruth and myself.

Second, I call to Ruth's attention the power that she has in the therapeutic relationship. I expect her to take responsibility for herself, to become aware of the ways she relinquishes her power in her relationships with others, and to take increasing charge of her life.

Third, I consistently attempt to demystify the counseling process. I do this by sharing with Ruth my own perceptions about what is going on in our relationship, by making her an active partner in determining any diagnosis, and by engaging in appropriate and timely self-disclosure.

Role-Playing Ruth's Marriage

In one session Ruth and I do some role playing in which I play John. She tells me (John) how frightened she is of making demands on me for fear that I might leave. Out of that session Ruth begins to be aware of how intimidated she has allowed herself to become. She continues to set John up to punish her by giving him the power to make her feel scared and guilty. As a homework assignment I ask her to write a letter to John saying all the things she really wants him to hear, but not to mail it. The writing is geared to getting her to focus on her relationship with her husband and what she wants to be different. (In an earlier session I gave her a similar assignment of writing a detailed letter to her father, which she agreed not to send to him but to bring in for a session with me.) I make the observation to Ruth that in many ways she is looking to John for the same things she wanted from her father as a child and adolescent. Further, she assumed the role of doing whatever she thought would please each of them, yet she typically ended up feeling that no matter how hard she tried she would never succeed in gaining their approval. I try to show her that she will have to change her own attitudes if she expects change in her relationships, rather than waiting and hoping her father or her husband might change. This is a discovery for her, and it represents a different direction for her life.

Holding a Joint Session With John

Ruth expresses her interest in having John come to a few counseling sessions with her, yet she is ambivalent about it. Initially she gives a list of reasons why she is sure that he will never come to any kind of counseling. After some discussion with me, she does agree to ask him to attend at least one session (which we will also role-play first). To her surprise, John agrees to join her. Here are a few excerpts from this initial joint session:

RUTH: I brought John here today even though I don't think he really wanted to be here. [*Notice that she speaks for him.*]

JERRY: John, I'd like to hear from you about what it's like for you to be here today.

JOHN: When Ruth asked me, I agreed because I thought I might be of some help to her. I couldn't see any harm in giving it a try.

RUTH: Now that he's here, I don't know what to say.

JERRY: You could begin by telling him why you wanted him here.

RUTH: It's that our marriage just can't go on this way much longer. Things are no longer satisfactory to me. I know that for many years I never complained—just did what was expected and thought that everything was fine—but the truth is that things are not fine by me.

JOHN [*Turning to me*]: I don't know what she means. Our marriage has always seemed OK by me. I don't see the problem.

JERRY: How about telling Ruth this?

I want Ruth and John to talk to each other directly rather than talking about each other. My guess is that at home they are very indirect. By having them speak to each other in this session, I get a better sense of how they interact.

RUTH: See what I mean! Everything is fine by John—I'm the one with the problems! Why is he so content while I'm so discontent?

JERRY: You're looking at me as you say this. Your message will be more powerful if you tell John directly what you would like to be different in your relationship.

RUTH: Why, John, am I the only one who is complaining about our marriage? Can't you see anything wrong with the way we're living? Do you really mean that everything is just fine by you?

JERRY: Ruth, let me make a suggestion. You are asking John questions. Instead of asking him these questions, try telling him what it is like for you to be in this relationship with him.

RUTH [*Again turning and addressing me*]: But I don't think he ever hears me! That's the trouble—I just don't think he cares or listens to me when I talk about our life together.

JERRY: So here is an opportunity to test out your assumptions. I hope you are willing to hang in with him and keep on talking.

RUTH [*With raised voice and a great deal of emotion*]: John, I'm tired of being the perfect wife and the perfect mother, always doing what's expected of me. I've done that for as long as I can remember, and I want a change. I feel that I'm the one holding together our family. Everything depends on me, and all of you depend on me to keep things going. But I can't turn to any of you for emotional support. I take care of everybody and everything, but I don't feel cared for.

JERRY: Tell John how that affects you and what you want from him.

RUTH: I'm tired of the way things are with us [*Pause*]. There are times that I need to know that I matter to you and that you appreciate me.

JOHN: Well, I do appreciate your hard work. I know you do a lot in the home, and I'm proud of you.

JERRY: How does it feel to hear John say that to you?

RUTH: But you never say that you appreciate me. I need to hear that from you. I need to feel your emotional support.

JERRY: Yet right now he is telling you that he appreciates you. So, how is it for you to hear what he just said?

I am calling to Ruth's attention that in this brief interaction, for one short moment, her husband responded to her in a way that she says she would like him to. Yet she does not acknowledge what he did say, which is what she says she'd like to hear more of.

> RUTH: I like it when you tell me that you appreciate me. It means a lot to me.

> JOHN: I'm just not used to talking that way. You know how I feel about you.

> JERRY: John! That's just the problem. You don't often tell Ruth how you feel about her and what she means to you, and she is not very good at asking for that from you.

> RUTH: Yeah, I agree. I'm missing affection from you. It's so hard for me to talk about my life with you—about you and me—about our family—oh! [*Ruth's tears up, she lets out a sigh, and then she grows quiet.*]

> JERRY: Don't stop now, Ruth. Keep talking to John. Tell him what your tears and the heavy sigh are about.

My hunch is that Ruth often feels defeated and stops there, seeing herself as misunderstood. I am encouraging her to stay with herself and continue to address John. Even though John is looking very uncomfortable at this point, he sounds receptive.

> JOHN: Sometimes I find it hard to talk to you because I feel I can never do enough. How can I be sensitive when you don't tell me what you want?

> JERRY: John, she is telling you right now what she wants. How is it for you to hear what Ruth is saying to you?

> JOHN: She is right. I should listen more often.

> JERRY: So, are you willing to listen to Ruth a bit more right now?

> JOHN: Yes.

> RUTH: You may not know how important going to college really is for me, John. I so much want to finish and get my credential. But I can't do that and be responsible for the complete running of our house. I need for the kids to pitch in and do their share instead of always expecting me to do everything. I need some time to myself—time just to sit and think for a few minutes—when I'm at home. And I'd like to be able to sit down with you after dinner and just talk for a bit. I miss talking to you. The times we do talk, the topic is household maintenance.

> JERRY: What are you hearing, John, and how does it sound to you?

> JOHN: Well, we do talk about chores. I just don't understand what she wants me to say.

John continues for a time with a critical voice. Yet eventually he does admit that the children don't help as much as they could and that he might be willing to do a bit more around the house. He adds that the way he grew up men were supposed to work outside of the house and women were supposed to stay home and take care of the family. He admits that he doesn't know how to begin making changes to these well-established patterns.

RUTH: Well, I'd really like your help at home. What about spending time with me? Is that possible?

JOHN: Yes. Too often I just want to relax after working all day. I want it to be positive at home after a long day.

JERRY: It sounds as if both of you would like to talk to each other. Would you be willing to set aside some time during the next week when you can have some uninterrupted conversation?

Together we develop a realistic contract that specifies when, where, and how long they will spend uninterrupted time with each other. John agrees to come in for another joint session. I let him know that it will be important that we explore messages that he has embraced unthinkingly and determine if there are ways he might modify his version of what constitutes a "natural" role for women and men. I point out to both of them that they have bought into a fixed vision of whose responsibility it is to maintain the family. They may want to begin to question these stereotyped gender-role expectations and consider redefining their roles. At a future session we will focus on what both John and Ruth have learned about roles and division of responsibilities, deciding if these values are functional in their marriage.

In the meantime I ask Ruth to monitor what she actually does at home for 2 weeks and to keep these notes in her journal. I suggest that she write down a specific list of the changes she wants at home. We pursue our individual sessions, working mainly on what she wants in her life for herself, and at times what she wants in her family situation.

PROCESS COMMENTARY Ruth and I spend several sessions working with her part in creating and maintaining the difficulties she is experiencing in her marriage. I challenge her to stop focusing on John and what he can do to change and, instead, to change her own attitudes and behaviors, which may lead to changes in her relationship with him. Ruth begins to see how difficult it is for her to make requests of John or to ask him for what she needs emotionally. Although she initially resists the idea of telling him directly what she wants with him and from him, she eventually sees some value in learning to ask for what she wants. Ruth has decided in advance that he (and others) will not take care of her emotionally, and with this expectancy she has blocked off possibilities of feeling emotionally nourished by others. She often becomes aware of slipping into old patterns, many of which were developed as a child, yet she becomes increasingly able to avoid these traps and to behave in more effective ways.

Ruth and I spend considerable time in our sessions talking about messages she received about gender roles. Up to this time she had not really given much thought to the impact her socialization continues to have on her, nor had she reflected on how she (and John) have uncritically accepted stereotyped gender roles. Much time is devoted in our sessions to reviewing and critically examining decisions she made about herself as a wife and mother. Ruth is realizing that her definition of herself is rather restricted, and now she is beginning to think about how she wants to expand her options.

Some Final Thoughts

A significant contribution of feminist therapy is the emphasis on assisting clients in becoming aware of typical gender-role messages they have grown up with and have incorporated from society. Feminist therapy involves a cultural critique of traditional assessment and treatment approaches. As Drs. Evans, Seem, and Kincade demonstrate in their collaborative approach to counseling Ruth, the empowerment of the client is given primary emphasis. Many traditional theories place the cause of problems within individuals rather than with external circumstances and the environment. This has led to holding individuals responsible for their problems and not giving full recognition to the social and political realities that create problems. The feminist approach requires that therapists work toward social justice by addressing oppressive structures in society rather than expecting individuals to merely adapt to expected role behaviors.[4]

Questions for Reflection

1. How might you integrate concepts and techniques from the other therapy orientations you've studied with feminist therapy? Are there any theories that you think would not fit with a feminist perspective? If so, which ones, and why?

2. What themes from the feminist approach would you most want to incorporate in counseling Ruth?

3. Feminist therapists believe in the value of educating clients about the therapy process and stress the importance of an egalitarian relationship. What other counseling approaches share this orientation? What are your thoughts about demystifying therapy and establishing a collaborative relationship with a client such as Ruth?

4. Feminist therapy takes a dim view of traditional diagnosis and assessment. What other therapies share this view? At this point, what are your thoughts about the use of the *DSM-IV-TR* as a basis for making an assessment and arriving at a diagnosis? To what extent do you think that traditional diagnosis contributes to blaming the victim?

5. Feminist assessment and diagnosis requires a cooperative and phenomenological approach. If you accept the feminist perspective on assessment and diagnosis, what problems might you expect to encounter in an agency that required you to come up with a diagnosis during an intake session?

6. What would you say to Ruth if she is enrolled in a managed care program that permits only six therapy sessions, and then only if a suitable diagnosis is submitted to the health provider program?

7. Feminist therapy focuses on gender-role and power analysis. What ways might you employ these interventions in your work with Ruth and John during a conjoint session? To what degree have you thought about how your gender-role socialization has influenced your views of what it means to be a woman or a man? How might your views influence your work with a client like Ruth?

8. As you read about the basic tenets of feminism, to what extent do you think it is appropriate for a therapist to teach clients ways of challenging the status quo and a patriarchal system? What modifications, if any, might you make in applying feminist therapy to clients who embrace cultural values that keep women in a subservient role?

9. How well does feminist therapy fit with your counseling style? What aspects of this approach do you find most useful? Which aspects might you want to modify to fit your personal counseling style?

Notes

See the *DVD for Theory and Practice of Counseling and Psychotherapy: The Case of Stan* and Lecturettes, Session 10 ("Feminist Therapy Applied to the Case of Stan"), which deals with Stan's exploration of his gender-role identity and messages he has incorporated into being a man.

1. We made a commitment to feminist collaboration in writing for this chapter and the order of our names holds no meaning. This is truly a collaborative piece with each of us contributing equally to its content and effort.

2. A more detailed description of feminist therapy can be found in chapter 12 of Corey, G. (2013), *Theory and Practice of Counseling and Psychotherapy* (9th ed., Belmont, CA: Brooks/Cole, Cengage Learning). See also Evans, K. M., Kincade, E. A., & Seem, S. R. (2011). *Introduction to feminist therapy: Strategies for social and individual change.* Los Angeles: Sage.

3. The source for making a traditional diagnosis is the *DSM-IV-TR*. American Psychiatric Association. (2000). *Diagnostic and statistical manual of mental disorders* (4th ed., text revision). Washington, DC: Author.

4. For more information on this model, see Worell, J. & Remer, P. (2003). *Feminist perspectives in therapy: Empowering diverse women.* New York: Wiley; and Brown, L. (2010). *Feminist therapy.* Washington, DC: American Psychological Association.

CHAPTER ELEVEN

Case Approach
to Postmodern Approaches

General Overview of Postmodern Approaches

A major goal for postmodern therapists is to create a context in which clients can create new stories that highlight their ways of being. Therapy provides the opportunity for clients to take apart (or deconstruct) the dominant story they bring to therapy. Clients are encouraged to rewrite these stories by looking at their past and rewriting their future.

Postmodern therapists view clients as the experts on their own life. The therapist is not the expert but assumes the role of a curious, interested, and respectful partner in the therapeutic relationship. The therapist and clients together establish clear, specific, realistic, and personally meaningful goals that will guide the therapy process. The therapist explores with clients the impact their problems have on them and how they are taking action to reduce this impact. Through the use of questions that challenge clients to separate themselves from problem identities, therapists assist clients in reauthoring their stories and in constructing a more appealing story line. It is essential that the story being authored in the therapy context be carried out into the social world where clients live.

Because this approach emphasizes the collaborative nature of therapy, clients are the primary agents in deciding when they have achieved their goals and when they are ready to terminate the therapeutic relationship. This approach to therapy emphasizes a time-effective format. It is appropriate to end therapy when the client finds solutions that work.

A Client-Directed, Solution-Focused Brief Therapist's Perspective on Ruth

by John J. Murphy, PhD

My approach borrows primarily from solution-focused brief therapy (SFBT) as developed by de Shazer and Berg,[1] early brief therapy models (Erickson, Mental

Research Institute), and client-directed, outcome-informed practice.[2] Core elements include an irrepressible belief in the ability of clients to resolve problems and to improve their lives when encouraged to (a) clearly describe what they want (goals), and (b) apply what is "right and working" in their lives toward solutions (exceptions and resources). I view Ruth as the expert on herself and build a collaborative partnership in which her preferences and perceptions have top priority.

A classmate told Ruth that I am a solution-focused brief therapy practitioner and suggested she call me.

> RUTH: I know you're very busy, but I've never been in counseling and have a few questions.
>
> THERAPIST: That's fine. I'd have questions too, so ask me anything you want.
>
> RUTH: Well, I wasn't sure how you schedule appointments. I have a husband and four teenagers, and I'm a substitute teacher, so I'm kind of worried about fitting this in with everything else. I know I shouldn't feel that way, but I'm just trying to figure out how to do this.
>
> THERAPIST: That's perfectly understandable. You've got important people and responsibilities in your life, so it makes sense to think carefully about the schedule. Maybe you could give me two or three times that would work best for you and we could go from there. How does that sound?
>
> RUTH: Good.
>
> THERAPIST: Okay. What other questions do you have?

First impressions are powerful, and I want Ruth to know from the start that I work for her and not the other way around. The accommodating nature of SFBT is conveyed by inviting Ruth to take the lead in the scheduling process ("Maybe you could give me two or three times") and validating her concerns about scheduling ("That's perfectly understandable"). This short exchange illustrates the client-directed practice of putting Ruth first throughout the change process. We will return to this conversation later.

Foundations and Assumptions

The following empirical foundations and clinical assumptions guide every aspect of my work with Ruth.

🪶 Empirical Foundations   Findings from psychotherapy outcome research suggest that therapeutic success rests largely on the activation of "common factors of change" that operate across different theoretical orientations.[3] These elements include client factors (resilience, social supports, and other resources), relationship or "alliance" factors (client perceptions of respect from the therapist, collaboration on therapeutic goals and tasks, client feedback), and hope (positive expectancy of change). Client factors are by far the most powerful ingredients, with alliance being the second most important element of successful outcomes. Empirically speaking, the client and alliance are the heart and soul of effective therapy. These findings urge me to (a) ensure that Ruth and her resources remain at center stage, (b) deliberately build and monitor the therapeutic alliance, and (c) boost hope by focusing on future possibilities rather than past problems.

Change is the essence of therapy, and common factors provide the most reliable roadmap to achieving change. In every contact I have with Ruth, I will seek to mobilize these potent ingredients of change. Common factors also drive the following assumptions.

🐾 Clinical Assumptions

1. *Every client wants to change and offers a unique set of resources for doing so.* SFBT assumes that clients enter therapy because they are "stuck" versus sick, and that they have the desire and ability to change in meaningful ways. Solutions are enhanced by building on "what's right" and "what's working" for the client rather than focusing on what is wrong and not working. Trusting Ruth to resolve her problems in her own unique way enables me to become more relaxed, accessible, present, and open to new solutions than would be possible within a traditional doctor–patient relationship in which Ruth is treated as a passive follower. I enter the relationship fully confident that Ruth offers a one-of-a-kind set of client factors that are waiting to be discovered and deployed in the service of her goals.

In the words of a wise 10-year-old client: "Counselors just don't understand . . . we have the answers, we just need someone to help us bring them to the front of our head. It's like they're locked in an attic or something."[4] The last thing Ruth and most clients need from me is a reminder of what is wrong with them or their lives. Treating Ruth as a capable partner in the solution-building process not only boosts her confidence and hope in the possibilities of therapy but mine as well.

2. *Alliance enhances solutions.* Alliances are built on mutual trust, respect, and collaboration, and client participation is the centerpiece of an effective therapeutic alliance. Ruth will have a voice and choice in every aspect of therapy from crafting goals through evaluating and terminating services. If my ideas and methods are not working for Ruth, I will change them rather than calling her resistant or otherwise discounting her dignity and choice. This is not to be confused with a nondirective approach in which therapists refrain from providing any direction regardless of client preferences. I will not hesitate to offer suggestions, but will do so in a collaborative manner ("Ruth, would you be willing to initiate a conversation with John one or two evenings next week and observe what happens?"). In short, the therapy process will be leveled in ways that give Ruth a valid and ongoing voice in her own care.

3. *No problem is constant; there are always fluctuations and exceptions.* Regardless of how constant some problems may seem (and they certainly seem that way when they're happening to us), problem patterns fluctuate. SFBT practitioners call these "exceptions" to the problem, and I will work with Ruth to identify and increase these exceptions.

4. *Small changes lead to larger changes.* The systemic idea that small changes can ripple into larger changes provides hope for clients and practitioners. In contrast

to the medical-diagnostic notion that one must thoroughly assess and under-stand the problem before successfully treating it, SFBT maintains that effective solutions are not always directly related to the problems that bring clients to therapy. Sometimes one small change (waking up 20 minutes earlier each morn-ing) leads to larger and more significant changes (exercising more). I will be on the lookout for small changes and will encourage Ruth to do the same.

5. *If it works, do more. If it doesn't, do something different.* These two statements summarize the practical nature of SFBT. The first emphasizes the importance of utilizing "what is working" in Ruth's life. Building on what already exists is a more respectful and efficient route to solutions than starting from scratch by teaching brand new skills and actions. Exceptions and other natural resources in Ruth's life were there before I arrived and will be there when I leave. There-fore, positive changes built on Ruth's indigenous resources are more likely to be maintained after therapy ends than changes resulting from therapist-directed strategies. The second statement urges us and clients to hold lightly to ideas and techniques, and to be willing to let them go and try something different when they are not working. The value of any technique rests on its acceptability and usefulness to clients. With these points in mind, the next section outlines the key tasks and techniques of client-directed SFBT.

Tasks and Techniques

Every technique is a means to an end and not the end itself. I never become too attached to a particular idea or technique or try to force it on Ruth. That would be disrespectful to Ruth and damaging to the alliance. No single strategy works with every client; I customize every technique to Ruth instead of squeezing her into my favorite methods. I will present ideas and suggestions in an invitational manner rather than a dictatorial way, giving Ruth full veto power. Although the following tasks and techniques of SFBT are numbered here, they often overlap in practice.

Task 1. Orient Clients to the Therapy Process.   This step is important for all clients, especially for those like Ruth who have never participated in therapy. The following techniques help to ease clients into therapy and prepare them for what to expect:

- *Arrange the setting to promote comfort and collaboration.* Provide a clear line of vision between you and the client; position yourself at or below the client's eye level to support the collaborative aspect of SFBT.
- *Use simple icebreakers and compliments.* Use icebreakers and small talk such as asking about hobbies or commenting on local events, especially for first-time clients who are apprehensive about therapy; compliment clients for being there and having the courage to address their concerns.
- *Provide an orientation statement.* Orientation statements have been shown to improve clients' hope and therapeutic outcomes. Here is a condensed example: "My goal is to be useful to you, so I'll need to know what you want from therapy and how our meetings are working for you. I want you to feel free to ask me questions and tell me if things aren't working so that we can change it and make it better. How does that sound?"

≋ Task 2. Build Cooperative Alliances. A strong alliance is the glue that holds everything together in therapy. One size does not fit all when it comes to building alliances. Some clients want a listener and sounding board, others want expert advice, and others prefer a combination of these positions. Client preferences may differ during the course of therapy, so I will need Ruth's feedback to ensure that I'm being helpful. Here are a few methods for building cooperative, change-focused therapeutic alliances:

- *Listen and learn from clients.* I will approach Ruth as a foreign ambassador approaches a new and unfamiliar culture,[5] listening without judging as she describes her concerns, perceptions, and goals.
- *Validate perceptions and feelings.* Therapy works best when clients openly express their thoughts and feelings without fear of reproach or criticism. Resolving problems is hard enough without having to defend oneself in the process or try to save face, and validation removes the need to do so. Ruth can focus more intently on reaching her goals if I validate her initial thoughts and feelings: "No wonder you're really down. It's perfectly understandable to feel that way."
- *Present ideas from a position of curiosity and flexibility.* Whenever I am tempted to think I know what is best for a client, I recall one of my mother's favorite sayings: "No one likes a know-it-all." Wise words for life in general and therapy in particular. I wrap ideas and suggestions in invitational phrases that convey Ruth's freedom to accept or reject them: "Could it be that . . . ?"; "I wonder what would happen if you tried. . . ."
- *Obtain systematic and ongoing feedback from clients.* Obtaining ongoing feedback from Ruth enables me to continue what is working for her and change what is not. Many SFBT practitioners use informal scaling questions to assess progress ("On a scale of 0 to 10, with 0 being 'the worst it can be' and 10 'the best,' how would you rate the past week?"). I prefer using two ultra-brief, client-rated, paper-and-pencil measures of outcome and alliance—the Outcome Rating Scale (ORS) and the Session Rating Scale (SRS)[6]—which have been shown to dramatically improve client outcomes. The ORS, administered and discussed at the start of every session, assesses Ruth's perceptions of progress in key areas of life such as personal well-being and family. The SRS, administered at the end of the session, assesses the extent to which Ruth experienced an effective alliance during the meeting: being heard and understood, addressing relevant topics, and experiencing a good fit with my approach and style. I will encourage Ruth to be brutally honest in her feedback because that is the only way we can detect and correct emerging alliance problems.
- *Ask versus tell.* Asking questions enables Ruth to describe things in her own words and style. Although counselor training programs rightfully discourage students from pummeling clients with a barrage of closed, interrogation-style questions, some open-ended questions can enhance solutions by providing space for Ruth to be heard and to reflect on future possibilities: "Tell me more about your concerns"; "What do you think needs to happen to make things a little better at home?"; "Who will be the first to notice when things get a little better, and how might they react?"

🔹 Task 3. Develop Useful Goals.   Clear goals are to SFBT what clear maps are to navigation. Well-formed, client-driven goals keep therapy on track and provide concrete benchmarks for evaluating effectiveness. The following techniques are helpful in partnering with clients to develop goals:

• *Ask miracle and scaling questions.* The miracle question is commonly used in SFBT to elicit goals: "Suppose a miracle happened while you are sleeping tonight and your problems completely vanished. What would be different about the next day? What will your husband and kids notice that's different?" Scaling questions can help to identify goals as well: "On a scale of 0 to 10, where 10 is 'the best it can be' and zero is 'the worst,' where would you rate things at school right now? What would the next highest number look like?"

• *Remember the 5-S guideline.* The 5-S guideline is a useful way to remember the five features of effective goals in SFBT: significant, specific, small, self-manageable, and start-based. I will help Ruth to develop significant goals ("What is most important to you right now?") and to translate vaguely stated wishes ("feeling better" and "being happier") into specific, observable indicators of progress: "What would we see if we watched a video of you feeling better and being happier?" I will also encourage her to focus on goals that are sufficiently small and self-manageable: "What will you be doing differently when this mark (pointing to one of her ORS ratings) moves from 5.9 to 6.0?"; "Of all the things that you would like to change, which one(s) do you have the most control over at this time?" Like many clients, Ruth might initially describe her goals as the end or absence of something undesirable such as worrying less and being less depressed. When this happens, I can encourage positively stated, start-based goals by asking "instead-of" questions: "What would you rather be doing instead of worrying?" Describing her goals as the start of something desirable ("spending more alone time with John") might be more energizing for Ruth because people generally are more motivated to work toward what they want than away from what they don't want.

🔹 Task 4. Build on Exceptions and Other Resources ("Client Factors").
This task is at the core of client-directed SFBT. Exceptions are times and situations in which the presenting problem is absent or less noticeable. Once exceptions are discovered, we can explore the conditions under which they occurred (what, when, where, how, with whom) and encourage clients to replicate them in the future. We can use the same process to discover and build on other client resources such as special interests, talents, social supports, resilience, and coping skills. In addition to exploring these factors in my meetings with Ruth ("Tell me about a time when you felt a little less depressed this week; How have you managed to handle everything at school and home?"), I will review available reports and records with an eye toward exceptions and resources. Sometimes client factors jump right out and fall in our lap. At other times it is more like panning for gold because these valuable assets, though plentiful, can remain hidden from sight until we actively seek them out. The following techniques will help me to discover and build on exceptions and other resources in Ruth's life:

- *Identify and build on exceptions.* I will listen for exceptions in Ruth's comments. For example, the italicized words in the following statements provide hints of exceptions: "I feel tired *most* of the time; I get angry at John about something *almost* every night." Exception-finding questions include "When is this problem absent or less noticeable?"; "Has anything changed for the better since you called to schedule this appointment?" Once an exception is discovered, I can explore exception-related conditions and encourage Ruth to replicate these conditions: "What was different about last Wednesday when you felt better and more efficient? What will it take to make that happen more often?"
- *Identify and build on other resources.* The following strategies help to identify Ruth's resources and explore how she might apply them toward her goals: "It took strength and determination to break from your parents' religion. I wonder how that same strength and courage might help you take on a goal or action that seems a little risky right now but will help you move closer to the life you want. What do you think?" "Of everyone you've ever known, who do you look up to and respect most? What would this person advise you to do?" "How have you kept things from getting worse?"

ꕤ Task 5. Change the Doing or Viewing of the Problem.

In addition to utilizing exceptions and other resources, I can invite Ruth to change the doing and viewing of the problem—that is, to try something different instead of more of the same. Changing *anything* in the problem pattern can lead to "a difference that makes a difference."

- *Encourage clients to change the doing.* Changing the doing involves altering any aspect of one's performance of or response to the problem. Examples include the following: "Ruth, are you willing to do something really different the next time you feel really down?" After hearing Ruth say that she "worries constantly" and has tried many methods to stop without success, I might invite her to schedule two intensive 5-minute worry sessions—one in the morning and one in the evening—to give her concerns the full and undivided attention they deserve instead of trying to do so amidst the distractions of work and home responsibilities.
- *Encourage clients to change the viewing.* When I observe Ruth's persistent yet futile efforts to stop worrying, I could relabel worrying as being "cautious" or "analytic" and invite Ruth to list situations in which caution is helpful along with times when it is not helpful. This reframes worry from a dysfunctional habit to a cognitive tool that is helpful on some occasions. As Ruth begins to view worry in a different light, she might become more relaxed and accepting of herself and her cautious, analytical leanings.

ꕤ Task 6. Evaluate and Empower Progress.

I will evaluate Ruth's progress on an ongoing basis and empower improvements whenever they occur. In addition to using the ORS and SRS to assess services and outcomes from Ruth's perspective, we can use other evaluation sources and methods at Ruth's discretion (keeping an activity log or charting physical exercise). The following techniques can empower positive changes:

• *Give clients credit, explore the personal and social impact of improvements, and consult clients for advice.* "How did you manage to make these improvements?" "How do your husband and kids treat you differently now compared to before?" "What have these improvements taught you about yourself?" "What is the biggest difference between the *old* you and the *new* you?" "What advice would you have for a friend who wanted to worry less and enjoy life more?" "May I consult you in the future for ideas that might help others?"

• *Write letters.* Letters written by the therapist can promote and empower progress by keeping the conversation alive between sessions and reinforcing therapeutic themes and messages. Among other purposes, therapists' letters compliment clients ("I am impressed by your openness to try new things"), create intrigue ("I wonder what you'll do differently this week"), boost hope and agency ("Your accomplishments during the past 2 weeks are incredible, and I can't wait to learn more about how you did it"), and invite alternative self-stories and attributions ("We could use more courageous and determined people like you in the world"). Getting feedback from the therapist between sessions can assist clients in applying what they are learning to daily life.

Assessment and Evaluation

Solutions do not always flow logically from problems, and I believe diagnosis is unnecessary and sometimes counterproductive to helping people change. I have generally found that diagnosis constricts rather than expands clients' views of themselves and their possibilities. However, many clients and agencies need a diagnosis for record-keeping and reimbursement purposes. If I needed to assign a *DSM-IV-TR* diagnosis, I would tell Ruth that the diagnosis may or may not be helpful to her and enlist her participation.

We would discuss Axes I, III, IV, and V of the *DSM-IV-TR* system in a transparent and collaborative manner. I would defer on Axis II (personality disorders) because it describes people in totalizing language that equates the problem with the person. For Axis I, we decide on an Adjustment Disorder with mixed anxiety and depressed mood. Ruth decides to list her weight concerns on Axis III. Of all the components in the multiaxial system, Axis IV is the most compatible with SFBT's systemic belief that most problems result from an increase or combination of psychosocial, situational, and environmental stressors, not from defects or pathologies inside the client. We list several factors on Axis IV, including life transitions (graduation and pending job decisions, obtaining her credentials, launching children) and concerns about John's adjustment to Ruth's career pursuits. After a brief explanation and discussion of Axis V (Global Assessment of Functioning), we decide on a GAF score of 70.

With diagnosis behind us, we can get down to the business of change. I view assessment as an ongoing process of discovery and exploration involving the following methods and considerations.

1. *Review documents for strengths, resources, and other client factors.* I review all reports, records, and other documents for client factors that can promote solutions and help with alliance-building. For example, I search for areas of common interest and connection with Ruth, such as our mutual experience as

teachers and parents. Ruth's autobiography and intake summary provide many client factors that can be incorporated into therapy. Here are just a few: (a) As an adolescent, Ruth courageously stuck to her values instead of succumbing to peer pressure (maybe she could call on that same courage and discipline to "resist" cooperating with the oppressive habits that hold her back from the life she desires); (b) she broke away from her childhood religion because she had "outgrown" it (perhaps her current unrest is a signal that she has outgrown one stage of life and needs to move on to another stage); and (c) she entered school as a nontraditional student and received her teaching degree while raising a family, a compelling testimony to her multitasking skills (Ruth and I will explore how these skills can be used to create more time for herself and her career while maintaining her parental and spousal responsibilities).

2. *Consider who else to include.* I begin by meeting with Ruth alone, but her concerns about John raise the possibility of couple sessions along the way. I will explore Ruth's concern about John wanting things to stay the same. In addition to validating this concern ("I can see why you're worried about this"), I can ask Ruth to reflect on the similarities between John's apprehension and her own fears about the future. I would raise the same question to John as a way of building mutual empathy.

3. *Administer the ORS and SRS at every session.* The ORS provides an accurate, client-based method of monitoring Ruth's goals and evaluating services. When ORS scores increase from one session to the next, I will empower these changes and ask what it will take to sustain them. When scores decline, we will consider what we can do differently to improve things. The SRS provides an ongoing snapshot of the alliance from Ruth's perspective, along with the opportunity to adjust my approach in accordance with her feedback. Here are a couple illustrations:

ORS Discussion

> THERAPIST: Your ORS mark on the personal well-being scale tells me you had a pretty tough time last week. Can you tell me about that?
>
> RUTH: I went back to eating more at night, and I haven't done that for a while.
>
> THERAPIST: Is there anything else that accounts for your lower rating this week?
>
> RUTH: No, that's it.
>
> THERAPIST: OK. What do you think might help improve the evening situation?

SRS Discussion

> THERAPIST: Your SRS scores look like things went pretty well for you this time.
>
> RUTH: Yes.
>
> THERAPIST: Your mark on the "Goals and Topics" line is not quite as high as the others. Can you help me out there?
>
> RUTH: Well, we talked mostly about me making a list of what I needed to do to move forward on getting my credentials. That's something

I definitely need to do, and it really helped to map it out here. But I'm still worried about how John is handling this, and he doesn't seem to want to talk about it with me.

THERAPIST: Does that explain the lower mark on Goals and Topics?

RUTH: Yes. I know we can't talk about everything and we only have so much time.

THERAPIST: That's true, but we can definitely talk about it at our next meeting.

RUTH: That sounds good.

THERAPIST: We can also invite John to join us if you think that would be helpful. Sometimes couples find it easier to talk about things with a third party. I'm not sure how it would work with you and John, but it is something to consider.

RUTH: Hmm. I don't know. I'll definitely think about that.

The Therapeutic Process

There is little distinction between assessment and treatment in SFBT because every interaction is approached as a solution opportunity. This section includes additional dialogue to supplement prior examples of therapeutic tasks and techniques. Process commentary is embedded within the dialogue to highlight specific techniques.

We now return to my first contact with Ruth when she phoned to inquire about scheduling. The following exchange illustrates how several techniques can be woven into a short slice of conversation.

THERAPIST: Before we stop, I can give you a quick sense of how I work with people. Is that OK with you?

RUTH: Sure.

THERAPIST: Thanks. I'll need to ask you what you want from counseling and how you will know if our work is successful, things like that [*Focusing on Ruth's hopes for counseling*]. These are hard questions, and we'll take things one small step at a time [*Inviting Ruth to begin thinking about these questions without pressuring her into answering them immediately*]. You know yourself and your life better than anyone else does, so I'll need your feedback about how the counseling is working so that I can be as useful as possible to you [*Assuring Ruth that her opinions and judgments take precedence over mine or anyone else's*]. One thing I've learned is that everyone is different, and different things work for different people. We might come up with some ideas right away or it might take us a while. Either way is fine. How does that sound to you?

RUTH: That sounds good. I'm probably making more of this than what it is. I've just heard different things about therapy from some of my friends, and I wasn't sure exactly what to expect. That's one of my problems. I overanalyze everything and make it more difficult than it really is.

THERAPIST: That makes sense. This is a big step, and you want to make sure it's right for you, and to make sure you're spending your time and money on something that's worthwhile [*Joining and validating*]. In fact, with everything else going on in your life, I'm wondering how you found the courage to take the step of making this call [*Complimenting Ruth and assigning a positive attribution to her decision to take action*]. Maybe I'll find out more about that when we meet next week.

The next exchange occurs early in the first session and illustrates how Ruth's decision to seek help serves as an empowering starting point for exploring other positive attributes and resources.

THERAPIST: Some people have a really tough time taking action and trying something different to make their lives better, even when they aren't happy. Where did you find the courage and energy to call me?

RUTH: I don't know. Courage isn't a word I associate with myself. I guess I've been feeling more desperate about things, and then my friend Carol mentioned counseling last week at lunch.

THERAPIST: Well, desperate or not, I think the fact that you moved from thinking about it to taking action says something important about you [*Complimenting Ruth for doing something she may have dismissed as trivial and ascribing a noble motive to it*]. Does that make sense to you?

The following dialogue, also taken from the first session, picks up as Ruth explains her lower mark on the personal well-being subscale of the ORS.

RUTH: It seems like I go through most days on autopilot, like I'm half there and half somewhere else.

THERAPIST: Where would you rather be instead of on autopilot? [*I ask an "instead-of" question that invites Ruth to think about what she wants to do more of (start-based goal) rather than less of.*]

RUTH: I want to be "there" and present instead of somewhere else. I would enjoy things more if I could be more involved in whatever I'm doing instead of thinking about other things.

THERAPIST: That makes sense. Tell me about a recent time when you felt a little more "there" and present than usual [*Searching for an exception*].

RUTH: Well, I was helping John wash our car Sunday and remember thinking, "Wow, this is really nice." I felt real light and relaxed.

THERAPIST: I wonder what was different about that time compared to other times [*Exploring the exception*]?

RUTH: I don't know. It didn't last very long once we started talking about money, but it was nice while it lasted.

THERAPTIST: OK, but it was nice while it lasted. I'm still wondering what was different about that short window of time when things were looser and more relaxed [*Gently returning to the exception question*].

RUTH: I think it was just that both of us were in a silly mood, which doesn't happen much these days.

THERAPIST: Any theories on how this happened?

RUTH: Not really.

THERAPIST: Do you see it as more of a random event, or was there something that either of you did to make it happen [*Exploring Ruth's view of the exception*]?

RUTH: A little of both, I guess. It started out kind of random when he accidentally squirted me with the hose, but then we both got into it and started joking around and enjoying each other.

THERAPIST: It might be interesting to be on the lookout for those "better times" this week, and to observe what you and John are doing to make them happen and keep them going [*Inviting Ruth to focus on future exceptions and on what she and John are doing to initiate and sustain them*].

Future Sessions and Termination

I continue (a) to listen and look for exceptions and other resources that can be applied toward solutions, (b) to empower any small changes in the direction of Ruth's goals, (c) to obtain Ruth's feedback on the outcome and fit of services, and (d) to remind myself and Ruth to do more of what is working and less of what isn't. As a teacher who appreciates the power of the pen, Ruth would probably respond well to periodic letters aimed at acknowledging small victories, boosting hope, reinforcing therapeutic themes, and otherwise sustaining the therapeutic conversation between sessions. The following letter was written during a short break at the end of a session in which Ruth reported marked improvements in taking better care of herself and becoming more accepting of her "cautious" tendencies.

> *Dear Ruth,*
> *I remain impressed by your genuine commitment to create a fuller life for yourself and for your family. In a world where talk is cheap and action is rare, your willingness to stand up to fear and try new things is very inspiring. One of the greatest benefits of my work is meeting people who have the courage to be vulnerable in the hope of becoming stronger. You are one of those people, and I am privileged to work with you. I'm always curious about how people make important changes like the ones you have made, so I'd appreciate it if you would continue to make note of the things you do to create a fuller and more satisfying life for yourself and your family. I look forward to finding out what you discover when we meet again in two weeks. JM*

Ruth and I will collaborate on the decision to end formal therapy. The aim of client-directed SFBT is to help Ruth establish positive momentum toward her major goals as efficiently as possible without imposing a preestablished cap on the number of sessions. The SFBT motto on the ideal number of sessions is "just enough and not one too many." The "brief" in SFBT does not mean clients are rushed into solutions against their will or otherwise squeezed into a one-size-fits-all format. Therapy looks different for different clients because it is driven by *their* goals and preferences, not mine. The main reason SFBT is briefer than other approaches, sometimes only a single session, is that change occurs faster when therapy focuses on what clients view as important and on what they already have and are already doing to make life better.[7]

A Narrative Therapist's Perspective on Ruth

by Gerald Monk, PhD

Introduction

Ruth contacted me because she has heard that I work from a narrative perspective, which she thinks might be a good fit for her. Ruth wants me to help her get clarity about what she might do with her life. What she wants most of all is certainty about what will make her happy without cost to others. She wants to know whether she should continue to stay married to John. She wonders whether she will survive without him at worst, or be miserable on her own at best. She is not sure that John will survive without her, and that worries her. Ruth is fearful of the judgment that she will incur from God, her father, and her children if she were to live a life that is not influenced by servitude, compliance, and emotional caregiving toward her husband and her soon to be grown children. She is frightened by attacks of anxiety, periods of depression, the prospect of dying and going to hell, her aging body, and her weight gain.

Basic Assumptions

A narrative approach involves entering a therapeutic situation with a range of specific assumptions. These assumptions have been largely pieced together into what is called narrative therapy by Michael White and David Epston.[8]

At the heart of this practice is the notion that we live our lives according to the stories people tell about us and the stories we tell ourselves. The story is not merely viewed as a means by which real experiences are accounted for. Rather, the story constructs "real experiences" and actually shapes our reality. Narrative practitioners contend that we construct what we see as well as describe what we see.

Significant therapeutic importance is placed on how people story their experiences and perform these stories in their lives. Narrative therapists work from the premise that our narratives do not encompass the full richness of our lives but only selected experiences. Other lived experiences are often overlooked, never noticed or understood, or are overshadowed by dominant problem-saturated stories. It is these overlooked lived experiences that are the material of interest in the narrative approach. Although a client is often strongly influenced by a problem-saturated story, a narrative therapist recognizes that this person also has many desirable lived experiences. These experiences are the basis from which an alternative, more preferred story line can be developed.

Narrative therapists maintain that problems are identified within socio-cultural and relational contexts rather than existing within individuals.[9] The therapeutic endeavor concentrates on the socially constructed dialogue and the narrative accounts that clients present. Narrative practitioners maintain that one's identity or personhood is developed, sustained, and transformed in and through relationships, both immediate and within the society at large. Narrative therapists challenge traditional Western psychology, which defines adjustment in terms of dominant cultural values, and recognizes the potential negative effects of therapies that pathologize and categorize human beings when they do not conform to stereotypical health standards. Instead, narrative therapists hold knowledge tentatively and assist clients in identifying resources so they can experience a heightened sense of agency or ability to act in the world.

Narrative therapists consider problems through a political lens, whether an overt cultural problem such as racism or a more covert pressure such as "healthy" relationships, and invite clients to explore cultural practices that produce dominant, oppressive narratives. Clients are encouraged to reflect on where we get our restrictive notions and how these ideas produce a negative effect on us or others. Narrative therapists "deconstruct" or "unpack" the cultural assumptions that contextualize client problems and invite clients to identify dominant cultural practices or certain mainstream belief systems that attempt to define and regulate them.

Narrative Techniques

Narrative techniques are constructed around the assumptions just described and include externalizing, mapping the effects, deconstruction, co-authoring alternative stories, several kinds of questions, and building an audience as a witness to the emerging preferred story.

🐾 Externalizing Conversation
"The person is not the problem. The problem is the problem." This catch phrase, coined by Michael White, is associated with narrative therapy because of its emphasis on separating the problem from the person rather than demanding that the person own the problem. This is perhaps narrative therapy's most distinctive feature. The method employed to separate the person from the problem is referred to as *externalizing conversation.* Externalizing conversations create space between clients and problems to counteract oppressive, problem-saturated stories, thereby altering clients' relations to problems. Externalizing requires the therapist to identify discourses (cultural ideas and beliefs) that are problematic and oppressive and to identify the effects of these discourses on clients. This externalization allows clients to locate problem stories within a community context rather than within themselves.

Although externalizing descriptions are typically developed in consultation with clients, narrative practitioners actively contribute in this process by identifying externalizing descriptions that fit with the problem's central themes and the wider sociocultural milieu. In fact, narrative practitioners use externalizing conversations to interrupt the tendency of the community or individuals to pathologize people into positions of helplessness, guilt, and shame. For example, a therapist's externalizing language is captured in these questions: "To what extent is this notion of the perfect wife contributing toward the distress that you currently feel?" "How do you manage to fulfill all of the demands placed upon you when fear continues to undermine your confidence?"

🐾 Mapping the Effects of the Problem Story
The full effects of the problem story have seldom been grappled with by the person seeking help. Clients often fear that they might be overwhelmed by their difficulties. When externalized

descriptions of problems are embedded in the conversation, their effects on clients are examined in a more dispassionate light. Clients feel less shamed and blamed. When the problem influences are examined in a systematic fashion, people feel listened to and that their concerns are taken seriously. They become more mindful of the burden they have been operating under, and after hearing and using externalized descriptions, they are more motivated to move away from the harmful effects of the problem. The externalized problems are understood in terms of the length of time they have been around (length), the extent to which they have had an impact on the person's life (breadth), and the strength and intensity of their influence (depth).[10]

Here are some examples of questions exploring the length, breadth, and depth of the problem-saturated story:

Length Questions
- How long has this problem been around?
- When did it start?
- If things keep going like this, what length of time do you think you might be wrestling with this problem?

Breadth Questions
- How widely spread is this difficulty?
- To what extent is it troubling you on a day-to-day basis?
- How are your present difficulties affecting your mental health, relationships with yourself, friends, children, husband, wife, siblings, physical well-being, your work, leisure time, spiritual well-being, plans for your future, ability to have fun?

Depth Questions
- What level of distress has this problem been causing you?
- At what times is this problem most difficult to handle?
- When is it less difficult?
- On a scale of 1 to 10, how impactful is the problem right now if 10 indicates the problem is in charge of you and 1 indicates that you are completely in charge of it? What score would you give it at its worst? At its best?

🌿 **Deconstructive Practices**   Frequently, people are unaware of how discourses restrict their knowledge, volition, and ways of being in the world. Alternative, more preferred ways of living may remain out of reach, unavailable, or unattainable. Deconstruction questions involve challenging taken-for-granted assumptions about how life must be lived, feelings that must be felt, and behaviors that must be performed. Here are some examples of deconstruction questions:

- What ideas do you have about being female that explain why you acted that way?
- Where and how did you learn these ideas?
- Who in your life keeps reminding you that you should continue to live by these ideas?
- What areas of your life keep reinforcing these ideas about how you should think, feel, and act?

❧ **Co-Authoring a Preferred Story**   The biggest challenge in constructing a non-problem-saturated story, or what is called an "alternative story," lies in the contrast between the fragility of the emerging story and the intensity and strength of the problem story. Problem stories typically take hold over a long period of time and often are experienced as true accounts of what is taking place in clients' lives. Just as the problem story has grown in strength, so must the alternative story develop sufficient plot strength to be vibrant and potent enough to challenge the authority of the problem-saturated story. The alternative story needs to be fleshed out in sufficient detail in the counseling sessions so that it remains compelling and strong.

The alternative story has a beginning in the early life of the client. It is the task of the practitioner to rediscover with clients their demonstrated abilities and strengths in their early life that have become eclipsed by chronic problem issues. A narrative practitioner notes these competencies and returns to them when a preferred client narrative is being constructed. Moments of creativity, capacity, and capability are woven together into a story that will endure in the face of the problem-saturated stories that a client may experience.

Unique outcome, unique account, redescription, and unique possibility questions are all examples of questions that help elicit the client's preferred story.[11]

❧ **Unique Outcome Questions**   Client competencies are the unique outcomes (sparkling moments that stand apart from the problem story) that provide the material that can be storied into an enlivening narrative. In collaboration with the client, the practitioner locates desirable experiences the client can reflect on that can be used to assemble a new plot for the alternative story. For example:

- Can you tell me about moments recently when this anxiety and distress has subsided even for a short time?
- Have you had any brief flashes of clarity amidst the confusion? Tell me about these momentary insights.
- Are you saying some things to me that hint at possible creative solutions to the dilemma that you face? Say more about this.

❧ **Unique Account Questions**   These questions assist clients in giving an account of how they were able to accomplish the desirable, favored moments. They provide opportunities to promote encouragement and optimism and help to build a sense of competence and capacity for people struggling with issues that attempt to incapacitate them. Here are two examples:

- How were you able to speak out and stand up for yourself when it seemed like everything and everybody else were wanting you to go along with their ideas for you?
- What is it about you that gives you the strength to ask for new possibilities for your life when you have been instructed to conform to certain prescriptions of how to be a woman?

❧ **Redescription Questions**   Redescription questions invite people to reflect on new emerging or submerged preferred identities. They provide an opportunity for clients to explore other ways of being in the world that are in contrast to the ways they are currently adopting. They get at people's preferences for their personal development and the kinds of new relationships they are establishing. Here are some examples:

- What does this action, series of thoughts, or feeling responses tell you about yourself that you have not previously been in touch with?
- Now that you are prepared to question and reexamine the direction your life is taking, what does this behavior suggest to you about the personal qualities and abilities you are exhibiting right now?

❧ Unique Possibility Questions   Unique possibility questions move the focus into the future. They encourage people to reflect on what they have currently achieved, and based on these successes, they invite people to consider what their next steps might be. Here are some examples:

- Given your present discoveries and understandings, what do you think your next steps might be?
- When you are acting from this preferred identity, what actions will it lead you to do more of?
- Now that you have observed people responding in a supportive manner to your self-caring, what plans do you have for yourself to not let go of your ability to nurture yourself?

❧ Building an Audience   Identities or ways of being are not performed in a vacuum. We are forever presenting ourselves to an audience—those significant others in families and communities whose opinions and viewpoints have immense influence on us. Sometimes this audience is critical and scathing. When significant others are consistently negative, they act as powerful definers of how we perceive ourselves and the dominant stories we carry about our lives. Thus, dominant problem stories often are cultivated under the gaze of scornful or judgmental observation.

Emerging alternative stories that carry with them the possibility of a preferred self-description must be nurtured by an audience of significant others who will notice and take delight in this desired self-depiction. An appreciative audience can verify the changes being made as real and sustainable. A common form of narrative questioning might begin with the request that the client identify a person who would be least surprised to learn of the changes he or she is now making. Clients can be asked what this valued person might say or do if informed about the emerging new story.[12]

Preparing for a Therapeutic Conversation With Ruth

Narrative therapy is essentially a therapy of questioning, conducted by a therapist who works from a nonexpert position of respectful and persistent curiosity and naive inquiry. I view Ruth as the senior author in the therapeutic conversation. She is the expert on her own life and will be consulted in regard to what she would like to achieve, how long she would like to attend sessions, and who she would like to include in future meetings. Therapy is generally a playful and optimistic activity in which Ruth is viewed as somebody who already has a variety of resources, abilities, and insights that she can capably bring to bear on her problem concerns. Together we discover her talents and capacities, which provide the basis for narratives of strength and resiliency, and we seek to understand the problem-saturated stories that restrain Ruth from attaining the level of personal satisfaction she would like to achieve.

Through a systematic process of careful listening and curious and persistent questioning, the therapeutic task is to co-construct enlivening alternative client narratives with Ruth. This is done within a spirit of partnership and collaboration, and Ruth can decline to answer any questions she finds intrusive or distressing. In the narrative conversation, I address seven domains in assisting Ruth with her concerns, although in practice they may not be followed in a specific order. I want to assist Ruth in some of the following ways:

- Story the problem-saturated narratives that feature prominently in her life.
- In a focused and systematic way, consider and experience the effects of the problem narratives on her life.
- Determine the extent to which she would like something different than her present circumstances.
- Deconstruct discourses that have a negative impact on her.
- Story a range of preferred alternative narratives that lie outside the problem-saturated stories.
- Reflect on how preferred narratives invite Ruth to construct new, more preferred identities.
- Build an audience to the emergence of Ruth's preferred identities.

Like many other narrative therapists, I view Ruth's concerns within the context of her life. I see us as two cultural beings doing the best we can to sustain ourselves in the face of a world that is challenging, fast changing, and unpredictable. As we work together, we are both making sense of our lives and producing meanings that take us forward, whatever they might be.

Initial Assessment and Evaluation

I begin my interview with Ruth by inviting her to tell me the concerns she has and what she is hoping to accomplish in our meetings together. I want to understand what help she would like from me. I explain the philosophy and practices underpinning narrative therapy because I want to be as transparent as I can be about what I am here to do. From a narrative perspective, I am not at all invested in producing a *DSM-IV-TR* diagnosis to guide my work with Ruth. I am concerned about the inadvertent effects of labeling Ruth's experience in this way, and I am opposed to the pathologizing tendencies that the *DSM-IV-TR* promotes. The *DSM-IV-TR* focuses on inadequacy and personal failure rather than on solutions and attention to resources and competence. It is seldom useful in helping me know what to do. I believe that Ruth is in a continual state of reinventing her identity, and such labeling invites a static perspective about her future directions. It also fails to address the significance of interpersonal and cultural factors that shape Ruth's experience.

However, if a *DSM-IV-TR* diagnosis were required, Ruth and I would work in a collaborative manner and probably choose what I would call a "cultural description" (what others may call a diagnosis) that Ruth is comfortable with. I would emphasize to Ruth the somewhat subjective, arbitrary nature of the exercise and the significant variation in diagnoses that are made by practitioners using this system.

Therapeutic Processes and Procedures

🐾 Telling Problem-Saturated Narratives   Ruth tells me about a number of her concerns, including her feelings of confusion, depression, inadequacy, distress, and anxiety. While Ruth still has concern with the panic attacks, the yoga class she is taking has decreased their frequency. Ruth also expresses concerns about her weight problems. However, right now Ruth is requesting very specific help—she wants advice about what she should do in relation to her marriage. She doesn't want marital counseling, but she wants to explore her own feelings about whether "she still loves John." She wants to get as clear as possible about whether she should try to salvage her marriage with John or leave him. She thinks some of the difficulties she is having with Jennifer (her daughter) relate to her current lack of communication and cooperation with John.

Despite entering into counseling, Ruth can barely believe she is asking herself these questions, let alone telling somebody else. Ruth feels like she is really letting John down by exploring her confusion, uncertainty, and ambivalence about their relationship. She wants lots of assurance that what she is doing is not evil and full of betrayal.

> RUTH: I can't believe I am telling you about my inner thoughts about my future. It is scary to say these things out loud.
>
> THERAPIST: Tell me more about that.
>
> RUTH: Well, I felt like I would always be married to John. Even though we have had some terrible times together, I have never, until very recently, faced the prospect that I could leave John. The fear of judgment from my children, from John, from my father, and fear of some kind of divine punishment—that I would go to hell—has stopped me from even considering anything but staying together. But right now I have been honest enough to accept the fact that I hate the kind of life I have been living and shudder to think that I may continue to live this life until the day I die.
>
> THERAPIST: Ruth, tell me about your life right now and how it got to be this way [*An invitation to tell the problem-saturated story*].

Ruth talks about how desperately unhappy she is. She talks about the fact that John was OK about her pursuing a teaching credential but has continued to be somewhat resentful about her developing her own professional interests. She feels like she can't really talk to John about how alone she feels. She lies alone at night wishing she were living somebody else's life. She talks some more about how scared she is to make any life changes. She is worried that things could get even worse.

I ask Ruth to tell me the story of her relationship with John from when they first met. She described the euphoria of falling in love and the profound sense of security she felt being with him. Ruth felt protected from the world. John was so strong, so secure within himself, so confident. He was also a good provider. Their relationship worked well for her for the first 15 years, but in the last 5 years things have started to deteriorate. She described feeling taken for granted by John and by the children as they reached adolescence. Ruth feels like a chauffeur, a housemaid, a cook, a counselor, a financial planner, and a caregiver/nurse. She reports feeling unfulfilled and unsupported. Ruth talks about her fear of speaking honestly to John about the depth of the despair she feels.

> THERAPIST: What's stopping you from speaking to John about your present feelings?

> RUTH: I really don't know. I guess I am just terrified that my world is going to come crashing around my ears if I tell people how I really feel.

> THERAPIST: How long do you think fear and terror has stopped you from expressing your heartfelt thoughts? [*I introduce externalizing conversation into the interview.*]

> RUTH: When I think about it, I have always been scared of speaking out. From as early as I can remember, I have been frightened about so many things.

Ruth speaks at length about how fear has silenced her in many different areas of her life on so many occasions. I am very curious about Ruth's relationship with fear. I enter the next phase of the narrative conversation.

❧ Exploring the Effects of the Problem Narratives on Her Life   I begin by exploring with Ruth the effects of being silenced by fear. I ask Ruth what contributions fear and terror have made to her life. What has it added? What has it taken away? What has the fear cost her? What has the impact of fear had on her health? Her relationships? Her career? Her spirituality? Her ability to enjoy her life? These questions help us map the effects of the problem.

Ruth talks about some of her fear. She is afraid of what is involved in pursuing her career. She feels that the fear she is feeling stops her from taking risks to build new friendships. Ruth speaks about being afraid of what Jennifer might do if she is more honest with her daughter. Most of all, fear is causing her misery because she feels she can't speak openly with John about how she is feeling about her life. Ruth agrees that this state of affairs is far from ideal!

> THERAPIST: Do you think there might be a relationship between being silenced and living with fear and the depression, anxiety, panic attacks, and confusion you speak of? [*Exploring themes and plotting connections within the problem story.*]

> RUTH: I think there is a relationship between these feelings and being able to speak openly about what is going on.

> THERAPIST: Ruth, tell me how big you think fear is right now as you think about talking to John about what is really going on. Out of

10, how much do you think fear is silencing you from sharing your thoughts and feelings with John? [*Further mapping the effects of the problem according to depth.*]

RUTH: I guess it's just about 10 because I just feel so terrible. I feel so unhappy. He has no real idea about how unhappy I am.

🌱 Making a Decision to Create an Alternative Narrative   At this stage, I encourage Ruth to begin creating an alternative narrative.

THERAPIST: Ruth, you have been speaking fully about the kind of life you have led with fear, and at times terror, dominating the quality of your relationships with your family and friends, your career, and diminishing your ability to play, have fun, and create a life of your own design. I am wondering if you feel ready to take on this pervasive fear, or do you feel that fear might still be serving you well?

RUTH: I know that being so afraid has closed in on my life in so many ways. I feel ready to take this on, but it would be too overwhelming to become so honest with myself and everybody else in lots of areas of my life all at once.

THERAPIST: So you would like to challenge fear and express yourself more openly, but you want do so in small steps. Is that right?

🌱 Understanding the Discursive Constraints   As Ruth is motivated to diminish the fear and anxiety that has dominated so much of her life, I ask her if she is willing to explore some of her life experiences that have contributed to the fear and anxiety she has felt. Ruth has made a link between the desire to step outside of her duties as a wife and a mother and the fear of doing so. She remembers the consequences as a young child of wanting to play and have fun, and the tensions and judgments that arose in the family if she participated in activities that weren't related to caring for others.

THERAPIST: Ruth, where did you learn how to be a woman, a wife, a parent?

RUTH: I don't know. I haven't really thought about it.

THERAPIST: Well, I am just wondering where you got the ideas of being very caring and putting your own needs aside to focus on other people's needs, sometimes at the expense of your own.

RUTH: I guess I mainly got the ideas from my Mom and the way my Dad treated my Mom, and the way he still treats her.

THERAPIST: Do you think you live your life according to the ways your Mom modeled how you should be a woman, mother, and wife?

RUTH: I'm not sure. I don't think I have really examined whether I live the same kind of life that my mother does. I know she would never have considered developing a career or going to college. In that way, we are quite different.

THERAPIST: Yes, that does seem to be a real difference. I am wondering if you can identify areas where you are the same?

RUTH: Well, I think Mom sees relationships in pretty traditional terms. The man is the head of the household, the primary income earner, the protector, if you like. The woman's job is to rear the children, to look after and take care of the house, and I guess to take care of the husband.

THERAPIST: How many of these ideas have you taken on board that your mom trained you in?

RUTH: Well, I guess for the first 15 years I've followed in Mom's foot-steps. That is the kind of woman I have been for virtually all my married life. Now, this is the problem. I feel like I want to stop doing that. I don't want to keep feeling responsible for John's happiness at the expense of my own. I don't want to keep living my life through John. But this is what I hate. I feel so guilty for wanting to establish my own career. And yet I feel really resentful of John when he doesn't support me and help me with the kids. I am also sick of being some kind of domestic slave. Sometimes I feel really clear about wanting a very different life, and then I start feeling really guilty and bad. I get so confused, and then I get depressed again.

THERAPIST: What areas of your life keep reinforcing these ideas about how you should think, feel, and act?

RUTH: Well, I think my Mom and Dad sure reinforce the kind of mother I should be. Dad has been really opposed to me training as a teacher. He feels it is taking me away from my duties as a parent. Mom is asking me whether I still cook for John and the children since I started my teacher training. I guess those are some obvious examples. There are lots of other subtle ones. Anyway, I just get this really yuk feeling when I am wanting to do career stuff, develop new friendships, and want John to get more involved in helping with the kids and around the house.

As Ruth and I work together, we mutually identify a number of cultural influences that are shaping Ruth and her experiences. My task here is to work with her to deconstruct some of the cultural discourses that might play a cen-tral role in producing the conflicts, depression, anxieties, tensions, ambiguities, and fears Ruth experiences. On the white board, Ruth and I work together and identify the following cultural discourses as being influential in her defining herself as a woman:

- As a woman, you are a worthy person if you live your life to serve others.
- As a woman, you are a selfish and unworthy person if you consider your own needs and want to have fun in your life.
- A woman should put aside her own career aspirations to fulfill the needs of a man.

As Ruth looks at this list, she agrees that these are the very beliefs held by her husband, and by her to some extent. These are also common cultural ideas about women that circulate in many societies.

THERAPIST: Ruth, do you think there is any relationship between the fear and anxiety you experience and the efforts you are making to continue to fulfill these prescriptions about the kind of life you should be leading?

RUTH: Oh, yes, there is. I guess I have believed that these ideas about womanhood were true and it was my job to fulfill them. I have really started to question these beliefs in the last 5 years. I think I have been faithfully living by these ideas for virtually all my life. But I really don't know whether this is going to help. I guess I want some specific advice about what I should do.

THERAPIST: OK, let's figure out what you are already doing to challenge these beliefs before I give you any suggestions. Is that OK with you?

RUTH: Sure, but I don't see what I am doing to challenge these beliefs. I feel like a complete weakling living the kind of life I am leading. I wish I were more courageous.

THERAPIST: Ruth, I would like to ask you some questions about your ability to challenge others and speak about things that you care about.

RUTH: OK, but I don't think there is anything much to say about courage. I don't have any.

Building the Alternative Story At this point, we turn to the storying of Ruth's preferred narrative.

THERAPIST: Ruth, I am intrigued that you are not aware of the occasions when you have been courageous and have challenged the kind of fear that had closed in so much on your life. I am really excited to start making some connections with you about the many moments you have mentioned already in this session when you were being an active participant in your life. For example, tell me what it was like to make a decision to come to counseling.

RUTH: What do you mean?

THERAPIST: Well, you knew you were going to start examining your life in a way you haven't done before, and that must be pretty scary.

RUTH: You're right. I was terrified to make the appointment. I was thinking to myself, "What if I find out things about myself that I don't like?" You know, I am still really scared about where this is going to go.

THERAPIST: Would it be true that last year you would have been seriously challenged by fear and not made an appointment, and yet recently you decided you could make an appointment and start talking with me as openly as you have [*An identified unique outcome*]?

RUTH: Yeah, but I have been feeling so desperate, I just had to go ahead and do something. I have been feeling like I am going crazy.

THERAPIST: OK, I hear that. However, despite feeling desperate, how did you prepare to face fear so directly and start talking about your life so openly with me [*Unique account question*]?

RUTH: I dunno, I just said to myself one day, "I can't stand this anymore, I have got to do something."

THERAPIST: What do you think you might have said to yourself in the face of "Oh, my God, my life could completely change in ways I can't predict. I have got to do something." Did you say, "I can do this?" What did you say?

RUTH: I really don't know. I think I just said, "Ruth you have got to do something." I don't want to keep doing what I have been doing.

THERAPIST: OK, you knew you wanted something more, and you were prepared to go for it in spite of the fear.

RUTH: Yes, I guess so.

THERAPIST: OK, so we have one example of your ability to demonstrate courage and face fear. You were saying earlier that you feel like fear is about 10 and that you are almost completely silenced by it. Is that right?

RUTH: Yes.

THERAPIST: Well, as I am having you reflect more on these issues, I am wondering if there are even just a few occasions where you speak up about feelings you are having in day-to-day interactions with John.

RUTH: I usually don't tell John what I am feeling, and frankly I don't think he is interested most of the time.

THERAPIST: Can you think of an occasion in the last week where you have said to John something you feel strongly about and you didn't let fear silence you?

RUTH: Well, I guess there was an occasion on Tuesday when I said to John I needed his support when the children are rude. I told him in no uncertain terms that I wanted him to speak up and challenge the children when their tone of voice is rude.

THERAPIST: What was it like to tell him that?

RUTH: It felt good, but I'm not sure it made much difference.

THERAPIST: In that moment, how much were you in charge of yourself, and how much was fear in charge?

RUTH: I felt pretty confident saying that. It is more difficult to talk about my feelings for him and about our marriage.

THERAPIST: What would you rate fear in that moment?

RUTH: Oh, about a 3.

THERAPIST: Earlier you said you were excited about what could be in your life even though fear was really huge. You have been willing to talk openly and honestly with me to gain more understanding of yourself.

❧ Developing the Alternative Story

In this phase of the narrative interview, I am storying lived experiences with Ruth about her courage, her ability to be decisive, to take risks in the face of not knowing, and being willing not to be controlled or stifled by fear. We speak together about a number of unique outcomes, occasions when Ruth has demonstrated courage in the face of serious fears. These include making a decision to train as a teacher, completing university studies, taking huge risks by leaving her parents' fundamentalist church, the courage to speak about shaming experiences about playing doctor when she was a child, her ability to care for her siblings when she was a child, and her ability to reflect now on her right to have fun and joy in her life.

We speak about the strengths and abilities required to raise four children, to "make a marriage work," and her ability to know that she has a right to be excited about her life. All of these lived experienced are linked together into a narrative of resilience and strength. To thicken the plot of the story of risk-taking, courage, determination, and having the right to enjoy life, I need to story with Ruth the courageous events that had recently happened and link them to events featured throughout her life. This includes eliciting occasions from as early as she can remember when Ruth displayed acts of courage. These memories are folded into the narrative that honors her own journey throughout her life. Ruth feels very excited and more potent as she reflects on these events.

It is not enough just to construct a lasting preferred narrative of strengths and abilities. We also need to reflect on how these actions influence Ruth's evolving and changing identity. In other words, I am interested in assisting Ruth to revise her understandings of herself as she reflects on these preferred narratives. I continue to move into exploring the unique account questions to further thicken the plot of this emerging story.

THERAPIST: Ruth, we have spent some time reflecting on the many, many instances when you have demonstrated courage in the face of fear and the unknown. What explanation do you give of your ability to have a history of courage, determination, and a willingness to take risks [*Unique account question*]?

RUTH: Well, to tell you the truth, it comes as a bit of a shock to think that I have been kind of brave at different stages in my life. It is surprising to put all of those experiences together and realize there really is something to all of this.

THERAPIST: What does this say about the kind of person you are?

RUTH: Well, I guess it says that I can be gutsy sometimes.

THERAPIST: Do you like that description about yourself?

RUTH: I do, but it still feels a little strange to describe myself in these terms.

THERAPIST: OK, I understand that. You want to get used to that?

RUTH: Yeah, I do.

THERAPIST: What title would you give this story of courage that we have been exploring together [*A question to concretize the alternative story*]?

RUTH: It is really hard for me to think of this. I am not really creative in that way.

THERAPIST: Would you like to have a name for this story? The story tends to be much more present for you when you name it. Are you willing for us to name it together?

Ruth and I go back and forth, and we eventually come across a title that is fitting for Ruth. We call it "Ruth's coming out." I then explore with Ruth the impact of the redescribing questions.

THERAPIST: What does it mean for you now to think of yourself as gutsy when you consider facing John and telling him what is honestly going on for you?

RUTH: Well, I think it helps. I will still feel scared, but I really want to be more honest with John. I think I am prepared to face him. We keep getting stuck in an argument, and I keep ending up feeling blamed. So often I feel like I have done something wrong, and I end up feeling guilty. To tell you the truth, I don't feel very hopeful for our relationship. All he really wants me to do is to go back to the kind of person I was before.

⚛ Recruiting an Audience I explore with Ruth the possibilities of recruiting an audience who will provide support for her as she moves more fully into her preferred story of "Ruth's coming out." Depending on how our work goes together with Ruth, John, and their children, it might be possible for Ruth's own family to appreciate her growing confidence, stronger voice, and ability to take more risks and be more honest. What is more realistic at this juncture is to engage Ruth to consider people in her life now who can support her, applaud her efforts, and cheer her on.

THERAPIST: I have been wondering as we have been working together, who would be least surprised to hear your "Ruth's coming out" story? You know, if they were to hear about this whole story of you who takes risks, challenges others, faces fear, who might say, "Sure, I'm not the least surprised to hear that Ruth did that"?

RUTH: Well, the only person I can think of now is my maternal grandmother. She would not be surprised by my "coming out story."

THERAPIST: What would your grandmother say to you if she were sitting in the room with us now?

RUTH: Well, she might say, "Ruth, you have got what it takes. Trust yourself. It will all work out."

THERAPIST: What is it like to hear that?

RUTH: It is really good. It encourages me.

Ruth and I talk some more about the people in her life and what they would say to her if they listened in on our conversation. Ruth identifies two of her friends that she would like to bring into the loop and be much more open with about what is going on in her relationship with John. She thinks she will get some support from these friends.

Future Challenges

In future sessions, we will come back to these cultural ideas that have been so influential in producing anxiety, depression, and confusion in Ruth's life. Ruth is coming to awareness that many of the troubles she is experiencing are not caused by personal deficits or difficulties in communicating. Rather, they are about the discursive clashes that invade her world. These culture clashes pull men and women in different ways. For example, "A woman's job is to stand by her husband no matter what the cost, versus men and women have the right to an equitable and respectful relationship."

There are flashes of awareness in Ruth that John is not a bad person intent on thwarting her plans. Rather, she is beginning to see that John is subject to cultural messages about how to be a man and a husband just as much as she is shaped by the cultural messages about how to be a woman and a wife. Knowing this doesn't mean it is going to be easy for Ruth to accept John's traditional beliefs about important familial matters when they are in opposition to her changing viewpoints. The difference for Ruth involves her knowing that the challenges she is experiencing with John aren't about her going crazy. It is about something much bigger than her.

Concluding My Work With Ruth

Ruth is already changing her sense of herself, and she knows a little more about what is possible in her life. She is connected more with her ability to take risks and express herself more openly and honestly, and she is more understanding about her confusion and anxieties about what she wants and what she is to do. There also is a qualitative shift in the extent to which she feels frightened. She is more trusting of herself in the face of the consequences of her decisions. However, there is a lot more to do.

Ruth doesn't know for sure whether she should continue to stay married to John, but she is now prepared to explore what it will mean to stay together as intimate partners. She is more confident in her ability to survive and less burdened by worrying about John's future. Issues about her relationship with the children remain a concern to her. She is more trusting of herself to handle her father's reactions to her, including blaming and judgment, and recognizes that this relationship will always be a struggle for her. Our work together has provided a strong foundation to address these ongoing concerns. Her story, "Ruth's coming out," is important to her and reminds her of her new emerging identity as a gutsy Ruth. Ruth is motivated to do more in future counseling sessions. For instance, she wants marital counseling, she wants a closer yet more respectful relationship with her children, and she wants to address her problems with body image and weight.

Ruth and I have established a strong collaborative partnership, and she is beginning to believe in her own expertise. She feels more sure of herself, knowing that many of the struggles she faces are less to do with some kind of personal deficits, malfunctions, and dysfunctions occurring within her and more to do with the clash of cultural expectations required of her as a woman, mother, and partner. As she enters into the next stage of her personal work, she is becoming less willing to internalize inadequacy and more willing to exter-nalize and challenge the cultural prescriptions that have constrained the kind of life she wishes to lead.

At this point, Ruth doesn't have all the answers to her questions, nor may she ever have such answers. She still doesn't know whether she will leave John, defy the God that her father introduced to her, change her body shape, or ever be completely free of sadness and anxiety. However, she is certain that what-ever she is yet to come up against, she has the strength and courage to step forward into the unknown.

Narrative Therapy: A Remembering Conversation with Ruth

by John Winslade, PhD

Introduction

In his final book before he died in 2008, Michael White[13] outlined a series of dif-ferent "maps" with which to chart several different kinds of narrative therapy conversations. These maps are formulated as different types of questions to be asked at different stages of a therapeutic process. They provide the counselor or therapist with a series of guideposts for structuring and shaping a conversa-tion so that it is purposeful and does not just wander aimlessly. The most well-known of these maps is the reauthoring map in which a therapist helps a client create a story of identity that differs in significant ways from a problematic story that has been governing his or her life. In the description and example of narrative therapy that Gerald Monk elaborated, this was the map he used to guide the process of the conversation.

Other maps for therapeutic conversation have emerged in the field of nar-rative practice, and the one that I want to feature in this conversation is called the "remembering map." It instigates a different kind of conversation that still aims to construct a narrative that can be sustaining and invigorating for a client. It is still about privileging the stories people tell and the stories that are told about them. In addition, it builds on a different foundation of reconstitut-ing one's memory of a person who is no longer alive as a significant touchstone in the ongoing process of living. In this section I elaborate the principles of a remembering conversation[14] and illustrate how it might be constructed through an imagined dialogue with Ruth. This dialogue might take place in a subse-quent session to the one that Dr. Monk modeled.

Key Concepts and Goals

A narrative orientation assumes a central role for stories in the construction of people's identities. We become the persons in the stories we tell about our-selves. Sometimes the stories we tell about ourselves are shaped by the stories that others tell. A person's story about his or her worth as a person is inevita-bly influenced by what the cultural world specifies in order to consider oneself worthwhile. For example, one might internalize the need to exhibit a certain body shape to be admired by others, or as a woman to take on family respon-sibilities and suppress her own career intentions, or to only expect certain economic opportunities as a result of one's social class. Another person might accept his diagnosis as scientifically correct and not contest it for fear of being classified as a difficult or resistant patient. Or someone might be convinced that her desired relationships and connection with others indicates a pathological dependency or incomplete ability to express the independence of thought nec-essary to be a good citizen. These internalizations are expressions of dominant discourse in the world around us. They are powerful enough that it is difficult not to internalize them and take them on as part of our identity.

At the same time, any story that is told about a person or by a person has a partial quality to it. Any identity story is inherently unstable because it is a selection of plot events, characterizations, and themes from among a range of possibilities for inclusion. Any story can be retold. The points of resistance to dominant stories can be considered entry points to counter narratives (or alter-native stories, as Dr. Monk referred to them) that can be established as the basis for living differently. But such narratives need to be built up and strengthened in order to withstand the ongoing force of a dominant narrative. They need to have meaning performed around them in order to become sustainable.

All of this is consistent with the reauthoring version of narrative practice. A remembering conversation, however, diverges from a reauthoring conver-sation in its emphasis on the concept of membership. Remembering means reinvigorating a person's sense of connection with the members of the club, or associations, or networks of her or his life. A membership club includes all those who have been significant influences on a person. It is not just the nuclear family of origin that has received so much attention in the history of therapy. It also includes extended family members, friends, mentors, teachers, partners and spouses, and children born into, or adopted into, a membership club. It may even include well-known authors or public figures whom a person adopts as significant influences on his or her decision making.

From a narrative perspective a person's identity does not achieve stabil-ity through being individuated from the influences of those who populate a person's membership club. Identity is instead formed out of the composite influences of all the members of a membership club. From among these per-sons and influences, the individual can still shape his or her own life by arrang-ing and structuring the status and rank of the membership club. Those who are granted the privilege of lifelong membership are held closer to the center, and those who are more temporary influences are relegated further to the outside of the circle. Sometimes those who gain automatic life membership (for instance parents) can abuse their privileges and be moved further toward the periphery. The membership club is always in the process of being reconfigured.

From among the members of the membership club a person might adopt characteristics, learn to emulate actions or personal styles of living, take on principles and values, copy behaviors and speech patterns, or incorporate information about him- or herself through another's eyes. Identity is thus formed out of the cumulative influences of a network of persons, rather than just out of the individual personality or through the actualization of the core inner self. Narrative practice fits well with a multicultural orientation because it privileges the cultural influences around us as shaping, but not permanently fixing, our stories of who we are. It is the role of culture in our lives to exert this shaping influence. In order to learn about a person it is, therefore, necessary to learn about the cultural influences that surround the person, rather than to think of him or her primarily as an isolated individual.

The idea of the membership club arose first in the concept of handling grief. The Western cultural perspective in grief psychology is that, when someone dies, they should be immediately cut out of a person's membership club and that death brings the end of relationship with that person. Accepting this perspective as "reality" is simply assumed in many grief counseling approaches. This idea has met repeated challenges from a variety of cultural perspectives in recent decades and has been challenged from within psychology. People are now considered to have "continuing bonds"[15] with their loved ones who are no longer alive. Many people experience the ongoing sense of connection with their dead loved ones as comforting and helpful rather than distressing. It may be, therefore, that the idea of "saying good-bye" to those who have died actually makes the experience of grief harder. This idea led Michael White[16] to write a seminal article, "Saying hullo again," in which he stressed the ongoing incorporation of dead loved ones into one's narratives of living.

The value of this idea lies not only in the practice of grief therapy but has wider application in helping people deal with a range of life problems. If the voice of the dead does not have to be banished by saying good-bye, then it can more easily be remembered as an ongoing influence and consulted as a resource for living in the future. Remembering conversations can be used to help someone like Ruth access stories from others in her membership club who are no longer alive but with whom she might still have a sense of connection. These stories can be incorporated into Ruth's story of herself as useful sources of strength for the task of becoming the person she wants to become.

Themes in Ruth's Life Serving as a Focus for Therapy

As I read the story of Ruth's life, I am struck by the gaps in it with regard to her membership club. There is no mention of extended family: grandparents, cousins, aunts and uncles. Her parents are apparently still alive; she has her husband John and her children; but there is no mention of significant friends, people in either of the churches listed with whom she connected, or teachers or mentors who have inspired her. Her story is not unusual in this respect because it reflects many of the Western cultural expectations about the individual and the patterns of urban living that have created the nuclear family as we know it, including the role of women as caregivers who consider their own careers as of secondary importance to those of their husbands. None of this is Ruth's fault, nor does her "failure" to feel comfortable in the position she finds herself indicate a personal pathology. She should not be considered to have something wrong with her so much as to be expressing a preference for something different in her own experience of life.

If we practice "double listening"[17] we might hear every problem or so-called "pathology" as an expression of a preferred life story or an intention to create something different. Double listening is the practice of consistently hearing the contradictory directions within a person's story—on one hand, the direction that the problem is taking her, and on the other hand, the direction she would prefer for herself. Ruth may be experiencing something of a struggle to give expression to her preferences, perhaps because her cultural context does not provide enough support for her personal hopes and dreams. The aim of a therapeutic conversation is to assist Ruth to connect more fully with her sense of agency and her preferred values and commitments in life.

In her earlier therapy conversation with Dr. Monk, Ruth refers to some of these preferences. One example lies in her preference to be someone who speaks up on her own behalf, who does not accept her children being rude to her, who wants her husband to listen to her, who has an intention of becoming an elementary school teacher, who makes her own decisions about her religious expression even if it does not please her father. Each of these expressions of her preferences for her life are openings to a counter story to the problems she is struggling with. Dr. Monk invites Ruth to deconstruct some of the cultural constraints operating to interfere with her development of this counter story. If we imagine that my meeting with Ruth takes place in a subsequent session, I would hope to build a conversation that strengthened the counter story that emerged in that session.

One way to do this would be to engage in a remembering conversation with Ruth about her relationship with someone who means something to her and who would value and appreciate what she is doing. In other words, I would be listening for someone in her membership club who might be an ally in her struggle so that she does not have to feel so alone with it. This person need not even be alive, although there is nothing to prevent her from identifying support from those in her membership club who are alive.

Initial Assessment and Evaluation

Like Dr. Monk I have grave concerns about the assumptions of power built into the process of assessment in therapy. Except in the case of assessing actual imminent danger, I avoid as much as possible any operation of assessment protocols upon a person. Standardized assessment processes like those advocated in the *DSM-IV-TR* are especially dangerous for a person in Ruth's position. They constitute an expression of "normalizing judgment"[18] and preclude the possibility of the client having a conversation with a person who takes a nonjudgmental position. From a narrative perspective, they set up a relational context that gives far too much authority to what is in the therapist's head and at the same time removes it from the client. This is therapeutically counterproductive and may be considered ethically suspect.

Narrative practice does not completely deny assessment and evaluation. In narrative practice the person who should in most circumstances do the work of assessment is not the therapist but the client. At the very least, any assessment should be collaborative. It is more productive in narrative practice for a therapist to engage with a client to help the client evaluate and assess the effects of a problem in his or her life. The deconstruction of the effects of cultural prescriptions in a person's life are a form of evaluation—not of an individual but of the cultural context. It turns normalizing judgments back on themselves.

When people are grieving the loss of someone they care about, we should specifically avoid any assessment of pathology in mourning. People are disrespected if a therapist decides that they are grieving abnormally, or too long, or too briefly, or without enough tears being shed, or are in a state of denial, or are crazy to be still talking to their dead loved one. Assessments that contain such evaluations of grieving will inevitably leak into the conversation in ongoing expressions of disrespect. Much more useful might be invitations issued to clients to evaluate for themselves the meaning of a dead loved one in their lives and the usefulness of continuing to maintain a sense of connection with that person.

Therapeutic Processes and Procedures

Narrative practice is founded on the technique of asking questions that are intended to open up and expand upon new territories for living in therapy. It is important, however, to emphasize that narrative practice is about a different form of listening as well. What distinguishes the listening in narrative therapy from some other approaches is that the emphasis is less on simply listening "to" the client and more on what the therapist might be listening "for." Narrative therapists are hearing, at the same time, a person's struggles or problems and their expressions of their resistance to those problems (hopes, dreams, intentions, preferences, commitments, and so on). This is a form of listening that consistently treats a person as capable of having agency and of being resourceful, rather than focusing too intently on a person's problems. In remembering conversations, this might mean listening both to the effects of dominant cultural assumptions about grief on a person's experience and to the personal sense of relationship and connection with a dead loved one that can become a resource for living. Or it might mean listening both for the problem stories that are constraining a person's vitality in life and for the voices of loved ones in a person's membership club who might support expressions of vitality in the face of such constraints. In other words, narrative listening stands for an ethic of always listening not just for problems but also for the stories that can counter those problems.

Narrative listening involves carefully listening for the resonance in the words that people utter. When such resonance is heard, it is not immediately paraphrased into the therapist's words but allowed to linger in the mind of both the therapist and the client. It may be written down for future reference or as material to give back to the client in a therapeutic letter. Michael White and David Epston[19] are well known for developing the idea of writing letters to clients that record on paper what was said in a therapy session so that it can continue to reverberate longer in consciousness than the spoken word might.

On this basis of listening, a remembering conversation proceeds through asking a series of different classes of questions. These questions start with a simple request to tell the therapist about the person's relationship with her or his dead loved one and proceeds from stories that are located primarily in the past toward stories about present relationship. The movement is from talking about the person who has died toward folding what is remembered into the person's identity story as a resource for ongoing living. These questions assume that the client has already mentioned in conversation that there is someone he or she cared about who is no longer alive. They are not prescriptive questions so much as samples of the kinds of questions that might be asked.

Introduction Questions
- What can you tell me about who this person was before he or she died?
- What are you most vivid memories of him?
- What kind of person was she?
- What did he like doing?
- What was her profession, and what did she enjoy?

Deconstructing Cultural Messages About Death
- What did people say to you after his death that was helpful or unhelpful?
- What cultural practices about grieving have you found helpful or unhelpful?
- What messages did you get about the right way and the wrong way to grieve?
- What effect did those messages have on you? What do you think about those messages?
- Which of those messages are you choosing to ignore and which to take seriously?

Meaning Making Questions
- What did knowing this person mean to you?
- What contributions did she make to your life?
- What did you enjoy about your relationship with her?
- What kinds of things did he say to you that were important?
- What kind of things did she teach you about life?

Ongoing Connections Questions
- How has your relationship with him developed since his death?
- What significant conversations have you had with other people about her?
- Are there times, places, rituals, songs, where you notice the connection with him? Are there times or contexts where you notice her significance for you more than others?

Subjunctive Identity Questions
- Are there things happening in your life at present for which it would be helpful to recall things about her?
- In what ways might remembering his teachings, words, and example be of assistance to you now?
- What might she appreciate about how you are handling the events of your life right now?
- What would it mean to him to listen to this conversation we are having today about him?

Folds of Identity Questions
- How would you notice that you were living with his voice closer to you?
- What difference would it make in your life if you were to do this?
- What possibilities open up when you live from this place?

- Where does this conversation take you?
- How does remembering her make a difference to your handling of the other issues we have been talking about?

The questions listed under the heading "subjunctive identity questions"[20] importantly use verbs that are in the subjunctive mood. The subjunctive represents the language of "as if . . ." rather than the language of reality. These questions invite a client to step into a world of what might be, rather than what is. This phrasing is a useful bridge between the present and the past. Also, you will notice that in remembering conversations there is no use of the practice of externalizing. Death or grief are not externalized, but a counter story to the pain of grief is implicitly developed through the practice of remembering.

Therapy in Action

In the process of reviewing the progress of her alternative story, Ruth comments on the difficulty she has in sustaining it in some circumstances.

RUTH: When I am thinking about it on my own it is not hard to think of myself as a gutsy and brave person as we talked about, but sometimes that sense of myself just seems to melt away when I am talking to my father, or to John, or even to my daughter Jennifer. I need to hold onto it in order to be that brave and gutsy person more often.

THERAPIST: OK. Sounds like a project you want to work on—to hold on to that brave and gutsy sense of yourself. Is that right?

RUTH: Yes that's exactly right.

THERAPIST: Well, one thing I recall was that at the end of our last conversation you were mentioning your grandmother as one person who would not be surprised about you being able to identify instances where you had been gutsy and brave. Do you remember that?

RUTH: Yes, I remember saying that. I had a very special relationship with my grandmother and I sometimes felt much closer to her than to my parents.

THERAPIST: Would you mind if I asked you some more about your relationship with her? Would that be of interest to you?

RUTH: Yes, that would be fine. I like talking about her. Although it has been harder since she died last year. I have missed her a lot. Her name was Marisol. But I used to know her as Nana.

THERAPIST: So what kind of person was your Nana Marisol? I'd like to learn something about her and what she meant in your life.

Ruth proceeds to talk for some time about her Nana, recalling some stories about her life. She also responds to my questions about her relationship with her Nana. She speaks of how she spent a lot of time with her Nana as a young child when her mother was ill and how she came to feel very special in her Nana's presence. Marisol would often scoff jokingly about her father's religious strictness and was the only person who could openly tease him about that. Ruth used to listen openmouthed and amazed at her gall. She was also the person with whom Ruth felt she could most easily confide about personal issues as a young person and even as an adult.

As she talks about Marisol, Ruth becomes quite animated and her eyes repeatedly tear up as she thinks of this very special relationship and of how she misses her Nana since she has died.

> THERAPIST: So I am interested, then, in how you have continued to think about her and to stay connected with her in the last year since she died.
>
> RUTH: Oh, I think about her on most days. I have little moments of sadness or sometimes I laugh when I think about her, because she would say really cheeky things sometimes that would bring anyone who was acting high and mighty down to earth in a moment.
>
> THERAPIST: Are there any special things that trigger your memory of her and help you to keep it close?
>
> RUTH: Well, I don't visit her gravesite. That has no special value for me. In fact the one time I did go there I found it creeped me out. It's more like when I listen to some old silly song on the radio and I remember that she used to sing that while she was doing things at home. She had a strong voice and could really sing, sometimes better than the recording artist.
>
> THERAPIST: Any particular song you remember?
>
> RUTH: Yes, that's funny when I think about it. She used to really belt out that song by Helen Reddy about: *I am strong; I am invincible; I am woman.* She used to get me to sing it too when I was young. When I was at school, she was always trying to teach me something with it.
>
> THERAPIST: Is that a special memory for you?
>
> RUTH: Yes, it is.
>
> THERAPIST: What is special about it?
>
> RUTH: Well, it's like a refrain that I run through my head sometimes when things are difficult.
>
> THERAPIST: How is that useful for you?
>
> RUTH: It reminds me that I am not someone to be pushed around. I have my own strength, and I can stand on my own feet in life.
>
> THERAPIST: As you stand on your own feet and have that refrain running through your head, is it like your Nana is standing alongside you?
>
> RUTH [*Suddenly tearful*]: You know, I have never thought of it like that, but that is such a lovely thought. And it fits exactly. I have always had a sense of being stronger when I think of her and her influence in my life.
>
> THERAPIST: So how might it be useful to you to remember that she is, in a way, standing beside you as you go through life?
>
> RUTH: Well, it might mean that I would be less susceptible to the doubts that come rushing in every time I try to stand strong.

THERAPIST: What would she do that would help banish those doubts?

RUTH [*laughs suddenly*]: Well, I just had this funny image of her with a bat standing there and knocking those doubts away before they get to me.

THERAPIST: And if she could do that, what difference would it make for you now?

RUTH: It would help me to stand firm and not go all weak-kneed when I need to demand something that is important to me in my marriage or with my children. And it would also help me to feel more confident about taking on this new job as an elementary school teacher.

THERAPIST: So let me ask something else. This is kind of an unusual question. What do you think it would mean to Marisol, if she could speak to us now, to know that she was helping you to stand strong and be gutsy and brave?

RUTH [*Again suddenly very moved*]: Oh, I think it would mean a lot to her. I can see her face beaming with pride and satisfaction. And she would be nodding as if to say, "I told you so!" She might even start to sing [*Laughs*].

THERAPIST: What would it be like for you to hold onto that image of her standing beside you, beaming with pride and satisfaction, and maybe even singing, and keep it close to you, particularly in times when things are more difficult for you?

RUTH: You know, I really like that idea. Cause I often feel that I have to do it all on my own. And this means that I am not so alone after all.

THERAPIST: Is that a helpful feeling?

RUTH: Yes, it is.

THERAPIST: What difference do you think it might make?

RUTH: Well, it might make me able to face things more calmly, make better decisions and speak clearly without being tied up in knots inside.

The conversation went on to discuss the situations Ruth was struggling with in her current life in which she was struggling to stay strong. Each of these was revisited with a sense of her Nana Marisol standing by her side and batting away doubts, then beaming with pride at what she was doing. With her Nana beside her, Ruth started to feel less shaky in some of these situations and started to work out more clearly what she wanted in her marriage and in her family. She also became more and more convinced that she was going to pursue her career as an elementary school teacher and make a difference in the lives of the children she taught.

🌿 **Concluding Commentary**   What stood out most for me in this conversation with Ruth was the sense I got of meeting Ruth's grandmother, Marisol. It was as if she came alive for me as we talked about her. The room seemed to become more populated and to have another presence in it. It was also noticeable that Ruth took on a different quality of speech as she spoke of her grandmother. She could easily imagine what her grandmother would have said, and she seemed to gain strength for herself as she did so. There was some sadness and she was definitely missing her grandmother, but she was also becoming more determined to honor Marisol by listening to her in a new way. She resolved to deliberately echo some of Marisol's hopes and dreams for Ruth in the way she dealt with the problems she was struggling with. In a curious way, even though her grandmother was no longer alive, she did not feel so alone as she imagined Marisol beside her.

Jerry Corey's Work With Ruth From a Postmodern Perspective: A Commentary

Introduction

In this chapter three different contributors have presented postmodern approaches to counseling with Ruth: Dr. John Murphy (solution-focused brief therapy), and Dr. Gerald Monk and Dr. John Winslade (both demonstrating narrative therapy, but from different perspectives). Because of these in-depth discussions, I will deviate from the usual format of discussing at length my particular perspective and only briefly mention of a few aspects of working with Ruth from the solution-focused and narrative perspectives. Then I will show how I might build on earlier work from these theories in thinking about Ruth's case.

Basic Assumptions

Narrative therapy emphasizes the value of devoting time to listening to clients' stories and to looking for events that can open up alternative stories. Like Drs. Monk and Winslade, I make the assumption that Ruth's life is affected by powerful cultural stories. Her life story influences what she notices and remembers, and in this sense her story influences how she will face the future. Although I am somewhat interested in Ruth's past, we will not dwell on her past problems. Instead, our focus will be on what Ruth is currently doing and on her strivings for her future.

I make the assumption that many of Ruth's problems have been produced by the contradictory cultural messages she has received from society about what kind of person, woman, mother, and partner she should be in the world. Part of our work together will be to look for personal resources Ruth has that will enable her to create a new story for herself. In short, from the narrative perspective my commitment is to help Ruth rewrite the story of her life. The collaboration between Ruth and me will result in her reviewing certain events from her past and rewriting her future. Working within a postmodern approach, our collaboration will be aimed at freeing Ruth from the influence of oppressive elements in her social environment and empowering her to become an active agent who is directing her own life.

The Therapeutic Process

The heart of the therapeutic process from the postmodern perspective involves identifying how societal standards and expectations are internalized by people in many ways that may constrain and narrow the kind of life that they might otherwise lead. Second, it focuses on how identifying a client's resistances to limiting cultural restraints provide the basis for the construction of an alternative story. Ruth's preferred story will be constructed based on her ability to embrace what she might regard as desirable cultural meanings and her ability to resist limiting cultural prescriptions. Ruth's autobiography provides me with significant clues to the unfolding story of her life.

Both narrative therapy and solution-focused brief therapy can help Ruth feel motivated, understood, and accepted. A method of supporting Ruth with the challenges she faces is to get her to think of her problems as external to the core of her selfhood. A key concept of both solution-focused therapy and narrative therapy is that the problem does not reside in the person. Even during the early sessions, I encourage Ruth to separate her identity from her problems by posing questions that externalize her problem. I view Ruth's problems as something separate from her, even though her problems are influencing her thoughts, feelings, and behaviors. While she presents many problems that are of concern to her, we cannot deal with all of them at once. When I ask her what one problem most concerns her right now, she replies, "Guilt. I feel guilty so often over so many things. No matter how hard I work at what is important to me, I generally fall short of what I expect of myself, and then I feel guilty." Ruth feels guilty because she is not an adequate daughter, because she is not the mother she thinks she should be, because she is not as accomplished a student as she demands of herself—when she falls short of "perfect performances" in these and other areas, guilt is the result.

My intention is to help Ruth come to view her problem of guilt as being separate from who she is as a person. I ask her how her guilt occurs and ask her to give examples of situations when she experiences guilt. I am interested in understanding how her guilt has been influencing her life. I also ask questions that externalize the problem, such as "What is the mission of this guilt, and how does it recruit you into this mission?" "How does the guilt get you, and what are you doing to let it become so powerful?" "How has guilt dominated and disrupted your life?" "What does guilt whisper in your ear?"

In this narrative approach, I follow up on these externalizing questions with further questions aimed at finding exceptions: "Has there ever been a time when guilt could have taken control of your relationship but didn't? What was it like for you? How did you do it?" "How is this different from what you would have done before?" "What does it say about you that you were able to do that?" "How do you imagine your life would be different if you didn't have this guilt?" "Can you think of ways you can begin to take even small steps toward divorcing yourself from guilt?"

My questioning is aimed at discovering moments when Ruth hasn't been dominated or discouraged by the problem of guilt. By identifying times when Ruth's life was not disrupted by guilt, we have a basis for considering how her life would be different if guilt were not in control. As our therapy proceeds, I expect that Ruth will gradually come to see that she has more control over her problem of guilt than she believed. As she is able to distance herself from defining herself in terms of problematic themes (such as guilt), she will be less burdened by her problem-saturated story and will discover a range of options. She will likely focus more on the resources within herself to construct the kind of life she wants.

Some Final Thoughts

In close alliance with the work of Drs. Murphy, Monk, and Winslade, my approach emphasizes Ruth's personal strengths rather than her liabilities. Both solution-focused brief therapy and narrative therapy are based on the optimistic assumption that people are healthy, competent, resourceful, and can be trusted to use their resources in creating better solutions and more life-affirming stories. I value building on a client's strengths, which is part of a number of theoretical models—Adlerian therapy, humanistic therapies, cognitive behavioral therapies, feminist therapy, and reality therapy. The postmodern approaches are distinct in that they encourage Ruth to create a richer life story by exploring new cultural meanings that are desirable to her. In this sense, therapy is a new beginning.

Questions for Reflection

1. In reflecting on the separate contributions of Drs. Murphy, Monk, and Winslade, what are some basic assumptions that all of these therapists share? How do these assumptions differ from the assumptions of traditional approaches to therapy?
2. What are the main differences you notice in reviewing each of the therapeutic styles in this chapter?
3. What are your thoughts about the manner in which diagnosis is viewed by both the narrative and solution-focused approaches? What do you think about working with Ruth to collaboratively establish a diagnosis?
4. What are your reactions to the specific techniques used by each of the therapists in this chapter? What techniques would you want to incorporate into your therapeutic style? What kind of questions do you find particularly useful?
5. Explain how the factors of the *client* and the *therapeutic alliance* represent the heart and soul of change in Dr. Murphy's client-directed SFBT approach.
6. What are some ways that Dr. Murphy was "client-directed" and "outcome-informed" in his work with Ruth?
7. What are some advantages to externalizing the problem from the client? How might you attempt to do this with Ruth? Are there any disadvantages to this approach?
8. Asking clients to think of exceptions to their problems often gets them to think about a time when a particular problem did not have such intense proportions. What advantages can you see in asking Ruth to talk about a time when she did not have a given problem? How might you build on times of exceptions?
9. Review the lists of questions that Drs. Monk and Winslade asked of Ruth. How could you apply this line of questioning in working with clients?
10. What are your thoughts about Dr. Winslade's approach to assisting Ruth in exploring her grief? How does his remembering perspective differ from traditional ways of viewing grief?

11. In what ways are some of the basic ideas of narrative therapy compatible with a multicultural perspective on counseling practice? What applications do you see for using narrative therapy with culturally diverse client populations?

12. How well does solution-focused brief therapy fit with your counseling style? What aspects of this approach do you find most useful? Which aspects might you want to modify to fit your personal counseling style?

13. How well does narrative therapy fit with your counseling style? What aspects of this approach do you find most useful? Which aspects might you want to modify to fit your personal counseling style?

Notes

See *DVD for Theory and Practice of Counseling and Psychotherapy: The Case of Stan and Lecturettes,* Session 11 ("Solution-Focused Brief Therapy Applied to the Case of Stan"), for an illustration of techniques such as identifying exceptions, the miracle question, and scaling. See also Session 12 ("Narrative Therapy Applied to the Case of Stan"), which focuses on Stan creating a new story of his life and for my presentation of ways that narrative therapy and solution-focused brief therapy can be applied.

1. de Shazer, S., Dolan, Y., Korman, H., Trepper, T., McCollum, E., & Berg, I. K. (2007). *More than miracles: The state of the art of solution-focused brief therapy.* New York: Haworth Press.

2. Duncan, B. L., Miller, S. D., & Sparks, J. A. (2004). *The heroic client.* San Francisco: Jossey-Bass.

3. Wampold, B. E. (2010). The research evidence for the common factors models: A historically situated perspective. In B. L. Duncan, S. D. Miller, B. E. Wampold, & M. A. Hubble (Eds.), *The heart and soul of change: Delivering what works in therapy* (pp. 49–83). Washington, DC: American Psychological Association.

4. Murphy, J. J., & Duncan, B. L. (2007). *Brief intervention for school problems: Outcome-informed strategies* (2nd ed.). New York: Guilford.

5. Murphy, J. J. (2008). *Solution-focused counseling in schools* (2nd ed.). Alexandria, VA: American Counseling Association.

6. Miller, S. D., & Duncan, B. L. (2004). *The Outcome and Session Rating Scales: Administration and scoring manuals.* Chicago: Author.

7. For a more complete discussion of the key concepts and methods I applied to the case of Ruth, see my book: Murphy, J. J. (2008). *Solution-focused counseling in schools* (2nd ed.). Alexandria, VA: American Counseling Association.

8. Michael White and David Epston are the principal founders of narrative therapy: White, M., & Epston, D. (1990). *Narrative means to therapeutic ends.* New York: Norton.

9. Excellent overviews of these ideas can be found in the following sources: Freedman, J., & Combs, G. (1996). *Narrative therapy: The social construction of preferred realities.* New York: Norton; Monk, G., Winslade, J., Crocket, K., & Epston, D. (1997). *Narrative therapy in practice: The archaeology of*

hope. San Francisco: Jossey Bass; and Madigan, S. (2011). *Narrative therapy.* Washington, DC: American Psychological Association.

10. Winslade, J., & Monk, G. (2007). *Narrative counseling in schools: Powerful and brief* (2nd ed.). Thousand Oaks, CA: Corwin Press.

11. White, M. (1989). The process of questioning: A therapy of literary merit? In *Selected Papers* (pp. 37–46). Adelaide, Australia: Dulwich Centre. For a useful discussion of various kinds of questions asked in narrative therapy, see Madigan, S. (2011). *Narrative therapy.* Washington, DC: American Psychological Association.

12. See Recruiting an audience. In M. White (1995), *Re-authoring lives: Interviews and essays.* Adelaide, Australia: Dulwich Centre.

13. White, M. (2007). *Maps of narrative practice.* New York: Norton.

14. Hedtke, L., & Winslade, J. (2004). *Remembering lives: Conversations with the dying and the bereaved.* Amityville, NY: Baywood.

15. Silverman, P., Klass, D., & Nickman, S. (Eds.). (1996). *Continuing bonds: New understanding of grief.* Philadelphia, PA: Taylor and Francis.

16. White, M. (1989). Saying hullo again. In M. White (Ed.), *Selected papers* (pp. 29–36). Adelaide, Australia: Dulwich Centre.

17. White, M. (2007). *Maps of narrative practice.* New York: Norton.

18. Foucault, M. (1965). *Madness and civilization: A history of insanity in the age of reason.* New York: Random House.

19. White, M., & Epston, D. (1990). *Narrative means to therapeutic ends.* New York: Norton.

20. Hedtke, L., & Winslade, J. (2005). The use of the subjunctive in remembering conversations. *Omega, 50*(3), 197–215.

21. See Corey, G. (2013). *DVD for Theory and Practice of Counseling and Psychotherapy: The case of Stan and lecturettes.* Belmont, CA: Brooks/Cole, Cengage Learning.

CHAPTER TWELVE

Case Approach to Family Therapy

General Overview of Family Systems Therapy

Depending on the specific orientation of a family systems practitioner, this approach has a variety of goals. For a therapist working with families, goals might include resolving the presenting problems of the client and the family; resolving a family crisis as quickly and efficiently as possible; creating an environment where new information can be infused into a system, allowing the family to evolve on its own; restructuring a system so that autonomy by all family members can be encouraged; changing the rules and patterns of interaction among family members; teaching communication skills; and teaching problem-solving skills.

A diversity of techniques may be employed, depending on the therapist's theoretical orientation. Because the therapist joins with the family, intervention strategies are best considered in conjunction with the personal characteristics of the therapist as well as what is in the best interests of the family. Outcomes are evaluated on the basis of the particular orientation of the therapist, yet a primary criterion is the degree of relational change that occurs among members of a family. In all couples and family therapy models, change needs to happen relationally, not just intrapsychically.

In this chapter, two family systems therapists join forces to provide their way of working with Ruth. This reconceptualized session with Ruth and her family, new to this edition, is so compelling that I have let it stand alone. In this chapter you will not find my own way of working with Ruth following this guest presentation.

A Family Systems Therapist's Perspective on Ruth

by Mary E. Moline, PhD, Dr.PH, and James Robert Bitter, EdD

Introduction

Family therapy calls for a conceptual shift from practicing individual therapy, for the family is viewed as a functioning unit that is more than the sum of the roles enacted by various members. The family provides a primary context for understanding how individuals function in relationship to others as well as how they behave within the system. Actions by any individual family member will influence the actions and reactions of others in the family, and their reactions will have a reciprocal effect on the individual. The transactions that occur between the individual and other family members shape the person's concept of self, relationships both within and outside of the family, and each member's worldview.

For a family with members who demonstrate a poor sense of self, a developmental approach might be integrated with a systems model. In the case of Ruth, a systemic family approach requires an assessment of her family system that includes her husband, her children, and her parents. An even more comprehensive systemic assessment could include examining her relationships (interactions) with other important units such as church, work, and friends. No rules dictate how much of her system of relationships the therapist must work with; rather, this will depend on the therapist's clinical judgment. Conceptually (or symbolically), however, the therapist will make interventions with Ruth that will enable her to deal with her husband, children, and parents, even though they may not be physically present in the therapy session.[1]

Confidentiality and Dealing With Secrets

A decision family therapists often make prior to a client's first visit is whom they will see. Many insist that a client's entire family be seen during the first visit. Given the variety of systemic approaches available, the therapist may decide to see only the concerned client in the beginning and later invite others in his or her system to attend therapeutic sessions. In that case, the matter of confidentiality must be addressed. The therapist needs to decide if what a client reveals in an individual session will be kept secret. It should be noted that many systems therapists avoid seeing the concerned client first, partially because of the problems involved with deciding how to deal with this client's disclosures in family sessions. To be clear, though, once a person has been seen individually, except in cases of harm prescribed by state laws, family practitioners who belong to AAMFT, APA, or ACA are bound to keep those sessions confidential—even after family therapy begins.

A safe rule in working with families is not to keep secrets. Present this policy in writing and encourage clients to discuss its ramifications. This contract informs clients of the risks involved with the therapy process. This definitely applies in those situations where the law mandates that the therapist reveal information indicating that clients are likely to harm themselves or others and in child abuse cases. Even when the law does not mandate revealing a secret, it is advisable to inform clients of any policies that apply to dealing with secrets. If secrets are kept, the therapist will certainly have a difficult time doing effective therapy with various parts of a family system. The therapist can easily forget what may not be said when the entire family gets together. For this reason, many family therapists refuse to become entangled in keeping secrets and let this be known from the outset. Of course, clients in family therapy should be clearly informed about the legal limits of confidentiality from the beginning, just as would be the case for individual therapy.

Considering the Cultural Perspective

Family therapists are concerned about how the family is influenced by their ethnic and cultural perspective. What might be observed as an ineffective hierarchical structure in a White, middle-class family may be quite normal if observed in a Latino, middle-class family. For example, in a Latino family, having the grandmother take on the parent role for the grandchildren may be culturally normal. However, a grandmother in Ruth's family taking on the parent role might create problems in the system. If the grandmother in Ruth's family is Ruth's mother-in-law and she is forming a coalition with Ruth's husband regarding the rearing of their children, this would definitely impair Ruth's role as the parent—and would most likely lead to difficulties in the spousal subsystem. Thus it is important to consider the family's cultural perspective before determining whether certain behavior is to be considered a problem. What might be considered enmeshment in one family may be normal for another family.

Key Themes and Issues

Ruth's problems could be viewed from a developmental approach, with the theme of family stages becoming central to the treatment process. Or Ruth's family could be assessed from a structural perspective, in which case the boundaries of the system as well as rules for communicating are also quite important. It may even hold true that the themes or issues to be examined determine the theoretical approach. In Ruth's case, we approach treatment from a structural intergenerational model, integrating some ideas and processes developed by Murray Bowen, Salvador Minuchin, and Alfred Adler and his followers. Our rationale for working from this integrated perspective is that Ruth's primary concern regarding change is related to a significant transition in the *family life cycle:*[2] Ruth is returning to school and hopes to begin a career as a teacher. Her children are getting older as Ruth reaches middle age, and she is facing an empty nest in just a few years.

We view treatment in four phases: *forming a relationship, conducting an assessment, sharing our hypotheses,* and *facilitating change.*

Forming a Relationship

The first phase is related to what Minuchin[3] called *joining* or entering the family system in collaboration and mutual respect, as in Adlerian therapy; with warmth and genuineness, as in Satir's model; and curiosity, interest, and exploration, as in the Bowen model.[4] Good therapeutic relationships are often initiated with the first phone contact, so we recommend that most family practitioners answer their own phones and make their own appointments. From the very first session, good therapeutic relationships start with efforts at making contact with each person present. The therapist meets each person with openness and warmth. A focused interest on each family member often helps to reduce the anxiety that family members may be feeling.

Therapeutic process and structure are the responsibility of the therapist. It is important for family members to introduce themselves and to express their concerns, but the therapist should not focus too tightly on content issues. Systemic understanding is facilitated more by *how* questions than ones that begin with *what, why, where*, or *when* (questions that tend to overemphasize content details).[5]

Change in both individuals and in human systems starts with understanding and accepting things just as they are.[6] The family practitioner's skill in communicating that understanding and empathy through active listening, validation and encouragement, and support facilitates a working alliance and stimulates family resilience, which in turn leads to the greatest amount of success in therapy.

The first phase, then, involves meeting Ruth and John anew—even if Ruth has already been seen individually by one of the therapists; we start with the couple, asking them to attend each session, and we begin phase two by assessing John's and Ruth's families of origin.

Systemic Assessment

Family counselors and therapists use many different approaches to assessment, including multigenerational maps; family life cycles; consideration of internal parts, sequences, family rules, and communication; order and power within the family; family routines and rituals; and issues related to culture and gender. Most often, we start with genograms[7] and then conduct other assessments related to differentiation and triangulation, family interactions during a typical day, birth order and multigenerational patterns, and boundary issues.

Because family therapists enter the system as change agents, they have a special obligation to be aware of their own family-of-origin issues and to be sensitive to their interactions with the whole family as well as the "identified" client. A family is an interactional unit; it has its own set of unique traits. It is not possible to accurately assess an individual's concern without observing the interactions of the other family members and to consider the broader contexts in which the person and the family live. Ruth is embarking on a journey that will affect those closest to her: her husband, her children, her family of origin (parents and siblings), her peers, and her therapist. In addition, assessments made about her will evolve and change as the therapeutic process progresses.

Our initial assessment starts with both Ruth and John present for the first visit. During this first session, we assess Ruth's presenting problem by asking them about their marital history and about their relationships with the children. We already know from an intake interview on the phone that Ruth both highly desires a new career and is frightened of making changes in her life. We also know that John is resisting her changes and prefers that Ruth remain her "old self."

Their positioning with each other almost automatically leads to additional questions: What kind of relationship do they have that prevents her from changing and him from wanting change? Do they lack the ability to negotiate a different relationship, and if so, why? To address these questions and as a means of enhancing their relationship, we choose to examine their families of origin, assessing the patterns that affect the presenting problem and may have been present in the family over a span of three generations.

The final part of the assessment involves the entire family. There are many different aspects to this assessment. We start with a simple observation about who sits where and what coalitions and alliances seem to take place. We want to see if the children have noticed differences in how their parents are handling family life and what meaning it has for them. We want to address developmental transitions, both those that are individual and those that are part of the family life cycle, that may be occurring. We are most interested in how the members function together, and for this part of the assessment, we ask about a typical day.

In Ruth and John's family, traditional, gender-determined roles still dominate a typical day in the household. Ruth gets up first and prepares breakfast and fixes lunches for her children. She checks with John to see what his needs are for the day, and to the best of her ability, she tries to find time in her day to handle his concerns. John gets ready for work and generally leaves without having breakfast or getting involved with his teenage kids. Ruth finds that she has to remind two of the youngsters every day to take homework with them and to finish breakfast and bring their dishes to the sink. It is with Jennifer, however, that she interacts the most. She does not always like what Jennifer wears to school or in public; she tries to get information about her day from her, but it is like pulling teeth; she reminds Jennifer of appointments or lessons, but she is blown off. There is conflict, but it is routine conflict, and it is always the same.

When everyone is out the door, Ruth cleans up the mess, and then she gets ready for school—whether that involves studying or going to campus. It will take up most of the rest of her day. She will slip home between classes to prepare a meal for dinner and leave a note for Jennifer to put it in the oven at a certain time. Jennifer will lose the note or claim to never have seen it, and everyone will complain that there is no dinner on the table at a reasonable hour. Jennifer will ask her father several times a night, "When is Mom going to be done with all this school stuff and take care of us the way she should?" Her father does not answer her, but he occasionally shrugs, giving Jennifer the sense that he agrees with her.

When Ruth gets home, there are dishes in the sink left for her to do. There are issues between the kids to be addressed. Her husband is wondering if dry cleaning was picked up that day. And Ruth often eats what is left of dinner alone, reading from one of her books. Then, she studies, and she is the last to go to bed.

Key Issues in Family Therapy

Ruth appears to be unable to define herself separately from her husband and her children. Her struggle with her identity leads us to examine her process of *differentiation* (or identity) as a central issue. Key family issues that we would assess include the ways in which anxiety is perpetuated through rigid (inflexible) patterns of three-person systems (known as *triangulation*), patterns across multiple family generations, and ways in which her current family structures and uses communication. We borrow the concepts of differentiation and triangulation from Bowen's approach to family therapy.[8]

🐾 Differentiation   Ruth appears to be struggling with developing a sense of self that is separate from her family and possibly from her family of origin. Her decision to develop an identity separate from her parents, husband, and children is known in Bowen's terminology as the "process of differentiation." The less differentiated people are, the more they invest their energies in relationships to the degree that they do not have a separate identity. Ruth is so concerned about what her husband and children will think if she pursues her own goals that she becomes immobilized. In interactions with her husband, John, she is easily triggered by even implied criticism; rather than participating in an adult-to-adult manner in these conversations, she becomes emotionally reactive. The goal for Ruth from a systemic perspective is to increase her level of differentiation. This does not mean that she will selfishly follow her own directives; rather, it implies that she can determine the direction of her life.

What keeps Ruth from having a sense of self is that she usually interacts with others through triangulation. This is a process by which a person (A) does not directly communicate information with another person (B) but goes through another individual (C). Gossip is a form of triangulation. It is an indirect and often ineffective form of communication. For example, Ruth may wish to communicate that she is upset with her husband, but she chooses to tell her daughter instead. In relaying the message, her daughter asks, "Why did you hurt mom's feelings?" This results in a confused and poorly delivered message. Ruth's indirect communication is a manifestation of her lack of differentiation. Her style of communication keeps her emotionally fused to others, including, as we will see, her parents, husband, and children. In her case, the more fused she has become with others, the less she has been able to understand what she values and believes. To some degree, her value system has become identical to those of the people with whom she is fused. Fortunately, it appears that she is at least examining a desire to become a separate individual from John and that she is considering what the consequences will be if she does acquire a new sense of identity.

🐾 Anxiety   Ruth's fused relationship with John gives her a sense of well-being. When she attempts to change her relationship to others in her system (parents, husband, and children), however, the level of stress (anxiety and emotional distress) increases in the system. Her inability to reduce anxiety and emotional distress is exhibited by physical symptoms such as panic attacks, difficulty breathing, and inability to sleep. Her referring physician has determined that there is no organic or physical causation. Depending on the outcome of her medical evaluation, she may be given medication as a way to control her symptoms so that she will be more amenable to psychotherapy. We do not recommend medication for removing anxiety symptoms because we value working through the issues that are leading to the panic attacks rather than merely numbing the symptoms.

Ruth is anxious that her movement away from homemaking and into teaching may threaten her family. Such anxiety is typical of clients who exhibit a diminished sense of self. A differentiated person makes decisions confidently about the direction of his or her life and is willing to face the consequences of those decisions as necessary. Ruth's anxiety, however, is not a one-way street. The anxiety that is manifested in Ruth's family system pertains to the intensity, duration, and types of tensions that are occurring among the members. Anxiety is occurring because John and the children fear the possible changes taking place with Ruth. They may assume that her changes imply that she no longer loves them. One way of examining this anxiety and how it is manifested is to work with Ruth from a natural systems (Bowen) perspective. The goal is to explore the processes within the family system that bring about Ruth's symptoms, including the manner in which family members form triangles.

❧ Transgenerational Patterns of Interaction   A triangle (three-person relationship), according to Bowen's theory, is the smallest stable unit of human relations. *Triangulation* consists of redirecting a conflict between two people by involving a third person, which stabilizes the relationship between the original pair. In other words, if two people are threatened by conflict, a third person is introduced in an attempt to create an overt appearance of togetherness. Actually, the conflict and the focus on the third person serves the purpose of reducing the tension between the two people.

This concept can be applied to Ruth's case. To assess her panic attacks and determine her level of differentiation, the therapist can assess the patterns of interaction in her current family as well as the relational patterns that have occurred in previous generations and have been transmitted from generation to generation. As mentioned, this involves examining the triangular process.

Looking at the situation between Ruth and John provides examples of triangular relationships. Because this couple is not able to discuss emotionally charged issues, there has been a tendency to focus on a particular child within the family. Jennifer, who is seen as the rebel, gets considerable attention. John may not have learned how to share the feelings of loneliness that he experiences when he considers Ruth working outside the home. Likewise, she cannot share how angry she feels about his not accepting her need for a career apart from her roles as wife and mother in the family. Instead of dealing directly with each other about their concerns as a couple, they argue about their daughter Jennifer. In this sense, Jennifer's actions stabilize her parents' relationship; she may even sense that she is keeping them from breaking up.

Consider this example as yet another illustration of the nature and functioning of triangles. Jennifer comes home and tells her mother she is angry that there is no food on the table. She also begins to complain about all the time her mother spends at school and accuses her of neglecting the children. If Ruth allows herself to become anxious about Jennifer's response, Ruth may not be able to sit down and tell her daughter about the importance of school in her life. If her identity (self) is influenced strongly by Jennifer's values, she may go to John and say, "Jennifer is at it again. She is so disrespectful." Then, suddenly, Ruth may begin to experience physical symptoms, including shortness of breath. In his attempt to reduce her anxiety, John may approach Jennifer and say, "You've made your mother very upset. You will stay home tonight."

This example provides a further illustration of the nature of interlocking triangles. These indirect relationships do not solve family problems; rather, they increase the chances that symptoms will be maintained. Ruth and Jennifer do not discuss their upset feelings toward each other; instead, John takes on their anxiety.

Every family system forms triangles, but when one triangle becomes the consistent or persistent pattern of communication, symptoms tend to arise. Ruth's anxiety sometimes escalates into panic attacks, and sometimes, it sinks into depression. Jennifer, on the other hand, may not be allowed to have peer relationships, and any of her attempts to define herself separately from the family triangle will lead to anxiety among key family members. Again, several possibilities arise: Jennifer may be rebellious and act out, or she may turn her angry feelings inward and become depressed or engage in self-harm. It is likely that she will develop psychosomatic symptoms because that is her mother's pattern for relieving stress.

In any family triangle that involves the parents and a child, we are most concerned with the spousal relationship, in this case Ruth's relationship with John. To help Ruth attain her goal of determining her own direction without experiencing anxiety, we want to observe and understand the patterns that characterize her relationship with John. How and why do they avoid emotionally charged topics? With whom in the family do they form alliances? How are triangular relationships in Ruth's current family a manifestation of patterns that go back over one or two generations in Ruth's and John's families?

Whatever the marital relationship patterns are, it is most likely that they will become apparent by studying patterns that have been passed on over several generations. This method of interacting and relating is often referred to as the family emotional system. An exploration of both John's and Ruth's families of origin may determine patterns of closeness, conflict, and distance that are transmitted from one generation to the next. The goal of therapy from this perspective is the reduction of anxiety expressed in the system so that all the members of the family can improve their sense of self, a goal that fits Ruth's case well.

❧ Rigid Boundaries

The structural approach pays particular attention to concepts such as the family system and subsystems, boundaries, power, and transactional patterns. Observed from a structural paradigm, a theme in Ruth's case is that the family structure appears to have rigid boundaries. Boundaries are the rules that define who participates and how members of a family interact with one another and with "outsiders." Ruth says on the phone that she is concerned about "losing" her children. They are appropriately trying to join peer groups outside the home, which worries her. They are at an age (16 to 19) when it is time for them to gain an identity outside of the family.

It appears that Ruth's family does not have mutually agreed-upon rules that would help it through this developmental stage. This is understandable, for her family of origin was characterized by rigid rules. Now, her current family may be struggling with the transition from a family with children to a family with adolescents and young adults. Thus the rules may be "adolescents will not challenge their parents" and "parents will decide what adolescents do with their time." These rules may be appropriate for children but not for adolescents. If a family keeps these rules and adolescents agree to abide by them, the family has rigid boundaries. Its rules for communication are closed. They do not change, even when the need to do so is appropriate to a new developmental stage.

In working with Ruth's family we want to ascertain who is interacting with whom and by what rules. We might start with this question: "Are coalitions of two people who join together against another occurring in this family?" If Ruth is having a difficult time defining herself within this system, perhaps her children and her husband are having the same difficulty. We also want to ascertain whether rules for communication are closed (no opportunity for change) or open (constantly changing), whether relationships are distant or enmeshed, and who has personal power within the system. If Ruth is having a hard time defining herself outside this system, it may be that her children and her husband are having the same struggle. Structural family therapists focus on the interactions of family members to determine when, how, and to whom individuals presently relate, an assessment that leads to an understanding of the organization or structure of a family.

❧ A Typical Day   In addition to multigenerational and structural perspectives, we know that family process is lived out in the day-to-day routines and repeated interactions that are both familiar and distinctive in any family system. We often ask a family to tell us what happens during a typical day, starting with who gets up first and ending with the last person to go to bed. We are looking for the details of the family's life together, for areas in which stress and distress occur, for the roles each person plays, for routines and patterns, and for opportunities for growth and change.

Working with Diagnosis

In general—and when possible—family therapists avoid psychiatric diagnoses because these formulations are most often considered to be part of an individual rather than symptoms of a relational difficulty. Rather than thinking of problems as something that a person *has* or *is*, family practitioners see problems as something the family, most often as a unit, needs to address. Even the language of family therapy avoids descriptions related to the verbs "to have" or "to be." Indeed, postmodern approaches to family therapy even go so far as to name and externalize problems, creating space for the family and its members to take a stand in relation to the problems they face.

Still, we recognize that many family practitioners work in agencies or practices that require diagnoses for third-party payments. When this happens, we believe both ethically and systemically that the family should be involved in any decision about the labels and diagnoses assigned to individuals or to the unit. Psychiatric labels are likely to stay with people a long time—and they often have ramifications in the future that neither the practitioner nor the clients have anticipated.

Ruth was referred for therapy because of her general anxiety symptoms, which interfered in many areas of her functioning. Taken together, these symptoms could justify the diagnosis of "panic disorder without agoraphobia" because her anxiety is not due to direct physiological effects of a substance or a general medical condition, and they meet the criteria delineated in the *DSM-IV-TR*.[9] Ruth has said that she has concerns about having additional anxiety attacks and that she sometimes feels that she is "going crazy."

Although Ruth's main reason for seeking therapy was her generalized anxiety, her relationship problems with her parents and with her spouse are certainly factors contributing to, if not causing, the symptoms of anxiety and panic. The V-codes of parent–child relational problem and partner relational problem (nonreimbursable *DSM-IV-TR* diagnoses) also seem appropriate for a number of her behavioral patterns. Her relationships with her parents are characterized by impaired communication, rigid discipline, and overprotection, all of which are associated with clinically significant impairment of the way she functions as an individual and in her family. Likewise, her relationship with her husband is marked by ineffective communication and fear of losing his support, which also affects her functioning. On the GARF (Global Assessment of Relational Functioning), an experimental scale in the *DSM-IV-TR*, Ruth and her family would receive a rating of 61, indicating that the relationships are at the bottom level of somewhat unsatisfactory (with real difficulties) and are close to falling into the range of clearly dysfunctional.

Assuming that the family, and especially Ruth, is comfortable with these diagnostic categories, we have provided her insurance company with a description that is acceptable for billing purposes, and we have maintained an emphasis on the relational aspects that will become central to family counseling and therapy.

From Shared Hypothesis to Facilitating Change

Ruth's goal for her therapy is the reduction of symptomatic behaviors (panic attacks). From a family systems perspective, the goals of therapy include (1) reducing triangles that have prevented her and others from obtaining a confident position in the system; (2) restructuring her immediate system so autonomy by all family members will be encouraged; (3) changing patterns of interaction, not only among family members, especially between Ruth and John, so that relationships are more flexible and able to cope with changes as the family moves to the next developmental stage; (4) reducing the presenting symptoms; and (5) creating an environment in which all members of the system feel secure and, indeed, are reinforced as they make needed changes. In family practice, these goals are articulated with the family, and family members participate in framing these goals and prioritizing them. Assessment does not end with such a conversation, but it does enter into a stage of continuous development. As more information is learned about the family and its individual members, the hypotheses that guide therapeutic interventions are shared and change is facilitated based on a collaborative, mutual understanding of what is happening in the family and the change that is sought.

Phase 1: Session With Ruth and John

Because we are still gathering information about the family system and are interested in the dynamics within the spousal subsystem, our first session is with Ruth and John alone. Our goals for the first session are (1) to obtain a working and therapeutic relationship with Ruth and John; (2) to assess John's willingness to be involved in the treatment process; (3) to encourage John's participation as a critical actor in this family act; and (4) to explore family-of-origin dynamics to shift the focus from symptoms (Ruth's panic attacks) to process (who says what to whom and under what circumstances). This shift will help put Ruth's problems in a larger context, minimize blame, and reduce Ruth's anxiety.

After introductions, we begin with Ruth's and John's concerns regarding this session. We address them individually.

THERAPIST: How were you feeling before you got here, and how is it to be here?

RUTH: I'm a little nervous to have John here with me.

THERAPIST: Could you explain what you mean by a little nervous?

RUTH: I guess I'm afraid that he may be here to make sure I continue to do things his way.

THERAPIST: [*Pause*] To do things his way. Do you mean that he might like life in your family to stay the way it has been for quite some time?

RUTH: Yes, and that he'll be upset if I talk about wanting to make changes, such as going to work—and that he'll try to pressure me not to.

THERAPIST: John, to what degree do you think Ruth's concerns are realistic?

JOHN: Well, to some degree her concerns are realistic. At first, when she asked me to come here, I was angry, because I thought she was inviting me because I was the one with a problem. Then I decided that I'd give it a try.

Answers to the question "How were you feeling before you got here?" bring out into the open each person's reactions and get dialogue going. Their answers also provide clues to what each needs to feel more relaxed as we get to know each other. John and Ruth seem to be willing to be honest with each other. Neither hesitated, and yet both were nervous in sharing their concerns. Their honesty and willingness to share their reactions are signs that the prognosis for change in their relationship is good. Ruth's anxiety may be reduced as they learn to negotiate a new relationship.

Other questions pursued during the beginning of the first session include (1) "Who said what to whom to convince you both to come to this session?" and (2) "What do you both hope to have happen during this session, and what do you expect from counseling?" These questions help us to ascertain how each attaches meaning to therapy. Because it appears that John has a desire to be a part of the therapeutic relationship, we continue to gather background information on both of them. This is done in the form of a genogram.

A *genogram* is an organized map, or diagram, of each person's family over three generations. It is a method by which therapist and client shift from examining a symptomatic individual (Ruth) to a family systems conceptualization of the problem, and it often gives an indication of possible solutions. In obtaining this transgenerational history, we acquire a history of the nuclear family (Ruth and John's family) as well as a history of her extended family and a history of his extended family.

While developing a genogram, we try to determine the following: (1) *relationship patterns* that have been repeated from one generation to the next, which explain the context in which the presenting problem or symptoms developed; (2) the occurrence, if any, of *emotional cutoffs,* which are a means by which people attempt to distance themselves from a fused, or overly close, relationship; (3) *triadic relationships* (triangles), which denote conflict, fusion, or emotional cutoffs; and (4) *toxic issues* such as religion, gender independence, money, politics, and divorce, which create in our clients emotional reactivity to other parts of the system.

The genogram work with Ruth and John generates a lot of information about their current family, their families of origin, their mothers' families and their fathers' families: occupations; educational background; dates of birth of both Ruth and John and their children; dates of marriage, separation, or divorce; names of former spouses and children; miscarriages, stillbirths, and adopted or foster children; where all of the children now live; dates and types of severe illnesses; passages such as promotions and graduations; demographic data; cultural and ethnic data; socioeconomic data; military service; religion; addictions such as drugs, alcohol, and sex; abuse of old people, children, or adults; and retirement or unemployment dates. This information forms a database that will be used as a context for family interaction patterns. After gathering this information, we prepare a summary that organizes and presents useful information in our effort to understand Ruth and John's relationship.

๙ Summary   Through the process of using the genogram to understand the family system, we learn that John has unresolved feelings toward his mother. John's triadic relationship (fused with his father and emotionally cut off from his mother) seems to have kept him from forming a healthy, individuated relationship with Ruth or with any other woman. His parents were unable to resolve their conflicts, and so one parent moved closer to him, just as the other was emotionally cut off in an effort to reduce the stress and anxiety in the marital dyad. John and Ruth discovered that they were continuing the same pattern that was evident in John's family of origin. Their identities were blended (fused) to the extent that they were unable to discuss the emotionally laden issue of gender independence, and so they have chosen not to relate to each other. In an attempt to dissipate their anxiety, they triangled Rob into their relationship (see Figure 12.1). John, like his father before him, chose to tell his son about his unresolved feelings toward his wife. Rob began to distance himself from his mother, most likely for reasons he cannot completely understand. This triangle left Ruth feeling isolated and without support. She felt that her

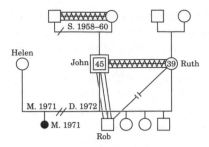

FIGURE 12.1 Multigenerational Triangles, Showing Repeated Structural Patterns With Emphasis on John's Family

family really did not appreciate her. But an emotional revelation during therapy helped give Ruth and John a new perspective on the family's problems.

In addition, a new option for interacting has opened up. John finds that he is able to break the *family rule* of not discussing emotionally charged issues, especially with a woman, a rule that prohibited Ruth from exploring with him how each of them felt as she was trying to become a more independent person within this system. When she decided to make some changes, she inadvertently influenced him to change. This is a good example of how change in one part of the system will result in change in other parts of the system.

Phase 2: Ruth's Genogram

Our genogram work starts by asking Ruth and John to gather information from their parents and siblings and any other family members willing to discuss their family stories. The purpose of gathering such data is not to help them change others in the system but to assist them in making individual changes that can result in a healthy relationship.

Ruth finds in going to her parents' home, and separately approaching each of them, that her mother is freer to discuss the family and their issues than her father. However, her father does give her some illuminating details about himself. The process of gathering information is an intervention within itself. Ruth is breaking the family taboo about asking questions of her superiors and also is inquiring about their own feelings in regard to others.

Mother's Family Ruth discovers that her mother is relieved to tell her about the family. Her mother, Edith, says she is the eldest of three siblings. She explains that she felt burdened by the role of caretaker for her brother and sister. She also says her father was abusive toward her and punished her severely if she did not obey him. He was not a religious man and was a heavy drinker. Edith decided at an early age not to try to relate much to her father. Her family members never discussed their feelings about one another. Conflict arose when religion was brought up or when she talked of going on to college. Her father and mother sat down with her and explained that they could not afford to send her (but they did send her brother) and that she would not be permitted to bring the subject up again.

Edith tells Ruth that she never heard a supportive word from any member of the family. Also, there was a rumor that Edith's mother had been sent to a hospital for what was known then as a nervous breakdown. This incident was never discussed among family members, and Ruth had never heard about it. She asks why her mother never spoke about this incident, and Edith weeps, saying that she was never allowed to discuss it. This is the first time Ruth has seen her mother cry, much less express emotions. In addition, her mother shares that she sees Ruth as the most stable person in the family. This is the first positive remark Ruth can remember receiving from her mother.

🍃 Father's Family

Ruth's father, Patrick, is less cooperative. He asks her a number of questions about her need to know family information. We have advised her that it is best not to tell the family that her questions are part of a therapeutic process. She chooses to say that they are part of an educational experience, which is true. Her father begins by saying that he is uncomfortable with giving her any information about his family. This is the first time he has admitted a feeling to her. When she asks about his reasons, he says families should keep their lives private. He believes only God should know what really goes on inside a family. Ruth does not react to her father but simply accepts whatever he feels comfortable revealing.

Patrick goes on to tell her that his older brother died at birth and that his youngest sister committed suicide. Her death left him as the only child of a fundamentalist minister and a mother that he knew little about. This is the first time her father has ever shared anything about himself. It allows Ruth to see her father in a different light. She also gains a sense about herself that she never had before. She discovers that she can handle discussing emotionally laden issues with her father. In the past, she would never have permitted herself to do so. She also feels more grown up with her father. It is as if he is treating her as an equal for the first time. Her genogram evolves as shown in Figure 12.2.

🍃 Ruth's Interpretation of Her Genogram

Ruth develops her own understandings regarding her place and her process in the family. Here are some of her discoveries:

- A toxic issue in this system over the years is a female notion of independence from the family.
- Over three generations the eldest daughters have been emotionally cut off from their fathers and have remained distant with their mothers, and the mothers and fathers have stayed in conflicted marriages.

One hypothesis regarding this pattern is that what controls anxiety in this couple's relationship is for the husband and wife to deflect their attention to the eldest daughter. The toxic issue that evokes the process is the desire of the eldest daughter to move physically and emotionally away from the fused triad (mother/father/daughter).

Ruth begins to understand that when she became the focus of attention in her family, her parents' communication with each other increased. When she tried to move out on her own (emotionally and physically), her parents would

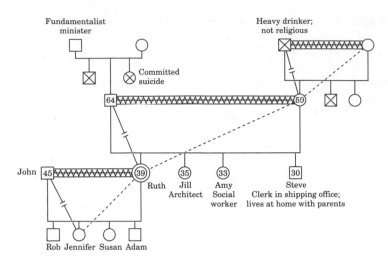

FIGURE 12.2 Multigenerational Triangles and Repeated Structural Patterns in Ruth's Genogram

---

focus on her. They were unable to work out their personal conflicts and instead chose to argue about her. When Ruth complied and the family appeared calm, her mother and father approved of her and had little more to say to each other.

In a therapy session, we discuss Ruth's understanding of these patterns carried on from one generation to the next:

THERAPIST: Ruth, what are you learning from the work you're doing with your family?

RUTH: I'm beginning to realize that whenever I made an independent move, I began to feel guilty. My movement created a great deal of reactivity from my parents, and in my desire to reduce their anxiety, I decided not to have a career. In some ways, I believe, I was keeping them together.

THERAPIST: Do you see any correlations between what you did in your family of origin and what you're currently doing in your own family?

RUTH: I'm seeing that I've continued the pattern. If John even hints at being uncomfortable with decisions I make independently from the family, I feel guilty, and it feels like my responsibility to reduce his stress. And I guess I'm continuing this pattern with my children. I make them feel guilty if they try to become independent from the family.

THERAPIST: Do you still believe John doesn't want you to become your own person?

RUTH: Not anymore. It is becoming clearer to us how we've brought the patterns of our own families of origin into our marriage. We're getting along much better. In fact, John has actually encouraged me to take courses next semester.

THERAPIST: Have your panic attacks continued during this time?

RUTH: I still get anxious, but now that I'm beginning to see what this is all about, I haven't had a panic attack for quite a while now.

This work accomplished with John and Ruth is a greatly condensed example. It could take months for Ruth come to these conclusions. For a time, we might meet weekly with the family, and then at a later time meet less frequently.

Phase 3: Presenting Ruth With the Idea of Family Therapy

As often happens when the couple starts to improve their relationship, Ruth and John report that since they began to come to therapy, Adam has been acting out more at home and at school. Adam and Ruth are having more arguments, usually centering on her request to have him clean up his room or do his homework. Before she entered treatment, they were very close, going to the movies and attending school events. John, too, is frustrated with Adam; he is most concerned about the trouble that Adam is having at school.

We recommend to Ruth and John that they consider bringing their entire family into the therapeutic process. Ruth and John, having explored their intergenerational dynamics in depth, have made some significant changes. According to both of them, their relationship has improved, and Ruth is feeling far less guilt and anxiety about her decision to return to school. However, she complains that their children are still resisting change, and especially her changes. Adam and Jennifer have told her that they prefer the "old mom" and do not want their lives to become unsettled.

Based on our discussion, Ruth and John decides to ask the children to join them in therapy. All of the children agree to participate, which can be considered a good sign. But Rob, the elder son, is reluctant. He feels that he does not have any problems, and he does not understand why he should attend.

THE FIRST SESSION Jim asks the family members to be seated wherever they want. Mary thanks the family for coming and addresses each member by her or his first name. We note that the purposes of this full family meeting are to establish the goals for counseling or therapy and to assess with them whether further sessions might be helpful to the family. We also discuss the limits of confidentiality and the reporting laws for the state.

⚡ The Presenting Complaint   It is apparent that there is some confusion over why everyone needs to be present. Therefore, we ask Ruth to explain her concerns to the family and her hopes for these sessions.

RUTH: Since John and I have been in therapy, I've seen this family change. Adam, you've been more moody. We've been arguing more, and you seem unwilling to take any suggestions of mine to get your homework done or to clean your room. I believe our marriage is improving, but my relationship with the children, and especially with you, Adam, is getting worse.

We observe that Ruth and Adam sit next to each other. John sits next to me (Mary), and Jennifer sits between Adam and Susan. Rob, who is 19, sits away from the rest of the family. We ask each member for his or her observations regarding the family. We also ask them: "If you could get something from this session for yourself, what might that be? Would you like to have a different relationship with anyone in your family?"

🍃 **The Family Interaction** Here are some excerpts of a dialogue among the family members, and with us, during this first session with the family. Those present in the family include Ruth, John, Rob, Jennifer, Susan, and Adam.

JOHN: Since Ruth and I began to improve our relationship through counseling, Adam has become less obedient and cooperative, especially with Ruth. Yesterday, Adam yelled at Jennifer, and when I tried to punish him, Ruth told me to leave him alone and let them work it out by themselves. I disagree with her new idea of how to discipline these children.

ROB [*Interrupting and in anger*]: You should listen to Mom. She knows more about what is going on in this family than you do.

JIM: Rob, you sound angry at your father. If that is true, can you tell him why you are upset, and would you share that directly with your father? [*Jim has Rob face his father.*]

ROB [*Looking at Jim as if he was odd, but he faces Dad directly*]: You are on everyone's case, and you don't have a clue as to what is going on in this family. Mom is more reliable and has backed off from telling us continually what to do. She's not on my case as much as she was before.

JIM: Rob, would you tell your mother what you mean by "being on your case"?

ROB: Mom would always want to know where I was going and what I was doing. She would clean my room without my permission.

JIM: Rob, you're talking about your mother as though she weren't in the room. How about talking directly to her over there?

ROB: You're asking me to do something I'm not comfortable with. Why can't I just explain myself to you?

JIM: You have said you're uncomfortable with the way things are in this family. You would like more of a voice in how you are treated in your family. One way for that to happen is to talk directly to your parents so they receive clearly the messages you want them to understand. Try this out and see if it doesn't give you a stronger position in the family.

ROB: That's kind of hard for me to do. It's not something that I usually do.

MARY: I can understand that, Rob. But I believe you are up to the task. Jim and I are not just asking you to deal directly with your family, but for each of you to talk directly to one another. It also helps Jim and me to better understand your position in this family.

ROB: OK. I also want to say something about Dad. I feel he's too hard on Adam.

JIM: So, Rob, there sits your dad. Can you tell him directly what you mean by your statement that he's too hard on Adam?

ROB [*Reluctantly*]: Dad, you're always upset when Adam starts arguing with his sisters or me. And you're getting on my case lately. If I'm not home by 10, you get all bent out of shape, just like Mom used to do.

JIM: John, how is it for you to hear what Rob is saying to you?

JOHN [*Looking to Jim*]: I don't believe I have to take this. I never corrected my father.

MARY: John, would you please sit closer to Rob and tell him directly how it is for you to hear what he is saying to you?

JOHN [*Moves his chair closer to Rob*]: Well, it does make me upset. Don't you know how much your mother and I care for you?

ROB [*Facing his father and looking surprised*]: No, I don't know you care.

JOHN: Well, I do care about you—about all of you. And if you don't know that, then that is the real tragedy of us as a family. Maybe we are all just so busy or maybe we don't know how to take the time to say that we care. But all of you—Rob, you are my firstborn—we love all of you so much.

ROB: I don't know what to say, Dad, except that it often seems like rules are more important to you than I am. I want to believe that you love all of us, and I want to see it more.

MARY: It seems that the two of you have more to talk about. I'm hoping that you two will continue this dialogue before the next session. Is that possible?

Both agree to meet outside and before the next session. They agree to go out for lunch and discuss their relationship. They agree to report at the next family session what occurred.

MARY: I would like to make sure that we get to each person in the family before this session is over. [*She turns to Jennifer.*] What would you like to say about being here and what you would like for yourself in these sessions?

JENNIFER [*Looking to Ruth and Susan*]: Susan and I like the idea of coming here because the family seems so different since Mom and Dad went to counseling. But we feel that Mom has abandoned the family.

JIM: Would you tell your mother what you mean by "abandoning the family"?

JENNIFER: Well, Mother, you don't do our wash anymore. We have to make our own lunches. You're arguing more with Adam and me. I want to stay out of the house when the bickering begins, especially between you and Adam.

MARY: Ruth, how do you respond to what Jennifer just said to you?

RUTH: It's hard to hear Jennifer disapproving of my going to college or my wanting her and the children to become more independent from me. I think that's why it's so difficult for me to get a job outside the home. I'm torn between making my own happiness or my family's happiness.

MARY: How do you respond to what your mother just said, Jennifer?

JENNIFER: I'd rather not respond right now.

MARY: That's OK, you don't need to answer now. I hope we can get back to what's going on between you and your mother later in this session. [*She turns to Susan.*] How, specifically, would you like things to be different for yourself with each member of your family?

SUSAN: Jennifer and I would like more of Mom's time.

MARY: I hear that it is important to you to have more time with your mom, and it may also be true for Jennifer, but right now, I want you to talk just for you, and we will let Jennifer say later what she would like to be different.

SUSAN: Well, I'd like to say that I agree with Rob that Dad is not as nice as he used to be since Mom got into counseling. He's nicer to Mom but seems more upset with all of us and . . .

JOHN [*Interrupting*]: How can you say that I'm not nice to you? I do the best I can, and nobody appreciates that!

JIM: Is that what you were trying to tell your father, Susan? Did he hear you correctly?

SUSAN [*Turning to Jim*]: No.

JIM: Would you mind telling your father what you'd like from him?

SUSAN [*With tears in her eyes*]: Dad, it's not that we don't appreciate how hard you work. It's just that I don't hear anything nice from you anymore.

MARY: Susan, if you could have one thing different with your father, what would that be?

SUSAN: That we could do something together without getting into a fight.

MARY: How would that be for you, John?

JOHN: Well, if I could find the time, I'd like to do more with Susan. But I don't know what a father does with a 17-year-old.

MARY: Why don't you ask her?

JOHN [*Looking at Susan, after a long pause*]: Well, what do you think?

SUSAN: We could go to a movie.

MARY: Is that something you'd like to do with Susan?

JOHN: Yeah, if we could ever agree on a movie.

MARY: I am guessing that the important thing is spending time together, not what movie you see, and I hope the two of you will make the time to talk with each other about what both of you want. [*She turns to Adam.*] Adam, what would you like to say about yourself?

ADAM: I think it's unfair that my family picks on me.

MARY: Who in this room picks on you, and would you tell them directly?

ADAM: Susan, you've been picking on me. And Jennifer just sits around and smiles. And, well . . . [*fidgeting and looking to the floor*] Dad and Mom have been upset with me a lot lately and . . .

JOHN [*Interrupting*]: When have I been upset with you that you didn't deserve it?

RUTH [*Interrupting and turning to John*]: I think you ought to let Adam finish.

MARY: Ruth, how about letting John speak for himself? [*She looks to John.*] What would you like to say to Adam?

JOHN: I feel that everyone is picking on me, and it's getting me mad!

JIM: John, I can understand that you might feel as if you're being picked on. But another way to look at this is to consider that what they're telling you is a sign that they trust you enough to be open and honest with you about their feelings. Maybe these are things that they haven't been able to express to you until now.

JOHN: Well . . . I don't know . . . But I do want my kids to be able to talk to me.

JIM: I believe that about you, John. A short time ago Adam said some things to you, and you seemed to be very emotionally moved. Is there anything you'd like to say to Adam?

JOHN: It's very difficult to hear what you had to say, Adam. [*He turns to Jim laughingly.*] Did I do it right this time?

JIM: Not a bad start; I hope you'll continue to talk. [*He addresses all the family members except Ruth.*] Several of you have mentioned that your mother's counseling has affected your lives. Some of you have even said that you felt abandoned by her. Would each of you be willing to talk to your mother?

SUSAN: Mom, it's hard to see you being different. I was so used to you taking an interest in us, even though at times I complained. You did so much for us, but I guess you have a life of your own too.

ROB: I think you're right on, Susan!

ADAM: Mother, I miss you not sticking up for me more. I don't like fighting with you, but at times I find myself starting a fight with you.

MARY: Do you think the fighting and missing your mom are related?

ADAM [*Thinking for a while*]: Maybe!

JENNIFER: I like talking like this. We never do this at home, and we're not even fighting right now.

MARY [*Turning to Ruth*]: How is it for you to hear that?

RUTH: It feels good to see my family talking about themselves and realizing that I don't have to take so much care of them anymore.

JIM: Our time is almost up, but before we close, I'd like to ask each of you if there are reasons you might want to return.

All of the family members feel that it is important to return, because they like what has happened during the session. They are agreeable to attending another session the following week. Jim notes that there have been some agreements made during this session, like dad and Rob talking further about their relationship and perhaps dad and Susan spending some time together. He wonders if the rest of the family might consider some additional suggestions. Because the family members are open to this idea, he suggests the following assignments:

- For Ruth: Avoid interfering when one of the children is attempting to interact with John.
- For Jennifer: Take the initiative to ask your mother to do something with you before next week, such as going shopping or spending 20 minutes together.
- For Ruth and John: Continue to discuss what you would like to do with each other and what you would like to do separately. When you do start to focus on the children, try to talk instead about yourselves.

The family members are asked if they have any objections to these assignments and if they would be willing to follow through with them by the following week, at which time they will meet again with both therapists. All feel that they can complete the assignments.

It is important that families work on issues outside of therapy as well as during therapy. In this way, they can observe that they have the strength to make their own changes. By taking this responsibility, they empower themselves. The only family member not given an assignment is Adam. This is an attempt to keep the other family members focusing away from him and keep him from continuing to be identified as a "patient" or "problem" in this family.

PROCESS COMMENTARY We set out to observe the structure of the family by (1) allowing the members to sit where they wanted to and (2) attempting to get a clearer picture of the family's transactional patterns. We assume, in observing the structure of this family, that Ruth's change has produced stress among the siblings. There was stress between Ruth and John, but initial sessions with them seems to have reduced it. Ruth appears to have rigid boundaries with Adam. Her ability to make changes has strengthened her boundary with Adam, and he is reacting to those changes. No longer does she feel the need to give in to his demands. But conflicts have increased in their relationship. Her changes are resulting in new strains on this relationship. If Adam can have a closer relationship with his siblings or other peer groups, he may be able to better adjust to this change. Jennifer also appears to be having difficulty with the changes, not only with Ruth but also with the fact that the spousal subsystem is becoming stronger. We repeat: If change occurs in any one part of the system, change will occur in the other parts. In other words, changes in Ruth and changes in Ruth and John's relationship have affected the equilibrium of this family. Whenever possible, therefore, it is important to have the whole family enter treatment so that the changes that occur are productive for the system as well as for each individual within it.

In this family, there is an enmeshment among members. They lack a clear sense of their individuality and roles in the family. Families such as this one are prone to conflict and confusion, and the behavior of one member or unit, in this case both Ruth and John, immediately affects the other members of the family.

Ruth and John are forming a new relationship. She is learning not to maintain her role as peacemaker, and he is learning to be more supportive of her. As a result, the other family members are being forced to learn to deal with one another. Until this session, they have been increasing the conflict among themselves and with Ruth to bring her back into her previous role as mediator. In family therapy terms, this is known as an attempt to maintain homeostasis, which involves prompting a return of the family to the former status.

This family system is relatively functional. Its members were able to make some strides in communicating in the session, especially considering that they generally have not expressed their own feelings with one another. John and Ruth's exploration of transgenerational patterns has assisted them in learning how to express these feelings, and that change helped them facilitate the children's flexibility, difficult as it has been at times. Intergenerational patterns of not expressing feelings and allowing independent thought are not likely to continue. Because these patterns do not change overnight, the family still has considerable work to do. A committed effort aimed at modifying these patterns will not only free this family to be more honest and open, but it will also benefit future generations.

The family has an excellent chance of making these structural changes:

- Becoming more direct with one another
- Taking the focus off of Adam as a problem
- Reducing the coalition that Adam and Ruth have against John
- Reducing the enmeshed (overly close) relationship Ruth has with Adam so she can have a closer relationship with John and so Adam can have appropriate closer relationships with his siblings and other peers

The chances are that the entire family will not always be included in future therapy sessions. Instead, therapy may include parts of the system (John and Rob), the spousal subsystem (Ruth and John), or the sibling subsystem (Rob, Jennifer, Susan, and Adam). Ruth and John will need to continue strengthening their independence from each other as well as their togetherness.

Some Final Thoughts

As work with this family illustrates, neither any individual in the family nor the family as a unit is blamed for a particular dysfunction. Actions by any individual family member will influence all the others in the family, and their reactions will have a reciprocal effect on the individual. The family is empowered through the process of identifying and exploring internal, developmental, and purposeful interactional patterns. At the same time, a systems perspective recognizes that individuals and families are affected by external forces and systems. If change is to occur in families or with individuals, therapists must be aware of as many systems of influence as possible.

Questions for Reflection

1. What differences do you see between working with Ruth in individual counseling and using family therapy? Do you think that including her husband or family in a few sessions will promote or inhibit her progress in individual therapy?

2. Can you see any complications arising from having Ruth both in individual and family therapy at the same time, and if so, what are they? How could you address any potential problems? In the family therapy approach, do you see any disadvantages in not meeting with her individually in therapy?

3. What possible ethical issues are involved if you do not suggest family therapy for Ruth, given clear indications that some of her problems stem from conflicts within her family?

4. Can you think of areas in your relationships with others where you demonstrate the attitude of acceptance? In what ways might learning to be accepting of a significant other benefit a relationship?

5. Can you identify some specific behaviors that Ruth and John changed, even though therapy did not focus directly on asking for behavioral changes?

6. If you were conducting family therapy in this case, whom would you consider to be your primary client? Would your client be the family as a system? Ruth? John? Jennifer? Adam? Susan? Rob? Can you see any ethical binds if you develop an alliance with certain members of this family?

7. How do you think your own relationships with an intimate partner or in your family of origin might either help or hinder you in working with this family? Can you see any possible sources of problems or potential countertransferences? If you become aware that you have unfinished business with either your family of origin or your present family, what course would you probably take?

8. If you were working with Ruth's family, with whom might you be most inclined to form an alliance? Which person do you think you would have the most difficulty working with, and why?

9. If you and Ruth were from different cultures, what factors would you as a family therapist want to address with both her and the members of her family? What role might cultural factors play in understanding the structure of this family? How might the interventions you make vary depending on the cultural background of the family involved in the therapeutic process?

10. Do you have any bias toward Ruth because of her desire to change her role within the family? Does her thinking fit with yours regarding female roles in the family? Regarding male roles in the family? What do you think about the way that values around gender roles were handled by both therapists in this chapter?

11. How well does family therapy fit with your counseling style? What aspects of this approach do you find most useful? Which aspects might you want to modify to fit your personal counseling style?

Notes

1. As a basis for understanding the guest contributors' presentations of family therapy perspectives on working with Ruth, refer to Corey, G. (2013). *Theory and practice of counseling and psychotherapy* (9th ed.). Belmont, CA: Brooks/Cole, Cengage Learning. Chapter 14 ("Family Systems Therapy") contains a comprehensive overview of the approaches to family therapy, along with a comprehensive list of references and recommended readings on family therapy.

2. For a complete description of the family life cycle, see McGoldrick, M., Carter, B., & Garcia-Preto, N. (Eds.). (2011). *The expanded family life cycle: Individual, family, and social perspectives* (4th ed.). Upper Saddle River, NJ: Prentice-Hall.

3. For an updated explication of structural family therapy and Minuchin's approach, see Minuchin, S. (2011). *Families and family therapy* (2nd ed.). New York: Routledge.

4. For a complete review of the major family systems approaches, see Bitter, J. (2009). *Theory and practice of family therapy and counseling*. Belmont, CA: Brooks/Cole, Cengage Learning.

5. Sam Gladding makes this point in Gladding, S. (2010). *Family therapy: History, theory, and practice* (5th ed.). Upper Saddle River, NJ: Merrill/Prentice-Hall.

6. Acceptance and validation are central to the model described by Virginia Satir and Michele Baldwin in their 1983 book: *Satir: Step-by-step*. Palo Alto, CA: Science and Behavior Books.

7. For a complete explanation and instruction in the development of genograms, see McGoldrick, M., Gerson, R., & Petry, S. (2008). *Genograms: Assessment and intervention* (3rd ed.). New York: Norton.

8. For a complete presentation of the Bowen model, see Bowen, M. (1978). *Family therapy in clinical practice*. New York: Jason Aronson.

9. All psychiatric diagnoses emanate from the American Psychiatric Association. (2000). *Diagnostic and statistical manual of mental disorders* (4th ed., text revised) (*DSM-IV-TR*). Washington, DC: Author.

CHAPTER THIRTEEN

Counseling Ruth From Multicultural Perspectives

Introduction

Race, ethnicity, gender, age, socioeconomic status, religion, lifestyle, and sexual orientation are crucial factors to consider when establishing a therapeutic relationship with clients. To learn to appreciate the subtle aspects of working with cultural themes in the lives of clients, Jerome Wright, a colleague and friend who teaches social work practice and cultural diversity courses, provides the following exercise for his students. He gives Ruth's case to his students and asks them to form small study groups to research the cultural variables that would apply if she were from each of these ethnic groups: Asian American, Latina, or African American. The students also are asked to think of issues that would be involved if Ruth were being counseled from a feminist perspective and special issues to consider if she were a lesbian. Each of the study groups have the freedom to present its findings in any way it deems fit, as long as the members do so as a group. Some did role-playing situations, others invited guest speakers who represented the group they were studying, and others found interesting ways to involve the class in their presentation.

Therapists who are *not* members of the groups their clients identify with must be culturally sensitive to their differences. Those who share their clients' group must engage in a personal assessment of the meaning associated with their life experience and be aware of how their own culture influences their behavior, assumptions, and biases, and how these factors are likely to influence the manner in which they work with clients who differ culturally from them. There is no automatic bonding between client and therapist based on race, ethnicity, sexual orientation, age, life experience, or any other key variable. Indeed, socioeconomic differences are often reflected in embarrassment and discomfort. In short, there are no "natural matches" between client and therapist based on group similarity. Individual differences oftentimes trump group collectivity (Jerome Wright, PhD, personal communication, March 8, 2011).

Becoming immersed in the study of cultural diversity is not without its dangers. Accepting stereotypes and applying general characteristics of a particular group to every individual within that group is problematic. Indeed, the differences among individuals within a given ethnic group can be as great as the differences between groups. Knowledge of the client's culture provides counselors with a conceptual framework, but knowledge of a client's cultural values is only the beginning. Counseling across cultures is personally demanding, but it can also be rewarding.

This chapter focuses on how to work with Ruth from various multicultural perspectives. Different contributors show how they would counsel Ruth assuming she is a Latina, an Asian American, or an African American. The multicultural perspectives are not separate theories; diversity perspectives can be incorporated into any of the theories considered in previous chapters. Each contributor in this chapter draws from his or her own integrative therapeutic approach when counseling Ruth. As you read about the themes in Ruth's life in the following pages, be aware of how cultural variations can easily be woven into the fabric of the counseling process.

Ruth as a Latina: An Integrative Culturally Grounded Perspective

by Andrés J. Consoli, PhD, Robert C. Chope, PhD, and Melissa L. Morgan, PhD

Introduction

Our integrative culturally grounded perspective on Ruth as a Latina is based on the following counseling principles:

1. Every counseling encounter is a cross-cultural one, typically across multiple dimensions, and requires both cultural competence and cultural humility.
2. The therapeutic alliance is central to effective counseling.
3. As treatment progresses, so does the alliance, from an empathic and respectful bond to a secure base for deliberate risk-taking.
4. Counseling should be tailored to fit clients' strengths and difficulties.
5. Counseling is best aimed at enlisting clients' self-healing capacities.
6. To learn more about strengths, self-healing capacities, and cultural norms, directly and sensitively question the client.
7. Overall, counseling should transcend *traditional* approaches and focus on the main forces of change: motivation, learning, meaning-making, and facilitative context.

Throughout this discussion we give our combined input on aspects of Ruth's therapy. However, Ruth's therapy sessions are conducted by a single therapist, a bilingual Latino professional who is an immigrant from a country other than the one Ruth's parents came from.

Initial Interview and Assessment of Ruth

Ruth is a Latina born in the United States to immigrant parents who impressed upon her the importance of "fitting into" the "American culture" to avoid experiencing the segregation they once experienced themselves in the predominantly White community in which they live.[1] Ruth reports that she met John, a Caucasian, at a church function, and he seemed to be a "shoe in" based on what her parents had wanted for her. She describes John as a color-blind individual when it comes to racial and ethnic differences and one who embraces traditional values concerning gender roles. She credits her recent college courses with awakening in her an interest in her Latina roots.

🐦 **Initial Interview**   We start the session by discussing confidentiality and its limitations. We then acknowledge the information we already have about Ruth and encourage her to discuss what is going on in her life that has prompted her to seek counseling. We honor her risk-taking in seeking counseling, and we inquire how we can best be of help. We foster her inquisitiveness and cultural wonderings. As topics related to culture and her identity arise, we acknowledge that our experiences are different from hers and ask her to describe her experience of "being Ruth." We acknowledge her self-abnegation and dedication to her family. We are attentive to her ambivalence about embarking on the counseling experience, and we understand the stigma she has previously associated with counseling. We are particularly attentive to the potential dissonance between her view of self as "living for others" and seeking counseling for "herself."

Throughout the initial interview we seek to enact collaboration and convey a message of appreciation for her perspectives. We welcome the questions she raised in her autobiography and encourage her to frame such questions as hypotheses that we can work on in a collaborative way. The following exchange takes place near the end of the first session.

THERAPIST: Ruth, we have a few minutes left in our session, and I want to check in with you and ask what it has been like for you to be in counseling today.

RUTH: I didn't know I had so much to say! I guess you got it all out of me. You are good!

THERAPIST: I thank you for the compliment. I wonder about other explanations you may have about how much you had to say.

RUTH: You seem very interested in me. I am not used to this kind of attention.

THERAPIST: Say more about what it was like for you to be here today and receive complete attention.

RUTH: That's it! You are persistent. You don't let me off the hook easily.

THERAPIST: Ruth, you are very perceptive. Now if I were not persistent, what would happen? [*We explore this together a bit more.*]

In closing, I sense your hesitations about coming to counseling; where are you now with respect to pursuing counseling?

RUTH: Well, it is hard for me to commit to something.

The therapist feels pulled to make a decision for Ruth but refrains and instead asks Ruth what she needs to make this decision. She commits to a next appointment and asks for a reminder call the night before.

Assessment We ask Ruth to complete a life history questionnaire covering presenting complaints; view of self with respect to strengths and shortcomings; goals and expectations for counseling; family, cultural, educational, employment, and medical history; prior counseling experiences; and current expectations for counseling. We organize the information from the clinical interview into a *DSM-IV-TR* multiaxial assessment and supplement it with two additional dimensions. The first dimension involves paying close attention to our reactions while working with Ruth: What do we feel inclined to do when we are in her presence? To what extent might this reflect how others could feel in her presence? The second dimension consists of collaboratively identifying, attending to, and building upon her personal strengths and accomplishments.

Ruth's assessment indicates a "dysthymic disorder," a "generalized anxiety disorder," and a "binge eating disorder" based on long-standing, chronic dissatisfaction with herself coupled with worries or apprehensive expectations and maladaptive coping strategies. We do not have a clear sense of an Axis II diagnosis and are cautious about it due to the danger of pathologizing what are otherwise traits congruent with traditional gender expectations. As we are not medically trained, we record nothing on Axis III expect self-reports or a quote from Ruth's personal physician. She presents several psychosocial challenges that, while noted in Axis IV here, must be listed on Axis I should they become the principal focus of clinical attention: phase of life problems; parent–child and partner relational problems; problems on occupation and identity; and religious or spiritual problems. Finally, we record a current GAF score of 55 (moderate symptoms and difficulties) in Axis V, and 65 for the past year. The GAF difference indicates a worsening of symptoms and difficulties, creates a sense of urgency for the work, and underscores the need for therapy.

Following the *DSM-IV-TR* cultural formulation, we indicate that Ruth self-describes as "Latina" and possesses moderate Spanish speaking capacity. She quotes her mother describing Ruth's problems as *"nervios"* and *"ataques de nervios."* She has not used traditional healers or *curanderos/as,* and lives in a predominantly White community with a White spouse.

In conceptualizing Ruth's strengths and difficulties, we consider Ruth's loyalty to her family of origin and commitment to her role as a wife, mother, and daughter while we seek a balanced understanding of the assimilation strategy emphasized by her parents. This strategy perhaps has been one of survival, but it also might shed light on Ruth's self-perception as "weird," especially in a predominantly White community, and Ruth's feelings of anxiety, depression, guilt, and shame. Ruth's own cultural identity development and family scripts help us understand her personal struggles and some aspects of her present disputes with her daughter, who is close to the age that Ruth was when she married and became a mother. We wonder *with* Ruth about how cultural dimensions can help us understand her circumstances while providing a platform for change. Based on our assessment of Ruth, we collaboratively establish the beginning goals of treatment.

Goals of Therapy

We work with Ruth in discerning the meaning of the assessment results. We establish immediate goals addressing urgent matters, such as safety and stabilization, followed by short-term and long-term goals for counseling. We explore Ruth's time availability, commitment level, readiness for counseling, and resources to accomplish the treatment goals. We arrive at a mutually agreed-upon counseling contract for 20 sessions, once a week.

We are particularly mindful of Ruth's suicidality in light of her statement, "I worry about death—about my dying—a lot," and her diagnoses, and we address this straightforwardly with her. Two important goals of therapy are symptom reduction and creating a strong support network that affirms and sustains her personal and career aspirations.

We decide together to work toward more clarity on Ruth's gender and relationship roles and her satisfaction with these roles. We pointedly reflect back to Ruth the strengths we have noted in her thus far and discuss with her a continued identification of these important factors that could lead to increased overall well-being. She likes the idea of "focusing on what is good, not just what is bad." She said she gets enough "bad" feedback from her parents.

Key Issues and Themes

We anticipate Ruth may have some difficulties in following through with counseling, and that she may be hesitant, such as she has been with her exercise routine and job offer. An area of concern pertains to her perception of the lack of support from her spouse regarding possible changes in her. Another concern is the catastrophic response she anticipates from her father if he were to learn about her being in counseling.

We pay particular attention to Ruth's tendency to treat us in the therapeutic relationship in much the same way she is accustomed to being in her other relationships. She wants us to be the "experts": "Tell me what I have to do and push me to do it." She may express worries that she is not a good enough client. She is especially concerned that her therapy will become "boring and stale," much as she thinks of her life. From time to time she may look after us, perhaps even complimenting us regularly.

In light of her nascent cultural interest, Ruth is attentive to our degree of comfort when discussing cultural matters so as to discern the safety of such explorations. Our knowledgeable, receptive, respectful, and inviting stance toward cultural matters plays a significant role in establishing a solid relationship, as does our office décor.

We entertain, but do not impose, three cultural constructs with Ruth. The first one pertains to her gender role and has been termed *"marianismo"* in the Latina literature. *Marianismo* is a female gender socialization process modeled after the Virgin Mary. Women are expected to be selfless, self-sacrificing, nurturing, pious, and spiritually stronger than men while living under the 10 commandments of *The María Paradox*.[2] The second one captures her devotion to her family and has been termed *"familismo,"* meaning Ruth embraces a collectivistic worldview and is willing to endure sacrifices for the sake of her immediate and extended family.

The third addresses the importance of fostering Ruth's *confianza* in us, a multi-layered concept that implies confidence, trust, security, intimacy, and familiarity, and facilitates treatment adherence. In developing the therapeutic alliance, we remain attentive to gender differences and the traditional gender roles she has been surrounded with in both her family of origin and her nuclear family. We explore Ruth's degree of comfort in working with a male therapist and are watchful about our limited understanding of what it is like for her to be a Latina woman living in a predominantly White social context.

In light of her anxiety and depressive features, as well as a possible eating disorder, we wonder with Ruth whether perfectionism, intolerance of uncertainty, and need to control play a role in her struggles with initiative and lack of satisfaction with realized outcomes, resulting in feelings of inadequacy and guilt. It becomes apparent that Ruth's worries are expressed in fears of catastrophic failures lurking around every developmental milestone despite having accomplished much in life already, which she alternatively acknowledges, "I've been the superwoman," or minimizes by saying, "I haven't done enough." We encourage her to explore unrealistic expectations she may have about her participation and progress in therapy and about us as her therapists.

Therapeutic Process and Techniques

Our therapeutic endeavor is directly influenced by Ruth's ongoing assessment and by the therapy goals we collaboratively develop. This includes addressing the "greatest catalyst" triggering her consultation: "her physical symptoms and her anxiety." Because of our commitment to strengthening the therapeutic relationship, we ask Ruth to complete the client version of the Working Alliance Inventory (WAI) by the third session.[3] We also complete the therapist version of this instrument. We use the results to monitor and work on the alliance over time, administering the WAI at regular intervals.

We continue to monitor Ruth's mood difficulties through repeated usage of the Beck Depression Inventory FastScreen,[4] paying close attention to her responses to items 2 (hope) and 7 (suicidality), and Ruth's worrying through the Worry Questionnaire.[5] We work with Ruth on her mood and anxiety difficulties. She will challenge her debilitating moods and anxiety-inducing, catastrophic cognitions. Through her therapy we anticipate that Ruth will construct an alternative story, one that is life affirming, to replace the problem-saturated story she tells herself over and over. We recognize the formative nature of her upbringing, and we believe that Ruth's current circumstances may shed equal light on her difficulties in finding joy in her life today. We invite Ruth to reflect upon what she is doing in her daily life that leads her to conclude that she has a "boring and stale" life.

> RUTH: If I speak up, I am afraid people will think I'm weird. I am afraid of saying the wrong thing, of getting dizzy, or losing control. . . . It is easier if I don't say anything.
>
> THERAPIST: And then what happens?
>
> RUTH: I think of my parents telling me not to stick out, to fit in, but then I feel guilty for not saying anything or for having said something and now wondering what people are going to think of me.

THERAPIST: And then?

RUTH: Back to boring and stale . . . it is safer that way. But then I feel bad about myself; I turn to food and feel guilty for overeating.

THERAPIST: Ruth, you are indeed in a difficult position, with plenty of reasons for continuing the way you are, a budding desire for things to be different, yet a nagging fear of what may happen if you do act differently. At the same time, I am struck by the fact that you are here, in counseling, with me, and you have taken much risk in looking at yourself, your values, and your actions. How do you reconcile it all?

RUTH: ¡La que no arriesga no gana! [*The one who doesn't take risks doesn't win.*]

THERAPIST: Ruth, I am delighted you are even taking the risk of using your Spanish. How does this *dicho* [*saying*] capture your work in counseling?

RUTH: I know I have to if I am going to turn things around. I feel safe here.

THERAPIST: I am curious as to how you and I have made it safe here for you to explore being different.

RUTH: I don't feel judged by you.

THERAPIST: And that's from my end. What is it that you contribute?

RUTH: Honesty . . . I don't feel the need to be perfect here. I just am.

THERAPIST: I am wondering about ways in which you are already doing some of this elsewhere.

As our alliance becomes stronger, we work with Ruth on curtailing avoidance strategies and co-creating relevant exposure exercises with response prevention within the session and eventually outside the session. Whenever Ruth has a tendency toward avoiding a life situation, we suggest that she ask herself this question: "Am I better off avoiding this challenge, or would it be better for me to take a different action?"

We explore with Ruth her relationship to her body, exercise, and food. She might think more about the range of activities that give her pleasure and bring joy into her life. This would include inviting Ruth to talk about the quality of her sexual life, even though such a conversation may be somewhat awkward initially. We appreciate that it may take some time for Ruth to be more open with us, particularly with a male therapist. We discuss her exercise and relaxation repertoire, the role that food plays in her life, and the familial and cultural scripts that are shaping her views of self and others. We might suggest a referral to a dietician and a personal trainer to get her going on a relevant exercise routine, but only when we think there is a good chance Ruth is open to considering these referrals.

We entertain the possibility of internalized oppression, self-hating ways of relating to self born out of assimilative processes with respect to her "Latina roots" and are watchful of such matters in relation to her body image and expectations of self. We maintain a stance that is not neutral about these matters. Our stance is characterized by a broad latitude of acceptance. It may turn out that our work with Ruth centers on her accepting herself and learning to love herself in spite of her imperfections. We also ask her to question what she learned about the standards of beauty and encourage her to watch relevant movies such as *Real Women Have Curves*.

We discuss with Ruth the importance of support groups that scaffold her explorations and expansive values such as participating in a relevant book club, taking further courses that could pertain to understanding more about ethnic identity, or volunteering at a civic or social service organization. The latter is an important alternative considering her career aspirations and the need to build her résumé and letters of reference.

Overall, we balance the treatment focus between symptoms and cultural and relational themes. We enlist Ruth in seeking cultural expressions that capture her strengths and dilemmas. She finds herself spending increasing amounts of time talking with her parents, siblings, and even her children about their ethnic roots. These novel explorations are captured in a cultural genogram that she constructs over time and with the help of her parents. She volunteers further *dichos* and song lyrics that support her explorations on gender and personal realizations even when such explorations challenge prior held values. Although John initially appeared somewhat puzzled by her cultural interests, she has enticed John to do his own cultural explorations, which have made for some lively discussions during family gatherings. She rejoices in the feelings of excitement and curiosity that she and her family are experiencing.

Twenty sessions later, Ruth's counseling is well on the way and her symptoms have decreased. She is ready to involve other people in treatment such as her husband or the daughter with whom she is having difficulties. It is an opportune time to explore her career aspirations more directly through a new counseling contract as well. We turn to these aspirations now.

Ruth, as a newcomer to the job market, needs all the support she can muster, and her counselor can help with that. She wants to be recognized for who she is and for who she might become without alienating her family. At the same time, she will need the support or, at the very least, the tacit acceptance of her family in this undertaking. It may be appropriate to enlist her family and extended family members to create the necessary support system that will nurture her aspirations. However, this may prove to be a challenge because neither Ruth's husband nor her father is likely to encourage her intention to seek a career outside of the home. Bringing other family members into the process increases the chances for support while gaining allies to her career aspirations. Extended family members can offer some practical advice, which we would assist her in thinking about so that she could determine if she wanted to follow the advice she is getting.

Ruth's siblings can offer a wealth of emotional support and human resources. And in looking for work, apprenticeships, volunteering, or part-time projects, family members can be used to generate ideas. In short, we want to work with Ruth in establishing, maintaining, and fostering a strong network. She can let everyone in her family address book know what kind of work she is looking for by sending out a broadcast letter. She is likely to find that these human connections will be a most important asset in her job search.

We assist Ruth in honing in on her interests, skills, and talents. She may not be as interested or committed as she once was with respect to becoming an elementary school teacher, and this may account for her "dragging her feet" at pursuing it. Therefore, some exploration of career interests may be appropriate. Ruth has accrued both specific and transferable skills, and we will engage her in figuring out what these are. She would need to work on a résumé and cover letters based on her talents. This is an area in which we would offer suggestions and feedback on her actions.

In light of Ruth's limited work experience outside the home, she might try several part-time positions for a while, creating a portfolio career path. We help Ruth stay focused and flexible, regularly reviewing her decisions while treating her goals as hypotheses. We prepare her for job interviews while emphasizing creativity, as creative questioning has become a significant part of the job search process. She may benefit from reading books like *How Would You Move Mt. Fuji?*[6] We work with Ruth in maintaining vision, flexibility, and adaptability along with realistic expectations. We anticipate that this will be a challenging aspect for her in light of her perfectionism and fear of failure.

Concluding Comments

As goals are achieved, we discuss the transition in the therapeutic relationship. We eschew the finality of the word "termination" and embrace the concept of "transition." We remain open to seeing Ruth for future counseling sessions if she determines this would be in her best interests. The scientific literature highlights the likelihood of lapses and relapses among people living with anxiety, depression, eating difficulties, ethnic identity exploration, and career indecision. In light of this, we encourage a follow-up appointment with Ruth 6 months after her final session.

Ruth as an Asian American: A Multicultural Integrative Perspective

by Grace A. Chen, PhD, and Alvin N. Alvarez, PhD

Introduction

Recognizing the diversity within the Asian American community is the first step in working with Ruth as an Asian American. One of the fastest growing racial groups, the Asian American community encompasses 43 distinct ethnic groups (Thai, Chinese, Vietnamese, Filipino, Pakistani, and so forth). Despite presumptions of their academic and financial success, certain Asian ethnic groups have the lowest levels of academic achievement and highest levels of poverty in the country. Working with a refugee from Laos with limited academic and socioeconomic resources is significantly different from working with a third-generation Japanese American who comes to counseling with a greater likelihood of both economic resources and a familiarity with Western culture. Consequently, recognizing Ruth as an Asian American should be a catalyst for an additional assessment of her ethnicity, generational status, socioeconomic status, acculturation level, and linguistic fluency. For the purposes of this case, we will assume that Ruth is a Chinese American immigrant who arrived in the United States when she was 10, is fluent in English, has college-educated parents, and comes from a middle-class background.

Our work with Ruth as an Asian American is grounded in a number of fundamental tenets of multicultural counseling. Namely, we assume the following: (a) the therapist's and the client's cultural backgrounds shape their expectations of the process and outcome of counseling; (b) the effectiveness of counseling is directly related to the therapist's awareness and knowledge of Asian Americans and her or his ability to work with the client in a culturally congruent manner; (c) counseling occurs within a larger sociocultural and sociopolitical context; and (d) interventions may occur at the level of the individual, group, or system.

Assessment of Therapist

A central tenet of multicultural counseling holds that cultural competence is reflected in therapists' awareness, knowledge, and skills with Asian Americans. It is critical for therapists to receive training on counseling Asian Americans as well as to reflect on their limitations and biases in working with Asian Americans *prior* to delivering services. It is imperative for therapists to engage in a candid assessment of their own comfort with and ability to raise issues of race and culture in a counseling session. The ability to address and name the cultural dimensions in a client's life are significant contributors to the success of multicultural counseling. Finally, it is also our belief that this self-reflection on the part of the therapist should occur regardless of whether the dyads are of the same race and ethnicity or not.

We present Ruth's therapy experience from the perspective of working with a White American female therapist of English and German descent. In this particular case, we believe the therapist will need to evaluate her knowledge of Chinese Americans and their history in the United States, their cultural values, expectations about help-seeking, conceptualization of psychological well-being, family and gender roles, and communication patterns. Although the therapist has worked with a number of Asian American clients and feels culturally competent, the therapist will need to assess her own socialization experiences around Chinese Americans and consider how that shapes her expectations and assumptions of such clients. A self-assessment of the therapist is essential because her experiences with and knowledge of Asian Americans in general may differ from Ruth's specific experiences.

Assessment of Ruth

Assessing Ruth's presenting concerns is valuable for (a) organizing the information that has been obtained, (b) developing a coherent yet tentative conceptualization of her presenting issues, (c) prioritizing and developing therapeutic goals, and (d) implementing relevant interventions. Our assessment is formative and informal, being based on the information currently available, and is open to revision as counseling proceeds. Although developing a more formalized diagnosis, such as using the *DSM-IV-TR*, can be helpful in conceptualization, we are reluctant to do so unless required to by institutional or financial expectations. Consistent with multicultural counseling principles, our hesitance in this area stems from our awareness of the sociopolitical context and stigma associated with diagnostic labels and their potential effects on the therapeutic relationship.

With this in mind, our informal assessment of Ruth's presenting concerns is centered on the following areas: (a) depression symptoms: suicidal ideation, melancholic mood, binge eating; (b) anxiety symptoms: physical tension, obsessive worrying, insomnia; (c) phase of life issues: career exploration and changing role in the family; and (d) multicultural considerations: cultural influences and pressures, racial and gender stereotypes, and religious identity.

Key Issues

From a multicultural counseling perspective, distinctions between race and ethnicity need to be acknowledged in order to work effectively with Ruth. The racial category of Asian Americans is a sociopolitical construct historically rooted in a system created to exclude "non-White" individuals from many privileges and rights in the United States. Racial stereotypes, such as the model minority, are often reflected in media portrayals of Asian Americans. Thus Ruth's racial identity is a psychological construct based on how she experiences racial categorization, which is imposed on her by American society. However, one's ethnic background is usually associated with a particular culture's values, beliefs, traditions, and language. For Ruth, her ethnic identity is based on how she views herself in relation to her Chinese culture. Although racial and ethnic identities are interconnected, recognizing the differences between the two is important in understanding Ruth as an Asian American of Chinese descent. Therapists who focus only on ethnicity or only on race may overlook a significant aspect of identity by failing to consider how both may affect Asian Americans.

It is important also to consider where spirituality fits into Ruth's self-identity as her religious confusion seems to be a significant piece of her presenting concern. Ruth has multiple social identities—being Chinese American, a woman, a spiritual person, and an Asian American. The therapist needs to assess the saliency of Ruth's various social identities to understand what aspects of her identity have meaning for her and, equally important, which social identities are not salient for her.

Another key issue to consider is how Ruth's distress manifests itself in her physical and mental health. A common response to difficulty or lack of opportunity to express emotions, particularly among Asian Americans, is for individuals to convert their anxiety and depression into bodily symptoms. Because Ruth seems to have little social support, it is important to be aware that her physical health is also negatively affected by her current concerns.

Goals of Therapy

Consistent with the collaborative stance inherent in multicultural counseling, we work *with* Ruth in identifying and prioritizing the goals of counseling. To initiate the process, we focus on the following immediate goals: (a) establishing a safe, trusting therapeutic relationship with Ruth; (b) providing psychoeducation about counseling, given Ruth's limited experience with counseling and its potential stigma; and (c) conducting a suicide assessment, given Ruth's comments about death.

In the near term, we work with Ruth on symptom reduction, with anxiety as a major presenting concern. In addition to working toward symptom relief, we focus on helping Ruth understand her presenting concerns within a cultural context. Specifically, we work with her in obtaining insight into how the cultural intersections of ethnicity, race, gender, and religion influence (a) her identity as a Chinese American woman, (b) her familial obligations and relationships, (c) her expectations of academic and career achievement, and (d) her body image and sexuality. In the long term, we work on empowering Ruth with the ability to recognize, deconstruct, and determine the cultural dimensions of her identity. Thus we work toward developing Ruth's self-affirming racial, ethnic, gender, and religious identities and her ability to respect and balance her needs as an individual with the needs of the group (in this case, parents, partner, children and church). We are aware that a White therapist addressing cultural issues needs to avoid a "color-blind" approach while being careful not to assume that culture is the primary concern. Being new to therapy, Ruth may be uncomfortable and cautious around a White female therapist. We do not want her to feel that we are assuming her race and ethnicity are her most significant social identities; we want her to recognize that we want to get to know her as a person *and* understand how she identifies with her Chinese heritage.

Therapeutic Process and Techniques

BEGINNING PHASE

Psychoeducation About Counseling   In the beginning phase of counseling, it is critical to address Ruth's expectations of counseling. Multicultural counseling research has consistently demonstrated that high rates of premature termination are a risk for Asian Americans in counseling. Cultural stigmas—such as "counseling is for crazy people"—reflect both attitudes toward mental health and toward therapists. Cultural expectations about self-disclosure and saving face for oneself and one's family also are potentially limiting factors. When we consider matters such as cultural prohibitions, Ruth's own expectations of counseling, her limited experience with counseling, and the referral by her physician, it is essential that we explore Ruth's commitment and intrinsic motivation to stay in counseling as that may affect her ability to address therapeutic issues in depth. During our initial session we explicitly address Ruth's expectations about counseling and our respective roles in counseling.

THERAPIST: Ruth, I know you mentioned that you've been to a counselor a few times as part of a class. But I'm wondering what it's like for you to come on your own to talk with me?

RUTH: Well, to be honest, it's kinda strange, and I always thought only crazy people came in here. Sorry about that!

THERAPIST: No need to apologize. I think a lot of people think that, particularly if they're not familiar with counseling.

RUTH: Oh, absolutely! If my father found out I were here, he would flip out.

THERAPIST: What do you think is behind all of that?

RUTH: Well, you're not supposed to talk about your business with a stranger. It's just such a shameful thing. Plus to talk to a therapist, well you gotta be really crazy if you need to do that.

THERAPIST: So, you're crossing a lot of lines by coming in here?

RUTH: Yeah, I never thought of it that way. But I guess that's why I'm kinda nervous about all of this.

THERAPIST: Well, I wanted us to talk about it directly because I think it's important to give you credit for taking such a big step outside of your comfort zone.

RUTH: Thanks, I appreciate that. I was wondering if you thought I was nuts or something.

THERAPIST: No, I don't think you're nuts at all. From what I can see, the things that are happening in your life and your reactions to them are pretty normal.

RUTH: Really?

THERAPIST: Absolutely. But since you're fairly new to counseling, I'm wondering if it would be helpful for us to talk more about who comes to counseling, what they do here, what I do in all of this, and how this all works.

RUTH: That sounds good!

THERAPIST: So, let's start with any questions you might have about all of this. What do you want to know?

❧ Acculturation and Enculturation   A central issue from a multicultural perspective involves the degree to which Ruth identifies with her social identities: ethnicity, race, gender, and religion. Multicultural counseling is based on the premise that culture, broadly defined, influences how clients view counseling and the help-seeking process. Culture also influences notions of psychological well-being, expectations of oneself and the counselor, expectations of the process and outcome of counseling, as well as symptom manifestation. Yet culturally competent counselors also recognize the heterogeneity in how individuals identify with their various cultures. In other words, the psychological salience of an individual's culture and the degree to which that individual identifies with that culture, varies from one person to another. For instance, although Ruth is biologically Chinese American, she may not identify with being Chinese, and her cultural worldview and identity may be more aligned with White Americans. Similarly, although Ruth's religious identity has been salient for most of her life, her relatively recent ambivalence about her beliefs suggests that her religious identification may be shifting. Hence, we incorporate questions about race, ethnicity, religion, and gender in our initial meetings to better understand Ruth's cultural frames of reference.

THERAPIST: I noticed that your parents emigrated here from Hong Kong.

RUTH: Yes, we came here when I was little—around 10 or so.

THERAPIST: What was that like for you? Growing up here in a Chinese family?

RUTH: Well, you know my dad was a Baptist minister. So, he was pretty strict. You know, the traditional Chinese dad . . . didn't say much but you knew he expected certain things from you.

THERAPIST: You used the phrase "traditional Chinese dad." Even though I have a sense of what you're getting at, I'm wondering if you could tell me what that means for you.

RUTH: Hmm. My parents have always been proud to be Chinese, and they expected us to be the same . . . so, we had to know how to speak Cantonese, how to read and write in Chinese, and we were expected to celebrate Chinese holidays.

THERAPIST: So, being Chinese is important to your parents.

RUTH: Oh yeah. Big time. And being a devout Baptist is very important too.

THERAPIST: Well, how about for you? How important is being Chinese and Baptist to you?

RUTH: As a kid, I really hated being Chinese. Everyone doing the "ching-chong chinamen" song and pulling their eyes when I walked by! Kids made fun of the food I brought for lunch. I hated standing out, and I just wanted to be normal. But when I got older, I realized that there's a lot about me that's pretty Chinese and it isn't all bad. Being part of my dad's Baptist church was all I knew, and over the years I found that I'm more comfortable with a less fundamental congregation, but it's hard to explain that to my dad.

Recognizing the saliency of Ruth's ethnic identity and conflict about her religious identity early in the counseling process, we continue to explore the many cultural dimensions of Ruth's concerns.

🌺 Therapist Multicultural Competency   Because the therapist and Ruth are of different ethnic and racial backgrounds, acknowledging their differences is part of being a multiculturally competent therapist. However, the therapist and Ruth are both women and may have similar experiences from that perspective. Acknowledging both similarities and differences can help to create a therapeutic alliance that Ruth can use to understand her struggles better. One approach to addressing cultural and racial differences is to bring it up as an explicit topic of discussion, but we decide to integrate our knowledge and awareness of cultural issues by weaving comments throughout our assessment with Ruth and let the discussions occur organically.

THERAPIST: Ruth, we talked a lot about your childhood experiences growing up in your family and your parents' expectations of you.

RUTH: Yeah, we sure have.

THERAPIST: I sense it was difficult for you growing up because you felt different from other kids.

RUTH: Even though I am more comfortable with my culture now, I feel guilty that I didn't like being Chinese when I was younger.

THERAPIST: I honestly can't imagine growing up being made fun of because of the way I look and because of my culture. That must have been embarrassing, so it makes sense that you didn't like the part of yourself—being Chinese—that made you feel different. And yet you still figured out what was meaningful to you about being Chinese. With you being a mother, I'm guessing this topic has come up for you as you raise your children.

RUTH: Oh, most definitely! Because I know what it was like growing up feeling different, I always tried to talk to my kids about how special their Chinese heritage is but also how other people may treat them differently because of it. Do you have kids?

THERAPIST: Yes, I do, so I understand talking to them about their identities and cultural heritage. Of course, even though we are both mothers, I don't want to assume that I know exactly how you feel because I'm not Chinese American and we've had different life experiences.

By weaving our knowledge and limitations into our discussion, we demonstrate that we understand and respect Ruth's unique experiences as a Chinese American woman. We want her to feel comfortable talking openly about being a Chinese American woman without feeling like she has to "teach" us. For instance, Ruth talked about having some apprehension of how she'll be perceived as a teacher. She is afraid that students may expect her to be a pushover as a "passive Asian female," which reflects her real fear that she fulfills that stereotype. We can validate Ruth's fear and express that we know how frustrating it is to deal with stereotypes.

MIDDLE PHASE

Symptom Reduction In response to Ruth's expressed hope for the therapist to "tell her what to do," we explain to Ruth that there is no "right" way for her to live her life. At the same time, it is important to address Ruth's expectation that counseling will give her concrete suggestions. Thus we begin the process of symptom reduction to provide Ruth with psychological relief as well as a tangible outcome from counseling. This is consistent with what scholars have referred to as the concept of "gift-giving" in multicultural counseling. The "gift" in this case may involve providing Ruth with an understanding of anxiety, recognizing her symptoms and triggers, as well as expanding her coping repertoire with deep breathing exercises, meditative practices, muscle-relaxation techniques, distraction exercises, and thought-stopping techniques. Insofar as Ruth experiences positive outcomes from such gifts, it is more likely that she will remain committed to counseling. Additionally, it is important for the therapeutic relationship that Ruth feels that we are responding to her direct requests for help. Through discussions about how counseling involves various techniques, Ruth understands that utilizing concrete techniques are only part of how she can use counseling.

❧ **Cultural Analysis**   After engaging Ruth's commitment to counseling, one focus of the middle phase of counseling involves a cultural analysis of her presenting concerns. In contrast to the individual and intrapsychic focus of traditional Western psychotherapy, multicultural counseling is based on the belief that it is facilitative for clients to recognize the role of culture and larger systems of oppression in their lives. We strive to shift Ruth's understanding and attributions of her presenting concerns from a purely intrapsychic and self-blaming focus to an understanding of her presenting concerns within a cultural context. For instance, it is important for us to help Ruth recognize that her inability to define who she is apart from her roles of daughter, wife, and mother is normative given traditional Chinese gender roles based on patriarchy and sexism. Additionally, we consider how her strict religious upbringing reinforced those traditional gender roles. We talk about cultural and religious influences within the context of her family of origin in order to recognize that family cultures are unique as well. We will work with Ruth to recognize that her lack of a self-determined identity is culturally influenced rather than a reflection of a deficiency on her part.

> THERAPIST: Ruth, you've talked about being a daughter, a wife, and a mother. It makes me wonder what your family taught you about what women were supposed to do in their lives.
>
> RUTH: Well, my mom didn't work, and she mostly just looked after us kids.
>
> THERAPIST: So, that seems pretty traditional to me.
>
> RUTH: I guess so.
>
> THERAPIST: Did you know any other Chinese women or women from your church who had careers or went to college?
>
> RUTH: Well, in my mom's generation and at church, no way! Some of my friends went to college, but they were still expected to raise families and watch over the kids after college.
>
> THERAPIST: What's the underlying message for women in your family?
>
> RUTH: I guess that your family and being a mom is number one.
>
> THERAPIST: It doesn't seem like you've had much support or encouragement to be anyone other than a mom or a wife.
>
> RUTH: Exactly. Even John doesn't like all these courses I've been taking.
>
> THERAPIST: And how is that for you?
>
> RUTH: Well, I know he makes sense about taking care of the kids. But sometimes I just get really upset because it feels like it's always about him and the kids. What about me?

Discussing cultural influences in Ruth's life provides a better understanding of her presenting concerns in that Ruth feels torn between two cultures that sometimes have competing values. For instance, for this case, we assume her husband is a traditional Chinese man who does not want Ruth to work because he's concerned about how he would look as a husband and father who is expected to provide for the family. If Ruth starts working, John fears that others will think it is because he is not able to support his family. Consequently, he would "lose face" in the community. Ruth understands his fear but questions if that is enough reason for her to give up her dream to teach. She struggles with balancing her own needs with the cultural expectations her husband has for their family. We acknowledge her dilemma by sharing with Ruth that balancing cultural values is a common struggle for Asian Americans. Fulfilling her own needs is a mainstream American value that is strongly encouraged, whereas "saving face" and focusing on the family is an important Chinese cultural value.

🏵 Emotional Expression   As the prior scene suggests, the middle phase of counseling may elicit a great deal of anger and frustration from Ruth as she awakens to the effects of gender and cultural socialization on her life. In racial identity terms, this dissonance-inducing period will be a time of confusion, anger, and resentment. Therefore, we work to provide a space and a relationship where Ruth's anger and resentment can be expressed, normalized, and validated. In a family where gender roles and a cultural system devalue self-assertion and the expression of negative emotions from women, counseling becomes a rare opportunity for Ruth to express herself without judgment.

LATER PHASE   Throughout counseling, our interventions are aimed at helping Ruth feel more empowered to make decisions for herself. To continue this process, we focus on enhancing Ruth's social support system by exploring venues—including support groups, cultural groups, and student organizations—as a way for Ruth to meet with other Asian American women or women of color who are also balancing family life with school. Similarly, bibliotherapy in areas such as women's studies or Asian American literature may further expose Ruth to the struggles that she shares with other women. In particular, the cultural and gender dimensions of body image will be explored in conjunction with a referral to a nutritionist. In addition, we encourage Ruth to discuss with her pastor and other members of her church how gender, race, and ethnicity may be integrated into her religious views. Career counseling may be vital in helping Ruth to recognize the influence of ethnicity, race, and gender on her choices to enter education. We also address the value of being active in the community to (a) solidify Ruth's connections with other Asian American women, (b) provide Ruth with a constructive outlet for addressing racism and sexism, and (c) increase her sense of self-efficacy in dealing with societal oppression.

Concluding Comments

In the later phase of counseling, Ruth's growth is manifested in a personally meaningful definition of herself that integrates her personal identity with that of her social identities as a Chinese American, as a woman, and as a Christian. Ruth also recognizes that this growth is only the beginning of a continually evolving process. Questions remain about her relationships with John and her children and how these relationships may need to be redefined. Similarly, Ruth's relationship with her own parents and the role of religion, gender, and family obligation continue to be relatively unexplored areas, but Ruth faces these concerns with a renewed and self-affirming sense of self. Consequently, in honor of that strength, we candidly examine these remaining concerns in Ruth's life and her plans to address these issues in the future. We discuss and anticipate times of relapse as well as steps to maintain progress such as follow-up and maintenance sessions, couples counseling, and family therapy.

As illustrated by the case of Ruth, multicultural counseling is complementary to treatment rather than being in competition with other theoretical and treatment approaches. Our emphasis on the cultural dimensions of Ruth's presenting concerns does not diminish the significance of addressing and treating her phase of life concerns or her symptoms of anxiety or depression. We believe that multicultural counseling can be integrated with other theoretical approaches insofar as therapists remain cognizant of the cultural factors that influence their own assumptions and practices, as well as the counseling experience and presenting concerns of their clients. In effect, multicultural counseling challenges therapists to situate themselves and their clients within a cultural context.

Ruth as an African American: A Spiritually Focused Integrative Perspective

by Kellie Kirksey, PhD

Introduction

Ruth, an African American female, is seeking counseling in a private practice setting. By entering therapy Ruth is engaging in a healing modality that is not typically embraced by her culture. She may have heard a number of negative messages about seeking counseling such as these:

- Therapy is for crazy people.
- Don't tell your business to strangers.
- What happens at home, stays at home.
- Talk to your preacher or minister if you have a problem.
- You can't trust the system.
- If you are a Christian, you have Jesus and therefore do not need an intercessor.

These are challenging perceptions, and historically, in many cases, these beliefs were the basis for survival.

When Ruth phoned to make her initial appointment, she requested an African American, Christian, female therapist. I don't market myself as a Christian counselor, but I see spirituality and faith as important variables in the healing process. Ruth proceeds to schedule an intake interview. I introduce myself and begin by asking her to discuss her perceptions of counseling. During the intake process, I talk about what counseling entails and how we will meet our goals. I acknowledge the courage it took for her to take this significant step in the healing process. I also inform her that the initial session is about laying the groundwork for counseling, and asking questions is part of the assessment and consequent treatment.

I invite Ruth to explore her beliefs and attitudes about seeking professional help and encourage her to talk openly about any concerns or fears she has about beginning counseling. I tell her that I am not the keeper of answers to her life problems, but simply a collaborator in this process. I operate with the assumption that individuals who come to me already have answers within themselves. Although I have expertise in facilitating the therapeutic process, I view clients as the experts on their own lives.

Assessment of Ruth

Ruth was referred for counseling by her primary care physician due to anxiety, panic attacks, and general feelings of sadness and frustration. She reports being brought up in a strict home where it was not acceptable to express emotions. As an adult, she has consistently repressed her feelings and experienced guilt when attempting to express her dissatisfactions. This way of responding to the world was modeled by her mother and grandmother. She has recently returned to school and is the only African American woman in her program. Her inability to express her honest reactions when she encounters discriminatory and racist comments in the classroom is causing her significant distress.

It is critical to ask Ruth about her race and ethnicity. I pay careful attention to how she defines herself. She tells me she is "Black, just like you." I tell her, "I was born in Cleveland, my husband is Haitian, although we are both 'Black,' our cultures are worlds apart, and this affects how we see the world." The questions I pose to Ruth assist me in knowing more of who she is and how she sees herself in relation to her cultural group and the world. I am interested in hearing her talk about both the specific challenges and the strengths she experiences in belonging to her racial and ethnic group. Ruth mentions resiliency as a particular strength of her race. This information is important as we move into the treatment phase.

I ask Ruth about her religious and spiritual background in our initial session. My goal is to learn what kind of religious practices, if any, were used in her family of origin. We explore the following questions: (1) Is religion an important part of your daily life? (2) What religion is practiced in your home? (3) What aspects of your religion/spiritual practice provide the most support for you? (4) Define your spiritual connection. Ruth's answers let me know how relevant religion and spirituality might be to our therapeutic work together.

This conversation reveals Ruth's ambivalent feelings toward counseling. She states if she were truly living by the Word of God, she wouldn't need a stranger to help her deal with personal issues. Because of her ambivalence, I lean away from a traditional multiaxis diagnosis and focus on building a collaborative relationship in which she feels free to co-create a new healthy life story.

Goals of Therapy

We will use a collaborative integrative approach to meet the following treatment goals:

1. Establish a therapeutic relationship built on trust and mutual respect.
2. Explore and deconstruct the cultural and societal messages that have played a role in her feelings of unworthiness and victimization.

3. Create a new, healthy narrative that supports her in being more authentic in her life.
4. Increase her ability to trust her inner wisdom and spiritual connection.

Key Issues and Themes

Ruth is entering therapy with a host of personal concerns, one of which is her lost sense of self, both culturally and as a woman in society. She has lived most of her life as a people-pleaser and has accepted the myth of the strong African American woman. Viewing herself as "superwoman," she has assumed the role of caretaker to everyone. In doing this she has become self-sacrificing and overextended physically and emotionally. Ruth's challenge is to learn self-care, healthy interpersonal boundaries, and to speak her truth as an African American woman.

As a woman of African descent who has been raised to never disclose family business, it is important that I acknowledge her courage in breaking the silence and doing something that generations before her have been hesitant to do. It is vital that she understands my office is a safe and nonjudgmental zone and she can trust me. I tell her about the limitations of confidentiality as a way of furthering this safety.

Ruth's anxiety is a major presenting concern; it has led her to control others, repress her feelings, and engage in unhealthy eating patterns. She tends to pacify her fear and frustration with food, leading to binge eating and weight gain. We will work on mindfulness strategies to assist her in becoming more aware of her automatic emotional eating and in making more life-affirming decisions.

Ruth feels that in the midst of being there for others she has lost sight of herself. She has never allowed herself to explore what it means to be an African American woman in society. As she is confronted with discrimination and bias on the college campus, she is more determined to explore those social and cultural issues that have defined her existence.

Therapeutic Process and Procedures

Ruth's primary task in therapy is to teach me who she is. I remind her that she is the expert on her life and has the answers for improving her life within her. Our joint partnership involves being intentional in discovering those answers and putting them into practice.

The therapeutic goals collaboratively developed will be accomplished through the use of psychoanalytic, cognitive behavioral, existential, and postmodern therapy approaches. I draw from the psychoanalytic approach during the initial stage of counseling to identify repressed emotion. This approach is used to bring unconscious material to the forefront and to aid Ruth in accessing early experiences. I ask her to bring in old photos that will stimulate a discussion of childhood experiences that may be affecting her current level of functioning.

I begin to weave in the cognitive behavioral perspective by allowing Ruth to witness the language she uses in relation to herself. I keep a list of statements she makes so we can reflect on how her negative language patterns influence her. Once she realizes how often she calls herself "foolish," or "stupid," she becomes more aware of her negative, self-defeating thoughts and how this affects her behavior. Cognitive behavioral strategies assist her in recognizing the negative self-talk that contributes to her sense of fear and panic. These strategies give her a framework for being more proactive in her life and help her see that changing her thoughts lead to behavioral change.

Existential theory, as well as some postmodern ideas, will be woven into Ruth's treatment. These approaches facilitate increased awareness on a variety of levels, including mind, body, and spirit. I encourage and challenge Ruth to be more mindful of who she is, what she is doing, and where she is going. Once she begins to explore some of her existential concerns, it becomes easier to work on shifting how she sees herself.

Because Ruth has indicated the church is a guiding force in her life, I invite her to call on her spiritual connection to assist us in our work together. I view her spiritual connection as whatever source she goes to for spiritual strength, comfort, and direction. She tells me that her spiritual connection is Jesus, and we proceed with our work; in a clear voice we invite Jesus into our session to guide and protect us on our journey of healing and self-discovery.

I tailor my therapeutic style to the specific needs of my clients. I realize that my ability to facilitate growth in my clients is consistent with my willingness to challenge my own personal struggles. In my work with African American clients, I give special attention to generational transmission or those tendencies, traits, and habits that are consciously or unconsciously passed along. Use of genograms (family maps) is helpful in the early phase of therapy as we explore these generational patterns.

The Beginning Phase of Therapy

Ruth is quite talkative in our initial sessions. She feels comfortable because she respects her doctor who referred her and she is relieved to have a place to be heard. Ruth has spent an enormous amount of time both in class and at home repressing her true feelings. She is relieved to have a safe place to speak her mind. Ruth is encouraged to take note of the pace of her breathing. I talk to her about the role breathing plays in decreasing anxiety. I demonstrate diaphragmatic breathing and ask her to practice at home. Ruth is also encouraged to write in a journal daily to release her pent-up emotions and frustrations. She reports feeling like she has already made progress and is glad she has something to do between sessions.

🐦 Process Commentary   The breathing activity is a way of assisting Ruth in becoming more aware of her body, what she is doing with her body, and what her body can do for her. As she continues her breathing exercises, her ability to relax will increase as her level of anxiety decreases. I continue to work with Ruth on body awareness and incorporate movement.

During the beginning phase of therapy we initiate affirmations and continue this practice until the end. These affirmations are born out of Ruth's own story. As I observe Ruth expressing phrases such as "I'm so stupid" or "I hate my life," I write down her affirmation on an index card. The affirmations are meant to cancel out her negative self-talk, increase awareness of inner dialogue, and replace a defeatist statement with a life-supporting phrase. The first card she receives has a separate statement on each side. I pass the card to Ruth with the words "I matter" and "I am worthy" written in black marker.

THERAPIST: Would you read those words out loud please? [*Ruth is silent and does not respond.*] How are you feeling as you look at those words?

RUTH [*Tears begin to stream down her face*]: I feel sad because I wish I felt this way about myself.

THERAPIST: As I listened to you share your experiences, I heard some harsh words.

RUTH: Yeah, it's all I heard growing up!

THERAPIST: Would you consider using kinder words?

RUTH: It just comes up before I can stop it!

THERAPIST: I am going to challenge you to monitor what you tell yourself. We know scripturally that "as a woman thinketh so is she." I'm challenging you to guard your thoughts and intentionally create something new in your mind. This entire process is about renewing your mind . . . forgiving yourself and others and moving forward.

RUTH: Easier said than done.

THERAPIST: That's why it is a practice—we practice new and different skills . . . try it on . . . see what it feels like.

Throughout our sessions I continue to discuss the importance of using positive self-statements, and I encourage Ruth to actively work on modifying her cognitions. We create a list of negative messages she has received from others and that she has told herself. Some of these automatic thoughts are related to her race, gender, and current stage in life. As she works on her list, she notices how her negative thoughts contribute to her poor self-image. I remind her that in future sessions we will explore positive, rational, coping statements to cancel negative self-statements.

The Middle Phase of Therapy

Once I have a sense that we have established a solid therapeutic bond, we begin to go into more existential work, focusing on Ruth's anxiety and how she feels about her place in the world as an African American woman. It can be expected that intense emotions will surface as she begins to really speak from her heart.

THERAPIST: How are you today?

RUTH: Sick and tired!

THERAPIST: OK. Tell me more about being sick and tired.

RUTH: Well, it's this school thing. I am going to finish. I know I'll succeed. It's just getting past all the mess that goes along with it! Sometimes it's the smallest things that get to me.

THERAPIST: Give me an example.

RUTH: Well, the other day I was in the college bookstore and an older White lady said to me, "You are such an articulate colored woman." For one, I thought I was hearing things, and for another thing, can't I speak like I have some sense and be Black? I was about two seconds from telling her off!

THERAPIST: I'm glad you curbed that impulse. What stopped you?

RUTH: I knew she didn't know better. She was old and had probably only seen someone like me on TV. There just aren't too many of us around the college, and I get tired of it sometimes.

THERAPIST: What feelings did you have after she made her comment?

RUTH: I mostly felt frustrated and sad. I can't say I was angry. A part of me could have cried because it just doesn't make sense that this old woman doesn't know that her comment was offensive. She didn't even know that we're called African American . . . huh, she could have at least said Black.

THERAPIST: What else? Remember how we talked about taking out the trash . . . now is a good time to get it out!

RUTH: I just get tired of people at the college sometimes. I want to be there and I will get my degree, but it would be nice to see more people that look like me. But no, I just get to be the poster child for all things Black. When we talk about diversity or multicultural issues in class . . . all the eyes roll toward me. Can't they see that they have some culture too! I don't get it. Then there's the conversations about family dynamics and poverty . . . well, I usually sit there feeling the heat. I think they see me as the older Black woman who was probably on welfare, crack, and has a different daddy for each of her kids . . . but somehow I made good and turned my life around, that I am the exception. It's like they think they know me because they have seen people that look like me.

THERAPIST: Do you really think that's what they think of you? And does it matter?

RUTH [*Heavy sigh*]: No. Who knows what they think. I don't care what they think. I just want to be able to go to school and do my thing. I don't want it to matter, but sometimes I feel like all I do is fight that stereotype.

THERAPIST: So do you?

RUTH: Do I what?

THERAPIST: Do you fight that image? Do you work to tear down that stereotype?

RUTH: Fight it how? Every time I raise my hand my professor shuts me down. See, in his world slavery has been abolished and racism doesn't exist. They think it's something we should just get over. I try to tell them it's alive and well and I live some aspect of it every day. If they really hear what I'm saying, then just maybe they have to be more accountable for their own biased views. I know my professor thinks I'm paranoid or hypersensitive when I tell him that we still get followed in stores or that my work seems to be scrutinized more than anyone else's in class. This is my world, so don't minimize my reality! I don't expect them to understand, but don't make it seem like I'm making this all up just to get pity. I don't want it and don't need it.

THERAPIST: When I was in school, I imagined that the next generation wouldn't have to deal with all this bias and judgment. But here we are, and it is still happening. It makes me so sad to hear you saying the same things we said 20 years ago, yet I am elated that you are in the trenches doing this.

RUTH: It's not easy.

THERAPIST: If it were easy, everyone would do it. Stay in your lane. God put you in this situation for a reason. Whenever you feel that heat rise inside of you, take a deep, slow breath, choose your battles, and share your truth. Let people know who you are as an individual. Telling your own story can break down the false images.

RUTH: They don't need to know my business. I don't need to tell them about myself.

THERAPIST: So you let the heat rise inside of you. Does that make you feel good?

RUTH: You know it doesn't or I wouldn't be here. Sometimes I speak up and become the angry Black woman who is sick of the foolishness, and there I go feeding into the stereotype.

THERAPIST: It's important to be aware of how we deliver our message. Sometimes we go right to our victim mode and that makes us defensive, and the anger can rise. It's not effective. That's the behavior that they've seen from us on TV. Don't perpetuate the myth . . . break it! What if you allowed yourself to detach from the victim and then speak, but just from your perspective?

RUTH: You got yours, Doc, you don't know what it's like.

THERAPIST: I have had to deal with some of what we are talking about, Ruth. It's a tough road. I was the first person in my family to go to college, and I lived in inner-city Cleveland with rats as big as cats in my house . . . college was not something we did. My game was called survival. I too had to realize that I couldn't do it alone and that I needed help to live a different life. My best friends' parents helped me get into college. It was tough, but we can't continue to function in isolation. . . . I couldn't do it alone, and neither can you. Going back to school is difficult under any circumstance. And here you are doing all types of things you never imagined yourself doing. Be proud of yourself, tell your story . . . it's powerful! It could be healing for others to hear more about who you really are.

RUTH: I guess I can give it a try. What I've been doing is not really working, and I can't continue to leave class tense and stressed out.

THERAPIST: That's a good attitude. You can also do some mental rehearsal and see yourself speaking more from your heart . . . not from your anger and frustration.

RUTH: OK, I can try that.

THERAPIST: I see a couple of things going on here. You're feeling isolated and alone at the college, and it's a struggle dealing with all the stereotypes. I can understand that. Your job is to consider who you can connect with to help you through this. You may need to step out of your comfort zone and actively seek out other people who are in a similar situation. Your college has an Office of Multicultural Affairs. Go to one of the meetings. There could be someone in another department who is feeling isolated and would like to connect with another student who is feeling isolated. It can be as simple as having coffee and conversation with this person.

RUTH: OK. That's a thought. I might be able to look into that.

❧ **Process Commentary**   I validate Ruth's feelings about being the only African American woman in her program. Her feelings of isolation, loneliness, and frustration are very real. It is helpful to simply allow her to be heard without interrupting the flow of her emotions. My use of self-disclosure may help her feel understood and less isolated. Because I am able to relate to Ruth's situation, it is likely that she will begin to feel it's appropriate and useful to express what she genuinely feels.

Encouragement is essential for Ruth. She doesn't receive a great deal of support and encouragement regarding her endeavors in her everyday life. Therapy is a place where she can be understood, encouraged, and affirmed. Teaching her to affirm and validate herself is a crucial aspect of our work together. She also has a pattern of doing everything on her own and then feeling overwhelmed and isolated. By connecting with the Office of Multicultural Affairs, she begins to build community and gain more strength and resiliency through her interactions with others.

Final Stages of Therapy

As we enter the final stages of therapy Ruth is aware that she can create a new story for herself. She knows that playing the victim is unproductive and leads to increased anxiety. No longer is she triggered by the behaviors and attitudes of others. As our time together comes to an end, we discuss the gains she has made through her work in therapy. She feels proud that she is now able to express her views at home and in the classroom without feeling overwhelmed or victimized. She reports feeling stronger in her cultural identity and no longer feels the need to defend herself. She has developed the habit of checking in with herself, tuning into her body, and doing what is necessary to return to a state of inner calm. She is writing her frustrations and success stories in her journal, thus more effectively managing her frustrations as they arise. Trusting her inner voice and setting clear boundaries are also gains that she has made.

Ruth can now say *no* without being riddled with guilt. She finds herself able to express opinions in class without being emotionally triggered. She has come to the conclusion that people don't have to understand her walk as an African American woman. She can simply meet people where they are and stand in her truth and integrity as a woman of African descent.

Ruth continues to work on issues such as building community, allowing herself to be vulnerable in relationships, and honoring her body as a temple through exercise and healthy nutrition. She has made amazing gains in these areas and continues to use cognitive behavioral strategies to support her continued growth.

As we transition from our weekly sessions, I tell Ruth that she can schedule sessions at any time for problems that might arise in the future. I thank her for allowing me the honor of sharing this journey with her and tell her that I, too, am changed because of our work together. We say a prayer and bid each other peace on our journeys.

Concluding Comments

Ruth showed great courage in staying faithful to her counseling process. This is still a new healing path for the majority of African American women. By taking this step she is validating a new way of wellness for herself and others. She has even given testimony in her new nondenominational church about the many tools God will use for the healing of our spirits.

Through having a safe place to discuss her feelings, she is able to give herself permission to live more authentically. She now realizes that her past behaviors were motivated by the fear that she would be misunderstood and judged if she expressed her true self. Counseling provided Ruth with the opportunity to explore and claim those things that she has been doing well in her life. She had been so preoccupied with what was going wrong that she could not recognize all the blessings and positive choices interwoven between the challenges. In therapy, she began to question her old patterns and to validate herself through positive self-talk and increased awareness of behaviors that have been effective for her. She has been able to draw on the strength and resiliency of our ancestors. In discussing the middle passage (the slave trade), Ruth felt proud when she realized that she is the descendant of those who survived.

Once she was able to connect with her spiritual side and say out loud that God is a kind, loving, and supportive God, she began to feel a greater sense of self-worth. She is now able to use her spirituality to affirm that she does not need to be all things to all people. Through her biblical studies, she has realized that it is natural to express a full range of emotions, including tears, anger, disappointment, sadness, and most important, love.

Ruth has begun to move through her life in a more mindful way. She has started to walk in the evening with her husband and is making healthier food choices. Her self-image has improved, and she is now living a more authentic life. She understands that life is a journey and she will encounter challenges along the way, but because of the time and effort she has devoted to her therapy, she now has a vast array of tools to cope effectively with whatever obstacles life brings her way.

Jerry Corey's Work With Ruth From a Multicultural Perspective

In my version of conceptualizing Ruth's case from a multicultural and diversity perspective, I am concerned with a number of factors. In the *DVD for Integrative Counseling: The Case of Ruth and Lecturettes,* Session 4 ("Understanding and Addressing Diversity"), I explore with Ruth how our differences might affect our work together. Not only is understanding her culture important, but our differences in age, gender, religious background, and educational background need to be considered. Ruth wonders if I will understand her because of our differences, which is material for exploration. I operate on the assumption that in counseling we can either choose to pay attention to cultural variables or ignore them. However, culture will continue to influence both Ruth's behavior and my behavior, as well as the direction that counseling takes.

It would be impossible for counselors who work with diverse client populations to have a comprehensive and in-depth knowledge of the cultural background of all of their clients. In Ruth's case, I believe she can teach me about those aspects of her culture that are important for us to attend to in our work together. Universal human themes unite people just as much as their differences enrich us all. We all need to receive and give love, to make sense of our psychological pain, and to make significant connections with others. However, in my work with Ruth I need to be aware of specific cultural values that are bound to influence the quality of our interactions. Any difference that has the capacity to create a gap in understanding should be explored in our therapy sessions.

The contributors in this chapter have written in some detail about counseling Ruth from an Asian American, Latina, and African American perspective, so my commentary will be brief. Mere knowledge about certain cultural groups is not adequate training to practice in culturally competent ways. In Ruth's case, I need to see her as a unique individual against the backdrop of her cultural group, the degree to which she has become acculturated, and the level of development of her racial identity.

The Many Faces of Ruth

Let's assume that Ruth is an Asian American. Depending on her degree of acculturation, I want to know something about the values of her country of origin. I may anticipate that she has one foot in her old culture and another foot in her new one. She may experience real conflicts, feeling neither fully Asian nor fully American, and at some points she may be uncertain about the way to integrate the two aspects of her life. She may be slow to disclose personal material, but this is not necessarily a reflection of her unwillingness to cooperate with the counseling venture. Rather, her reluctance is likely to reflect a cultural tradition that has encouraged her to be emotionally reserved. Knowing something about her case and about her background, I am aware that shame and guilt may play a significant role in her behavior. Talking about family matters is often considered shameful and to be avoided. Furthermore, in her culture, stigma and shame may arise over experiencing psychological distress and feeling the need for professional help.

Now let's assume that Ruth is a Latina and that she is cautious in attempting to maintain eye contact with me. It is important to accurately interpret nonverbal behavior, and I would probably err if I assumed that this behavior reflected resistance or evasiveness. Instead, she is behaving in ways she thinks are polite, for direct eye contact could be seen as disrespectful. I need to be patient while developing a working alliance with Ruth as Latinas have a tendency to reveal themselves more slowly than do many Anglo clients. Again, this does not mean that Ruth is being defensive, but it can reflect different cultural norms. She may not relate well to a high level of directness because in her culture she has learned to express herself in more indirect ways.

If Ruth were a Native American and if I were unfamiliar with her culture, I could err by interpreting her quiet behavior as a sign that she was stoic and unemotional. Actually, she may have good reason to be emotionally contained, especially during the initial meeting with a counselor of a different cultural background. Her mistrust does not have to be a sign of paranoia; rather, it can be a realistic reaction based on numerous experiences that have conditioned her to be cautious. If I did not know enough about her culture, it would be ethically imperative either that I learn some of its basic aspects or that I refer her to a counselor who was culturally skilled in this area. I don't burden myself with the unrealistic standard that I should know everything. It would be acceptable to admit to her that I lacked knowledge about her culture and then proceed to find a way to remedy this situation. Openness with a client can certainly be the foundation for a good relationship. Ruth can provide me with some information regarding what would be important for me to know about her cultural background.

Some Final Thoughts

Members of certain ethnic, cultural, and racial groups have encountered more than their share of discrimination based on being different. This factor needs to be addressed in therapy. As an African American, Latina, Native American, Asian American, or Pacific Islander, Ruth will share the experience of institutional oppression. She will know what it means to struggle for empowerment. This experience is bound to be reflected in the dynamics of our therapeutic relationship. I will need to somehow demonstrate my good faith and my ability to enter her world and understand the nature of her concerns. If I ignore these cultural realities, chances are that Ruth will not stay in therapy with me very long. However, I cannot emphasize enough the guiding principle of letting her provide me with the clues for the direction of therapy. In our initial encounter, I will want to know what it was like for her to come to the office and why she is there. Rather than having prior conceptions of what we should be doing in this venture, I will ask her what she wants and why she is seeking help from me at this time in her life. If cultural issues are present, I expect that they will emerge very soon if I am listening sensitively to her and attempting to understand her world.

Questions for Reflection

1. If your cultural background and life experiences are very different from Ruth's, will this present any particular problems in establishing a therapeutic relationship? If you do differ from her on any of these dimensions—gender, race, culture, ethnicity, socioeconomic status, age, value system, religion, spirituality, or sexual orientation—would you feel a need to discuss these differences with her? How might your differences affect your counseling with Ruth? Would any of these differences incline you to refer her to another therapist? What are the ethical considerations in referring Ruth to another therapist?

2. In examining your own belief system and life experiences, do you think you would have any difficulty working therapeutically with any particular racial, ethnic, or cultural group? If you expect that you might have difficulty, what are your concerns, and what might you do about them?

3. What specific aspects about each culture do you feel a need to understand to develop a therapeutic alliance and work effectively with a client? If you do not have this knowledge, how could you go about acquiring it?

4. How important is it that you are similar to your client in each of the following areas: age, gender, race, ethnicity, culture, socioeconomic status, spirituality, religion, values, sexual orientation, ability/disability, education, marital status, and family status?

5. Dr. Kirksey's work with Ruth is based on an integration of spirituality and religion in the counseling process. How important is it to ask clients questions pertaining to their spiritual and religious background during the intake session and the assessment phase?

6. What are some key questions you could ask clients to learn more about their cultural background? Why do you think it is important to learn how clients identify themselves culturally?

7. Cultural competence involves knowledge of your own biases and stereotypes, awareness of other cultural groups and practices, and the skills to form relationships across cultures. What competency area do you think you most need to improve, and how might you go about accomplishing this goal?

8. As Ruth's therapist, how would you respond to the issue of discrimination? What could you do to become more prepared to address this topic?

9. What direct experiences, assumptions, and beliefs do you have about Latinas/Latinos? About Asian Americans? About African Americans? How might this influence your conceptualizations, assessments, and interventions with such individuals?

10. As you consider the three selections on Ruth as a Latina, as an Asian American, and as an African American, what common themes do you notice?

11. What potential challenges do you think you will face in combining concepts from various multicultural perspectives in your work with a client who is culturally different from you?

12. Each of the contributors in this chapter draws from his or her own unique approach when counseling Ruth. What have you learned from these

contributors about how to work with the various facets of culture that you could apply to counseling Ruth? What aspects of the multicultural approach do you find most useful? Which aspects might you want to modify to fit your personal counseling style?

Notes

1. To maintain a broad stance, we will not identify a country of origin for Ruth's parents although we recognize the importance of such information with an actual client.
2. Gill, R. M., & Vásquez, C. I. (1996). *The María paradox: How Latinas can merge Old World traditions with New World self-esteem.* New York: G. P. Putnam.
3. Horvath, A. O., & Greenberg, L. S. (1989). Development and validation of the Working Alliance Inventory. *Journal of Counseling Psychology, 36,* 223–233.
4. Beck, A. T., Steer, R. A., & Brown, G. K. (2000). *BDI-FastScreen for medical patients.* San Antonio, TX: Harcourt.
5. Meyer, T., Miller, M., Metzger, R., & Borkovec, T. (1990). Development and validation of the Penn State Worry Questionnaire. *Behaviour Research and Therapy, 28,* 487–495.
6. Poundstone, W. (2003). *How would you move Mt. Fuji? Microsoft's cult of the puzzle—How the world's smartest companies select the most creative thinkers.* Boston: Little, Brown.

CHAPTER FOURTEEN

Integrative Approaches and Developing Your Own Therapeutic Style

This chapter is devoted to integrative approaches in counseling Ruth. John Norcross and I demonstrate how we would work with the themes of Ruth's life from a variety of therapeutic perspectives. Let me emphasize that no one single approach has a monopoly on the truth. There are many paths to the goal of providing Ruth with insight and mobilizing her resources so that she can take constructive action to give new direction to her life. Diverse therapeutic perspectives often complement one another. First, let's hear from John Norcross.

An Integrative Therapist's Perspective on Ruth
by John C. Norcross, PhD, ABPP

Introduction
Rivalry among systems of counseling has a long and undistinguished history, dating back to Freud. In the infancy of the field, therapy systems, like battling siblings, competed for attention and affection. Psychoanalysts, Adlerians, existentialists, and behaviorists, to mention a few, have traditionally operated from within their own particular theoretical frameworks, often to the point of being blind to alternative conceptualizations and potentially more effective methods.

Fortunately, the ideological cold war has waned and integration has become a therapeutic mainstay. *Eclecticism*—or the favored term, *integration*—is now well established as the most frequent orientation of mental health professionals.[1] Most psychotherapists now acknowledge the inadequacies of any one theoretical system and the potential value of others. Indeed, many young students of psychotherapy express surprise when apprised of the ideological cold war of the preceding generations.

Psychotherapy integration is characterized by dissatisfaction with single-school approaches and the concomitant desire to look across and beyond school boundaries to see how clients can benefit from other forms of behavior change. Integration refers not only to combining diverse systems of psychotherapy but also to blending psychotherapy with medication, spirituality, exercise, social support, sociopolitical advocacy, self-help, and other curative forces. Improving the effectiveness, efficiency, and applicability of psychotherapy is the goal of integration.

Many roads lead to an integrative Rome. The most popular roads or pathways to psychotherapy integration are *common factors, technical eclecticism, theoretical integration,* and *assimilative integration.*[2] My own integrative approach borrows from each of these roads in tailoring psychotherapy to the unique needs of the individual client, in this case, Ms. Ruth Walton. We strive to create a new therapy for each client by tailoring it to the particulars of the client according to general principles identified by research and experience. Remember, the integrative mandate is to improve treatment effectiveness, not to entertain the therapist or simply to borrow techniques from different schools.

Initial Consultation

As every counselor knows, and as the research demonstrates,[3] the therapy relationship is pivotal to the ultimate success of psychotherapy. I start in my initial contact with Ruth and with our nascent relationship using some standard open-ended questions.

> THERAPIST: Ms. Walton, what brings you here today? What do you want to accomplish?
>
> RUTH: Well, I don't know where to start. There's so much that has been troubling me, especially these anxiety attacks.

We begin with Ms. Walton's story and with respect. I address the client as Ms. Walton until, or if, she grants me permission to call her Ruth. In return, I request that she address me as "John" if she is so inclined (and not all clients are). Ruth begins to present her narrative and concerns. My primary task in the early sessions is to cultivate a warm, empathic, and supportive relationship, one in which Ruth will feel understood and prized. Using these Rogerian facilitative conditions increases Ruth's comfort and decreases her ambivalence.

Following about 30 minutes of Ruth's concerns and basic history, I inquire about her history of psychotherapy. Upon learning that this is her first experience and hearing the anxiety in her voice about pursuing therapy, I begin to explore and define our relationship.

> THERAPIST: How would a psychotherapist be most useful to you? What would he or she do? And not do?
>
> RUTH: Well, I am not sure. I suppose I most want a therapist to give me advice on how to resolve my problems.

Ruth's answer naturally segues into an exploration of our respective roles and her active collaboration in psychotherapy. She intellectually understands the importance of an active client but, emotionally, feels inadequate to the task.

RUTH: I probably won't make a very good client. I set goals but then cannot move on them.

THERAPIST: As you say that Ruth, I am struck by how often this hour you have put yourself down, saying self-deprecating and defeatist things. Are you aware of that too?

RUTH: Oh, not really. It seems that I cannot help myself. I probably do it automatically.

THERAPIST: What would you say to a therapy agreement that I politely note those times you put yourself down? Would you find that helpful in here?

RUTH: Yes.

THERAPIST: And once you become aware of it, I am certain that you will be able to control it.

Thus psychotherapy begins with both an explanation and an experience of the way we might proceed. To ensure that therapy proceeds with Ruth's informed consent and active collaboration, we jointly develop three between-session activities. First, Ruth will consider her preferences for a therapist. What would the therapist do and what should he or she avoid? Might Ruth be better served in her first counseling experience with a female therapist? Second, at my request, Ruth agrees to complete a life history inventory to systematically cover the essential ground. We will review her responses next session. And third, Ruth will prioritize her treatment goals. Among the desirable changes, which would she like to focus on at the outset?

All of these activities are designed to jumpstart the therapy process and to activate Ruth's collaboration despite her inexperience and understandable ambivalence about psychotherapy. Instead of only talking to Ruth about empowerment, we design therapy to actualize it. Instead of only offering Ruth support and affirmation, we contract for Ruth to offer it to herself.

Assessment of Ruth

As an integrative therapist, I am less concerned about formal diagnoses and more concerned with understanding Ruth in all of her uniqueness and complexity. At our second session, Ruth and I review her completed life history inventory and realize that we desire additional information on the breadth of her psychological suffering. I offer Ruth the opportunity to take a broadband psychological test—typically the Minnesota Multiphasic Personality Inventory or the Millon Clinical Multiaxial Inventory—on the office computer between sessions. She agrees, commenting, "I probably will look like a big mess and a bad client on it." I smile and playfully comment, "There you go again." This leads into a productive 10 minutes in which Ruth observes impressive early gains in catching and reducing her self-deprecation outside of our sessions. I congratulate Ruth on her early success and, in addition, on recognizing the success.

It is difficult to diagnose a person on paper and by long distance, but the severity and chronicity of Ruth's problems exceed those associated with an adjustment disorder. The clinical history, her autobiography, her life history inventory, and the psychological test results converge on a series of diagnosable disorders. On Axis I, these would probably entail "panic disorder without agoraphobia," "dysthymic disorder" (chronic dissatisfaction and mild depression), marital dissatisfaction or partner relational problem, partner–child relational problem (particularly with Jennifer), and a question of binge eating or an atypical eating disorder. But I would be careful not to over diagnose her eating behavior without additional information. On Axis II, Ruth probably suffers from a "dependent personality disorder" (living for others) and, on Axis III, overweight/obesity. Her physician has ruled out medical origins for her anxiety and depression. Ruth is also beset by myriad Axis IV psychosocial problems, including problems with her primary support group and occupational problems.

Most clients crave a coherent picture of their disorders and their origins. I offer Ruth a formulation on how her multitudinous problems are interconnected. For example, depression and anxiety are highly correlated, and in turn, both are perpetuated by dependency and unassertiveness. Relational problems and parenting conflicts are part and parcel of this constellation of problems. Following the assessment, I offer some tentative statements about the multiple, intertwined origins of her disorders. Such feedback usefully mentions the formative experiences of childhood (without encouraging pessimism or victimhood), leading to skill deficits and thinking patterns, intersecting genetic vulnerabilities (in cases of family psychiatric history), and culminating in a vicious cycle of life choices and behavioral enactments.

Ruth's autobiography contains several hints of an abusive father and definite reasons to explore the possibility of physical and sexual abuse as a child. Ruth's autobiography does not indicate any abuse, nor does it specifically disavow abuse. I wonder about a history of sexual abuse given her father's punitive punishments and the dynamics of her family of origin. I sensitively inquire about this possibility along with Ruth's own adult sexual functioning in the next session or two as our alliance solidifies.

With all clients, I conduct an assessment of their strengths. Ruth is encouraged to nominate her personal strengths, and I comment on some that she may have missed. She raised four children and is dedicated; she devoted herself to others and is responsible; she broke from a fundamentalist church to pursue her own values and is courageous; she described her life situation and is reasonably aware; she self-described herself as a late-blooming questioner and is open to the process. And she is here, in psychotherapy, despite her father's vehement objections and her husband's skepticism.

But assessment falls short for treatment purposes if we stop with disorders and strengths. It is frequently more important to know the person who has the disorder than the disorder the person has. What about Ruth as a person? What are her treatment goals, her treatment preferences, her readiness to change, and her personality style? Ruth has been so busy tending to others and concentrating on her problems that we do not hear much from her as a person.

Decades of empirical research have identified several cross-diagnostic client characteristics that serve as powerful indicators for treatment selection. Three of these are the *client's preferences,*[4] *stage of change,* and *resistance level.* For selecting the relationship and treatment to offer Ruth, these are as important as, if not more important than, her disorders.

❧ Ruth's Preferences and Goals

Ruth is hesitant initially to give voice to her preferences, consistent with her core dependency and deference to authorities. With encouragement, she brings a list into the second session as part of her between-session homework.

RUTH: It was hard to decide what I want from a therapist. In fact, it seems a little presumptuous. After all, you are the expert, right?

THERAPIST: Right, I am the expert on psychotherapy and behavior change. You are the expert on Ruth and what she wants. We will work together as a team pursuing your goals. I hear that it was difficult— and maybe new—to figure out what you want. Yes?

RUTH: Oh, yes. But it feels good.

THERAPIST: Feels frightening *and* good. That's how many of your changes might feel at first.

RUTH: Well, I wrote on my list that I would like to stay with you. I feel comfortable with you, and I don't know whether I would feel that with a woman therapist. And I would like you to push me a bit. I really liked doing things between appointments and our agreement for you to point out when I put myself down.

THERAPIST: I am heartened that you are finding your own voice, Ruth, and I will remember to end sessions with us developing between-session goals. Sounds like that will fit both of us just fine.

RUTH [*Smiling*]: Yes. And you know, almost nobody has ever asked me what I want.

THERAPIST: That's how therapy is a special relationship. It is all about you, your life, your growth.

Ruth decides to focus in early sessions on her panic attacks and her dependency. "The other stuff is less important, but I do want to get to them." It would be naive to assume that clients always know what they want and what is best for them. But if clinicians had more respect for the notion that their clients often sense how they can best be served, fewer mismatches would ensue.

❧ Ruth's Stage of Change

People enter the consulting room literally in different places or stages. Change unfolds over a series of stages: precontemplation, contemplation, preparation, action, and maintenance.[5] Ruth presents in the contemplation stage: aware of her problems and seriously thinking about overcoming them, but not yet taking specific action. People can remain stuck in the contemplation stage for years, as in Ruth's case. This is contemplation: knowing where you want to go, but not quite ready yet to go there.

Ruth presents for psychotherapy as a chronic contemplator seeking to move into action. She has failed resolutions to begin an exercise program, dragged her feet in becoming an elementary school teacher, and in general taken a postdated check from life. In her autobiography she wonders, "What if I open Pandora and too much comes out, and I get even more overwhelmed than I already ar

Psychotherapy is more effective when the treatment strategy and thera relationship are tailored to the client's stage of change and then evolve as the client moves along the stages during the course of treatment. With contemplators, my role as therapist is akin to a Socratic teacher who encourages clients to achieve their own insights into their condition. As Ruth enters the action stage, my stance is more like that of an experienced, supportive coach who has been through many crucial matches and can provide a fine game plan. The treatment methods of choice during contemplation are more exploratory, but those same methods are contraindicated once Ruth enters the action stage. Then, specific cognitive and behavioral methods are demonstrably more effective. The stages of change systematically guide me in tailoring the treatment and my relationship with Ruth.

Ruth's Resistance Level A person's tendency to react in opposition to external influence is an indicator for how directive a therapeutic stance to take. Research[6] has reliably found that directive methods work best among clients who have relatively low resistance, whereas nondirective methods work best with clients with high levels of resistance. Ruth, with a lifelong history of dependency and low reactance, will respond best to a directive stance on the part of the therapist. Moreover, this is in line with her treatment goals and therapist preferences.

Proceeding in a directive fashion in synch with Ruth's preferences and in accord with the outcome research is likely to enhance her eventual outcome. At the same time, we must be careful not to reenact, in conscious and unconscious ways, Ruth's unassertive and subservient relationship with the powerful therapist. Thus I will broach this concern early with Ruth and contract for an evolving relationship in terms of our respective roles.

> THERAPIST: I am comfortable in following your preference for a directive therapist with an action plan and using between-session goals, Ruth. Your preference also agrees with the research. My concern is that doing so may reinforce in here your tendency to behave dependently and defer to others. Does that make sense?
>
> RUTH: Yes. I haven't thought about it that way before. Hmm.
>
> THERAPIST: Might I suggest this: In the short run, I can be more directive, in the lead, so that you can become less panicky and depressed. Once that happens, in the longer run, then we ask and teach you to become more assertive, more in charge in our sessions. How does that sound?

This distinction between mediating goals and ultimate goals is almost always enthusiastically received. The mediating goal is to reduce symptomatic distress; the ultimate goal is to restructure interpersonal behavior. Psychotherapy can be more directive in the short term to work toward more mature and assertive relationships in the long term.

ree client characteristics—treatment preferences, stage of change,
level—in addition to diagnoses are evidence-based means of
ting treatment and enhancing eventual success. These cross-diagnostic
cteristics also underscore the potential for psychotherapy integration.
rapists will be directive *and* less directive according to the client's level of resistance; therapists will incorporate awareness-enhancing *and* action-oriented
methods depending on the client's stage of change. In this respect, ostensibly
contradictory therapy methods are, in fact, complementary when tailored to
the individual client.

Goals of Therapy

Adherents of single theoretical perspectives frequently but unknowingly dictate
therapy goals to their clients. They behave like the legendary Greek innkeeper,
Procrusteus, who owned a single hotel bed and stretched short guests and
trimmed tall guests to fit that bed. Clients are all too often fit to the one-size,
Procrustean bed when they receive the same assessment and the identical
treatment.

By contrast, integrative practitioners favor fitting the therapy to the client
and creating a new therapy for each client. It is Ruth's therapy, and her goals
should predominate. I value clinical theory and therapists' preferences, but
they should assume lower priority than the client's goals.

Ongoing assessment will, of course, refine Ruth's goals, and her early success will lead us to further goals. Ruth's immediate goals are to reduce her
panic attacks and dependency; phrased more positively, to increase calm/
relaxation and assertion/autonomy. That is where we begin, that is where Ruth's
commitment and action lie, and that is where initial success awaits us.

Therapeutic Process and Procedures

Early on I introduce panic control therapy (PCT), a multicomponent treatment that includes elements of cognitive therapy, behavior therapy, and exposure therapy. I educate Ruth about the nature and physiological aspects of
panic, train her in slow breathing, initiate cognitive restructuring directed at
negative cognitions related to panic, and ask her to repeatedly expose herself to feared physical sensations associated with panic. The efficacy of this
treatment has been demonstrated in numerous clinical trials; on average,
about 80% of PCT clients are panic free post-treatment, compared with 40%
of clients receiving relaxation training alone and 30% of clients on a waiting
list.[7] This treatment also fits well with Ruth's preferences for active methods,
between-session goals, and a directive therapist stance.

Within 8 to 10 sessions, Ruth is free of panic and brimming with confidence.
She succeeds without short-term anxiolytic medication, which she would accept
"only as a last resort." Ruth is ready to dive headlong into her dependency, which,
not surprisingly, is comorbid with panic disorder. We begin with education about
her unassertive, approval-seeking style through bibliotherapy. I offer Ruth a
selection of assertion self-help resources rated highly by mental health professionals.[8] In the existential tradition, I ask her to actively choose instead of
passively accepting a prescription. She selects one, and we begin with assertion

training in the behavioral and feminist traditions: exploring differences betwee. assertion and aggression; cognitive restructuring for her inevitable guilt when assertive; role-playing specific responses in session; tape recording her during role plays to fine tune her voice and words; and jointly developing homework assignments with family members.

"We are really cooking," Ruth enthusiastically asserts in session 15. Her panic is eliminated, and despite some anxious moments in challenging assertion situations, she is successful in asserting herself. I punctuate her success, comment on her newfound self, and reintroduce our agreement that she begin to exercise more direction in our therapy session.

Assertion is a goal not only outside therapy but within it as well. Now that Ruth has gained more confidence and our therapy relationship is firmly established, one method to engender assertion in the therapy hour is to request that Ruth ask for something in each session. Our exchange goes like this.

> THERAPIST: If you agree, let's spend a few moments on your asserting yourself in here, with me. Your therapy is going terrifically well, but we can always improve on something. What would you like to do differently—perhaps something I could do less of or something we can do more of to your liking?

> RUTH: It's going well. . . . I can't think of anything.

> THERAPIST: I appreciate that it is difficult and also appreciate that you would not want to offend me. Yet it is your therapy, and one of your goals is for you to be assertive in here, not only at home. What are you experiencing now as I say that?

> RUTH: Fear, fear that you might dislike me or abandon me if I complain.

Ruth's underlying identity or schema as inadequate is activated, which requires extensive emotional processing, cognitive restructuring, and active practice over the next five or six sessions. The emotion-focused work follows in the experiential or Gestalt tradition, including a few sessions with two-chair dialogues. The active practice occurs in her life and in our sessions, as we agree that Ruth will ask in every session for "something different," not necessarily a complaint about therapy or me. Ruth is able to do so, requesting that we spend more time role-playing assertive responses and that I not ask at the end of each session, "When would you like to schedule our next session?" She informs me that she understands why I do it—"it helps clients to take control of their therapy"— but she finds it annoying because I already know that she desires weekly sessions. I thank her for her candid feedback, agree that I have taken a good idea too far, and pledge to stop asking each session. Voila!

Ruth's emerging self is now confronted with endless choices in her life and in therapy. Should she remain in school? What about her marriage? What would she like to tackle in therapy? I participate in these discussions, of course, but ultimately Ruth will decide, knowing that I support her and her decisions. Here is how Ruth probably opts to tackle other areas on her own schedule:

• *Marital dissatisfaction:* Now that her distressing symptoms have remitted and her assertion skills are enhanced, Ruth opts to invite her husband in for several conjoint sessions to improve their communication and to clarify expectations about her education and occupation. "I am finishing school, and whether he likes it or not, I will become a teacher." Ruth startles her husband and me (ever the optimist) by asking her husband in the third conjoint session to devote the next session to their sex life. Voila again!

Sequencing Ruth's various goals in psychotherapy turns out to be crucial. I had casually suggested to Ruth earlier in therapy that perhaps it was time to invite her husband in for conjoint sessions. Ruth insightfully observed that, if we had done so early, she would have communicated as a submissive spouse requesting permission rather than as an assertive partner negotiating the relationship. Her wisdom shows us the way.

- *Discipline with Jennifer:* At the intersection of her assertion work and conjoint sessions, Ruth declares that she is determined to parent more assertively and insists that her husband back her up. Ruth consumes a self-help book on effective parenting in a few days and then invites Jennifer in to three sessions, each a month apart. Using communication and family therapy methods, I assist them in expressing feelings, repairing ruptures, and arranging a contingency contract. Jennifer will follow the signed behavior contract with her mother; compliance brings privileges (such as more freedoms) and violation brings punishments (such as being grounded). Both Ruth and Jennifer report sustained improvement in their relationship and household compliance. Relationship voila!

- *Weight reduction and body image:* Ruth tackles this goal reluctantly and with some honest resignation about the futility of quick weight-loss schemes. I suggest that perhaps our goal could first be to initiate an exercise plan and to confront gender-linked stereotypes about body image. With the money saved by moving from weekly to biweekly therapy sessions, Ruth decides to join a women-only exercise club, where she makes friends and consults a dietician monthly. We also spend several sessions examining, in the feminist tradition, the detrimental impact of social pressures on women's body image. Ever the eager student, Ruth pursues another self-help resource on overeating and gender.

- *Toward growth and pleasure:* As therapy winds down—our sessions now every 3 weeks—and as Ruth consolidates her progress, I wonder about her future. I gently suggest that the best protection to slipping back into panic, depression, dependency, stagnant relationships, and inactivity is self-nurturance. Ruth thinks on this for a few weeks and then, at our next session presents a self-nurturance list. This includes ongoing exercise at the gym, regular participation in her new church (which she finds comforting and calming), and a "girl's night" out with school friends at least once a month.

Over the course of Ruth's therapy, her efforts and success are remarkable. She transforms herself from a panicky, tired, underappreciated farm horse into a reassured, vibrant, affirming Pegasus. What psychotherapists do (and do not do) matters, but it matters less than Ruth's actions. I revel in the pride of her treatment success and remind myself of the blessings of being a psychotherapist. I express my admiration of and to Ruth, and of her ability to use what I offered. I anticipate the mutual sadness, the sweet sorrow of our termination.

Concluding Comments

The case of Ruth vividly demonstrates the value of psychotherapy integration. Her treatment combines individual sessions, conjoint couples sessions, sex therapy sessions, and mother-daughter sessions. Her integrative psychotherapy entails relationship stances and treatment methods associated with the psychodynamic, experiential, person-centered, cognitive, behavioral, exposure, systemic, and feminist traditions. Her integrative treatment blends psychotherapy, self-help, exercise, social support, and spirituality. Her case also usefully warns us of the danger of imposing narrow theories and singular treatments on complex clients. Had Ruth been offered only medication, only individual therapy, or only self-help, it seems doubtful that she would progress as quickly or as far. Beware of the propensity of theories to approach the proverbial elephant and discover only the elephant's trunk, leg, or tail. Let us discover, celebrate, and treat all of our clients in their glorious complexity.

I want to emphasize the centrality of a systematic, evidence-based integration in clinical work. Integration is more than borrowing techniques from various therapeutic approaches; it is a thoughtful and research-informed approach that seeks to improve treatment effectiveness. Gone are the days of haphazard eclecticism; we live in an era of *evidence-based practice*.[9] We conduct—and our clients deserve—a psychotherapy that integrates the best available research with clinical expertise in the context of patient characteristics, culture, and preferences. Research can increasingly guide us in creating a nurturing therapy relationship and in tailoring treatment to individual clients beyond their diagnoses; three examples illustrated with Ruth are her treatment preferences, stage of change, and resistance level. Each psychotherapist will establish his or her own integrative style on the basis of values, personalities, and life experiences. Let us also incorporate the research evidence into the integrative mix. In the end, our ethical responsibility is to the client's welfare; we strive to create for each client a new therapy that works.

Questions for Reflection

1. Dr. Norcross mentions some of the advantages of an integrative approach. What are your thoughts about the potential advantages, if any, of using an integrative perspective as a basis for your counseling practice rather than a single-school approach? What possible disadvantages, if any, do you see in psychotherapy integration?

2. Dr. Norcross states that treatment goals, stage of change, and resistance level are important client characteristics to consider when working with Ruth. To what extent would you consider each of these factors if you were working with Ruth? Explain.

3. Dr. Norcross writes: "We conduct—and our clients deserve—a psychotherapy that integrates the best available research with clinical expertise in the context of patient characteristics, culture, and preferences." What value do you place on understanding and incorporating evidence-based research in your style of counseling?

Jerry Corey's Integrative Approach to Working With Ruth

John Norcross demonstrated his way of drawing from multiple theoretical perspectives in counseling Ruth. He pointed out that you need to consider your preferences, values, life experiences, and personality when developing your own integrative style of counseling. In this concluding piece, I demonstrate my vision of applying an integrative perspective in counseling Ruth. For an illustration of my work with Ruth from an integrative perspective, see Session 9 ("An Integrative Perspective") of the *DVD for Integrative Counseling: The Case of Ruth and Lecturettes.*[10] This segment of the DVD is a useful supplement to this chapter.

Each therapy approach has something unique to offer in understanding Ruth. I draw from a combination of approaches to work with Ruth on a *thinking, feeling,* and *behaving* basis. Table 14.1 shows what I might draw from the various therapies as I conceptualize Ruth's case and work with her from an integrative perspective. But I am not suggesting that you incorporate concepts and techniques from each theory, for doing this can be overly ambitious. As I describe how I would proceed with Ruth based on the information presented in her autobiography and the additional data from the various theoretical perspectives chapters, parenthetical comments indicate from what theoretical orientations I am borrowing concepts and techniques in any given segment of work. Thus, in addition to seeing a sample of my style of working with Ruth, you will have a running commentary on what I am doing, why I am using particular techniques, and the direction of Ruth's therapy. As you read, think about what you might do that is similar to or different from my approach.[11]

TABLE 14.1 Major Areas of Focus in Ruth's Therapy

Orientation	Areas of Focus
Psychoanalytic Therapy	My focus is on ways in which Ruth is repeating her past in her present relationships. I have a particular interest in how she brings her experiences with her father into the session with me. I concentrate on her reactions to me because working with transference is a major way to produce insight. I am also interested in her dreams, any resistance or defensiveness that shows up in the sessions, and other clues to her unconscious processes. One of my main goals is to assist her in bringing to awareness buried memories and experiences, which I assume have a current influence on her.
Adlerian Therapy	My focus is on determining what Ruth's lifestyle is. To do this, I examine her interpretation of her early childhood experiences through her early recollections. My main interest is in determining what her goals and priorities in life are. I assume that what she is striving toward is equally as valid as her past

dynamics. The past, present, and future are all important. Therapy consists of doing a comprehensive assessment, helping her understand her dynamics, and then helping her define new goals.

Existential Therapy	My focus is on exploring with Ruth the meaning in her life. What does she want in her life? I am interested in the anxiety she feels, her emptiness, and the ways in which she has allowed others to choose for her. How can she begin to exercise her freedom? I assume that our relationship will be a key factor in helping her take actual risks in changing.
Person-Centered Therapy	I avoid planning and structuring the sessions because I trust Ruth to initiate a direction for therapy. If I listen, reflect, empathize, and respond to her, she will be able to clarify her struggles. Although she may be only dimly aware of her feelings at the beginning of therapy, she will move toward increased clarity as I accept her fully, without judgment. I am concerned with creating a climate of openness, trust, caring, understanding, and acceptance. Based on this solid relationship, she can move forward and grow.
Gestalt Therapy	My focus is on what is emerging in Ruth's awareness. I am guided by the shifts in her awareness, and together we create experiments that grow out of her awareness and her struggles. The emphasis is on our dialogue and the quality of our contact in the therapy sessions. I ask Ruth to bring her feelings, reactions, and experiences of not being accepted into the present by reliving them rather than by merely talking about past events. I am mainly interested in helping her experience her feelings fully, not in developing insight or speculating about why she behaves as she does. The key focus is on how Ruth is behaving and what she is experiencing.
Behavior Therapy	Initially I am interested in doing a thorough assessment of Ruth's current behavior. I ask her to monitor what she is doing so that we can have baseline data. We then develop concrete goals to guide our work. I draw on a wide range of cognitive and behavioral techniques to help her achieve her goals: stress reduction techniques, assertion training, role rehearsals, modeling, coaching, systematic desensitization, meditation, mindfulness, and relaxation methods. The emphasis is on learning new coping behaviors that she can use in everyday situations. She practices these in our sessions and elsewhere.

(continues)

TABLE 14.1 Major Areas of Focus in Ruth's Therapy *(continued)*

Orientation	Areas of Focus
Cognitive Behavior Therapy	My interest is on Ruth's internal dialogue and her thinking processes. I uncover the ways in which she is creating her problems through self-indoctrination and retention of beliefs that are not rational or functional. By use of Socratic dialogue I assist her in detecting her faulty thinking, to learn ways of correcting her distortions, and to substitute more effective self-statements and beliefs. I use a wide range of cognitive, behavioral, and emotive techniques to accomplish our goals.
Reality Therapy	Our work is guided by the principles of choice theory. Key questions are "What are you doing now?" and "Is this behavior helping you?" Once Ruth has evaluated her own current behavior and has decided what she wants to change, we collaboratively make plans. I get a commitment from her to follow through with these plans.
Feminist Therapy	My interest is to provide a context for Ruth to evaluate how oppression may be operating in her life today. As a woman she has learned to subordinate her wishes to care for her family, which makes it difficult for her to identify and honor what she wants out of therapy or her life. Because oppression profoundly influences Ruth's beliefs, choices, and perceptions, we will examine the cultural context of her gender-role socialization and how that is influencing her behavior now.
Postmodern Approaches	Rather than focusing on problems, I ask Ruth to look for exceptions to her problems or for times when she functioned without a specific problem. I also strive to get her to externalize her problem from the person that she is. The crux of Ruth's therapy is to conceive of the kind of life she would like to have, a life without the problems that are bringing her into therapy. The emphasis is on finding solutions rather than talking about problems.
Family Systems Therapy	My focus is on the degree to which Ruth has become differentiated from her significant others. We also examine ways in which anxiety is perpetuated by rigid interactional patterns and by her family's structure, and ways in which she can balance her role as a mother with taking care of herself.

Multicultural Perspectives   At the initial stage of counseling, and throughout the rest of the counseling process, I keep in mind how Ruth's culture is affecting her current behavior. I want to understand Ruth's subjective world and work within this framework. For the duration of therapy, she is asked to assess what she is getting from our work together, and I will make adjustments based on her input. From this perspective, counseling is focused on both her inner world and how the outer world is influencing her.

Initial Stages of Work With Ruth

I read Ruth's autobiography before our initial session, and I feel excited about working with her. I like her ability to pinpoint many of her concerns, and the information she provides is rich with possibilities. From her autobiography alone I do not have a clear idea of where our journey together will take us, for a lot will depend on *how far* Ruth wants to go and what she is willing to explore. However, reading Ruth's autobiography has given me many ideas of how I want to proceed, which I describe next.[12]

Our Beginning   I assume that Ruth, too, has some anxiety about initiating therapy. I want to provide her with the opportunity to talk about what it is like for her to come to the office today. That in itself provides the direction for part of our session. I want to get an idea of what has brought her to therapy. What is going on in her life that motivates her to seek therapy? What does she most hope for as a result of this venture? I structure the initial session so that she can talk about her expectations and about her fears, hopes, ambivalent feelings, and so forth. Because Ruth's trust in me will be an important part of the therapy process, I give her the chance to ask me how I will work with her. I do not believe in making therapy into a mysterious adventure. I am convinced that Ruth will get more from her therapy if she knows how it works, if she knows the nature of her responsibilities and mine, and if she clearly identifies what she wants from this process.

The Contract   I begin formulating a working contract that will give some direction to our sessions. As a part of this contract, I discuss what I see as my main responsibilities and functions, as well as Ruth's responsibilities in the process. I want her to know at the outset that I expect her to be an active party in this relationship, and I tell her that I function in an active and directive way (which is characteristic of most of the cognitive, behavioral, and action-oriented therapies).

I see therapy as a significant project—an investment in the self—and I think Ruth has a right to know what she can expect to gain as well as some of the potential risks. I begin by getting some sense of her goals. Although she is vague at first, I work with Ruth to help her define her goals as specifically and concretely as possible.

❧ Ruth's Self-Presentation   As a way of beginning the counseling process, I see value in first letting Ruth give her presentation of self in the way she chooses. How she walks into the office, her nonverbal language, her mannerisms, her style of speech, the details she chooses to reveal, and what she decides to relate and not to relate provide me with a valuable perspective from which to understand her. I am interested in how Ruth perceives the events in her life and how she feels in her subjective world. (This is especially important in the existential and person-centered models and in the postmodern approaches.) If I do too much structuring initially, I will interfere with her typical style of presenting herself. So I am mainly concerned with listening and letting her know what I am hearing.

I want to avoid the tendency to talk too much during this initial session. Being fully present in the therapy session and giving Ruth my sincere attention will pay rich dividends in terms of the potential for therapy. If I listen well, I will get a good sense of what she is coming to therapy for. If I fail to listen accurately and sensitively, there is a risk of going with the first problem she states instead of waiting and listening to discover the depth of her experience.

❧ Gathering Data   I did not begin the session by asking Ruth questions pertaining to her life history, but after Ruth talks about what brought her to therapy at this particular time I ask questions to fill in the gaps. This method gives a more comprehensive picture of how she views her life now, as well as events that she considers significant in her past. Rather than making it a question-and-answer session, I like the idea of using an autobiographical approach, in which Ruth writes about the critical turning points in her life, events from her childhood and adolescent years, relationships with parents and siblings, school experiences, current struggles, and future goals and aspirations, to mention a few. I ask her what she thinks would be useful for her to recall and focus on and what she imagines would be useful to me in gaining a better picture of her subjective world. In this way she does some reflecting and sorting out of life experiences outside of the session, she takes an active role in deciding what her personal goals will be for therapy, and I have access to rich material that will give me ideas of where and how to proceed with her.

Therapy Proceeds

I favor integrating cognitive work into therapy sessions and recommend some books to Ruth to supplement her therapy. These may include novels, books that deal with central areas of concern to her personally, and something on the nature of therapy. For example, I suggest that she read some books about women facing midlife crises, about parent–child relationships, about enhancing one's marriage, about sex, and about special topics related to her concerns. I find that this type of reading provides a good catalyst for self-examination, especially if these books are read in a personal way—meaning that Ruth would apply their themes to her life.

❧ Clarifying Therapy Goals   During the beginning stages, I assist Ruth in getting a clearer grasp of what she most wants from therapy, as well as seeing some steps she can begin to take in attaining her objectives. Like most clients, Ruth is rather global in stating her goals in her autobiography, so I work with her on becoming more concrete. When she looks in the mirror, Ruth says she does not like what she sees. She would like to have a better self-image and body-image and be more confident. I am interested in knowing specifically what she does not like, the ways in which she now lacks confidence, and what it feels like for her to confront herself by looking at herself and talking to me about what she sees.

Ruth reports that she would like to have more fun in her life. She can be helped to pinpoint specific instances in which she is overly serious and not having fun. We can further define what she would like to be doing that she considers being fun. We consistently move from general to specific; the more concrete she is, the greater are her chances of attaining what she wants.[13]

⚘ Importance of the Client–Therapist Relationship   One of the most significant factors determining the degree to which Ruth will attain her goals is the therapeutic relationship that she and I will create. Therapy is not something the therapist does to a passive client, using skills and techniques. Although I have expertise with respect to therapeutic interventions, Ruth is clearly the expert on her own life. I operate on the premise that therapy will be productive to the extent that it is a collaborative venture. Furthermore, Ruth will get the most from her therapy if she knows how the therapeutic process works. I strive to demystify the therapy process by providing information, securing her informed consent, sharing with her my perceptions of what is going on in the relationship, and by making her an active partner in both assessment and treatment phases. I am concerned with the potentially harmful uses of power dynamics in the client–therapist relationship, and I strive to build mutuality and a sense of partnership into the therapeutic endeavor.

Therapy is a deeply personal relationship that Ruth can use for her learning. The person I am is just as important as my knowledge of counseling theory and the level of my skills. Although I value using techniques effectively and have a theoretical base from which to draw a range of techniques, this ability becomes meaningless in the absence of a relationship between Ruth and me that is characterized by mutual respect and trust. Some of the questions that I am concerned with in forming our relationships are: To what degree can I be real with Ruth? To what degree can I hear what she says and accept her in a nonjudgmental way? To what degree can I respect and care for her? To what degree can I allow myself to enter her subjective world? To what degree am I aware of my own experiencing as I am with her, and how willing am I to share my feelings and thoughts with her? An authentic relationship is vital at the initial stages of therapy, and it must be maintained during all stages if therapy is to be effective.[14]

Working With Ruth in Cognitive, Emotive, and Behavioral Ways

My integrative style is a blend of concepts and techniques from many therapeutic approaches. As a basis for selecting techniques to employ with Ruth, I look at her as a *thinking, feeling,* and *behaving* person. Although I may have to describe the various aspects of what I am doing separately here, keep in mind that I tend to work in an integrated fashion. Thus I would not work with Ruth's cognitions, then move ahead to her feelings, and finally proceed to behaviors and specific action programs. All of these dimensions would be interrelated. When I am working with Ruth on a cognitive level (such as dealing with decisions she has made or one of her values), I am also concerned about the feelings generated in her at the moment and about exploring them with her. And in the background I am thinking of what she might actually *do* about the thoughts and feelings she is expressing. This *doing* would involve new behaviors that she can try in the session to deal with a problem and new skills that she can take outside and apply to problems she encounters in real-life situations. (As a basis for this integrative style, I am drawing on the cognitive and emotional insight-oriented approach of psychoanalysis; on the experiential therapies, which stress the expression and experiencing of feelings; on the cognitive therapies, which pay attention to the client's thinking processes, affecting behavior and beliefs; and on the action-oriented therapies, which stress the importance of creating a plan for behavioral change.)[15]

Exploring Ruth's Fears Related to Therapy   Ruth begins a session by talking about her fears of coming to know herself and by expressing her ambivalent feelings toward therapy:

> RUTH: Before I made the decision to enter therapy, I had worked pretty hard at keeping problems tucked away. I lived by compartmentalizing my life, and that way nothing overwhelmed me. But the reading I'm doing, writing in my journal, thinking about my life, talking about my feelings and experiences—all this is making me uncomfortable. I'm getting more and more anxious. I suppose I'm afraid of what I might discover.

From an existential perspective, I see this anxiety as realistic, and even useful. I surely do not want to merely reassure Ruth that everything will turn out for the best if she will only trust me and stay in therapy. I want to explore in depth with her the decision she must now make. There are risks attached to the process of looking at her life in an honest way. Although she has security now, she is paying the price in boredom and low self-respect. Yet her restricted existence is safe. The attractions of getting to know herself better and the possibilities for exercising choice in her life can be exciting, yet also frightening. At this point I hope Ruth will look at this reality and take a stand on how much she wants for herself and the risks she is willing to take in reaching for more.

Ruth Decides to Continue   Being in therapy is a series of choices. Not only does therapy open Ruth up to new possibilities by expanding her awareness and thus widening the brackets of her freedom to choose, but she makes choices all during the therapy process itself. I respect her choices, and I support her when she is struggling with difficult ones. I also push her gently and invite her to ask for more and to take more risks. Ultimately, she is the one who decides many times during our sessions the depth to which she is willing to go.

🐾 Ruth Works to Become Free   In one session Ruth expresses her desire to be liberated. I suggest that she imagine all the ways she has felt unfree and write down the messages she has heard. I ask her to write to herself as her father, and then again as her mother.

Here is the idea of "homework assignments" (borrowed from the cognitive and behavioral therapies), but I am stressing the feelings that go with such an exercise. In this way Ruth can review some earlier experiences, and I hope she will stir up some old feelings associated with these memories, which we can deal with in future sessions.

At the following session Ruth brings her journal and says she would like to talk about what it was like to write herself letters (as her father and as her mother), saying all that was expected of her. I ask her to share what this was like, and I pay attention to her body as well as her words. (Like the Gestalt therapist, I think the truth of one's messages are conveyed in voice inflections, postures, facial features, and the like. If I listen only to her words, I am likely to miss a deeper level of meaning. Like the person-centered therapist, I value listening to what she is feeling and expressing.) Although I think it is important that I reflect and clarify, I deem it crucial that I bring myself into a dialogue with Ruth. If I am having reactions to what she is saying or if she is touching something within me, sharing my present experience with her can facilitate her work. My own disclosure, at timely and appropriate moments, can lead to a deeper self-exploration on Ruth's part. I must take care not to disclose merely for its own sake; nor is it well to take the focus off of her. But even a few words can let her know that I understand her.

Ruth is talking about her mother's messages to her. As I listen to her, I notice that there is a critical tone and a sharpness to her voice, and she makes a pointing gesture with her finger. I get an idea that I want to pursue.

JERRY: Would you sit in this red rocking chair? Actually rock back and forth, and with a very critical voice—pointing your finger and shaking it—deliver a lecture to Ruth, who is sitting in this other chair.

RUTH: I want you to work hard and never complain. Look at how I've slaved, and look at how moral I've been. Life is hard and don't forget that. You're put on earth here to see if you can pass the test. Bear all your burdens well, and you'll be rewarded in the next life—where it counts!

There are many possibilities of places to go from here. (So far I have been using a Gestalt technique of asking her to "become" her mother in the hope that she can actually feel what this brings up in her as she relives the scene.) I ask her to sit in the other chair and be Ruth and respond to her mother's lecture. The dialogue continues with exchanges between her mother and Ruth, and finally I ask her to stop and process what has gone on. This technique also can be done with her father, and will likely be done in further sessions because her relationship with her father continues to have a powerful influence on her way of being and behaving.

Earlier I had suggested that Ruth write about all the ways she has not felt free in life. Her personal writing was a catalyst that stimulated some useful exploration in her therapy sessions. Now I ask Ruth to think about the times in her life when she felt the most free. I ask her, "If you were to awaken and a miracle happened when you were asleep, what would your life be like if you were really free?" By using this *miracle question* (a solution-focused technique), I am inviting Ruth to design the kind of ideal existence she would hope for. As an alternative, I might use the Adlerian "acting as if" approach:

> JERRY: Ruth, I know that you experience yourself as not being free most of the time, but I'd like you to try an experiment. For one week I would like you to consciously act *as if* you are free. For this period of time, operate on the assumption that you are the free person now that you'd like to be. Let me suggest that you write in your journal about your experience when you are acting as if you are really free.

It is likely that Ruth's sense of freedom exists on a continuum. When she describes a time when she felt relatively free, I would then pursue with her what she did to contribute to feeling free. What's more, I will ask her to come up with small steps she can take and is willing to take to move in the direction of increasing her sense of freedom. The various journal assignments are useful for helping Ruth carry out her own therapy at home; she can then bring into her therapy session topics she wants to pursue.

❧ We Work on Ruth's Cognitions   Gestalt techniques are very useful for assisting Ruth to get an experiential sense of the messages and values she has swallowed whole without digesting. My goal is to help her externalize these introjections so that she can take a critical look at them. I have an investment in getting her to look at this process and make her values truly her own.

I ask Ruth to identify as many family rules as she can that she recalls having grown up with as a child. She recollects parental messages such as these: "Don't think for yourself." "Follow the church obediently, and conform your will to God's will." "Never question the Bible." "Live a moral life." "Don't get close to people, especially in sexual ways." "Always be proper and appropriate." We spend time identifying and dealing with gender-role messages Ruth still struggles with, such as these: "Your main concern should be your family." "Don't put your career needs before what is expected of you as a woman." "Defer to what men want." "Always be ready to nurture those who need care and attention."

In addition to working with Ruth's feelings, I find it essential to work with her *cognitive structures*, which include her belief systems, her thoughts, her attitudes, and her values. (In behavior therapy attention would be given to beliefs and assumptions that have an influence on her behavior; in rational emotive behavior therapy attention would be paid to irrational beliefs and self-indoctrination; in Adlerian therapy we would look at her basic mistakes; in reality therapy the focus would be on values; and in feminist therapy we would do an assessment of the impact of gender-role messages.) I focus on the underlying messages Ruth pays attention to now in her life. I assume that her self-talk is relevant to her behavior.

❧ Ruth Brings Up Her Spirituality   Although I do not have an agenda to impose religious or spiritual values on Ruth, I do see it as my function to assess the role spirituality plays in her life currently and to assess beliefs, attitudes, and practices from her earlier years. Several times Ruth initiated a discussion about the void she feels in the area of religion. She was brought up with a strict fundamentalist religion and was taught that she should never question the religious and moral values that were "right." Eventually Ruth rejected much of the guilt-oriented aspects of her religion. However, even though she cognitively confronted many of the religious beliefs she was taught, on an emotional level she still feels a sense of unease and has yet to find what she considers a viable alternative to the religion of her parents.

Ruth lets me know that mainly what she remembers from her church experiences is feeling a sense of guilt that she was not good enough and that she was always falling short of being the person that her church and parents thought she should be. Not only was she not enough in the eyes of her parents, but she was also not enough for God.

Ruth is engaged in a struggle to find spiritual values that will help her find meaning in her life. Although formal religion does not seem to play a key role for Ruth now, she is struggling to find her place in the universe and is seeking spiritual avenues that provide her with purpose. She is floundering somewhat and realizes that this is a missing dimension in her life. She also lets me know that she is pleasantly surprised that I am even mentioning religion and spirituality; she was not sure that it was appropriate to bring matters such as religion and spirituality into counseling. She says that it was good for her to be able to initiate a discussion about her past experiences with religion and her present quest to find a spiritual path that has meaning to her. Ruth tells me about her intention to further explore in her sessions ways that she can enhance her spiritual life.

🪷 Ruth Brings Up Her Father   We devote several sessions to discussing how Ruth's father played a central role in the moral and religious values that she believed she had to accept to stay in his "good graces." Eventually, Ruth acquires the insight that she does not want to live by the religious dogma that her father preached, nor does she want to accept for herself the messages he continues to give her about the "right path for living."

As we explore the messages that Ruth was reared with, one theme seems to emerge. She has lived much of her life in ways that were designed to get her father's approval. She feels that unless she gets her father's acceptance and approval, she will never have "arrived." She reasons that if the father who conceived her could not love her, then nobody ever could. If this man does not show her love, she is doomed to live a loveless life! I proceed by using cognitive behavioral concepts and techniques to get her to critically evaluate some invalid assumptions she continues to make.

As much as possible, without pushing Ruth away, I invite her to explore her thinking and her value system, which appear to be at the root of much of her conflict. I am not imposing my values on her; rather, it is a matter of getting her to look at beliefs and values she has accepted to determine if she still wants to base her life on them. Does she want to spend the rest of her life in a futile attempt to "win over" her father? Does she want to continue making all men into her father? What will it take for her to finally gain her father's acceptance and love—if this is possible? What might she think of the person she had to become to gain his acceptance? I take this line of questioning in an attempt to get her to *think*, to *challenge* herself, and to *decide* for herself her standards for living.[16]

🌿 Dealing With Ruth's Past in Understanding Her Decisions   I have been talking about some of the early decisions Ruth made in response to messages she received from her parents. I very much value the exploration of a client's early childhood experiences as a basis for understanding present pressing issues. (The psychoanalytic approach emphasizes a reconstruction of the past, a working through of early conflicts that have been repressed, and a resolution of these unconscious conflicts. Family approaches encourage clients to work through conflicts with their parents.) I accept that Ruth's childhood experiences were influential in contributing to her present development, although I do not think these factors have determined her or that she is fixed with certain personality characteristics for life unless she goes through a long-term analytic reconstructive process. (I favor the Gestalt approach to working with her past.) I ask her to bring any unresolved conflicts from her past into the here and now through use of her imagination and role-playing experiments. In this way her past is being dealt with in a powerful way as it is being manifested in her current problems.

Overall, Ruth is a willing and motivated client. She is insightful, courageous, able to make connections between current behavior and past influences, willing to try risky behaviors both in the session and out of the session, and willing to face difficult issues in her life. Even under such favorable (and almost ideal) circumstances, I still think Ruth will experience some resistance. She debates about whether to continue therapy; at times she blames her parents for her present problems; and at other times she chooses to stay comfortable because of her fear of plunging into unknown territory. In short, I work with whatever resistance she shows by pointing out its most obvious manifestations first and encouraging her to talk about her fears and explore them. An effective way to deal with resistance is to recognize it and deal with it directly. This can be done in a gentle yet confrontational way, along with providing support to face issues that she might otherwise avoid.[17]

🌿 Working Toward Redecisions   I try to structure situations in the therapy session that will facilitate new decisions on Ruth's part. Her redecisions have to be made on both the emotional and cognitive levels. (In encouraging Ruth to make new decisions, I draw on cognitive, emotive, and behavioral techniques. I use role-playing procedures, fantasy and imagery, mindfulness approaches, assertion-training procedures, Gestalt techniques, feminist therapy social action strategies, solution-focused therapy techniques, narrative approaches, and family systems therapy methods.) She can spend years getting insights into the cause of her problems, but her willingness to commit herself to some course of action aimed at changing herself and also bringing about environmental change is more important.

🌿 Encouraging Ruth to Act   In many ways I look at therapy as a place of safety where clients can experiment with new ways of being to see what behavioral changes they really want to make. The critical point consists of actually

taking what is learned in the sessions and applying it to real-life situations. I consistently encourage Ruth to carry out homework assignments geared to having her challenge her fears and inhibitions in a variety of practical situations. Thus, if she says that she is yearning for a weekend alone with her husband yet fears asking for it because she might be turned down and the rejection would hurt, I challenge her: "If you don't bother to ask, chances are you won't have this weekend you say you want with John. You've often brought up in your sessions that you don't ask for what you want, and then end up feeling depressed and unloved. Here's your chance to actually do something different."

At various times I ask Ruth to decide what changes she wants to make in her life. Because she sincerely wants to be different, we use session time in role playing and behavioral rehearsal, and then I ask her to experiment with her new learning in different life situations, especially with her family. For me, translating what is learned in the sessions into daily life is the essence of what therapy is about.[18]

Evaluating Ruth's Therapy Experience

My style of counseling places emphasis on continuing assessment by both the counselor and the client from the initial to the final session. In my work with Ruth I bring up from time to time the topic of her progress in therapy. We openly discuss the degree to which she is getting what she wants from the process (and from me). If she is not successfully meeting her objectives, we can explore some factors that might be getting in the way of her progress. I could be a restricting factor. This is especially true if I am reacting to her strictly from a technical approach and am withholding my own reactions from her. If I am being inauthentic in any way in the sessions, I am certain this will show up in a failure on her part to progress to the degree to which she might have.

I also explore with Ruth some of the circumstances in her life that may be contributing to what appears to be slow or nonexistent progress. She has done a lot of changing, which may itself be creating new problems in her home relationships, and she may feel a need to pull back and consolidate her gains. There may be a plateau for a time before she is ready to forge ahead with making other major life changes. Still another factor determining her progress or lack of it lies within her—namely, her own decision and commitment of how far she wants to go in therapy. Is she willing to make some basic changes in her personality and create a new identity for herself? Is she willing to pay the price that changing entails? Does she merely want to solve some pressing problems on the surface while remaining personally unchanged? These are but a few of the factors we have to consider in understanding any failure in the therapy process.

How do Ruth and I determine the degree to which she is progressing? What criteria do we use to make this determination? I look at Ruth's work in the sessions and what she is doing outside of them as a measure of the degree to which therapy is working. Another important index is our relationship. If it is one of trust and if she is dealing with difficult personal issues in her therapy and also working on these issues outside of the sessions, then therapy is working. Also, her own evaluation of how much progress she sees and how satisfied she is by the outcomes is a major factor in assessing therapeutic results.

When is it time for Ruth to terminate therapy? This, too, is a matter that I openly evaluate at appropriate times and we explore in a collaborative way. Ultimately, I see termination as her choice. My hope is that once Ruth attains a degree of increased self-awareness and specific behavioral skills in meeting present and future problems, she might well be encouraged to end formal therapy and begin to become her own therapist. To keep her beyond this point could result in needlessly fostering her dependence on me, which is not too unlike the problem that brought her to therapy in the first place.[19]

Concluding Comments

Developing a counseling style that fits you is truly a challenge. It entails far more than picking bits and pieces from theories in a random and fragmented manner. As a counselor, you bring your background of experiences and your personality, worldview, biases, and unique talents and skills to your work with clients. You also bring to your professional work your theoretical preferences. As you take steps to develop an integrated perspective, think about these questions: Which theories provide a basis for understanding the *cognitive* dimension? Which theories help you understand the *affective* dimension? Which theories address the *behavioral* dimension? As you are aware, most of the therapeutic approaches you have studied focus primarily on one of these dimensions of human experience. The task is to wisely and creatively select therapeutic procedures that you can employ in working with a diverse population. Knowing the unique needs of your clients, your own values and personality, and the theories themselves is a good basis for beginning to develop a theory that is an expression of yourself.

It requires knowledge, skill, art, and experience to be able to determine what techniques will work best with particular clients and with certain problems. Practitioners are being challenged to incorporate evidence-based practice in their work, so keeping abreast of the research is a necessity today. But knowing *when* and *how* to use a particular therapeutic intervention is also an art.

Building your personalized approach to counseling is a long-term venture, I do hope that you will be patient with yourself as you continue to grow through your reading, thinking, and experience in working with clients and through your own personal struggles and life experiences.

How Would You Work With Ruth Using Your Own Approach?

Try your hand at achieving some synthesis among the various approaches covered in the previous chapters by drawing on each of them in a way that seems meaningful to you—one that fits your own personality and your view of people and the nature of therapy. Here are some questions to help you organize the elements of your approach.

1. What would you be thinking and feeling as you approach your initial session with Ruth? Use whatever you know about her from the material presented about her and her autobiography in the first chapter, as well as from the 13 chapters on her work with various therapists.
2. Briefly state how you see Ruth in terms of her current dynamics and most pressing conflicts. How would you feel about working with her as a client? How do you view her capacity to understand herself and to make basic changes?
3. How much direction do you see Ruth needing? To what degree would you take the responsibility for structuring her sessions? Where would you be on a continuum of highly directive to very nondirective?
4. If you were applying brief therapy with Ruth, what kinds of interventions would you be most interested in making?
5. What major themes would you focus on in Ruth's life, especially if you were working within the context of short-term therapy?
6. In what ways might you go about gathering life-history data to make an initial assessment of Ruth's problems and to determine which therapy procedures to use?
7. How might you help Ruth clarify her goals for therapy? How would you help her make her goals concrete? How would you assess the degree to which she was meeting her goals?
8. How much interest would you have in working with Ruth's early childhood experiences? Her current issues? Her future aspirations and strivings? Which of these areas do you favor? Why?
9. What value do you place on the quality of your relationship with Ruth? How important is the client–therapist relationship as a determinant of therapeutic outcomes?
10. Would you be more inclined to focus on Ruth's feelings? Her thought processes and other cognitive factors? Her ability to take action as measured by her behaviors?
11. How supportive might you be of Ruth? How confrontational might you be with her? In what areas do you think you would be most supportive? Most confrontational?
12. How much might you be inclined to work toward major personality reconstruction? Toward specific skill-development and problem-solving strategies? Toward social action strategies?
13. How might you explore Ruth's major fears, both about therapy and about her life?
14. What life experiences have you had that would most help you in working with Ruth? What personal characteristics might hinder your work with her?
15. How might you proceed in dealing with Ruth's parents and the role she feels that they have played in her life? How important would it be to focus on working through her attitudes and feelings toward her parents?
16. To what degree would you strive to involve Ruth's current family in her therapy?
17. How much might you structure outside-of-therapy activities for Ruth (homework, reading, journal writing, and so forth)?

18. What specific techniques and concepts might you derive from the psychoanalytic approach? From the experiential approaches? From the cognitive, behavioral, and action-oriented approaches? From the postmodern approaches? From systemic approaches? From the multicultural approaches?
19. Would you orient Ruth's therapy more toward insight or toward action? What balance might you seek between the cognitive aspects and the feeling aspects?
20. How might you make the determination of when Ruth was ready to end therapy?

An Exercise: Themes in Ruth's Life

A few of the major themes that have therapeutic potential for further exploration are revealed in these statements that Ruth made at one time or another:

1. You seem so distant and removed from me. You're hard to reach.
2. In spite of my best attempts, I still feel a lot of guilt that I haven't done enough.
3. I just don't trust myself to find my own answers to life.
4. I'm afraid to change for fear of breaking up my marriage.
5. It's hard for me to ask others for what I want.
6. I feel extremely tense, and I can't sleep at night.
7. All my life I've tried to get my father's approval.
8. It's hard for me to have fun. I'm so responsible.
9. I've always had a weight problem, and I can't seem to do much about it.
10. I'm afraid to make mistakes and look like a fool.
11. My daughter and I just don't get along with each other.
12. I give and give, and they just take and take.
13. I've lived by the expectations of others for so long that I don't know what I want anymore.
14. I don't think my marriage is the way it should be, but my husband thinks it's just fine.
15. I'm afraid to tell my husband what I really want with him because I'm afraid he'll leave me.
16. I fear punishment because I've given up my old religious values.
17. I wear so many hats that sometimes I feel worn out.
18. There's not enough time for me to be doing all the things I know I should be doing.
19. I'm afraid of my feelings toward other men.
20. When my children leave, I'll have nothing to live for.

Look over this list of Ruth's statements and select the ones that you find most interesting. Here are three suggestions for working with them. For each of the themes you select, (1) show how you would begin working with Ruth from each of the various perspectives; (2) take only two contrasting approaches and focus on these; or (3) combine several therapeutic models and work with Ruth using this synthesis.

Attempt to work with a few of Ruth's statements after reading both Dr. John Norcross's and my integrative way of working with her in this chapter. This would make interesting and lively material for role playing and discussion in small groups. One person can "become" Ruth while others in the group counsel her from the vantage point of several different therapeutic perspectives. Practicing a variety of approaches will assist you in discovering for yourself ways to pull together techniques that you consider to be the best.

Notes

See the *DVD for Theory and Practice of Counseling and Psychotherapy: The Case of Stan and Lecturettes,* Session 13 ("An Integrative Approach Applied to the Case of Stan"), which deals with termination and takes an integrative view of Stan's work and for my presentation of ways that an integrative perspective can be applied.

1. For a study on trends and practices among eclectic and integrative practitioners, see Norcross, J. C., Karpiak, C. P., & Lister, K. M. (2005). What's an integrationist? A study of self-identified integrative and (occasionally) eclectic psychologists. *Journal of Clinical Psychology, 61,* 1587–1594.
2. A fuller discussion and clinical examples of integration can be found in Norcross, J. C., & Goldfried, M. R. (2005). *Handbook of psychotherapy integration* (2nd ed.). New York: Oxford University Press.
3. Research on the therapy relationship and its association to treatment success are summarized in Norcross, J. C. (Ed.). (2011). *Psychotherapy relationships that work* (2nd ed.). New York: Oxford University Press.
4. Accommodating the client's preferences, when ethically and clinically feasible, modestly improves the effectiveness of psychotherapy and markedly reduces premature terminations. See Swift, J., & Callahan, J. L. (2009). The impact of client treatment preferences on outcome: A meta-analysis. *Journal of Clinical Psychology, 65,* 368–381.
5. For definitions of the stages of change and its clinical applications, consult Prochaska, J. O., Norcross, J. C., & DiClemente, C. C. (1995). *Changing for good.* New York: Avon. The relation between systems of psychotherapy and stages of change is considered in detail in Prochaska, J. O., & Norcross, J. C. (2010). *Systems of psychotherapy: A transtheoretical analysis* (7th ed.). Belmont, CA: Brooks/Cole, Cengage Learning.
6. Research on resistance (or reactance) level is summarized in a meta-analysis by L. Beutler & colleagues, in Norcross, J. C. (Ed.). (2011). *Psychotherapy relationships that work* (2nd ed.). New York: Oxford University Press.
7. Barlow, D. H., Gorman, J. M., Shear, M. K., & Woods, S. W. (2000). Cognitive-behavioral therapy, imipramine, or their combination for panic disorder: A randomized controlled trial. *Journal of the American Medical Association, 283,* 2529–2536.
8. For a compilation of psychologists' self-help ratings and recommendations, see Norcross, J. C. & colleagues. (2003). *Authoritative guide to self-help resources in mental health.* New York: Guilford Press.
9. Methods of implementing evidence-based practice (EBP) in mental health and the addictions are offered in Norcross, J. C., Hogan, T. P., & Koocher, G. P. (2008) *Clinician's guide to evidence-based practices.* New York: Oxford University Press.

10. In addition to the *DVD for Integrative Counseling: The Case of Ruth and Lecturettes*, the integrative perspective is addressed in more detail in chapters 15 and 16 of Corey, G. (2013). *Theory and practice of counseling and psychotherapy* (9th ed.). Belmont, CA: Brooks/Cole, Cengage Learning.

11. A useful resource for a more in-depth presentation of how to develop an integrative approach can be found in Corey, G. (2013). *The art of integrative counseling* (3rd ed.). Belmont, CA: Brooks/Cole, Cengage Learning.

12. The *DVD for Integrative Counseling: The Case of Ruth and Lecturettes*, Session 1 ("Beginning of Counseling"), provides a demonstration of my work with Ruth during the initial stage of counseling.

13. Refer to Session 3 ("Establishing Therapeutic Goals") in the *DVD for Integrative Counseling: The Case of Ruth and Lecturettes* for a demonstration of ways I assist Ruth in identifying concrete goals that will guide our work together.

14. Refer to Session 2 ("The Therapeutic Relationship") in the *DVD for Integrative Counseling: The Case of Ruth and Lecturettes* for a demonstration of some issues that are essential to developing a therapeutic alliance.

15. In the *DVD for Integrative Counseling: The Case of Ruth and Lecturettes*, Session 6 deals with the cognitive focus, Session 7 deals with the emotive focus, and Session 8 deals with the behavioral focus.

16. In the *DVD for Integrative Counseling: The Case of Ruth and Lecturettes*, Session 11 ("Understanding How the Past Influences the Present and the Future"), Ruth explores her feelings toward her father via a role play.

17. In Session 5 ("Understanding and Dealing With Resistance") in the *DVD for Integrative Counseling: The Case of Ruth and Lecturettes*, Ruth expresses some resistance toward continuing counseling.

18. In Session 12 ("Working Toward Decisions and Behavioral Change") in the *DVD for Integrative Counseling: The Case of Ruth and Lecturettes*, Ruth explores some of her early decisions and begins to make new decisions.

19. In Session 13 ("Evaluation and Termination") in the *DVD for Integrative Counseling: The Case of Ruth and Lecturettes*, Ruth and I review what she has learned in counseling and discuss future directions after terminating counseling.